CREDULITY

CLASS | NEW
200 | STUDIES
| IN
| RELIGION

EDITED BY Kathryn Lofton AND
John Lardas Modern

CREDULITY

A Cultural History
of US Mesmerism

EMILY
OGDEN

The University of Chicago Press
Chicago and London

The University of Chicago Press, Chicago 60637

The University of Chicago Press, Ltd., London

© 2018 by The University of Chicago

Published 2018

Printed in the United States of America

27 26 25 24 23 22 21 20 19 18   1 2 3 4 5

ISBN-13: 978-0-226-53216-5 (cloth)

ISBN-13: 978-0-226-53233-2 (paper)

ISBN-13: 978-0-226-53247-9 (e-book)

DOI: https://doi.org/10.7208/chicago/9780226532479.001.0001

The University of Chicago Press gratefully acknowledges the generous support of the Buckner W. Clay Dean of Arts and Sciences and the Vice President for Research of the University of Virginia toward the publication of this book.

Library of Congress Cataloging-in-Publication Data

Names: Ogden, Emily, author.

Title: Credulity : a cultural history of US mesmerism / Emily Ogden.

Other titles: Class 200, new studies in religion.

Description: Chicago : The University of Chicago Press, 2018. |
    Series: Class 200: new studies in religion | Includes bibliographical references.

Identifiers: LCCN 2017036849 | ISBN 9780226532165 (cloth : alk. paper) |
    ISBN 9780226532332 (pbk. : alk. paper) | ISBN 9780226532479 (e-book)

Subjects: LCSH: Mesmerism—United States—History—19th century. |
    Credulity—United States—History—19th century.

Classification: LCC BF1125 .O33 2018 | DDC 154.70973/09034—dc23

    LC record available at https://lccn.loc.gov/2017036849

For John, Luther, and Neil

**Out on Credulity! 't would swallow whole
A rabbit-belly'd elephant with foal!**
Laughton Osborn, *The Vision of Rubeta* (1838)

CONTENTS

FIGURES

ABBREVIATIONS

TEXTS

AM	Elizabeth Inchbald, *Animal Magnetism: A Farce, in Three Acts, as Performed at the New-York Theatre* (1809)
ANOM	Archives Nationales d'Outre-Mer, Aix-en-Provence, France
BJM	Joseph Rodes Buchanan, ed., *Buchanan's Journal of Man*
BMSJ	*Boston Medical and Surgical Journal*
BR	Nathaniel Hawthorne, *The Blithedale Romance*
C	Hannah Webster Foster, *The Coquette; or, The History of Eliza Wharton*
CW	Edgar Allan Poe, *Collected Works of Edgar Allan Poe*
E	J. Stanley Grimes, *Etherology; or, The Philosophy of Mesmerism and Phrenology* (1845)
L	William Leete Stone, *Letter to Doctor A. Brigham, on Animal Magnetism: Being an Account of a Remarkable Interview between the Author and Miss Loraina Brackett, While in a State of Somnambulism*
LBF	Marianne Dwight, *Letters from Brook Farm*
LMF	Margaret Fuller, *Letters of Margaret Fuller*
McLane Report	US House of Representatives [Secretary of the Treasury Louis McLane], *Documents Relative to the Manufactures in the United States*
MD	Herman Melville, *Moby-Dick*
MHH	J. Stanley Grimes, *The Mysteries of the Head and the Heart Explained: Including an Improved System of Phrenology; A New Theory of the Emotions; and an Explanation of the Mysteries of Mesmerism, Trance, Mind-reading, and the Spirit Delusion*
MHN	J. Stanley Grimes, *The Mysteries of Human Nature, Explained by a New System of Nervous Physiology: To Which Is Added, a Review of the Errors*

	of Spiritualism, and Instructions for Developing or Resisting the Influence by Which Subjects and Mediums Are Made
PDJ	*Providence Daily Journal*
PIA	Thomas C. Hartshorn, "Appendix" to *Practical Instruction in Animal Magnetism*, by J. P. F. Deleuze, trans. Thomas C. Hartshorn (1837)
PS	Perkins School for the Blind Archives, Watertown, MA
RS	Ann Braude, *Radical Spirits: Spiritualism and Women's Rights in Nineteenth-Century America*
"TR"	Irma Elizabeth Voigt, "Life and Works of Mrs. Therese Robinson (Talvj)"

PERSONAL NAMES

BK	Benjamin Kent
GC	George Capron
LB	Loraina (aka Lurena) Brackett; later married name Lurena B. Carpenter
SGH	Samuel Gridley Howe
TH	Thomas C. Hartshorn

ACKNOWLEDGMENTS

THIS BOOK'S EXISTENCE DEPENDS ON THE work of librarians, both living and dead, who have meticulously preserved the flotsam of antebellum American culture without demanding to know exactly what the use of every scrap of paper could be. For each physical card catalog in which my subject appeared under headings from "animal magnetism," "mesmerism," and "hypnosis" to "neurology," "faith healing," and "folk medicine;" for every inspired guess about a stray manuscript that might be of interest; for all the cheap newspapers, filled with the intent to be lost but preserved anyway, I have librarians to thank. I gratefully acknowledge the following institutions and the people who sustain them: the American Antiquarian Society, the American Philosophical Society, the Archives Nationales d'Outre-Mer, the Bakken Museum and Library, the Bibliothèque François-Mitterand of the Bibliothèque Nationale de France, the Harvard Libraries, the Massachusetts Historical Society, the National Air and Space Museum Archives, the National Library of Medicine, the New York Public Library, the Perkins School for the Blind Archives, the Rare Books Library at the University of Pennsylvania, the Albert and Shirley Small Special Collections Library at the University of Virginia, and the Yale Franklin Papers. I owe a particular debt to Jennifer Arnott, Paul Erickson, Jen Hale, Jacqueline Penny, and Michael Sappol, and to the American Philosophical Society for an early residential fellowship.

There can't be many happier ways to begin an academic career than by landing at the University of Virginia. Steve Arata, Anna Brickhouse, Mark Edmundson, Bruce Holsinger, Deborah McGrady, and Cindy Wall went beyond the call of duty both before I became their colleague and afterward. Francesca Fiorani has generously supported my research at every turn. Grants from the Buckner W. Clay Dean of Arts and Sciences and the

Vice President for Research have sustained each stage of the writing process, from fact gathering to publication.

It was my good fortune to spend three years at the Columbia Society of Fellows during the tenure of Eileen Gillooly, Chris Brown, and David Johnston. Eileen encouraged, and the Society of Fellows supported, the convening of a conference that would eventually give this book its title. David Russell and Brian Goldstone were ideal comrades in arms. The members of Columbia's Religion in America seminar, and especially its leaders Courtney Bender and Joe Blankholm, gave me a second disciplinary home. Funding from the Andrew W. Mellon Foundation made all these relationships possible.

For my education at the University of Pennsylvania, and for continued support and counsel in the years since, I can never repay my two dissertation advisers, Nancy Bentley and Amy Kaplan.

I am grateful to the friends, colleagues, and family members who have read this book in whole or in part, and whose suggestions have improved it: Todd Carmody, Mrinalini Chakravorty, Rita Felski, Jennifer Fleissner, Susan Fraiman, Erica Fretwell, Bernard Geoghegan, Iris Muchmore, Benjamin Reiss, and Lindsay Reckson. Nick Gaskill's summaries of chapters routinely showed me what point I was actually making. John Parker reads everything I write and is the constant interlocutor I couldn't do without. My parents have never wavered in their support of a long education.

I am lucky that Alan Thomas, Randolph Petilos, John Modern, and Kathryn Lofton had confidence in this book; my thanks go to all of them for shepherding it into print. Madeline Zehnder's meticulous assistance helped me prepare the manuscript for press in good time.

The dedication expresses my deepest debt and my highest hopes.

An earlier version of chapter 1 appeared as "Mesmer's Demon: Fiction, Falsehood, and the Mechanical Imagination," *Early American Literature* 47, no. 1 (2012): 143–70; and an earlier version of chapter 2 appeared as "Beyond Radical Enchantment: Mesmerizing Laborers in the Americas," *Critical Inquiry* 42, no. 4 (Summer 2016): 815–41, © 2016 by The University of Chicago, all rights reserved. I thank the editors for permission to include that work here.

OUT ON CREDULITY!

An Introduction

Out on Credulity! 't would swallow whole
A rabbit-belly'd elephant with foal!

Laughton Osborn, *The Vision of Rubeta* (1838)[1]

J. STANLEY GRIMES, AN AMERICAN MESMERIST, announced in 1845 that he had discovered the organ of the brain that accounted for enchantment. "Credenciveness" governed religious faith and overall gullibility; it accounted for why one might enter an apparently magical trance, believe in false gods, or fall for a confidence game (Fig. 1). Too much credenciveness meant "superstition, credulity."[2] Grimes explained that "prophets and seers and soothsayers of ancient times" had possessed a secret technique for heightening the organ's activity; their knowledge allowed them to propagate such lamentable errors as the Delphic oracles and the Shaker prophecies and gave them "unbounded sway over the minds of the ignorant masses."[3] His next step was not, however, the one we tend to expect of Enlightenment's heirs: he had no interest in stamping out either credenciveness or the techniques that had stimulated it. On the contrary, he wanted to perpetuate

---

Translations throughout the book are my own unless otherwise noted.

1. Laughton Osborn, *The Vision of Rubeta* (Boston: Weeks, Jordan, 1838), 68.

2. J. Stanley Grimes, *Etherology; or, The Philosophy of Mesmerism and Phrenology* (New York: Saxton & Miles, 1845), 169.

3. Ibid., 43.

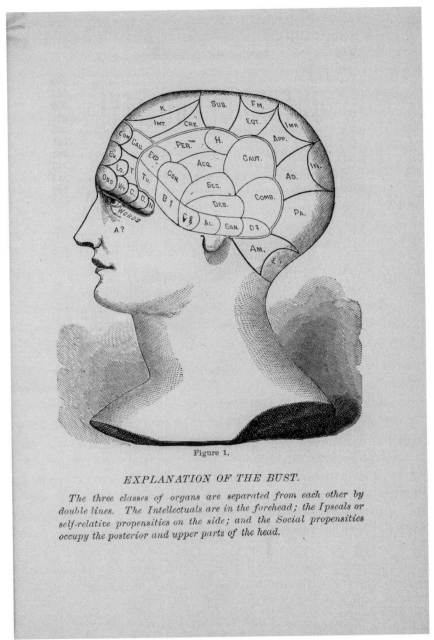

Figure 1.

EXPLANATION OF THE BUST.

The three classes of organs are separated from each other by double lines. The Intellectuals are in the forehead; the Ipseals or self-relative propensities on the side; and the Social propensities occupy the posterior and upper parts of the head.

Fig. 1. Bust showing the organ of Credenciveness. In J. Stanley Grimes, *The Mysteries of the Head and Heart Explained* (Chicago: W. B. Keen, Cooke, 1875), p. [1]. Credenciveness is marked "CRE." and appears above the temple, toward the crown of the head. Courtesy, American Antiquarian Society.

those techniques. He proposed first to explain the false priests' chicanery and then to appropriate it, redirecting their occult gestures toward new rational ends. He proposed, in a word, to practice mesmerism.

Mesmerists, who were active in the United States between 1836 and the Civil War (1861–1865), offered an applied science of excessive belief, or *credulity*. Not all practitioners tied credulity to a phrenological organ, but most shared Grimes's conviction that when they entranced their subjects with precisely choreographed gestures, thus inducing a suite of phenomena including delusion, thrall, and prophetic knowledge, they were updating false religion for modern use. Employed secretly, the mesmeric gestures abetted Delphic frauds. Employed openly and rationally, the same gestures served enlightened ends. Was the mesmerized subject fantastically obedient? Then mesmerism could help discipline workers. Was the subject clairvoyant? Then he could speedily communicate the price of cotton from north to south. Could the subject read minds? Her insight might aid in educating young people. All of these uses were proposed; the first and last were attempted. If one imagines that a person can be either a debunker or a practitioner of the occult, but not both at once, mesmerism poses a problem. Mesmerists did not believe in magic, but they did believe in the utility of others' belief. They were not enchanted themselves, but they were eager to use the enchantment of others.

"To enchant" has long been an ambivalent verb in English; it means to delight, and also to delude; to enrapture, and also to rape; to spellbind figuratively, and also to spellbind literally. When *disenchantment* was used to translate *Entzauberung* (literally, demagification) in Max Weber's foundational account, "Science as a Vocation," *enchantment* became the term for that state of the world before modernity when one is in awe but in error, like the propitiating savage. *Enchantment* became a periodizing word, that is: the world used to be enchanted, and now it is not. Whatever the shortcomings of this translation,[4] it does preserve Weber's own ambivalence about the transition he described. The world is enchanted when "the savage," deluded about reality, has "recourse to magical means in order to master or implore the spirits."[5] When the world is disenchanted, by contrast,

4. Jane Bennett, *The Enchantment of Modern Life: Attachments, Crossings, and Ethics* (Princeton, NJ: Princeton University Press, 2001), 57. On translation questions, see Michael Warner's review of John Modern's *Secularism in Antebellum America*: "Was Antebellum America Secular?" *The Immanent Frame* (blog), October 2, 2012, http://blogs.ssrc.org/tif /2012/10/02/was-antebellum-america-secular/.

5. Max Weber, "Science as a Vocation," in *From Max Weber: Essays in Sociology*, trans. and ed. H. H. Gerth and C. Wright Mills (New York: Routledge, 1948), 139.

everything is "in principle" manipulable through "technical means and cal-culations," and one can live bravely, honestly, but a little sadly in the face of this knowledge.[6]

In recent years, and to some extent as an attempted correction of Weber, scholars have taken a celebratory attitude toward enchantment. States of awe, and even magical practices, *can* persist in modernity, despite the best efforts of skeptics and disillusionment artists, and we are lucky—from an ethical, aesthetic, or political standpoint—that they *do* persist. As philosophers have sought ethical sources in wonder;[7] as literary critics have looked to aesthetic transports for new (or old) ways of reading raptly;[8] and as historians have drawn our serious attention to the occult,[9] the tone has been distinctly op-timistic.[10] The darker aspects of enchantment, which have belonged to that term for as long as it has been in use, appear not as its real features but as the paranoid overlay bequeathed to us by some combination of Weber and the Enlightenment. If we want to see enchantment accurately, on this view, we have to stop listening to the shrill warnings against it. Heeding these warn-ings will hinder us in our efforts; it will distort our understanding of what enchantment is.

I take a different view. Where recent work on enchantment has ac-centuated the positive, this book accentuates the negative. It recognizes that practitioners of modern enchantment may look like Grimes: contemptuous of the manipulated "masses," yet more than willing to try a little manipula-tion themselves. The book's tendency is not reactionary; the point is not to return to decrying enchantment. The point instead is to ask what those who decried enchantment were actually doing with it in practice. How were they

6. Ibid.

7. Bennett, *Enchantment of Modern Life*, 3–4, 12–13, 131–58.

8. Michael Saler, *As If: Modern Enchantment and the Literary Prehistory of Virtual Real-ity* (New York: Oxford University Press, 2012), 14, 57; Rita Felski, *Uses of Literature* (Mal-den, MA: Blackwell, 2008), 51–76.

9. Molly McGarry, *Ghosts of Futures Past: Spiritualism and the Cultural Politics of Nineteenth-Century America* (Berkeley: University of California Press, 2008); Alex Owen, *The Place of Enchantment: British Occultism and the Culture of the Modern* (Chicago: Uni-versity of Chicago Press, 2004).

10. On the cleansing of delusion from modern enchantment, see David Walker, "The Humbug in American Religion: Ritual Theories of Nineteenth-Century Spiritualism," *Re-ligion and American Culture* 23, no. 1 (2013): 30–74, esp. 57n6, and Tracy Fessenden, "The Problem of the Postsecular," in "American Literatures/American Religions," ed. Jonathan Ebel and Justine S. Murison, special issue, *American Literary History* 26, no. 1 (2014): 154.

using it? Like New York literatus Laughton Osborn, skeptics exclaimed, "Out on Credulity!"[11] Like David Reese, the author of *Humbugs of New-York* (1838), they deplored "such sublimated folly, such double distilled nonsense, as popular credulity is perpetually swallowing."[12] But meanwhile many of them were busily seeking employment for the very thing they spurned, as Grimes was. This study shows that the skeptic of this period sought to manage enchantment, not to suppress it. To confine, explain, and redeploy primitive religious power: these were the quintessential aspirations not just of mesmerists in particular but also of antebellum secularism in general. Skeptics' characterization of enchantment as the product of credulity cannot be ruled out of court as a secular prejudice, as recent scholarship has sometimes been inclined to do. Credulity is where critical thought about modern enchantment must begin.

The opening decades of the twenty-first century have seen a "wholesale shift in how secularization is understood," as John Modern puts it.[13] Inspired in part by the overwhelming evidence that spiritual belief has not receded from public life as some narratives of modernity promised, scholars have stopped approaching secularity as an "empirical description" of a historical moment from which religion has disappeared.[14] Instead, the secular is an imaginary,

11. Osborn, *Vision of Rubeta*, 68.

12. David Reese, *Humbugs of New-York: Being a Remonstrance against Popular Delusion* (Boston: Weeks, Jordan, 1838), 15.

13. John Lardas Modern, "Commentary: How to Read Literature, Win Friends, Influence People, and Write about American Religion," in "American Literatures/American Religions," ed. Jonathan Ebel and Justine S. Murison, special issue, *American Literary History* 26, no. 1 (2014): 195.

14. Ibid.; Talal Asad, *Formations of the Secular: Christianity, Islam, Modernity* (Stanford, CA: Stanford University Press, 2003); Dipesh Chakrabarty, *Provincializing Europe: Postcolonial Thought and Historical Difference* (Princeton, NJ: Princeton University Press, 2000); Tracy Fessenden, *Culture and Redemption: Religion, the Secular, and American Literature* (Princeton, NJ: Princeton University Press, 2007); Janet R. Jakobsen and Ann Pellegrini, eds., *Secularisms* (Durham, NC: Duke University Press, 2008); Janet R. Jakobsen and Ann Pellegrini, "World Secularisms at the Millennium: Introduction," *Social Text* 18, no. 3 (2000): 1–27; John Lardas Modern, *Secularism in Antebellum America* (Chicago: University of Chicago Press, 2011); Charles Taylor, *A Secular Age* (Cambridge, MA: Harvard University Press, 2007); and Bruno Latour, *Petite réflexion sur le culte moderne des dieux*

or a mind-set. It is a set of prescriptions impinging on those who, in Talal Asad's phrase, "*aim* at 'modernity.'"[15] Secular prescriptions may operate on multiple levels. They may organize relations between states and individuals around such concepts as human rights.[16] They may point to the nature and proper bounds of scientific knowledge, or to the correct procedures for "critical thought."[17] They may indicate how a subject should or should not comport herself, stipulating for example that the subject must demonstrate freedom from superstition; adopt a rational, calculating attitude toward social life; and make her own destiny.[18] Secular prescriptions may tell us, too, that we should conceive of social life as something calculable. In that case, hours worked, households counted, or texts distributed may be the measures by which we are to understand society, as in Modern's account of the "evangelical secularism" practiced by the American Tract Society.[19] Rather than representing enchantment's disappearance or exclusion, secularity ac-

---

faitiches (Paris: Synthélabo, 1996). I cite from Latour's second French edition, *Sur le culte moderne des dieux* faitiches, *suivi de* Iconoclash (Paris: La Découverte, 2009), and from the English edition, *On the Modern Cult of the Factish Gods*, chap. 1, "On the Cult of the Factish Gods," trans. Catherine Porter and Heather MacLean (Durham, NC: Duke University Press, 2010), 1–66.

15. Asad, *Formations of the Secular*, 13. According to Modern, secularity is a "prescriptive discourse": "Commentary," 195.

16. Asad, *Formations of the Secular*, 129, and chap. 4, "Redeeming the 'Human' through Human Rights," 127–58; Taylor, *Secular Age*, 419.

17. Latour, *Factish Gods*, 39; *Dieux faitiches*, 86; Bruno Latour, *We Have Never Been Modern*, trans. Catherine Porter (Cambridge, MA: Harvard University Press, 1993), which is a translation of his *Nous n'avons jamais été modernes: Essai d'anthropologie symétrique* (Paris: La Découverte, 1991).

18. Asad, *Formations of the Secular*, 79. Closely related secular subjects might be found in a number of studies. One example is Latour's figure of the "Modern": *Factish Gods*, 1–7, 45; *Dieux faitiches*, 15–29, 95; see also chapter 1 of the present volume. Another is Taylor's "buffered self," for whom "the possibility exists of taking a distance from, disengaging from everything outside the mind," though Taylor is inclined to see buffering as a fact, as well as a demand or prescription: *Secular Age*, 38; see also 134–35. A final example is Modern's account of antebellum subjectivity. While antebellum Americans imagined and prescribed "selves [that] have the capacity to access, immediately, their own thoughts" and that "are set apart from organized forces and systemic structures, a removal that guarantees both the political and epistemological premises of the agentive self" (*Secularism in Antebellum America*, 6), it would be more accurate, Modern says, to see the antebellum agent as "haunted" and undermined by these same organized forces and systemic structures (*Secularism in Antebellum America*, xxxiv).

19. Modern, *Secularism in Antebellum America*, 49–117.

cording to these scholars amounts to a new set of procedures for *regulating* enchantment—for deciding, much as Grimes did with his organ of credenciveness, when belief is to be censured as excessive or insufficient, and when it is to be praised for its compatibility with reason and productive labor. Key to the secular is not the disappearance of enchantment but its redescription as the appropriate target of particular administrative energies.

Thus it is necessary to rethink secularity's relationship to that which it condemns as a relationship of use, not a relationship of repression. When a secularist predicts the evanescence of magic or declares that it is already extinct, the question is not whether such statements are empirically true or false. The question is what work they do. Disenchantment narratives—accounts of how magical thinking recedes as human beings reach the mature or modern stage of their history—are to be evaluated in this light. One of the foundational texts of Enlightenment, Bernard de Fontenelle's exposé of how ancient oracles had worked through a combination of priests' subterfuge and dupes' foolishness, is a disenchantment narrative: the *Histoire des oracles* (1686), translated as *The History of Oracles, and the Cheats of the Pagan Priests* (1688). The American David Reese, too, was a Weberian avant la lettre, with his "humbugs" put forward by foreign mountebanks and gobbled up by "popular credulity."[20] Both of these authors, and countless others, target something recognizably similar to Weber's "enchantment": a passionate, and often craven, attachment to what does not exist; blockheadedness; credulity.

If we view secularity as a "prescriptive discourse," to borrow Modern's term, then we will be inclined neither to adopt nor to correct periodizing statements like Fontenelle's or Reese's.[21] We will be inclined, instead, to study their effects. As Modern writes, "Secularism . . . cannot be approached as an ideological ruse. It neither deceived nor promulgated inaccurate representations of reality" but was instead "part and parcel to the very constitution of the real."[22] Whether or not the statement "now that we are modern, we no longer propitiate spirits" is true—and it is at the very least misleading on multiple fronts—that statement still has imperative force, and it still issues permits for dominion. The imperative might be translated, for example: if you wish to be fully human, and to have the full

20. Reese, *Humbugs of New-York*, 19.

21. Modern, "Commentary," 195.

22. Modern, *Secularism in Antebellum America*, 9. See also Asad, *Formations of the Secular*, 12–13.

privileges thereof, abandon credulity. And the permission might be formulated: it is appropriate for us, the enlightened, to dominate them, the credulous. To illuminate such imperatives and permissions is in large part the aim of Dipesh Chakrabarty's discussion, in *Provincializing Europe* (2000), of the historicism within which "it could always be said with reason that some people were less modern than others, and that the former needed a period of preparation and waiting before they could be recognized as full participants in political modernity."[23] The drive to periodize, to make secular, to "aim at 'modernity,'" demands study in its own right, not because of the truth of the associated statements but because of their consequences.

Both Asad and Bruno Latour have, apparently independently, called such a study an "anthropology" of the secular or the modern.[24] As moderns scrutinized the curious beliefs of their anthropological objects without taking those beliefs to be true, so the moderns' own beliefs in progress, in the disappearance of spirits, and in empowered agents can now come under our scrutiny. From this perspective, enchantment is not a state of the world before the present period, though statements of that kind are undoubtedly a key part of modernity's foreign policy. Enchantment is the contraindication that goes with the secular prescriptions.[25] It is a taboo, if you will, that these modern savages scrupulously observe (even in the breach). *Enchantment* is, as Asad points out, best understood as a term applied "in retrospect" by those for whom "modernity is a *project*." While such people look to a "pre-modern" past, they construct that past as enchanted for the first time.[26] Enchantment can best be understood by looking at the historical moment of the accusers, rather than at the historical moment of the accused. And it can only be fully defined by reference to a particular set of secularists who say they see it.

The new secularity studies thus should prompt us to carry a new question to the nineteenth-century American occult: how was enchantment managed at the threshold of nineteenth-century modernity? Indeed, what *was* enchantment at that moment? *Credulity* poses these questions. Historicizing enchantment is distinct from offering a history of any particular modern religion—Mormonism, evangelical Protestantism, séance spiritualism, or

23. Chakrabarty, *Provincializing Europe*, 9.

24. Asad, "What Might an Anthropology of Secularism Look Like?" chapter 1 of *Formations of the Secular*, 21–66; Latour, *Factish Gods*, 5; *Dieux faitiches*, 24.

25. Modern, *Secularism in Antebellum America*, xvi, n. 1.

26. Asad, *Formations of the Secular*, 13–14.

vodou, for example—though American studies' recent turn toward religion and the secular has enriched our understanding of all of these persuasions.[27] This book reckons with the full contours of excessive belief as an accusation, a boast, and a practical label. Here, the phrase "modern enchantment" takes on an unanticipated meaning. Modern enchantment simply *is* credulity, at least where the antebellum United States is concerned; it is deception and thrall to false magic as this particular set of secularists saw these failings. I have culled my central term from the texts I study: when nineteenth-century Americans imagined superstitious savages and glassy-eyed religious wackos, credulity, not enchantment, was the insult they hurled.

I make no claim that this historically embedded term is infinitely transferrable to other places and times. I do want to argue, though, that modern enchantment in general has more to do with delusion than we usually think. Scholars often point out magical practices in modernity with a triumphant air of refuting the very existence of secularism. Yes, enchantment *can* be modern! has been the frequent subtext. It *does* persist after 1700 (or 1893, or 1789, or 1690 . . .)! It *can* have traffic with liberalism, feminism, science, and mature artistic production![28] When I say "modern enchantment," by contrast, I mean not to refute but to explore and to emphasize accusations of delusion. I ask, what do such accusations tell us about secularity, and what unexpected possibilities do they afford? On my view, the following (equally hyperbolic) exclamation might be closer to the truth: enchantment can *only* be modern! Instead of the titillating oxymoron we sometimes think it is, modern enchantment may actually be a redundancy. There is only modern enchantment, because declaring someone else's practice to be a primitive

27. Two recent periodical special issues testify to this interest: Peter Coviello and Jared Hickman, eds., "After the Postsecular," *American Literature* 86, no. 4 (2014); Jonathan Ebel and Justine S. Murison, eds., "American Literatures/American Religions," *American Literary History* 26, no. 1 (2014). Representative studies include: Toni Wall Jaudon, "Obeah's Sensations: Rethinking Religion at the Transnational Turn," *American Literature* 84, no. 4 (2012): 715–41; Justine S. Murison, "Obeah and Its Others: Buffered Selves in the Era of Tropical Medicine," *Atlantic Studies* 12, no. 2 (2015): 144–59; Gregory S. Jackson, *The Word and Its Witness: The Spiritualization of American Realism* (Chicago: University of Chicago Press, 2009); McGarry, *Ghosts of Futures Past*; and Jared Hickman, "*The Book of Mormon* as Amerindian Apocalypse," *American Literature* 86, no. 3 (2014): 429–61.

28. Michael Warner has noted the oddity of such positive uses of *enchantment*, at least if we mean the term in its Weberian sense: "In English, 'enchantment' is associated with positive affects such as wonder and reverence, and only under the sway of such associations, I think, can anyone imagine that 'reenchantment' would be a good thing, let alone a change that could be willed into being": Warner, "Was Antebellum America Secular?"

remnant implies an imagined renaissance in the present (no matter how early on the historical time line the declaration occurs).[29] There are no doubt multiple—if you like your history local, then countless—modern enchantments. But if we are talking about enchantment at all, we must be talking about a modernizing gesture.

Let me be systematic in distinguishing my use of modern enchantment from three ways that others have used that and similar terms, all of which aim more or less to detach enchantment from delusion, rather than to treat the two as inextricable. My division of these narratives into types is only a heuristic; there are overlaps between the types, and no scholar's work can be reduced to any one of them. The first type imagines the possibility of enlightened enchantment. There is, after all, a way to enjoy enchantment's affects of wonder and spellbinding without the delusion and the thrall. Experiences of wonder are accessible even to unsuperstitious moderns—through fiction, art, and nature, usually—without the experience devolving into opiated escapism. Take, for example, *As If* (2012), in which Michael Saler hails the late nineteenth-century advent of a reading practice he calls the "ironic imagination." A reader with an ironic imagination can "inhabit the imaginary worlds of fantastic fiction for extended periods without losing sight of the real world."[30] Saler's approving title for this attitude is "Delight Without Delusion."[31] Or take Jane Bennett's *The Enchantment of Modern Life* (2001), where Bennett aims to recover enchantment as an experience that is both available in modernity and valuable as an ethical resource: enchantment energizes us to care about others and about the world.[32] Bennett limits enchantment to the realms of affect and aesthetics, not magic: it is a "pleasurable feeling" of "fullness, plenitude, or liveliness."[33] But even within these limits Bennett worries about the "dangers" of "the link between enchantment and mindlessness, between joy and forgetfulness," and she assumes her readers will, too.[34] She promises a moderate regimen: "small, controlled doses" of "a certain forgetfulness" and "moments of enchantment rather than an enchanted way of life."[35] We can have enchantment's moods of awe without its

---

29. On early disenchantments, see Taylor, *Secular Age*, 43–45, 77.
30. Saler, *As If*, 14.
31. Ibid., 57.
32. Bennett, *Enchantment of Modern Life*, 12.
33. Ibid., 5.
34. Ibid., 10.
35. Ibid., 10.

slavish religious beliefs; its raptures without its glazed-over enthrallment to mass culture; its pleasures without its mortal injuries to our free will.

The enlightened-enchantment approach has advantages. It may be empirically true that modern readers experience an ironic double position like the one Saler describes: delight, and not delusion; a pleasant buzz, and not a bender. For that matter, it may be empirically true that premodern readers did, too. The disadvantage of this approach, though, is that valorizing detachment, as both Saler and Bennett do, amounts to a repetition of secular prescriptions against delusion rather than an analysis of them. Recognizing the "dangers" of "forgetfulness" and of "losing sight of the real world" is a maneuver that belongs squarely in secular discourse. Tracy Fessenden has pointed out "the lingering impress of the secularization narrative even on some newer works of scholarship that seek to revise or rethink their relationship to its plotline."[36] In "The Problem of the Postsecular," she observes that by retaining what is basically the division between good religion (wonder, ethical resources) and bad religion (doctrine, fixed identities, thrall), scholars are reinstating, rather than analyzing, the secularization narrative.[37]

A second approach to modern enchantment is one for which the persistence of magical practices after 1800 (or whenever the great divide is taken to be) proves the secularization thesis wrong: secularity is a ruse.[38] Alex Owen's *The Place of Enchantment* (2004) is a case in point here.[39] Owen's object of study is what she variously calls "fin-de-siècle enchantment" or "newly configured enchantment in the modern period:" the late nineteenth-century British occult.[40] That milieu can "challenge . . . our traditional understanding of modern culture as characterized by a strictly secular-scientific outlook, and of occultism as necessarily opposed to the dictates of rationalism and out of synch with reality." Actually occultism was "committed to the guiding principle of reason and played to a formalized concept of rationality even as it contested a strictly secular rationalism."[41]

36. Fessenden, "Problem of the Postsecular," 157.

37. Ibid., 165.

38. John Warne Monroe, *Laboratories of Faith: Mesmerism, Spiritism, and Occultism in Modern France* (Ithaca, NY: Cornell University Press, 2008), 6–7; Corinna Treitel, "What the Occult Reveals," *Modern Intellectual History* 6, no. 3 (2009): 612. See Modern's argument against this position, *Secularism in Antebellum America*, 9.

39. A. Owen, *Place of Enchantment*, 8–16.

40. Ibid., 12, 15.

41. Ibid., 12.

Though Owen's book "in no way seeks to dissociate itself from the relevance of a secularization paradigm for the modern period," it nonetheless does seek to show that enchantment and belief are seamlessly compatible with the secular.[42] Owen had to contend with a prior generation of scholars ready to dismiss the occult as "a retrogressive throwback or a fringe aberration,"[43] and those of us who study the occult now owe a debt to her and others like her who have shown that it merits serious attention.[44] What is missing here, though, is an acknowledgment of the tension between secular ideals and the occult. Downplaying the threat that the occult represented for many would-be secularists, as Owen's approach does, has some significant drawbacks. It tends to take attention away from the important self-definitional work secular ages have done around the occult. While it is true that such practices as British occultism and American mesmerism thrived after 1800, it is also true that many would-be moderns called their thriving a travesty and a shame. These practices were not modern, according to such detractors; they were atavistic throwbacks, last vestiges of a darker age. The role of the historian certainly is not to adopt such a position. But on the other hand, if historians ignore such positions as false, they miss secularity itself. Occult practitioners often thought they were aiming for modernity; detractors found their aim to be abysmally poor. Neither side of the debate can be safely ignored.

The third type of modern enchantment thesis takes occult practices to be so much at odds with the secular consensus surrounding them that they are a source of radical alternatives. I call this the *radical enchantment position*.[45] In American studies especially, the occult has lent itself to what Robyn Wiegman has called the "political imaginary of the alternative that

---

42. Ibid., 10–11.

43. Ibid., 15.

44. See, among others, ibid.; Ann Braude, *Radical Spirits: Spiritualism and Women's Rights in Nineteenth-Century America* (Boston: Beacon Press, 1989); Monroe, *Laboratories of Faith*; McGarry, *Ghosts of Futures Past*; Stefan Andriopoulos, *Ghostly Apparitions: German Idealism, the Gothic Novel, and Optical Media* (New York: Zone Books, 2013); John Durham Peters, *Speaking Into the Air: A History of the Idea of Communication* (Chicago: University of Chicago Press, 1999); Alison Winter, *Mesmerized: Powers of Mind in Victorian Britain* (Chicago: University of Chicago Press, 1998); Corinna Treitel, *A Science for the Soul: Occultism and the Genesis of the German Modern* (Baltimore: Johns Hopkins University Press, 2004).

45. I make this argument at greater length in Emily Ogden, "Beyond Radical Enchantment: Mesmerizing Laborers in the Americas," *Critical Inquiry* 42, no. 1 (Summer 2016): 815–19.

governs the field."[46] American studies, according to Wiegman, has tended to ally itself with positions that seem to offer a vantage point of exteriority to American power, by virtue of being themselves subject to "exclusion, subordination, and exploitation."[47] Ever since Ann Braude argued in *Radical Spirits* (1989) that séance spiritualism fostered feminist politics, enchanted states have seemed to offer a position exterior to the national consensus.[48] A variety of practices bringing do-it-yourself revelations achieved in altered states of mind—from revivalism to spiritualism to vodou—have taken the starring role in such stories.[49] For Nancy Ruttenburg, witchcraft and Great Awakenings hosted "the untheorized experiential beginnings of political life for persons without a public voice within the culture."[50] For Molly McGarry, spiritualism may give us political resources in the present by "bring[ing] into focus the historical specificities of the marginal and local forms by which dominant practices were resisted, deflected, or shown to be imperfectly constituted."[51] Exterior to patriarchy, liberalism, secularity, and Whig history, radical enchantment has stood for our hopes. It has stood, and continues to stand in American studies, for an avant-garde aligned with marginalized subjects.

The radical enchantment model has its truth, too, especially for Braude and McGarry's subject, spiritualism. Both make convincing cases for spiritualism's relationship to, respectively, women's rights and queer identities. But as Wiegman is well aware, and as Fessenden has convincingly argued in connection with postsecular approaches to literary study, avant-gardism is closely tied to secularity itself. Fessenden remarks that "what is hardest to

46. Robyn Wiegman, "The Ends of New Americanism," *New Literary History* 42, no. 3 (2011): 399.

47. Ibid., 392.

48. Braude, *Radical Spirits*.

49. For Alex Owen, spiritualists were unconsciously "radical" in spite of their sometime refusal to transgress feminine norms: *The Darkened Room: Women, Power, and Spiritualism in Late Victorian England* (Philadelphia: University of Pennsylvania Press, 1990), 202; Nancy Ruttenburg, *Democratic Personality: Popular Voice and the Trial of American Authorship* (Stanford, CA: Stanford University Press, 1998), 3–5; Deborah Manson, "'The Trance of the Ecstatica': Margaret Fuller, Animal Magnetism, and the Transcendent Female Body," *Literature and Medicine* 25, no. 2 (2006): 300; Jaudon, "Obeah's Sensations," 718. Robert S. Cox has looked askance at radical enchantment: *Body and Soul: A Sympathetic History of American Spiritualism* (Charlottesville, VA: University of Virginia Press, 2003), 4.

50. Ruttenburg, *Democratic Personality*, 4.

51. McGarry, *Ghosts of Futures Past*, 12.

throw off of the secularization narrative's pressures . . . is the patterning of secular time. The secularization thesis keys the progressive emancipation of individuals and groups to movement forward in time. . . . The 'post-' of post-secular literary studies likewise implies fleetness in relation to obdurate and potentially confining tradition."[52] As Peter Coviello and Jared Hickman write, "unburdening from the secularization thesis is perhaps more easily described than enacted"; after "the demise of the secularization thesis, we are only now beginning to grasp how deeply we remain in it."[53] The liability of approaching enchantment as a radical alternative is that it leaves unexamined the relations between enchantment and disenchantment that happen within secularity— and that go well beyond repression of something standing "outside" the sec-ular consensus. We are unlikely to notice from this vantage point how calling a practice a delusion may incite that practice rather than repress it.

Studies falling under all three of these types are invested, to one degree or another, in defending enchantment against the charge of superstition or false consciousness. Enchantment is compatible with reason, say Saler and Bennett. It persists into modernity, says Owen, where it mixes with sec-ular values—calling into question whether there is any such thing as disen-chantment. Or as Braude and McGarry suggest, enchantment acts in secu-larity as the shelter for ways of life that, far from being retrograde, may be in the vanguard. These strands of thought about modern enchantment are ready for anything but a conversation about delusion. Even for historians of the occult who are less invested in secularity—such as Alison Winter in *Mesmerized* (1999) and Catherine Albanese in *A Republic of Mind and Spirit* (2007)—delusion has not been of primary concern. Winter's history of mes-merism in Britain makes the well-taken point that one ought not to apply present ideas about the divisions between science and pseudoscience to the past.[54] Albanese, writing about what she calls the American metaphysical religion tradition, makes an analogous argument, directed toward histori-ans of religion, against back-forming divisions between religion and cultic practices.[55] Both of these historians are careful to avoid applying present-

52. Fessenden, "Problem of the Postsecular," 157; see also Wiegman, "Ends of New Ameri-canism," 392.

53. Coviello and Hickman, "Introduction: After the Postsecular," in Peter Coviello and Jared Hickman, eds., "After the Postsecular," special issue, *American Literature* 86, no. 4 (2014): 646.

54. Winter, *Mesmerized*, 26.

55. Catherine L. Albanese, *A Republic of Mind and Spirit: A Cultural History of American Metaphysical Religion* (New Haven, CT: Yale University Press, 2007), 6–16.

day divisions between the reputable and the deluded to the past. But in the process, past accusations of delusion—with all they can tell us about the formation of a secular consensus—get short shrift.

Ann Taves observed in *Fits, Trances, and Visions* (1999) that "much of the writing [on trance experience] . . . has either taken the critics' charges of enthusiasm or fanaticism at face value or has focused exclusively on those who claimed to have experienced religion."[56] Taves's analysis of the field still resonates, in spite of the example that her own book gave us of how to place the traffic between "experiencing" religion and "explaining" religion at the heart of the matter.[57] Delusion was an empty nothing to Whig historians who contemned the occult. But the irony is that delusion has *remained* an empty nothing when historians recovering occult practice as a serious subject have strenuously rebuffed these earlier scholars' contempt. As David Walker points out, Albanese has even praised McGarry for her "refus[al] to be preoccupied with the too-easy discourse of fraud, the conventional ritual of denial that historians have often used to dismiss spiritualists from thoughtful examination."[58] But Walker sees that the time has come to turn the tables on this notion that describing fraud is easy. His response is to "admit to preoccupation precisely with the discourse of fraud . . . and to persistent concern with its historical and historiographical operations. Such discourse is never simple . . . and historians have still insufficiently attended not only to the types of 'thoughtful examination' that may occur in 'ritual[s] of denial' themselves but also to the ways in which spiritualists have assumed and enabled them."[59] I agree. The discourse of fraud, with its accusations of credulity and chicanery, demands a quantity and a quality of attention greater than what we have been giving it.

US mesmerism has also been understudied, and the two areas of relative historiographical neglect—delusion and mesmerism—probably have been sidelined for related reasons.[60] Those who do not want to talk about

56. Ann Taves, *Fits, Trances, and Visions: Experiencing Religion and Explaining Experience from Wesley to James* (Princeton, NJ: Princeton University Press, 1999), 4.

57. Ibid.

58. Albanese quoted in Walker, "Humbug," 57n6. Brackets are Walker's.

59. Walker, "Humbug," 57n6.

60. The last monograph on US mesmerism was published more than thirty years ago: Robert C. Fuller's *Mesmerism and the American Cure of Souls* (Philadelphia: University of Pennsylvania Press, 1982). In the meantime, studies of US mesmerism have appeared as parts of longer works: Taves, *Fits, Trances, and Visions*, 121–65; Albanese, *Republic of Mind and Spirit*, 190–206; Adam Crabtree, *From Mesmer to Freud: Magnetic Sleep and the*

delusion would be unlikely to talk about US mesmerism, because to address the latter without addressing the former would be to contort the facts, as Taves saw. Delusion was what mesmerists understood themselves to be practicing, and they said so explicitly: they manipulated and enhanced the credulity of their clairvoyants in order to know, to discipline, to entertain, and to cure. Nor were their deceptions held at the ironic distance we see in magic shows: their manipulations of the animal-magnetic fluid had the dead earnestness so often attached to discoveries of new forms of matter.[61] Comparing antirevivalist rhetoric to mesmerism, Taves has observed that both were "secularizing discourses" but that mesmerism differed from antirevivalism in one important respect: "while anti-enthusiasts *explained* involuntary bodily movements that appeared spontaneously, mesmerists also *induced* them."[62] Mesmerism sought to theorize enchantment and to incite it, by manipulating the animal-magnetic fluid. Beyond the bodily movements Taves notes, mesmerists also induced states of extreme obedi-

---

Roots of Psychological Healing (New Haven, CT: Yale University Press, 1993), 213–31; Alan Gauld, *A History of Hypnotism* (Cambridge: Cambridge University Press, 1992), 179–96, 231–34. Sheila O'Brien Quinn has also done important work on the topic: "How Southern New England Became Magnetic North: The Acceptance of Animal Magnetism," *History of Psychology* 10, no. 3 (2007): 231–48; "Credibility, Respectability, Suggestibility, and Spirit Travel: Lurena Brackett and Animal Magnetism," *History of Psychology* 15, no. 3 (2012): 273–82. Histories of mesmerism in other national settings also provide important context, notably Bertrand Méheust, *Somnambulisme et médiumnité (1784–1930)*, vol. 1, *Le Défi du magnétisme animal*, 2nd ed. (Paris: La Découverte, 2014); Nicole Edelman, *Voyantes, guérisseuses et visionnaires en France, 1785–1914* (Paris: Albin Michel, 1995); Darnton, *Mesmerism and the End of the Enlightenment in France*; and Winter, *Mesmerized*.

61. Generally speaking, scholars of deceptive entertainments such as magic or the hoaxes of P. T. Barnum have been more likely to focus on delusion than have scholars of the occult. See, for example, Simon During, whose history of fin de siècle British magic shows tells a story of enchantment and magic understood as premodern but then restaged as entertainment. For During, modern enchantment is to be found not among those who believe but among those who control "the technically produced magic of conjuring shows and special effects": Simon During, *Modern Enchantments: The Cultural Power of Secular Magic* (Cambridge, MA: Harvard University Press, 2002), 1. See also Neil Harris, *Humbug: The Art of P. T. Barnum* (Boston: Little, Brown, 1973); James Cook, *The Arts of Deception: Playing with Fraud in the Age of Barnum* (Cambridge, MA: Harvard University Press, 2001). Scholars of religion and the occult who have recognized delusion's importance include Taves, *Fits, Trances, and Visions*; Walker, "Humbug"; and Leigh Eric Schmidt, *Hearing Things: Religion, Illusion, and the American Enlightenment* (Cambridge, MA: Harvard University Press, 2000).

62. Taves, *Fits, Trances, and Visions*, 125.

ence and belief. With mesmerism there is no possibility of treating modern enchantment as an exterior space. Mesmerists both saw the credulity of somnambulistic subjects as a primitive remnant *and* sought to elicit that credulity as a thing of value. Thus, in their practice, enchantment stands revealed as a part of secular discourse, not an exception to it. Mesmerists were aiming at modernity—but this did not stop them from aiming other people away from it or from experimenting with, and hoping to control, the credulity of others.

This book's focus on the aiming of others *away* from modernity is its primary contribution to secularity studies. As mesmerists, and also debunkers of mesmerism, tried to be modern, I ask, what relations did they establish with the credulous? In posing this question, I take as starting points Asad's and Latour's descriptions of the subject position toward which moderns aspired. Latour defines his "Moderns" as those who are "freeing themselves from attachments to the past in order to advance toward FREEDOM," and who are heading toward a future in which "the distinction between Facts and Values will finally be sharp and clear."[63] Asad's "secular agent" represents the "metaphysical idea . . . of a conscious agent-subject having both the capacity and the desire to move in a singular historical direction: that of increasing self-empowerment and decreasing pain."[64] This agent's fundamental question is, "what should human beings do to realize their freedom, empower themselves, and choose pleasure?"[65] The figures of the secular agent and the modern allow these theorists to indicate demands implicit in secular discourse, not to describe philosophical accounts of subjectivity or subject positions realized in practice. Neither the modern's platform of FREEDOM nor the secular agent's program of a fully achieved self-knowledge and self-control are destined to be realized in practice. What *does* happen in practice, this book argues, is that the impossibility of these demands prompts a range of compensatory strategies: attempts to feel like a secular agent if one cannot be one. What distinguishes the present account from Asad's or Latour's, in fact, is just this interest in how people try to negotiate the impossible demand that they be empowered and free: my

---

63. Bruno Latour, *An Inquiry into Modes of Existence: An Anthropology of the Moderns*, trans. Catherine Porter (Cambridge, MA: Harvard University Press, 2013), 8; translation of Bruno Latour, *Enquête sur les modes d'existence: Une Anthropologie des Modernes* (Paris: La Découverte, 2012), 20–21.

64. Asad, *Formations of the Secular*, 79.

65. Ibid., 71.

interest is not in describing secular agency per se but in understanding the aftereffects of its inevitable failure.

By turning to mesmerism, a practice that applied itself with unusual industry to the task of finding delusion a useful place in modern life, *Credulity* shows how would-be moderns (a group that included debunkers such as Osborn or Reese and mesmerists such as Grimes) sought to establish the kind of mastery over credulous people that they could not establish over themselves. Mesmerists put forward the same taxonomies of excessive belief that others in diverse areas of American culture did, locating it among women, primitives, and the insane, and blaming it for everything from the election of the populist president Andrew Jackson in 1828 to the collapse of the financial markets in the Panic of 1837. Yet mesmerists were unusually frank in admitting their intention to augment and exploit others' gullibility. The attempt involved them in forms of agency quite different from those they originally sought to shore up: it involved them in conversion, in collaborative storytelling, and in dependence on their alleged dependents. My aim is to describe this whole pattern and the mutual imbrication of credulity and secularity that it implies—not to pit one phase against another (the secular versus the credulous). Modern enchantment, I argue here, is neither a cleaned-up version of old credulous practices nor a seamless integration of magic into modernity that proves disenchantment narratives like Weber's wrong. Modern enchantment is the negotiation between those who are aiming at modernity and those whom they see as nonmodern. It is the refracted and refractory array of results, some intended and some not, that arises from the attempt to manage credulity.

Mesmerism was accused of credulity, it claimed to control and employ credulity, and it furnished a space in which credulity could be enthusiastically embraced. Each of these modes coexisted with the others, but one can say that their historical emergence occurred roughly in the order in which I have named them. By 1784, some fifty years before US audiences saw mesmerism in action, they already knew it as the kind of falsehood by which the "credulity of the public" could be imposed upon.[66] Mesmerism had been practiced

66. Editorial headnote to [John Adams,] "Boston, Nov. 29: Extract of a Letter Dated September 8, 1784, Auteuil, near Paris," *American Herald*, Boston, MA, November 29, 1784.

in France starting in the late 1770s, when its namesake, the Austrian physician Franz Anton Mesmer, set up a treatment salon in Paris. He claimed to cure diseases by controlling the invisible fluid of "animal magnetism" with his hands; sometimes he also waved an iron rod in intricate circles and played music on a glass harmonica. In 1784 the French government appointed two academic commissions to investigate, with Benjamin Franklin, then resident in Paris, as the cochair of one of the two. Franklin's committee formulated an idea of credulity that would have a major influence in both religious and scientific circles. The commissioners hypothesized that because the patients had believed in mesmerism, their "imaginations" had manufactured in their bodies the effects that Mesmer told them to expect. Thus their passionate belief in the fluid of animal magnetism made that fluid appear to have an effect—even though it did not exist. Belief's physical effects via the imagination could in fact explain all the enchantments and enthusiasms of the past and present. American audiences learned about the triumph of Franklin before mesmerism was ever practiced in the United States, and so for them mesmerism was, first and foremost, an exemplary credulous error. Chapter 1 recounts this early history.[67]

Mesmerism's US founder, Charles Poyen, lamented Americans' skepticism, but his success in establishing the practice in 1836 partly depended on it, as chapter 2 shows. Born on a sugar plantation on the Caribbean island of Guadeloupe, Poyen was a slaveholder. He learned about mesmerism while in medical school in Paris. Since Franklin's time, practitioners had retooled their science as a means of explaining and exploiting credulity. Whereas the Franklin commission had called mesmerists' practice an *example* of excessive belief, proponents now claimed it was a means of *controlling* false belief. Poyen saw mesmerism used on nervous patients in Paris hospitals and on slaves on Guadeloupe plantations. With the help of Cynthia Gleason, a power loom weaver who turned out to be a gifted mesmeric clairvoyant, Poyen marketed mesmerism to the textile factory owners of New England as a means of managing their female laborers. The Franklin report had primed Americans for an association between mesmerism and

67. I draw here on Jessica Riskin, *Science in the Age of Sensibility: The Sentimental Empiricists of the French Enlightenment* (Chicago: University of Chicago Press, 2002), 189–225; Léon Chertok and Isabelle Stengers, *Le Cœur et la raison: L'hypnose en question de Lavoisier à Lacan* (Paris: Éditions Payot, 1989), 15–46, later published in English as *A Critique of Psychoanalytic Reason: Hypnosis as a Scientific Problem from Lavoisier to Lacan*, trans. Martha Noel Evans (Stanford, CA: Stanford University Press, 1992), 1–36; and Darnton, *Mesmerism and the End of the Enlightenment in France*.

credulity, and they were interested in Poyen's promise of discipline. One can draw an unbroken line from the Franklin commission's explanation of the prestidigitations of the ancient priests to mesmerists' explanation of the same. The commissioners theorized religious cheats and made mesmerism Exhibit A. Mesmerists of the nineteenth century also theorized religious cheats. But now mesmerism, instead of being Exhibit A, was the rational practice that systematized the formerly unsystematic art of priestcraft. Mesmerists practiced what they preached against. But they practiced it with the difference, in their minds critical, of having reduced the occult art to a technique. Enchantment, here, was not a radical or fringe practice; it was a management strategy.

Neither the Franklinian position, that mesmerism was an instance of credulity, nor the Poyenian position, that it was a profitable method for manipulating credulity, ever went away during the rest of the practice's US history. But chapter 3 demonstrates that soon after Poyen's arrival, complications emerged in his program. As mesmerism spread, attracting the curiosity of thousands and the sustained attention of such major authors as Edgar Allan Poe, Herman Melville, Harriet Beecher Stowe, and Nathaniel Hawthorne, Poyen's vision of credulity governed by a detached operator soon gave way to a more collaborative relationship between mesmerist and subject. That happened because of, not in spite of, the continued efforts to rein credulity in. The more urgent the need to demonstrate mastery, the more the object of that mastery had to be elicited. And the more one listened to credulity's siren song, the more fascinating it became. It turned out to be difficult to supervise others' enchantment without becoming enchanted oneself. The first distinctly American variation on the practice involved skeptics, mesmerists, and subjects alike in a web of mutual credulity. Adept "traveling clairvoyants" could voyage "in imagination" to distant cities, describing what they saw—but only if their interlocutors feigned credulity and pretended to be traveling, too. The pretense of belief had a tendency to become real. Through an account of the conversion of the prominent skeptic William L. Stone by the blind clairvoyant Loraina Brackett, I show how mesmerism became a place for rethinking the value of delusion. Poe took up traveling clairvoyance in his story "A Tale of the Ragged Mountains" (1844), where he used it to ask whether it might simply be a secular prejudice, better abandoned, to be ashamed to be taken in by a fictional account.

In the 1840s and 1850s, mesmerism's heyday, several competing branches emerged. Chapter 4 focuses on one of these, phrenomesmerism, as practiced by the Kentucky physician Joseph Rodes Buchanan. Buchanan promised that by stimulating the brain with the mesmeric fluid, he could produce an accurate map of the phrenological organs of character. This map would aid in education and self-culture, helping to form the kind of empowered subject Asad has called the secular agent. Yet such a map could only be drawn by the aid of people who were the very opposite of empowered. Buchanan called them "impressible"—that is, when mesmerized, they manifested the qualities of whatever organ the practitioner touched, even against their own personalities. Some impressible subjects could also read others' characters directly, by touching their skulls or holding scraps of their handwriting. Buchanan's practice offers a particularly crisp example of how enchanted states, here "impressibility," were tools to be used in secular projects, not modes of being that were excluded from a secular age. Phrenomesmerism is the basis for *The Blithedale Romance* (1852), in which Hawthorne uses Buchanan's science of character to indict the secular agent and explore tolerable forms of disempowerment.

Finally, chapter 5 shows that US mesmerism ended much as it began: with debunking. As versions of mesmeric practice proliferated, practitioners became focused on discrediting each other. Some, notably J. Stanley Grimes, devoted substantial portions of their careers to the task of showing that their rivals were self-deceived. In this distinctly Franklinian atmosphere, a new group of mesmerists emerged. The electrobiologists, as they were called, gradually jettisoned the idea of turning credulity to useful purposes. They focused on showing that instead of being an exceptional state, credulity was frighteningly common. Their subjects manifested a spectacular gullibility—seeing entire scenes playing out before them that were not real—without any concomitant gain in clairvoyance or insight. Electrobiologists' uncompromising sense that their technique permitted them to fool anyone anytime upset the delicate balance on which mesmerism had long depended: the claim to confine and control enchantment. Spiritualists took up the mantle that mesmerists had dropped. In spiritualist practice, too, the credulity of mediums would be profitably directed. Mesmerism's modern enchantments thus continued in a new form. A coda on Melville's *Moby-Dick* (1851) serves as a conclusion to the chapter and to the book.

Like mesmerism itself, *Credulity* has to do with a wide range of texts, not all of them true. Mesmerists and their debunkers repeatedly muddled fact, fraud, and fiction. Theorists doing their level best to be truthful nonetheless invented nonexistent fluids—or so their detractors said. Patients distinctly felt things that other people told them were not real. Skeptics conducted elaborate gaslighting campaigns to trick practitioners into betraying that they had been deluded—or that they had deluded others. Pseudomesmerists pseudoconfessed to pseudoseductions, in tracts that antimesmeric writers used to smear their opponents' names. Fiction is hardly out of place in such a milieu, and it provides an important perspective on mesmerism throughout this book. Many of the major fiction writers of the antebellum period wrote about mesmerism, and so did some who are less well remembered now. Temperance novelist T. S. Arthur imagines a mesmeric seduction in *Agnes* (1848), as do city mysteries writers George Lippard and Osgood Bradbury in *The Quaker City* (1845) and *Mysteries of Lowell* (1844), respectively. Since I am in pursuit here of the social effects of an imaginary—credulity—rather than, in the first instance, the physical effects of a magnetic fluid, fictional texts are helpful. Fiction writers, unconstrained by what can be demonstrated onstage in front of an audience, often tell us more about what mesmerists dreamed of achieving, even as they tell us less than factual accounts do about what practitioners actually accomplished. Besides, fiction writers, like mesmerists, often promised to govern credulity: the genre of the novel, in particular, characteristically claimed to help readers learn to distinguish truth from falsehood at the moment of its eighteenth-century origins.[68] Novelists had a professional stake in the question of how much gullibility was to be permitted. This book does not claim, however, that literary writers have a monopoly on the description of imaginary life, or that they have special insight into the workings of mesmerism that practitioners themselves could not achieve. Both imagination and insight are to be found in a wide range of mesmeric genres, from theoretical treatises to amateur performances to literary renderings.

It sometimes seems as though secularity is properly an object of study for historians of science and religion. But it would be a mistake for historians of literature to be diffident about the relevance of their subject matter to this topic. It is not just that literary texts may deal thematically with the secular. The target of secularizing energies is not religion but falsehood—including false religion, but also other trickery that may take credulous people in (confidence games, seductions, demagoguery). Fiction's status as a free-trade zone for untruth makes it a fertile space in which the boundary between acceptable and unacceptable falsehood can be defined. There is as much reason for theorists of fiction to talk about the secular as for theorists of religion to do so. Poe wrote hoaxes and worked in magazine genres

68. Catherine Gallagher, "The Rise of Fictionality," in *The Novel*, vol. 1, *History, Geography, and Culture*, ed. Franco Moretti (Princeton, NJ: Princeton University Press, 2006): 336–63.

where truth and fiction mixed. Melville, trying to escape the genre of the sea narrative, was accused of promiscuous mixtures of falsehood and auto-biography. Hawthorne flirted with the roman à clef form in his *Blithedale Romance*, a novel based on the Brook Farm community, though he denies any strict correspondence between characters and real-life figures in the "Preface."[69] For these authors, mesmerism's position on the line between modernity and credulity was productive. It allowed them to consider where that line should be drawn; to step over it momentarily; and, indeed, to look at the line directly and ask how, by whom, and for what purposes it had been put there. Those are my questions, too.

Credulity appears generally in triplicate in the secular encounter, subject at once to contempt, to employment, and to ardent practice. The same is true in the mesmeric scene. Rather than vying with one another, or repre-senting separate historical periods, these modes are mutually reinforcing. Practice does not compete with debunking and with instrumentalization; it feeds off both. Together these modes make up modern enchantment: the place, that is, of enchantment in secular discourse. Margaret Fuller saw this complex interplay at work in a review she wrote of Grimes's *Etherology*, the book that introduces the organ of credenciveness.[70] In the review, Fuller recounts meeting the clairvoyant Loraina Brackett at the Perkins School for the Blind in Boston.[71] Brackett's career as a clairvoyant was over by the time this encounter took place—probably in the early 1840s—but she was still "very susceptible to magnetic influences." As Fuller left, Brackett passed her a note that deeply impressed the other woman: it was a "token," Fuller thought, of "the same affinity that had acted" when the two women had met

69. Nathaniel Hawthorne, *The Blithedale Romance and Fanshawe*, ed. Fredson Bowers, vol. 3 of *The Centenary Edition of the Works of Nathaniel Hawthorne*, ed. William Charvat et al. (Columbus: Ohio State University Press, 1964), 1–3.

70. Margaret Fuller, "The New Science, or the Philosophy of Mesmerism or Animal Mag-netism" (review of *Etherology; or, The Philosophy of Mesmerism and Phrenology*, by J. Stan-ley Grimes), in *Life Without and Life Within; or, Reviews, Narratives, Essays, and Poems*, ed. Arthur B. Fuller (Boston: Brown, Taggard, & Chase, 1859), 169–73. First published in *New York Tribune*, February 17, 1845.

71. Brackett and the Perkins School are discussed further in chapter 3.

in Providence years before.[72] Fuller performs her struggle to name the "affinity." Is it "Credulity," she asks, as "the world at large" would have it? That had been the Franklin commission's position. Is it "a talisman of 'Credenciveness,'" as Grimes had claimed in the book she was reviewing? Grimes represented the view that Poyen and many other mesmerists took: that mesmerism could direct and employ credulity. Fuller suggests a third possibility: that the note represents "one of the clews granted . . . to the mysteries of future states of being, and more rapid and complete modes of intercourse between mind and mind."[73] Fuller shows herself drawn toward this last idea of credulity as a utopian "clew"—but her inclusion of the other two is not just a matter of strategic concession. She recognizes that in a period during which credulity is contraindicated, the positive qualities tied up in it— lowered social boundaries between herself and Brackett, for example—can be described only by a detour through the negative. Her hopeful maneuver is as much what the exclamation "Out on Credulity!" permits and entails as any gesture of denigration would be. This book aims to pursue all sides of the credulity accusation: its dismissals, its employments, its futuristic possibilities. As antebellum Americans aimed at modernity, credulity was not a name for what ought to disappear. It was a name for what could be profitably managed and for what, in the name of management, could be practiced with absorption and enthusiasm.

72. M. Fuller, "New Science," 173.
73. Ibid.

I

IT DOES NOT EXIST

Animal Magnetism Before It Was True

They are all able men and have published a masterly report, which shews very clearly that this Magnetism can never be useful, for the best of all possible reasons, viz.—*because it does not exist.*

John Adams on the Paris royal commissions
investigating mesmerism (1784)[1]

IN 1778, THE PRACTICE OF ANIMAL magnetism started in Paris. Magnetists enjoyed six happy years; then a star-studded panel of mostly French academicians declared, as John Adams put it, that their science *did not exist.* Late in 1784, the *American Herald* published a letter from Adams, then in France, to his friend the physician Benjamin Waterhouse, then in Boston.[2] The letter contained the first mention in the American press of both animal magnetism and its debunking at the hands of the French academicians. The Austrian physician Franz Anton Mesmer had been making a succès de scandale in Paris by claiming to cure illnesses with the invisible fluid of "animal magnetism" (*magnétisme animal*), a living analog to mineral

---

1. [John Adams], "Boston, Nov. 29: Extract of a Letter Dated September 8, 1784, Auteuil, near Paris," *American Herald*, Boston, MA, November 29, 1784. The author is identified in John Adams, "John Adams as He Lived," *Atlantic Monthly*, May 1927.

2. Adams, "Boston, Nov. 29;" Adams, "John Adams as He Lived."

magnetism that was distributed throughout the cosmos and was especially active in human bodies. ("Animal" is something of a misnomer; Mesmer meant *animal* as opposed to *mineral*, not as opposed to *human*. Think "vital magnetism.")[3] Adams aptly called Mesmer's practice "a kind of physical new light or witchcraft."[4] It mixed Bavarian exorcism, a practice Mesmer had claimed to explain with his own principles, with a view of matter that seemed vaguely drawn from Benjamin Franklin's *Experiments and Observations on Electricity* (1751).[5] According to Mesmer, imbalances in the magnetic fluid were at the root of all disease. By manipulating the fluid through gestures called the "magnetic passes," he could make his patients seize, shriek, go into hysterics, vomit, and, allegedly, get well. The theory was that magnetization cleared obstructions in the movement of the body's vital fluids. But Adams and other Anglophone observers were put more in mind of new-light Protestant convulsions in the Great Awakening.[6] The prodigies of animal magnetism took place in Mesmer's very public treatment salons, where the mise-en-scène showed the Austrian's flair for theater. The walls were padded and decorated with celestial symbols, the air vibrated with glass harmonica music, and the doctor wore purple—flowing violet robes, to be exact.[7] Some of the patients' fits bore a suspicious resemblance to or-

3. Jessica Riskin, *Science in the Age of Sensibility: The Sentimental Empiricists of the French Enlightenment* (Chicago: University of Chicago Press, 2002), 195–98.

4. Adams, "Boston, Nov. 29."

5. Benjamin Franklin, *Experiments and Observations on Electricity* (London: E. Cave, 1751); Riskin, *Science in the Age of Sensibility*, 196–99; H. C. Erik Midelfort, *Exorcism and Enlightenment: Johann Joseph Gassner and the Demons of Eighteenth-Century Germany* (New Haven, CT: Yale University Press, 2005), 2, 17–20.

6. Ann Taves, *Fits, Trances, and Visions: Experiencing Religion and Explaining Experience from Wesley to James* (Princeton, NJ: Princeton University Press, 1999), 121–22. "New-light" meant prorevival in the years of the eighteenth-century religious Awakenings: Taves, *Fits, Trances, and Visions*, 22. When Adams calls magnetism "a kind of physical new light," he is alluding to that tradition: Adams, "Boston, Nov. 29." On the difference between Anglophone and Francophone experiences of enthusiasm and involuntary convulsions, see Jan Goldstein, "Enthusiasm or Imagination? Eighteenth-Century Smear Words in a Comparative National Context," *Huntington Library Quarterly* 60, no. 1–2 (1997): 29–49.

7. Riskin, *Science in the Age of Sensibility*, 201, 224; Alan Gauld, *A History of Hypnotism* (Cambridge: Cambridge University Press, 1992), 5; Robert Darnton, *Mesmerism and the End of the Enlightenment in France* (Cambridge, MA: Harvard University Press, 1968), 8.

gasm.[8] "The thing is so serious," Adams told Waterhouse, "that the King has thought necessary to appoint a number of Physicians and Academicians, with your friend *Franklin* at their head, to enquire into it."[9]

This, to Adams, was the point of the letter. Forget the pretensions of the "German Empirick" Mesmer; the real marvel here was Benjamin Franklin's power of annihilation.[10] Franklin was by this time in semiretirement in the Paris suburb of Passy.[11] But he and the founder of modern chemistry, Antoine Lavoisier, cochaired one half of the dual investigating commission appointed by King Louis XVI to examine mesmerism. Franklin and his fellow commissioners had shown, Adams said, that "this Magnetism can never be useful, for the best of all possible reasons, viz.—*because it does not exist.*" Adams expected the commission's report to "annihilate the enthusiasm" for Mesmer's art.[12] Franklin's name became central to the American reception of the commissioners' report. The *Rapport des commissaires chargés par le roi de l'examen du magnétisme animal* (1784), drafted by commission member Jean-Sylvain Bailly and translated by William Godwin as the *Report of Dr. Benjamin Franklin, and Other Commissioners, Charged by the King of France with the Examination of the Animal Magnetism* (1785), would find an interested audience in the United States even though mesmerism had never been practiced there.[13] Magnetism slowly regained its footing in France after a brief intermission for the French Revolution; in the United States, by contrast, the successful introduction of the practice by Charles Poyen was still fifty years out.[14] So it would be fair to say that animal magnetism

8. Riskin, *Science in the Age of Sensibility*, 215–16; [J. S. Bailly], "Rapport secret sur le Mesmérisme, rédig[é] par Bailly," August 11, 1784, *The Franklin Papers at Yale*, accessed February 13, 2017, http://franklinpapers.org/franklin//.

9. Adams, "Boston, Nov. 29."

10. Ibid.

11. Simon Schaffer, "Self Evidence," *Critical Inquiry* 18, no. 2 (1992): 355.

12. Adams, "Boston, Nov. 29."

13. [J.-S. Bailly], *Rapport des commissaires chargés par le roi de l'examen du magnétisme animal* (Paris: Imprimerie du Roi, 1784); [J.-S. Bailly], *Report of Dr. Benjamin Franklin, and Other Commissioners, Charged by the King of France with the Examination of the Animal Magnetism, as Now Practised at Paris*, [trans. William Godwin] (London: J. Johnson, 1785), hereafter cited as *Rapport* and *Report*, respectively. Neither Bailly nor Godwin is named on the respective works' title pages. Godwin is identified as the translator in a letter from Benjamin Vaughan to Benjamin Franklin, October 1784, cited in Schaffer, "Self Evidence," 351n56.

14. Gauld, *A History of Hypnotism*, 111. Charles Poyen is discussed further in chapter 2 of the present volume.

came to the United States as a falsehood before it appeared there as a truth. In that intervening half century, magnetism was the quintessential example of modern idolatry. Guardians of public reason trotted out the 1784 report each time the crack-brained proponent of some new cure, prophecy, or electrical machine needed reminding of which side Franklin would have been on. As an exemplary falsehood, animal magnetism did a brisk trade.

Where does disenchantment actually put the things that do not exist; and what happens to them after that declaration? The 1784 commission report gives us a unique opportunity to ask those questions.[15] It is a canonical instance of disenchantment.[16] Faced with the claim that there existed something called "animal magnetism," the commissioners showed that this alleged entity was a fetish, cobbled together out of a couple of natural causes and a good deal of credulity. Disenchantment stories like to end with broken idols. But as with many a conventional generic ending, the truth is more complicated. After the idols stop functioning, they resume their activity in a new way, often enjoying long and eventful second lives. That liveliness, I argue in this book, takes place not in spite of disenchantment but in concert with it. The death knell the 1784 commissioners tried to ring was far less decisive than many observers had hoped it would be. Not only did the commissioners fail to obliterate animal magnetism—which, on the contrary, thrived throughout the first two-thirds of the nineteenth century— they also made a vital contribution to magnetism's later theoretical apparatus. Later magnetists would incorporate some of the commission's own anti-idolatry rhetoric, making the practice into a strange compound of the theories of its founder and of its first major debunkers. As for Poyen, the

15. Isabelle Stengers has seen hypnotic phenomena as an opportunity to ask about non-existence and the boundaries of science: Léon Chertok and Isabelle Stengers, *Le Cœur et la raison: L'hypnose en question de Lavoisier à Lacan* (Paris: Éditions Payot, 1989), later published in English as *A Critique of Psychoanalytic Reason: Hypnosis as a Scientific Problem from Lavoisier to Lacan*, trans. Martha Noel Evans (Stanford, CA: Stanford University Press, 1992); Isabelle Stengers, *L'Hypnose entre magie et science* (Paris: La Découverte, 2002); Tobie Nathan and Isabelle Stengers, *Médecins et sorciers*, 2nd ed. (Paris: La Découverte, 2004).

16. The investigation is canonical in the literal sense of being the frequent resort for historians of science considering the history of experimental evidence, including the control of the imagination and passions in experimental settings: e.g., Schaffer, "Self Evidence," 349–58; Chertok and Stengers, *Critique of Psychoanalytic Reason*, 1–36; Chertok and Stengers, *Le Cœur et la raison,* 15–46; Lorraine Daston, "Fear and Loathing of the Imagination in Science," *Daedalus* 134, no. 4 (2005): 21; Riskin, *Science in the Age of Sensibility*, 189–225.

success of his 1836 lecture tour in the United States owed a debt to the Franklin commission. Poyen considered mesmerism a means of manipulating credulity, just as, in a different way, the commission had. Mesmerism's long association with falsehood in the United States did not exactly hurt Poyen's cause; he simply had to twist that association in another direction. Poyen and the other early mesmeric practitioners in the United States would till the rich fields of a half century of their own disrepute. This chapter is a tour of those fields in the years before he came. It aims to describe what imagination was in the commissioners' hands and why imagination and other concepts of nonexistence like it were both the necessities and the scourges of enlightenment.

IDOL-FUNCTIONS

There is a surprising consequence involved in accusing other people of believing in things that do not exist. The aim is to deprive these idols, these nothings in the world, of their power. And yet the end result is to give some placeholder—"belief" or "idolatry" or "imagination"—all the power that the idols once had. As humbug-buster David Reese would write in 1838, by which time mesmerism not only still existed but was the primary target of Reese's ire, "an *idol* is nothing, and *error* is nothing, but these *nothings* are the most dangerous things in the world."[17] Reese was recalling some mixture of Francis Bacon's anatomy of the "Idols which beset men's minds" in the *Novum Organum* (*New Organon*; 1620) and Paul's declaration in the first letter to the Corinthians that "an idol is nothing in the world."[18] Whether early Christian or early modern, disenchantment—which is to say, the performance of recognizing intelligence in fewer objects than one's predecessors did—has

17. David Reese, *Humbugs of New-York: Being a Remonstrance against Popular Delusion* (Boston: Weeks, Jordan, 1838), [i].

18. Francis Bacon, *The New Organon*, book 1, para. 39. The quoted edition is *The Works of Francis Bacon*, 15 vols., ed. James Spedding, Robert Leslie Ellis, and Douglas Denon Heath (Boston: Brown and Taggard, 1860–64), 8:76, an American reprint of the standard edition of Bacon's *Works*, 14 vols. (London: Longman, 1857–74). The passage is translated differently in a more recent scholarly edition, as "*illusions* which block men's minds" (emphasis original; the Latin word *idola* is alternately translated as "illusions" or "idols"). See Francis Bacon, *The New Organon*, ed. Lisa Jardine and Michael Silverthorne (Cambridge: Cambridge University Press, 2000), 40. See also 1 Cor. 8:4 (AV).

often been plagued with the same problem.[19] To wit: if all those things that people "used to" believe—and that the wrong kind of people still believe now—are mere chimeras, then what explains their effectiveness? One can, if one wishes, sparingly decorate one's modern temple, distributing existence with a parsimonious hand and making a trash heap of idols outside the door. But doing so will not break the links of effectiveness that connect those idols to their human beings. If animal magnetism did not exist, for example, then why were Mesmer's patients convulsing? The debunker is obliged to supply an *idol-function*: a cause to account for the effects formerly attributed to the idol animal magnetism. The trouble is that whatever this idol-function may be, it necessarily must have many of the powers attributed to the idol itself. In the case of the 1784 commission, the idol-function was a combination of things, including credulity, imagination, and imitation. Imagination, the leading cause in this group, soon came to be almost as powerful and worrisome as animal magnetism. To disenchant, then, is to invent idol-functions that explain the behavior of other people. And it is often to become unnerved by these inventions of your own.

Whose behavior requires more explanation: the idolater who worships at the shrine or the disenchanter who breaks the idol, sets up an idol-function on the plinth, and then runs from it in fright? Since the 1996 publication of Bruno Latour's essay *Petite Réflexion sur le culte moderne des dieux faitiches* (*On the Modern Cult of the Factish Gods*), one of the sustained preoccupations of his work has been to shift the explanatory emphasis when it comes to scenes of disenchantment.[20] Disenchanters tell us it is belief itself that needs to be explained, but Latour turns the tables: his object of study is the disenchanting "Modern" who "believes that others believe" ("Est moderne celui qui croit que les autres croient").[21] An "agnostic," Latour's name for his own position, "does not wonder whether it is necessary to believe

---

19. Christian theology can be seen as a disenchantment in that it is a monotheism: the verse to which Reese alludes reads in full, "As concerning therefore the eating of those things that are offered in sacrifice unto idols, we know that an idol is nothing in the world, and that there is none other God but one": 1 Cor. 8:4 (AV). On Christian disenchantment, see Charles Taylor, *A Secular Age* (Cambridge, MA: Harvard University Press, 2007), 77.

20. Bruno Latour, "On the Cult of the Factish Gods," chapter 1 in *On the Modern Cult of the Factish Gods*, trans. Catherine Porter and Heather MacLean (Durham, NC: Duke University Press, 2010), 1–66; translation of Bruno Latour, *Sur le culte moderne des dieux faitiches, suivi de* Iconoclash, rev. ed. (Paris: La Découverte, 2009).

21. Latour, *Factish Gods*, 2; *Dieux faitiches*, 20.

IT DOES NOT EXIST

or not, but why the Moderns so desperately need belief in order to strike up a relationship with others."[22] The new secularity studies in general has made this correction: it explains the one who believes in belief rather than explaining the believer. As Charles Taylor comments, "the energy of disenchantment is double. First, negative, we must reject everything which smacks of idolatry." But the second energy is "positive," in that "we feel a new freedom in a world shorn of the sacred . . . to reorder things as seems best."[23] As an alternative to what he calls "subtraction stories," accounts of secularization that imagine it as a clearing away of superstition, Taylor proposes the view of secularization as an additive process, a construction of new "reference-points" for leading a life full of meaning.[24]

Latour, too, sees the Moderns as having added new ways of looking at the world rather than as having subtracted superstitions from it. The Moderns' chief peculiarity, on Latour's view, is their insistence that objects are either made by us (belonging to the realm of "values") or independent of us ("facts.")[25] An object may act on us, as such "facts" as the economy and the law of gravity do. Or it can be made by us—a puppet, a novel, a moral code—in which case we must recognize that all "its" actions are actually our own. Facts or values, but never both, the Moderns demand. Idols—or "primitive fetishes," to use Latour's term—represent for the Moderns the confusion of facts and values. In the fetish that we treat as though it had autonomy from us, we misrecognize the work of our own hands and imaginations as coming from outside of us. Thus in the discard pile of broken idols Moderns place any object that is allegedly both made *by* humans and capable of acting *on* humans.

This rigorous act of sorting leaves the Moderns obliged to explain how it could ever have seemed as though made objects could act on their creators. Here is where an idol-function comes in handy. Moderns use the idea of others' "belief" (*croyance*) to explain the apparent action of made objects as merely the function of the "believer's" weak psychology. Says Latour in the voice of the Moderns: "those empty-headed fantasies had to go

22. Latour, *Factish Gods*, 2; *Dieux faitiches*, 20.

23. Taylor, *Secular Age*, 80.

24. Ibid., 27.

25. Bruno Latour, *An Inquiry into Modes of Existence: An Anthropology of the Moderns*, trans. Catherine Porter (Cambridge, MA: Harvard University Press, 2013), 8; translation of *Enquête sur les modes d'existence: Une Anthropologie des Modernes* (Paris: La Découverte, 2012), 20; Latour, *Factish Gods*, 8; *Dieux faitiches*, 30–31.

somewhere . . . let's invent the notion of an interiority filled with hollow dreams." The psychological qualities of believers, "primitive, archaic, infantile, or unconscious human beings," explain how they can make the mistake of thinking a fetish is animate.[26] In the work of disenchantment—of distributing intelligence more parsimoniously than those who came "before" did—belief, as an idol-function, smoothes over the gap between the power that can no longer exist and that power's still-evident effects. For every chimera that apparently acted, Moderns supply a belief to explain the illusion of that action—and a credulous person to hold the belief. Latour's interest is primarily in the Modern, and not in the (alleged) believer. He aims to reduce or even remove the distinction between the two, insisting that in fact Moderns have an ability to move between facts and values similar to that of a worshipper of fetish gods (and far greater than they would avow).[27] But where does this leave belief and the complex relations that Moderns establish with it? Somewhere on the sidelines; in fact, Latour's ally, the ethnopsychiatrist Tobie Nathan, even goes so far as to say that belief does not exist: "Ah, my friend!" exclaims Nathan, "you must expunge from your vocabulary the words 'believe' and 'belief.' I can promise you: no one, no matter where, has ever believed in anything!"[28] Latour is more measured: "No one, in practice, has ever displayed naïve belief in any being whatsoever. If there is such a thing as belief at all, it is the most complex, sophisticated, critical, subtle, reflective activity there is."[29]

This is quite the suggestion, though Latour does not follow it up. What if belief and all those other hollow mental gymnastics that Moderns never tire of pointing out in others really *were* the sophisticated activities Latour envisions? What if, to put a finer point on it, the *relations* between the Mod-

26. Latour, *Factish Gods*, 40; *Dieux faitiches*, 87.

27. Latour, *Factish Gods*, 16-21; *Dieux faitiches*, 43–52.

28. Tobie Nathan, "Manifeste pour une psychopathologie scientifique," in Nathan and Stengers, *Médecins et sorciers*, 17. The original reads: "Ah, mon ami! Il vous faut supprimer de votre vocabulaire le mot 'croire' ou 'croyance.' Je peux vous l'assurer: nul ne croit en rien, et nulle part!" Latour conceived of his essay on the factish while spending a year as an intern in Nathan's ethnopsychiatry practice in Paris, where Nathan approaches the worldviews of his mostly African-immigrant patients not as belief systems but as worlds with which he enters into diplomatic relations. See Latour, *Factish Gods*, ix–x; *Dieux faitiches*, 11; Nathan and Stengers, *Médecins et sorciers*; and Tobie Nathan, *L'influence qui guérit* (Paris: Odile Jacob, 1994).

29. Latour, *Factish Gods*, 42; *Dieux faitiches*, 90.

erns and the "belief" that they in part invented were critical and subtle in the way Latour suggests? In that case, it might well be worth identifying the moments where Moderns invent and elaborate their own practices of "belief." What flexibilities are they permitting, or stumbling into, at those moments? Here I want to make *belief* a bit more specific. The word has many shades of meaning; *croyance*, the French term being translated, is similarly broad. But Latour is specifically invoking the derogatory use of belief: belief as what happens when weak-mindedness in one person meets trickery in another, or when a false priest manipulates a mark. I have found it preferable to use the term *credulity* instead because credulity is more clearly derogatory. It has less chance of creating confusion with liberal, potentially secularity-compatible forms of religious belief, or with a distinction as to degree of certainty (i.e., between belief and knowledge).[30] With *credulity*, the aim is to capture the Modern move of explaining the effectiveness of that which *does not exist*, as Adams put it, by reference to another's excessive tendency to credit implausible statements.

Rather than following Latour, then, down the road of seeing modern activities through the lens of the factish, I am following this other road he indicates: of considering credulity—which inevitably also means the relations Moderns enter into with credulity—as the most sophisticated activity imaginable. The essential preliminary work is to find the moments when Moderns think they are seeing credulity; later, we can ask what comes out of these acts of definition. The 1784 animal magnetism investigation was one of those moments. In explaining animal magnetism as the compound of belief and overactive imaginations, the commissioners made animal magnetism into a practice of credulity. They attributed to credulity all those powers that Mesmer had attributed to animal magnetism—the *nothings*, as Reese would later lament, that are the most powerful things in the world. The result of the commissioners' debunking was not that animal magnetism fizzled out; on the contrary, by the end of this chapter we will be able to say that calling animal magnetism pure credulity actually gave enlightened Moderns a reason to keep thinking about magnetism and eliciting its practice. And as soon as something is being incited—even if only so that it

---

30. Barbara Herrnstein-Smith has noted that this ambiguity is a potential problem with Latour's term *belief* in "Anthropotheology: Latour, Knowledge, and Belief" (paper presented at the conference "Recomposing the Humanities with Bruno Latour," sponsored by *New Literary History*, University of Virginia, Charlottesville, September 18, 2015).

can be managed—there is room for it to expand and change. Thanks to its initial debunking, animal magnetism could eventually become an instance of credulity deliberately practiced.

"UNE GRANDE INCRÉDULITÉ"

The commissioners who were appointed in 1784 had the puzzling task that disenchanters often face. Skeptical about the existence of the animal-magnetic fluid, they nonetheless found themselves confronted with magnetism's alleged effects on patients' bodies. If there was no such thing as animal magnetism, then whence the patients' convulsions, vomiting fits, and so forth? Franklin and most of his colleagues attributed mesmerism's remarkable effects to imagination, which was for them a mechanism by which belief could create physical symptoms in the body. If you believed in the efficacy of Mesmer's proceedings, then you would for that very reason be excited and affected by them. Your belief, not the animal-magnetic fluid, would be the cause of your convulsions. Other factors mattered, too: gender, class, degree of education, and presence or absence of a mob of other sufferers. The commissioners would ultimately claim not only that the patients' credulity, aided by their imaginations, *misled* the patients about their own experiences, but that the experiences were, if you will, *mis-had*. Imagination did not merely trick them into *thinking* they were feeling heat in a magnetized part of the body, or convulsing; it tricked them into *actually feeling* heat and convulsing. In other words, imagination made susceptible patients feel sensations and exhibit physical symptoms that had no other source beyond their thoughts. It was a robust machine for animating false idols and empowering nonexistent fluids.

The two Paris commissions investigating mesmerism came from the academic institutions most directly threatened by Mesmer's sensational cures: the Royal Society of Medicine and the Faculty of Medicine. To the Faculty of Medicine commission were also appointed six members of the Academy of Sciences, including the chairs Antoine Lavoisier and Benjamin Franklin and the eventual drafter of the report, astronomer Jean-Sylvain Bailly. The commissioners investigated the mesmerist Charles Deslon, one of Mesmer's pupils, in spite of Mesmer's protests that he ought to have taken center stage himself. Both commissions published their reports in August. Of the two reports, the Franklin–Lavoisier commission's report was by far the more influential.[31] It introduced the idea that imagination was responsible for the mesmeric effects, and it was also the report that Godwin chose to translate into English a few months later, with prefatory material including an original English introduction and a synopsis of M. A. Thouret's *Recherches et doutes sur le magnétisme animal* (1784), a historical survey of magnetism-like phenomena before Mesmer.[32] Throughout this book I refer to the Academy of Sciences–Faculty of Medicine report as the "Franklin report," even though Bailly drafted it; the misnomer captures the way this document would be received among Anglophone readers, starting with Godwin's free translation of the title: the *Report of Dr. Benjamin Franklin*.

The commissioners' target was not animal magnetism alone; they took aim, rather, at the resurgence of superstitious practices in what were supposed to be enlightened times. Mesmer and Deslon's public treatment salons struck the commissioners as a laboratory reproduction of darker ages, alarming but fascinating. Patients gathered around the *baquet*, a bucket filled with water and broken glass with iron bars protruding from it; they then applied the iron bars to the affected parts of their bodies. A rope bound the patients loosely to one another. Meanwhile Deslon's assistants exerted pressure on patients' stomachs and waved iron rods along the magnetic poles of their bodies. Music played in the background. Some patients felt nothing; others coughed or felt mild pains; but a third group were "agitated and tormented with convulsions . . . rendered extraordinary by their frequency, their violence, and their duration"; some also coughed up fluid.[33] "Nothing can be more astonishing," the commissioners acknowledged, "than the sight of these convulsions; he that has not had it, can have no idea of it."[34] It was hardly surprising that similar effects "seduced in former ages men,

---

31. Riskin, *Science in the Age of Sensibility*, 209; Gauld, *History of Hypnotism*, 26. There was also a minority report more favorable to animal magnetism published by Antoine-Laurent de Jussieu, member of the Royal Society of Medicine commission: *Rapport de l'un des commissaires chargés par le Roi, de l'examen du magnétisme animal* (Paris: Veuve Hérissant, 1784). On Jussieu's report, see Chertok and Stengers, *Critique of Psychoanalytic Reason*, 19–26; *Le Cœur et la raison*, 31–37.

32. Michel Augustin Thouret, *Recherches et doutes sur le magnétisme animal* (Paris: Prault, 1784), summarized in *Report*, 1–17. Godwin's translation was issued in December 1784, though 1785 is the date printed on its title page: [Advertisement], *St. James's Chronicle or the British Evening Post*, December 16, 1784.

33. [Bailly], *Report*, 23–28; *Rapport*, 3–7; see also Riskin, *Science in the Age of Sensibility*, 201.

34. [Bailly], *Report*, 27; *Rapport*, 6.

venerable for their merit, their illumination and even their genius, Paracel-
sus, Van Helmont and Kircher"—thus delaying the inevitable onset of enlightenment.[35] Even so, there was nothing in Mesmer's claims; the magnetic
effects were merely the products of imagination and fanaticism. Just as in
"theatrical representation, where the impressions are greater in proportion
to the number of the spectators," and in military camps, "where the enthusiasm of courage, as well as the impressions of terror, are propagated with so
amazing rapidity," the movement of a convulsion passed from one patient
to the next in the public treatment salons.[36] The same contagion could account for religious exercises such as those of French Protestants known in
the early eighteenth century for their spasmodic worship: "where fanaticism is the presiding quality, its fruit is the tremblers of the Cevennes."[37]
Though presented as a newfangled science, "the magnetism then is no more
than an old falsehood," the commissioners would eventually conclude with
a flourish.[38]

The commissioners' aim was not only to show that animal magnetism
was false but also to show how it had appeared to be true. Thus they also
needed an idol-function: something to substitute for animal magnetism
in producing the patients' physical exercises. Credulity played a key role.
Early on, they hypothesized that magnetism existed only for the gullible:
"the magnetism has seemed to have no existence for those subjects, who
have submitted to it with any degree of incredulity [*quelque incrédulité*]."[39]
Working in private, away from the distractions of the public process, they
had Deslon perform the magnetic gestures on a cross section of subjects:
learned and ignorant, rich and poor, male and female. They even tested it
on themselves.[40] The results suggested that magnetism, much like tyranny
and priestcraft, worked especially well on those who were poor, uneducated,
or female, though for any of these groups, intelligence could serve as a safe-
guard.[41] Against those who were "armed . . . with that philosophic doubt which
ought always to accompany inquiry," magnetism—much like enchantment—

35. [Bailly], *Report*, 99; *Rapport*, 57.

36. [Bailly], *Report*, 91; *Rapport*, 51.

37. [Bailly], *Report*, 92; *Rapport*, 52; on the tremblers of Cévennes, see Goldstein, "Enthusiasm or Imagination?" 44.

38. [Bailly], *Report*, 97–98; *Rapport*, 56.

39. [Bailly], *Report*, 53; *Rapport*, 25.

40. [Bailly], *Report*, 39–48; *Rapport*, 15–21.

41. [Bailly], *Report*, 52–53; *Rapport*, 24–25.

was powerless.[42] Just three patients exhibited effects that the commissioners could not explain away. These patients were all of "the lower class . . . while those of a more elevated rank, of more enlightened understandings, and better qualified to describe their sensations, have felt nothing."[43] The commissioners, on account of their "philosophic doubt . . . have felt none of those sensations."[44] Those who approached the magnetic process skeptically were, the commissioners maintained, unaffected, even if their nerves were susceptible. The well-heeled Madame de B—, for example, "felt nothing . . . she submitted to the magnetism with an extreme tranquility, which originated in the highest degree of incredulity [*une grande incrédulité*]."[45] Thus the rich and philosophical were immune to animal magnetism, while the poor and superstitious were vulnerable.

It took some doing to impose this degree of order on the results. Actually, sensations during the process of magnetism were far from unique to the lower class; even among the commissioners there were several who felt "irritation of the nerves."[46] But the *Report* attributes these sensations to preexisting illnesses or to the effects of pressure on the stomach, whereas what the ignorant felt was to be attributed to their credulity.[47] The commissioners expected to find superstition and dependence here, and so they knew they would find susceptible imaginations as well: "Let us represent to ourselves the situation of a person of the lower class, and of consequence ignorant," proposed the commissioners, "attacked with a distemper and desirous of a cure, introduced with some degree of ceremony to a large company, partly composed of physicians, where an operation is performed upon him totally new, and from which he persuades himself before hand that he is about to experience prodigious effects." Awed by the majesty of these physicians whose claims his education does not permit him to judge, this lower-class person is also "paid for his compliance," and "he thinks he shall contribute more to our satisfaction by professing to experience sensations of some kind."[48] Here is a person who will unconsciously produce the sensations the doctors seem to require. The credulous person's sensations

---

42. [Bailly], *Report*, 54; *Rapport*, 25.
43. [Bailly], *Report*, 52; *Rapport*, 24.
44. [Bailly], *Report*, 54; *Rapport*, 25.
45. [Bailly], *Report*, 47–48; *Rapport*, 21.
46. [Bailly], *Report*, 42; *Rapport*, 17.
47. [Bailly], *Report*, 42–43, 51–52; *Rapport*, 17, 23–24.
48. [Bailly], *Report*, 52–53, *Rapport*, 24.

when magnetized "were the fruits of anticipated persuasion, and might be operated by the mere force of imagination."[49]

Imagination had a heavy explanatory load to bear. It had to produce not just mild physical sensations, but astonishing crises. It had to do all this, moreover, without its operations becoming evident to the subject, who had to mistake those operations for the effects of an external fluid, animal magnetism. Imagination had to be the equivalent of an inner mechanism for manufacturing idols, cobbling together convulsions, peculiar sensations, and strange prestidigitations into the single object "animal magnetism" as though they were so many feathers, carved wooden bits, and beads. There was reason to think imagination might be capable of such a feat. Imagination was the power of calling up objects that were not—and perhaps had never been—present to the senses.[50] It allowed us, as Dugald Stewart explained in his *Elements of the Philosophy of the Human Mind* (1792), to "withdraw the attention at pleasure from objects of sense, and transport ourselves into a world of our own."[51] Nor was there anything out of the ordinary in the idea that the imagination could act on the body. This phenomenon had been observed in women whose unwholesome ideas during pregnancy engendered monstrous births.[52] In the French tradition, as Jessica Riskin has pointed out, the trouble with imagination was primarily that while memory was "cool and calm," imagination was "warm and vivid."[53] Memory, too, called up objects not present to the senses, but imagination did so much more realistically. Thus it could, as Riskin puts it, "hijack the senses," making one mistake inner vicissitudes for outer processes—exactly what happened to the mesmeric patients.[54]

With habitual magnetization, imagination could not only stretch and distort the inner narrative. It could also create a repeatable process in the body that would seem to indicate the presence of an external object—animal magnetism—where none was. Stewart distinguished imagination from "conception" (a faculty closely related to memory) in that, rather than being con-

49. [Bailly], *Report* 54; *Rapport*, 25.

50. Riskin, *Science in the Age of Sensibility*, 210.

51. Dugald Stewart, *Elements of the Philosophy of the Human Mind*, vol. 1, 5th ed. (London: Cadell & Davies, 1814), 516. Volume 1 first published in London in 1792.

52. G. S. Rousseau, "Pineapples, Pregnancy, Pica, and *Peregrine Pickle*," in *Tobias Smollett: Bicentennial Essays Presented to Lewis M. Knapp*, ed. G. S. Rousseau and Paul-Gabriel Boucé (New York: Oxford University Press, 1971), 79–109.

53. Riskin, *Science in the Age of Sensibility*, 210–11.

54. Ibid., 217.

fined to calling up an "exact transcript" of a past perception, imagination could "make a selection of qualities and of circumstances from a variety of different objects, and by combining and disposing these . . . form a new creation of its own."[55] In the case of habitual magnetization, imagination would aggregate effects that had initially come from pressure on the stomach or from the excitement of the public treatment salons: "The sensations having been felt once or oftener, nothing is now necessary, but to recal [sic] the memory of them, and to exalt the imagination to the same degree, in order to operate the same effects."[56] Thus while physical pressure and a crowd were necessary initially, later on, imagination alone could be enough.

Specifying the exact location of the body-mind nexus was an embarrassment, as it has ever been to those who attempt it; the commissioners hazarded that "the affections of the soul make their first corporeal impression upon the nervous centre" near the "diaphragm."[57] But if we grant the commissioners their equivalent to René Descartes's pineal gland, then the important point becomes visible: imagination was a remarkable tool for the creator of newfangled idols. Imagination could concoct animal magnetism out of the effects of a number of causes and then replay the tapes "by its sole instrumentality."[58] The commissioners called animal magnetism "chimerical [chimérique]," and it was a "chimera" in the strict sense.[59] The original chimera was a monster with a lion's head, a goat's body, and a serpent's tail. From a disenchanting perspective, the chimera was a creature that did not exist, made out of the parts of creatures that did. So too was animal magnetism, according to the commissioners: it was a compound of imagination, imitation (at the public process), and touch. P. T. Barnum, the great humbugger, would later sew together a desiccated fish and a dried monkey and call it the Feejee Mermaid.[60] Imagination did Mesmer's sewing for

55. Stewart, *Elements*, vol. 1, 5th ed., 481. Conception is similar to memory, though for Stewart, there is a distinction between the two: conception is the active calling up of a past perception; memory is the passive recognition that a present conception or object of the senses is the same as a past perception (133).

56. [Bailly], *Report*, 96; *Rapport*, 55.

57. [Bailly], *Report*, 88; *Rapport*, 49. On failed eighteenth-century efforts to assign a physiological basis to the imagination, see G. S. Rousseau, "Science and the Discovery of the Imagination in Enlightened England," *Eighteenth-Century Studies* 3, no. 1 (Fall 1969): 116.

58. [Bailly], *Report*, 90; *Rapport*, 50.

59. [Bailly], *Report*, 97; *Rapport*, 56.

60. James W. Cook, *The Arts of Deception: Playing with Fraud in the Age of Barnum* (Cambridge, MA: Harvard University Press, 2001), 73–118.

him. It could in theory make a chimerical object on behalf of any charlatan who was capable of managing excitement and ginning up awe-inspiring proceedings—all without the subjects having any suspicion of what was happening under their skin.

MANAGING AND CONTROLLING

It was all very well to identify the imagination's operation in everything from theater crowds to military mobs to religious meetings. But as John Adams noted from the beginning, doing so raised as many questions as it laid to rest. If it really was true that "this faculty of the mind can produce [such] terrible effects upon the body," Adams told Waterhouse, "I think you physicians ought to study and teach us some method of managing and controuling it."[61] It was not so easy to conceive of what this method might be. As Léon Chertok and Isabelle Stengers point out, the details of imagination's functioning were far from clear in the commissioners' account.[62] The *Report* sardonically notes that Mesmer protected the theory of animal magnetism from being experimentally disproved by making the fluid "perfectly insensible": "It is not, like the electrical fluid, luminous and visible; its action is not, like the attraction of the loadstone, the object of our sight; it has neither taste nor smell; its process is silent, and it surrounds you or penetrates your frame, without you being informed of its presence by the sense of touch."[63] But the same could be said of imagination. It, too, was perfectly insensible and all-important.

When the commissioners submitted personally to magnetization, they showed an anxious concern that their imaginations would be activated in spite of themselves. They were careful "not to observe too minutely what passed within them" because "to turn and fix in this manner ones [*sic*] attention upon oneself, is not perhaps itself entirely without its effects."[64] And indeed, some commissioners did feel physical effects while they were being magnetized; even this queasy balance of surveillance and inattention was not quite enough.[65] The trouble was that imagination operated below the

---

61. Adams, "Boston, Nov. 29."
62. Chertok and Stengers, *Critique of Psychoanalytic Reason*, 19; *Le Cœur et la raison*, 30.
63. [Bailly], *Report*, 30–31; *Rapport*, 9.
64. [Bailly], *Report*, 39–40; *Rapport*, 15–16.
65. [Bailly], *Report*, 42; *Rapport*, 17.

level of consciousness, a fact that Godwin neatly captured when he employed some license in translating the *Rapport*'s description of the mind-body nexus at the diaphragm. When imagination affects the diaphragm, sympathy between organs means that "the viscera of the lower belly then experience a reaction," accounting for the digestive problems caused by the imagination. Godwin inserts his own modifier for this chain of effects, one with no corresponding phrase in the French original: "by this automatous process," imagination causes convulsions (the original simply has "it is thus [*c'est ainsi*]").[66] *Automatous* could mean both automatic—that is, self-moving, like the circulation of the blood, after being set in motion—and autonomous, capable of starting *itself* in motion, like the rational soul.[67] One part of the body-soul complex, the imagination, could create mechanical effects that would actively mislead another part, the intellect. The education of the senses made this automatous usurpation less likely but did not rule it out. Management and control might well be a good idea. But how, exactly?

The one person who *did* evidently know the secret of managing and controlling the imagination was the magnetist. As Leigh Eric Schmidt observes, false priests often won a begrudging admiration from their debunkers on this score: "Those superior men who had this insider knowledge had autonomy; those capable of this instrumental inventiveness, however abused, had dominion. The rest were dupes—the weak, the servile, the ignorant, the dependent, and the female."[68] The commissioners readily acknowledged the magnetist's dominion. Animal magnetism was a chimera; and yet, according to the *Report*, "it is impossible not to recognize in these regular effects an extraordinary influence, acting upon the patients, making itself master of them, and of which he who superintends the process [*celui qui magnétise*], appears to be the depository [*dépositaire*]."[69] The word

66. [Bailly], *Report*, 88; *Rapport*, 49.

67. *Oxford English Dictionary* online, 3rd ed. (2011), s.v. "automatous, *adj.*," http://www.oed.com.proxy.its.virginia.edu/view/Entry/13476?redirectedFrom=automatous (accessed June 22, 2017). On mechanism and the body in the eighteenth century, see Simon Schaffer, "Enlightened Automata," in *The Sciences in Enlightened Europe*, ed. William Clark, Jan Golinski, and Simon Schaffer, 126–29 (Chicago: University of Chicago Press, 1999); Jessica Riskin, "Eighteenth-Century Wetware," *Representations* 83 (Summer 2003): 97–125.

68. Leigh Eric Schmidt, *Hearing Things: Religion, Illusion, and the American Enlightenment* (Cambridge, MA: Harvard University Press, 2000), 100.

69. [Bailly], *Report*, 28; *Rapport*, 7. The original reads: "On ne peut s'empêcher de reconnoître, à ces effets constans, une grand puissance qui agite les malades, les maîtrise, & dont celui qui magnétise semble être le dépositaire."

depository has fallen out of use in English since Godwin employed it in his translation; a close synonym would be *trustee*. A *dépositaire* might be the banker or custodian to whom one entrusts funds, the friend with whom one leaves a letter for safekeeping, or the confidant to whom one tells an important secret.[70] In the case of magnetism, the credulous patients in effect deposited with the magnetizer the power he had over them. Thus, in a scene where imagination was hard to describe and impossible to detect with the senses, there was one person with mastery over it: the magnetizer.

If the commissioners wanted to control the imagination, then Deslon himself might be their model. As Schmidt writes, "it was hard to dream about all the machinery of priestcraft without yearning to become a master of such technologies, without imagining a transfer of power from ancient magician to modern philosopher, scientist, and entrepreneur."[71] The commissioners' second round of experiments enacted just this transfer of power. When they wanted to test magnetic effects, they actually performed the magnetic gestures personally in some cases—a remarkable enough emulation of the false priest in itself. In some experiments their deceit went even further than Deslon's had: they pretended to magnetize the patients when they were not doing so, and they magnetized without allowing the patients to know it. "This mode of proceeding was not calculated to deceive them [the patients]," the *Report* protests; "it only misled their imagination[s]."[72] The commissioners used a placebo in the form of a sham device: they feigned the magnetic gestures with an iron rod but moved it with the magnetic poles of the body rather than against (this, according to Mesmer's theory, would have had no effect). Thus magnetism could not act, but the patient's *idea* of magnetism could. When magnetizing in secret, on the other hand, *only* magnetism could act; imagination could not be affected. Thus the commissioners could see both what imagination could do without magnetism and what magnetism could do without imagination.

While they manipulated imaginations and sham devices, the commissioners were in effect charlatans, though all the profits went to enlightenment. Latour has written that Moderns imagine only two stark options in a

70. *Oxford English Dictionary* online, 1st ed. (1895), s.v. "depository, *n.*," http://www.oed.com.proxy.its.virginia.edu/view/Entry/50382?redirectedFrom=depository (accessed June 22, 2017); *Le Robert: Dictionnaire historique de la langue française*, ed. Alain Rey (Paris: Le Robert, 2012), s.v. "dépositaire, *n.*"

71. L. Schmidt, *Hearing Things*, 100.

72. [Bailly], *Report*, 60; *Rapport*, 30.

scene of idolatry: "either you are cynically pulling the strings, or else you are being had."[73] With the sham-placebo experiments, the commissioners were certainly pulling the strings—and that to an almost farcical degree. Commissioner Joseph-Ignace Guillotin, inventor of the guillotine, later called the investigation "very important though highly ridiculous," and historian Riskin calls it a "comedy."[74] Had you been at Franklin's house in Passy on one day during the mesmerism trials, you could have enjoyed a different sight gag in every room. Here, Deslon magnetizing the aged Franklin, with little effect. There, a woman biting her own hand because she believed Deslon was magnetizing her from behind a door (he was not).[75] In another corner, a commissioner "personat[ing] M. Deslon" in front of a blindfolded woman, while carrying on a dialogue with his companions designed to make the woman think he was performing the magnetic passes.[76] In fact, pseudo-Deslon and his coconspirators were "sit[ting] quietly, occupied only in observing what would happen."[77] Soon the woman mounted a foot-stamping, hand-clapping crisis while the commissioners maintained the demure silence of successful pranksters. During another set of experiments the commissioners summoned the seamstress "Mlle. B." to a private house in Paris, where one of their number magnetized her secretly from behind a paper panel. Though this commissioner had succeeded in magnetizing people before, he came up empty now: holding an iron rod and gesturing vigorously for thirty minutes, he had not the slightest effect on Mlle. B. Things changed when he came into the room and magnetized Mlle. B. with his iron rod from a fully visible position. Soon she began chattering her teeth, stamping on the floor, and flinging her arms behind her in a spasmodic movement. This time, however, the commissioner had intentionally misused the iron rod. While he magnetized Mlle. B. "conformable to the . . . magnetic theory" the first time, moving the rod in the opposite direction from her body's magnetic poles, he moved the

73. Latour, *Factish Gods*, 7; *Dieux faitiches*, 28.

74. Joseph Ignace Guillotin to Benjamin Franklin, Paris, June 18, 1787, *The Franklin Papers at Yale*, accessed February 13, 2017, http://franklinpapers.org/franklin//, translated in Riskin, *Science in the Age of Sensibility*, 218.

75. [Bailly], *Report*, 69–71; *Rapport*, 36–37. See also Riskin, *Science in the Age of Sensibility*, 218–19.

76. [Bailly], *Report*, 70; *Rapport*, 38.

77. [Bailly], *Rapport*, 37, my translation. The original reads: "On a eu l'air d'adresser la parole à M. Deslon, en le priant de commencer, mais on n'a point magnétisé la femme; les trois Commissaires sont restés tranquilles, occupés seulement à observer ce qui alloit se passer."

rod *with* the poles on round two. Used in this way, the rod should have had no effect whatsoever—unless it was affecting Mlle. B.'s imagination.[78]

According to the commissioners' theory, the iron rod worked on Mlle. B. much as an idol might work on a primitive believer. She attributed the so-called animal-magnetic power to it, exciting her imagination; her imagination in turn caused her convulsions. The iron wand was a *fetish* to her, in the sense in which that term was used by the Encyclopedists and other eighteenth-century historians of religion; namely, it was a meaningless object to which she had falsely attributed meaning.[79] But the commissioners were fetishists too, in a sense closer to Freud's inflection of the concept in his 1927 essay on the topic.[80] For them, the fetish was not any particular object but the whole scene of the mesmeric experiment in which they controlled other believers. That scene was for them a way of forcing the imagination to show up—to be manageable and graspable—when it threatened to do none of these things.

In Freud's essay, the boy and future fetishist sees to his horror that his mother has no penis. At stake is more than an organ: to the son her loss, her castration as he thinks, spells a loss of power and pleasure to which he, too, might be subject. Symbolically to undo his mother's castration—which in fact never happened, except to him—is to preclude the possibility of his own. In substituting an object for the mother's phallus, he both retains and gives up his belief in his lost idol. This simultaneous retention of and relinquishment of the idol is to Freud the most important point. Freud's fetishist is less like a happy primitive than like a discontented or melancholy debunker of false gods. For the fetishist, "the woman *has* got a penis, in spite of everything; but this penis is no longer the same as it was before." Something else

---

78. [Bailly], *Report*, 79–83; *Rapport*, 43–45.

79. See William Pietz, "The Problem of the Fetish, I," *RES: Anthropology and Aesthetics* 9 (Spring 1985): 14; "The Problem of the Fetish, II: The Origin of the Fetish," *RES: Anthropology and Aesthetics* 13 (Spring 1987): 23; and "Fetish," in *Critical Terms for Art History*, ed. Robert S. Nelson and Richard Shiff, 2nd ed. (Chicago: University of Chicago Press, 2003), 307–9. Pietz distinguishes the fetish and the idol on the grounds that while the latter's "truth lies in its relation of iconic resemblance to some immaterial model or entity," the former has an "untranscended materiality" ("Problem of the Fetish I," 7). Both, however, are terms that attribute to the believer the mistake of seeing power in an object that has none; thus, the distinction is of limited importance for my purposes.

80. Sigmund Freud, "Fetishism" (1927), in *The Complete Psychological Works of Sigmund Freud*, vol. 21, trans. James Strachey (London: Hogarth and the Institute of Psychoanalysis, 1957), 147–57.

is now its "substitute" and "inherits the interest which was formerly directed to its predecessor"—an interest that has meanwhile increased dramatically because of the intensity of the boy's horror.[81] The fetish represents at once the acknowledgment of the mother's castration *and* the disavowal of that knowledge. Were one to apply the same principle to the scene of so-called primitive religious fetishism, it would yield the reading that the fetishist valued his object not because he believed absolutely in the power of the god behind it but because, on the contrary, he had reason to suspect the god did not exist. The fetish would only acquire its "extraordinary increase" in interest because it forestalled the horror of the god's loss—because it permitted the fetishist to remain frozen between knowing and not knowing.[82]

As for the commissioners, they, too, forestalled and acknowledged an unpleasant fact through their "very important, though highly ridiculous" manipulations of an iron rod. The commissioners knew that they might not be able to control imagination in themselves. Yet they did *not* know this fact—they repudiated it—at least so long as they managed to cast themselves in the roles of puppeteers to the patients, rather than puppets to their own imaginations. The patients' imaginations, which they controlled, served as proxies for their own imaginations, which perhaps they did not control. Though distantly, the commissioners' concept of imagination would contribute to "the discovery of the unconscious," as Henri Ellenberger once put it, and thus to the very possibility of both knowing and not knowing that is so central to the psychoanalytic thinking that informs my reading of them now.[83]

The commissioners' fetishism was, however, nothing so simple as the attachment to an iron rod. It was an attachment to the other's (fantasized) attachment to an iron rod. The pleasure, then, was not in the fetish itself, but in the supposed fetishism of the other, as played out in the scene of

---

81. Ibid., 154. On the relationship between Freudian fetishism and so-called primitive fetishism, see Pietz, "Fetish," 313–15.

82. Freud, "Fetishism," 154.

83. The classic account of the development from mesmerism to hypnosis to psychoanalysis is Henri Ellenberger, *The Discovery of the Unconscious: The History and Evolution of Dynamic Psychiatry* (New York: Basic Books, 1970), v, 101–2. See also Mikkel Borch-Jacobsen, *The Emotional Tie: Psychoanalysis, Mimesis, and Affect* (Stanford, CA: Stanford University Press, 1992), 39–61; and Adam Crabtree, *From Mesmer to Freud: Magnetic Sleep and the Roots of Psychological Healing* (New Haven, CT: Yale University Press, 1993), 351–60. I argue in this chapter and in the rest of the book that the Franklin report made its own substantial contribution to this tradition. In that argument I join Chertok and Stengers; see *Le Cœur et la raison*, 37; *Critique of Psychoanalytic Reason*, 26.

animal-magnetic debunking. That scene "suffer[ed] an extraordinary in-crease" in interest, as Freud tells us to expect with any fetish.[84] One of the commissioners' emulators spoke eloquently of debunking's pleasures. In 1796 a Mesmer imitator in the United States, Elisha Perkins, patented metal rods called "tractors" as a cure-all for disease.[85] When the rods made their way across the Atlantic to Bath, England, the physician John Haygarth repeated the Franklin commission's experimental design in an effort to debunk Per-kinism.[86] In *Of the Imagination, as a Cause and as a Cure of Disorders of the Body* (1800), Haygarth reports how he made wooden tractors, painted to resemble metal ones, and tried them on patients. The patients found themselves strongly affected—but this could only be from "mere Imagina-tion," since there was no magnetic virtue in a wooden tractor.[87] Haygarth's coconspirator Richard Smith, who repeated the experiment in Bristol, re-called faux-tractorizing his patients while trying not to laugh. "It was often necessary to play the part of a necromancer—to describe circles, squares, triangles, and half the figures of geometry, upon the part affected, with the small ends of the Tractors," he reported. "To a more curious farce I never was witness; we were almost afraid to look each other in the face, lest an involun-tary smile should remove the mask from our countenances, and dispel the charm."[88] One wonders if the commissioners, too, experienced this exhila-ration that is also an exquisite relief. In the world of dupes and false priests, they could reassure themselves, they were on the sovereign side.

QUIETUS

The mesmerism investigation allows us to articulate some of the ways be-lieving in others' belief works for Moderns more generally. First, such for-

84. Freud, "Fetishism," 154.

85. Elisha Perkins, *To All People to Whom These Presents Shall Come* ([Philadelphia: 1796]), broadside; Elisha Perkins, *Evidences of the Efficacy of Doctor Perkins's Patent Metal-lic Instruments* (New London: S. Green, 1797); James Delbourgo, *A Most Amazing Scene of Wonders: Electricity and Enlightenment in Early America* (Cambridge, MA: Harvard Uni-versity Press, 2006), 239–77.

86. John Haygarth, *Of the Imagination, as a Cause and as a Cure of Disorders of the Body; Exemplified by Fictitious Tractors, and Epidemical Convulsions* (Bath, UK: Cruttwell, 1800).

87. Ibid., 16.

88. Ibid., 17; see also 15.

mations as credulity and imagination are invoked as idol-functions: ways to explain why things that do not exist nonetheless attract subscribers. But the potency attributed to the idol-function then opens the way to a more diverse set of relations. I may wish, as Adams suggests, to manage and control the powerful force of imagination. That might mean identifying with the false priest as the one person in the magnetic scene who seems to be in possession of the secret of how to exert such control. Or I may become unsettled about the possibility that imagination might affect me without my knowledge, as the commissioners do when they test animal magnetism on themselves. Having started out to dismiss the credulity of others, I end up not being able to rule out the possibility that I am, myself, one of the credulous ones. That problem is susceptible only of compensation, not of solution. Perhaps I cannot master my own imagination, but just like the string-pulling priests of ages past, I can master other people's.

In a few ways, then, debunking begets more debunking. The task of deploring credulity is perennially incomplete and must always be repeated. This is a constitutive feature, not just a result of the accidental fact that there are always a couple of blockheads left somewhere in the world. Only when credulous people can still be spotted is there any way to enjoy the essential compensatory function of mastering someone else's imagination. Far from trying to stamp out errors like animal magnetism or "annihilate the enthusiasm" for them, as Adams imagined the *Report* doing, the debunker actually needs to find, even elicit, more credulity on which to work.[89] Looking at credulity this way—as something to be elicited, not repressed—raises the possibility that it might be an open-ended formation for the Moderns, one that would change and complicate itself through continued practice. That, as we will see, is what would happen with mesmerism: it would ultimately elaborate on the Franklin commission's accusations rather than wilt under them. Mesmerism would become the very place where one could enter into these pleasurable and relieving relations to others' credulity.

If debunking mesmerism was more about using the credulity of others than about correcting it, then the US reception has a certain piquancy. Discussion of mesmerism in the United States was an almost pure case of conjuring up others' belief in order to work upon it, since for all practical purposes there *were* no mesmerism believers in the United States when Adams announced in 1784 that animal magnetism *did not exist*. No one had really thought that it did. Most reacted at first with idle curiosity, as

89. Adams, "Boston, Nov. 29."

expressed by Hugh Williamson in a letter to Thomas Jefferson in December 1784: "We have lately heard strange stories concerning a certain Doctor in Paris who performed some thing in the Cure of Diseases like inchantment. Is there any useful discovery made?"[90] Jefferson, who was in Paris, had already started spreading the word about the Franklin commission, forwarding six copies of the *Rapport* to influential correspondents in the United States in November 1784.[91] "I send you a pamphlet on the subject of animal magnetism which has disturbed the nerves of prodigious numbers here," he wrote to Charles Thompson.[92] The *Rapport* "has actually given a quietus to a madness that was becoming epidemical," he told David Rittenhouse, sending the same thing.[93] With most of these dispatches he also enclosed, as he told James Madison in the covering letter to his copy, "an account of Roberts' last voiage thro' the air" and "some phosphoretic matches."[94] The Robert brothers, Anne-Jean and Nicolas Louis, had recounted the journeys of the hydrogen balloon they built in *Mémoire sur les expériences aérostatiques faites par MM. Robert frères* (1784).[95] Jefferson presented the matches as a new self-igniting technology. And imagination, as Jefferson saw, was an enlightened innovation, too, a means of dispatching not just the mesmeric error but any error to which credulity might give rise. He sent balloons for flight, matches for light, and imagination for disenchantment—a complete *Lumières* care package. Jefferson was constituting his own enlightenment by passing on news of an error his correspondents had never heard of, so that he and they could agree in decrying it.

Jefferson was also trying to kneecap the Marquis de Lafayette.[96] Lafayette had plans to take a post-Revolutionary victory lap in the United States

90. Hugh Williamson to Thomas Jefferson, Trenton, NJ, December 11, 1784, in Thomas Jefferson, *Papers of Thomas Jefferson*, ed. Julian P. Boyd, 42 vols. (Princeton, NJ: Princeton University Press, 1950–2016), 7:570.

91. On November 11, 1784, Jefferson wrote to Charles Thompson, James Currie, James Madison, John Page, David Rittenhouse, and Francis Hopkinson from Paris: Jefferson, *Papers*, 7:500, 502, 504, 514, 517–18.

92. Jefferson, *Papers*, 7:518.

93. Ibid., 7:517.

94. Ibid., 7:504.

95. Anne-Jean and Nicolas Louis Robert, *Mémoire sur les expériences aérostatiques faites par MM. Robert frères* (Paris, Imprimerie de P.-D. Pierres, 1784).

96. See Emily Ogden, "Mesmer's Demon: Fiction, Falsehood, and the Mechanical Imagination," *Early American Literature* 47, no. 1 (2012): 151. The present chapter is an altered version of the article (reprinted from *Early American Literature* 47, no. 1 (2012).

that winter, in his capacity as the young nation's military ally in its conflict with Britain. He was one of Mesmer's initiates, and he had every intention of spreading the "epidemical" madness of magnetism during his trip.[97] Jefferson hurried to inoculate his friends against Lafayette's efforts. Lafayette "had got a special meeting called of the philosophical Society at Philadelphia," according to Thompson, who was a member, "and entertained them on the subject for the greater part of an evening." Thompson was almost taken in: could it be that "the Shakers" had "by some means become acquainted with this fluid," and the agitations which "they ascribed to the influences of the divine spirit [were] the effect of this unknown agent[?]"[98] Thompson learned thanks to Jefferson that it was *imagination*, not animal magnetism, that should explain all false religious exercises. Thus he was saved in the nick of time from taking the heretical position that some observers were already proposing; namely, that imagination and animal magnetism might be one and the same.[99] "The report you sent me has removed this doubt," he told Jefferson, recanting.[100] Meanwhile Madison reported from Williamsburg that "the Marq. Le Fayette in his Journey thro' this Town had raised amongst us the highest Anxiety to know the real discoveries made in Animal Magnetism. But the Pamphlet you favoured us with, has effectually quieted our Concern upon that Score. The Matches," he added, "were the first seen here, and are indeed extremely curious."[101]

Jefferson had an enthusiastic general to outgeneral, and so his epistolary frenzy is understandable. But even after Lafayette had been sent on his way with polite nods and smothered looks of alarm, the Franklin report remained a touchstone. At every opportunity, American readers assured themselves that the first nation founded on enlightened principles was immune to this "art" by which "the credulity of the public, has been successfully converted into a mint for coining princely rewards," as the Boston *Herald* lamented.[102] In addition to the Adams letter, the original French report, and the Godwin translation, there were four periodical abridgments of the Franklin report, each reprinted multiple times in Atlantic-Seaboard publications during

97. Jefferson, *Papers*, 7:517, 8:17n.

98. Thompson to Jefferson, New York, March 6, 1785, in Jefferson, *Papers*, 8:15–17.

99. These observers included Charles Deslon himself, according to the commission report: [Bailly], *Report*, 100; *Rapport*, 58.

100. Thompson to Jefferson, New York, March 6, 1785, in Jefferson, *Papers*, 8:16.

101. James Madison to Thomas Jefferson, Williamsburg, VA, April 10, 1785, in Jefferson, *Papers*, 8:73.

102. Editorial headnote to Adams, "Boston, Nov. 29."

1784 and 1785 and each focusing on the commission's hypothesis of imagination.[103] As Jefferson drew his enlightened circle of acquaintances close via their shared disdain for animal magnetism, Americans would continue to treat magnetism as the falsehood over which one could reliably triumph, the instance of imagination that could be at any point resurrected so that it could be annihilated again.

Godwin recognized in his introduction to the English-language *Report* that it might well be "asked, why it should be thought necessary to give to the public a translation of papers, which may be thought interesting only to persons who have been witnesses of the imposture."[104] This would indeed be a puzzling question if the point of debunking were to suppress credulity for-

103. These four periodical abridgements determined the bulk of what American readers would have encountered. All quoted extensively from, or simply redacted, the *Report*. When I cite the following articles, I note the group number of the article from which I am quoting. The earliest group (Group 1) includes a number of reprintings of an article that had previously appeared in London: "A Wanderer," "To the Editor of the *General Evening Post*," *General Evening Post*, London, December 7, 1784. The earliest reprinting I have located was "Extract of a Letter from a Gentleman at Paris," *Columbian Herald*, Charleston, SC, February 10, 1785, and the majority of subsequent American printings mention this Charleston article as their source: *Independent Journal*, New York, March 9, 1785; *Pennsylvania Packet*, Philadelphia, February 23, 1785; "Charleston, Feb. 8, Extract of a Letter from a Gentleman at Paris," *Providence Gazette*, March 12, 1785; "Charlestown, (S. C.) Feb. 17, Extract of a Letter from a Gentleman at Paris," *Falmouth Gazette*, Falmouth, ME, April 2, 1785; "Charleston, (S. C.) Feb. 17, Extract of a Letter from a Gentleman at Paris," *Essex Journal*, Newburyport, MA, March 23, 1785; *Salem Gazette*, Salem, MA, March 22, 1785; "[Charleston, SC] February 10, Extract of a Letter from a Gentleman at Paris," *Massachusetts Spy*, Worcester, March 30, 1785; "Charlestown, Feb. 8: Extract of a Letter from a Gentleman at Paris," *American Mercury*, Hartford, CT, March 21, 1785; *New-Jersey Gazette*, Burlington, March 14, 1785, and elsewhere. A second, smaller group of newspapers (Group 2) gave a more detailed redaction of the Franklin report: "Account of the Report of the Committee, Appointed by Order of the French King, to Enquire into Animal Magnetism," *Boston Magazine*, May 1785, 163–66; *Massachusetts Spy*, Worcester, May 19, 1785; *New-Haven Gazette*, New Haven, CT, June 16, 1785. Group 3 comprises two nearly identical articles on Mesmer's "pretended discovery" that gave the first part of the Franklin report extensive treatment, appearing in New York and Philadelphia in the summer of 1785: "Animal Magnetism!" *New-York Journal*, June 30, 1785; "Animal Magnetism," *Pennsylvania Packet*, July 5, 1785. Finally, a sequel to Group 3 described the second part of the Franklin commission experiments (Group 4): "The Following Are the Principal Experiments, Made by the Commissioners Appointed by the French King," *Pennsylvania Packet*, Philadelphia, July 12, 1785; *New-York Journal*, July 7, 1785; *American Herald*, Boston, August 29, 1785; *Salem Gazette*, Salem, MA, August 16, 1785.

104. William Godwin, introduction to *Report*, xv–xvi.

ever. But that is not the point of debunking. The point is instead to master credulity—to make it one's marionette—and thus to line oneself up on the side of the puppeteers rather than on the side of the stooges. "Indeed it is not a little astonishing that, at the end of the eighteenth century, and in such a country as France, the world could have been so egregiously duped," lamented the *New-York Journal*.[105] Mesmer, the *Boston Magazine* commented, "is said to have amassed a very considerable fortune, at the expense of a credulous public."[106] When Jefferson reassured himself that mesmerism had "received it's [*sic*] quietus" or when Adams predicted that "the phrenzy" would "evaporate," these statements (which, by the way, proved untrue) are not to be analyzed as describing a state of affairs.[107] They are to be understood as performances of the speaker's knowingness about others' imaginations and as screens for his ignorance about his own.

Such performances remained common right up until Poyen's arrival on the scene in 1836, when mesmerism was to be practiced as a truth in the United States more or less for the first time. In spite of Lafayette's efforts and a few local publications and performances in the 1790s, mesmerism was best known as a falsehood until then.[108] Whenever anyone wanted to cast doubt on a cure, a subtle-fluid spectacular, or a religious manifestation, Mesmer's rout sprang to mind.[109] Revivals were a species of Mesmer's deception.[110] It was rumored in the late eighteenth century that Signor Falconi, an itinerant electrical demonstrator, knew how to perform animal magnetism.[111] As James Delbourgo and others have shown, American Enlightenment represented no easy "progress of reason against superstition" but was

105. "Animal Magnetism!" *New-York Journal*, June 30, 1785 (Group 3).

106. "Account of the Report of the Committee, Appointed by Order of the French King, to Enquire into Animal Magnetism," *Boston Magazine*, May 1785: 164 (Group 2).

107. Adams, "Boston, Nov. 29;" Thomas Jefferson to John Page, Paris, November 11, 1784, in Jefferson, *Papers*, 7:514.

108. On these earlier attempts, see Emily Ogden, "*Edgar Huntly* and the Regulation of the Senses," *American Literature* 85, no. 3 (2013): 430–31; Robert C. Fuller, *Mesmerism and the American Cure of Souls* (Philadelphia: University of Pennsylvania Press, 1982), 16–17; Gauld, *History of Hypnotism*, 179–81.

109. Ogden, "Mesmer's Demon," 147–52, part of whose argument I recapitulate here.

110. "Medicus," *Carolina Gazette*, August 26, 1802.

111. "Extract of a Letter from a Gentleman in Kingston to His Friend in Spanish-Town," *South-Carolina Gazette and General Advertiser*, July 15, 1785. On Falconi's demonstrations, see "Signor Falconi," *New-York Journal*, June 28, 1787, and Steven S. Tigner, "Magic and Magicians," *Handbook of American Popular Culture*, 2nd ed., vol. 2, ed. M. Thomas Inge, 673 (New York: Greenwood Press, 1989).

instead "a far more shadowy epistemological landscape . . . where the difference between knowledge and error was decidedly unclear."[112] Americans who worried that imagination would deceive them in religious, medical, and natural-philosophical enterprises could turn to the Franklin commission for support. Dugald Stewart, who was widely read in the United States, thought that students of the imagination owed a debt of gratitude to Mesmer. The facts in animal magnetism were "inestimable *data* for extending our knowledge of the laws which regulate the connexion between the human mind, and our bodily organization."[113] Benjamin Rush also acknowledged himself in Mesmer's debt: though he rejected the "futile pretensions of Mr. Mesmer," he was nonetheless "willing to derive the same advantages from his deceptions, which the chymists have derived from the delusions of the alchymists. The facts which he has established, clearly prove the influence of the imagination and will upon diseases."[114] When Perkins started peddling his magnetic tractors, relentless comparisons to Mesmer ensued. One paper disparagingly called Perkins the "modern *Mesmer*" and declared that in his experiments with the tractors, "the imagination only was affected."[115] Perkins's cures, said another, came from the "force of imagination," as "that eminent philosopher Dr. Franklin" had proved to be the case in "the pretended *Animal Magnetism*."[116]

The unanimity that animal magnetism was false gave it a special role. One could at any moment use it as Jefferson had: to constitute the community of the enlightened by excluding the dupes. Grant Powers's *Essay upon the Influence of the Imagination on the Nervous System, Contributing to a False Hope in Religion* (1828) and Amariah Brigham's *Observations on the Influence of Religion upon the Health and Physical Welfare of Mankind* (1835) both used animal magnetism to define the boundaries of true and false reli-

112. Delbourgo, *Wonders*, 3. Schmidt, Taves, and Sandra Gustafson all emphasize how the very process of policing the boundaries of rationality meant that natural-philosophical demonstrations were drawn toward passion, faith, and error: L. Schmidt, *Hearing Things*, 1–9; Taves, *Fits, Trances, and Visions*, 19; Sandra Gustafson, "The Emerging Media of Early America," *Proceedings of the American Antiquarian Society* 115, no. 2 (2005): 212.

113. Dugald Stewart, *Elements of the Philosophy of the Human Mind*, vol. 3 (Philadelphia: Carey, Lea, and Carey, 1827), 135. Volume 3 first published in London in 1827.

114. Benjamin Rush, "Extracts from a Pamphlet Lately Printed by Prichard and Hall," *Columbian*, March 1789, 165.

115. "Miscellaneous: Perkins's Metallic Points," *Bee*, New London, CT, January 17, 1798.

116. "A. B.," *Eastern Herald*, Portland, ME, March 9, 1797; see also "Extract of a Letter from a Physician in Philadelphia to His Friend in Wilmington," *Philadelphia Gazette*, April 8, 1797.

gion, as Ann Taves has pointed out.[117] Powers, a Congregationalist minister, wanted to restrain camp meetings because he considered them more fertile in apostasy and false hope than in real conversions. Brigham, a physician who would later become the director of the New York State Insane Asylum, was against camp meetings as well, for a different reason: the mental excitement and "bad air, in crowded tents" were sure to "prove injurious to health."[118]

Both Powers and Brigham offered the 1784 commission report as a means of giving an aggregate explanation for false religions of the past and present: all these were the work of the imagination. Powers proposes a thought experiment: "let us suppose that Mesmer and Deslon had been ecclesiastics; that they had inculcated the idea . . . that religion, in a high degree, produced similar effects on the human body . . . suppose they had endeavored by all possible means to excite their [the auditors'] apprehensions . . . and by hurried, boisterous, and long addresses, they had kept their minds strained intensely for hours in succession . . . have we not reason to believe, that similar effects would have followed?"[119] Functionally identical to animal-magnetic convulsions, according to Powers, were the exercises of the "*Areekee*," or "*Priests*," of New Zealand; the Kentucky revivalists of 1800–1803; the French prophets; the George Fox Quakers; and the "afflicted" in the Salem witchcraft trials.[120] Brigham rounds up some of the same suspects, plus "the negroes and savages of America [who] profess the worship of the Fetish gods,"[121] and such "semi-crazy papists and enthusiasts" as Saint Teresa, Jonathan Edwards's converts, and Abigail Hutchinson.[122] Since Mesmer had managed to create the same effects in his patients by means of the

---

117. Amariah Brigham, *Observations on the Influence of Religion upon the Health and Physical Welfare of Mankind* (Boston: Marsh, Capen, & Lyon: 1835); Grant Powers, *Essay upon the Influence of the Imagination on the Nervous System, Contributing to a False Hope in Religion* (Andover, MD: Flagg and Gould, 1828); Taves, *Fits, Trances, and Visions*, 123, 133–34.

118. A. Brigham, *Observations*, 156–57. On Brigham, see Benjamin Reiss, *Theaters of Madness: Insane Asylums and Nineteenth-Century American Culture* (Chicago: University of Chicago Press, 2008), 23, 35.

119. Powers, *Essay*, 23–24.

120. Powers, *Essay*, 22, 36–49, 54. On the Salem *afflicted* (a term for the accusers, not the accused witches) as participants in the American tradition of trance and religious ecstasy, see Nancy Ruttenburg, *Democratic Personality: Popular Voice and the Trial of American Authorship* (Stanford, CA: Stanford University Press, 1998), 31–82.

121. A. Brigham, *Observations*, xiv, quoting Franz Joseph Gall.

122. A. Brigham, *Observations*, 215; see also 210.

so-called animal magnetism, the spasms of these false religionists could not have anything to do with the Spirit, both Brigham and Powers argued.[123] They drew a picture of modern religion as worship in which the imagination was under control—all without actually having to explain exactly what imagination was or how one would manage it. They permitted their readers to condemn semicrazy and savage imaginations and thus take their places in the ranks of the rational.

READING FOR IMAGINATION

While one is occupied with recognizing and deploring the work of imagination in others, the question of whether one has one's own imagination under control fails to arise. That deferral may have been the payoff of learning about animal magnetism for American readers. It may be one reason that those readers, who were never very well versed in magnetism itself, became well versed in its falsehood between 1784 and 1836. During this period you could look up "Imagination, influence of, on the corporeal frame" in an encyclopedia and find—if not Mesmer's picture, at least the Franklin commission's damning account of him. The article on "imagination" in the first American edition of Rees's *Cyclopaedia* offers a detailed redaction of the Franklin report.[124] Imagination, especially in the "irritable female constitution," allows one "to give a rational explanation of many historical relations, which have been considered as altogether fabulous, or as direct violations of truth," including such things as "diabolical or daemoniacal possession; the power of incantations and amulets; the miraculous influence of relics; images of saints, &c . . . and many other circumstances."[125] In the *Domestic Encyclopaedia*, "Magnetism, Animal" figures as a "wild and incoherent system" fit only for the "fannatical and credulous."[126] An anonymous "gentle-

123. A. Brigham, *Observations*, 259; Powers, *Essay*, 23–24.

124. Abraham Rees, ed., *The Cyclopaedia; or, Universal Dictionary of Arts, Sciences, and Literature*, 1st American ed., 41 vols. (Philadelphia: Samuel F. Bradford & Murray, Fairman, 1810–1824), vol. 19, s.v. "imagination." See the subheading "Imagination, influence of, on the corporeal frame."

125. Ibid.

126. A. F. M. Willich and James Mease, eds., *The Domestic Encyclopaedia; or, a Dictionary of Facts, and Useful Knowledge*, 5 vols. (Philadelphia: William Young Birch & Abraham

man of Philadelphia" wrote in 1837, soon after Poyen's arrival, that "in the United States, especially, it would have been somewhat hazardous for any man of literary pretensions to couple [animal magnetism] with his name, except in the way of sneer and invective."[127]

Debunker-readers could align themselves against imagination by de-riding Mesmer's errors. As they shook their heads over poor, credulous fools, they mastered their own imaginations by proxy. To say that readers of exposés might have been performing this delicate projective substitution is only to suggest that they were as canny as novel readers. The Franklin report came out during the heyday of American seduction fiction. Like the *Report*, such novels occupy the paradoxical position of claiming to put the quietus on falsehoods, even as they portray imaginative errors that seem difficult to recognize and impossible to suppress. Reading novels would "habituate [the] mind to remark the difference between truth and fiction," William Hill Brown ventured, and yet the genre is known for portraying credulous heroines and—according to its detractors—inducing credulity in its readers.[128] In Brown's *The Power of Sympathy* (1789), the first American novel by some reckonings, an overeager suitor laments that "our imagina-tion dresses up a phantom to impose on our reason . . . we fall in love with the offspring of our brain."[129] The "paroxisms of passion" could cause "such a tumult—such an ebullition of the brain" as to "blind the eyes of the lover," one of Brown's level-headed characters explains.[130] Readers were invited to train in discerning falsehoods and controlling ebullitions, lest they join a cautionary parade of patsies: Susanna Rowson's "credulous girl," William

---

Small, 1803–1804), vol. 4, p. 8, s.v. "magnetism, animal." See also *Encyclopaedia Britannica: or, A Dictionary of Arts, Sciences, and Miscellaneous Literature; Enlarged and Improved*, 6th ed., 20 vols. (Edinburgh: Constable, 1823), vol. 12, pp. 398–400, s.v. "magnetism."

127. "A Gentleman of Philadelphia" [pseud.], *The Philosophy of Animal Magnetism, To-gether with the System of Manipulating Adopted to Produce Ecstacy and Somnambulism.—the Effects and the Rationale* (Philadelphia: Merrihew & Gunn, 1837), 11. Joseph Jackson, editor of a subsequent edition, attributed this anonymous text to Edgar Allan Poe, but the attribution has not been accepted: "*The Philosophy of Animal Magnetism* Identified," in *The Philosophy of Animal Magnetism* (Philadelphia, 1928), 14–31.

128. William Hill Brown, *The Power of Sympathy*, in *"The Power of Sympathy" and "The Coquette,"* ed. Carla Mulford (New York: Penguin, 1996), 53.

129. Ibid., 95.

130. Ibid., 10.

Hill Brown's "deluded female," and Hannah Webster Foster's coquette who "imagine[s] herself superior to delusion."[131]

Yet boiling brains, like automatous processes, were not exactly under conscious control. If they had been, perhaps it would not have required so many iterations of the seduction plot to make the point. As with the English translation of the *Report*, the error that seduction fiction was exposing was not exactly news. By the 1790s, devoted readers of the genre had surely started to notice a pattern: give way to sentiment, have sex out of wedlock, get pregnant, and die. Godwin was inclined to think that the reexposure of Mesmer's already-exploded falsehood required explanation. So too does the repeated exposure of seducers' wiles. These plots may give a compensatory pleasure analogous to the one involved in frowning on the errors of a mesmeric patient. Having raised the pedagogical demand that the imagination should be controlled, a novel such as Foster's *The Coquette* (1797) then offers a proxy for this impossible task: a credulous character whose transparency makes her easier to understand than the reader's own murky interior.[132]

Catherine Gallagher suggests in her essay "The Rise of Fictionality" that the "knowability" of novelistic figures contrasts favorably with the usual opacity of complex persons in real life: "if such a person [as the character] did exist, the usual boundary of personhood would be in place, and the reality created by the fiction would disintegrate." If it weighs on readers to find that their best efforts at introspection run aground on a puzzling opacity, fictional characters offer the balm of a projective substitution: characters' "knowability . . . produces a subtle sense of relief when we reflect on our own comparative unfathomability," Gallagher writes.[133] The pleasure we take in novelistic characters, then, comes from the fact that we find them easier to understand, more readable, than we find ourselves. The late eighteenth century has no monopoly on the unfathomable self. But still there

---

131. Ibid., 29; Susanna Rowson, *Charlotte Temple,* in *"Charlotte Temple" and "Lucy Temple,"* ed. Ann Douglas (New York: Penguin, 1991), 84; Hannah Webster Foster, *The Coquette; or, The History of Eliza Wharton*, ed. Cathy N. Davidson (New York: Oxford University Press, 1986), 55 (hereafter cited in text as *C*).

132. See Ogden, "Mesmer's Demon," 158–63, for an earlier version of this reading.

133. Catherine Gallagher, "The Rise of Fictionality," in *The Novel*, vol. 1, *History, Geography, and Culture*, ed. Franco Moretti (Princeton, NJ: Princeton University Press, 2006), 357. Gallagher sees the character as similar to Freud's fetish in this regard. As the Franklin commissioners used the imaginations of the mesmeric patients to substitute for their own unfathomable imaginations in my earlier argument, so, in Gallagher's argument here, the reader uses the character to substitute for his or her own unknowable self.

is, I would argue, a historical specificity to the difficulty of introspection. I would place the emphasis differently from the way Gallagher does: the fictional character does not substitute for the reader's entire self but rather for its unconscious and involuntary part, the imagination. The character, like the mesmeric patient, represents an imagination run rampant that the reader can fantasize about controlling.

Foster's *The Coquette* issues a tempting invitation to the reader: conduct a rational and virtuous surveillance over Eliza Wharton's imagination, since you cannot maintain one over your own. *The Coquette* fictionalizes the true story of Elizabeth Whitman, Eliza Wharton's namesake. Whitman was the unmarried daughter of a clergyman; she left home and died giving birth alone in a country inn.[134] Foster's epistolary novel is an experiment in understanding how a well-educated woman could be betrayed into a position like Whitman's; in real life, all the events leading up to the death at the inn remained mysterious. Given the end of Whitman's story, Foster reconstructs the beginning—and the beginning is imagination. Freed from an onerous engagement, Eliza Wharton describes herself as being carried away by her own imagination, though she only partly knows that this is what she is describing: "My heart beats high in expectation of its fancied joys. My sanguine imagination paints, in alluring colors, the charms of youth and freedom, regulated by virtue and innocence" (C, 29). Her virtuous correspondents see more clearly what these "charms of youth and freedom" really are. As one of Eliza's prudent friends writes to another about Eliza and her seducer Major Sanford, "though [she is] naturally penetrating, he has some how or other, cast a deceptious mist over her imagination, with respect to himself. . . . How prone to error is the human mind! How much lighter than the breath of zephyrs the operations of fancy! Strange then, it should ever preponderate over the weightier powers of the understanding!" (C, 111). In *The Coquette*, Eliza's imagination fabricates a reformed rake—a chimera if ever there was one—out of a heel and her own wishful thinking.

134. Whitman's story was reported in the *Salem Mercury* on July 29, 1788, and then repeated elsewhere: Cathy Davidson, *Revolution and the Word: The Rise of the Novel in America*, 2nd ed. (New York: Oxford University Press, 2004), 140–41. Gallagher might not count *The Coquette* as fictional, given that she defines fiction as "plausible" representation without "referential assumptions"; "Rise of Fictionality," 345. Eliza Wharton does refer, though in a distant way, to a real person. But because I am interested in the way fiction introduces its readers into the possibility of making credulous errors, I am less inclined than Gallagher is to define the novel in such a way that no confusion with reality would ever be possible. See chapter 3 of the present volume.

The zephyr imagination overwhelms the understanding here via the same avenues as in the Franklin report: it operates below the level of consciousness. Much of the drama of the novel lies in the fact that one cannot tell, during the first half of the text at least, whether Eliza is deceiving others—leading her suitors on, in other words—or is self-deceived, or is simply reluctant to take either of the poor marriage prospects offered her. Her two suitors represent unappealing extremes: one is a bore, the other a libertine. Eliza appears as a character in whom the deceptious imagination is probably operating—but she herself does not know to what extent. Foster uses physiological terms of art that signal the automatous imagination's effects on the body. "Alas!" Eliza writes to her mother, "can your volatile daughter ever acquire your wisdom?" (*C*, 39; cf. also 13). If Eliza is "volatile," then her animal spirits are prone to the speedy circulation that can hijack conscious thought—the same condition that afflicted mesmeric patients and religious enthusiasts. Eliza also explains that her seduction's "cause may be found in that unrestrained levity of disposition, that fondness for dissipation" that characterizes her (*C*, 145). *Dissipation* means frivolity, but it also indicates the animal spirits' near dissolution into gas underlying that frivolous state of mind.[135] Eliza is capable of analyzing her imagination's power, and yet imagination still mingles insidiously in her decisions. That, precisely, is the problem with this treacherous faculty. Our analytical efforts do not seem to disable it.

Critics have read *The Coquette* as divided between championing Eliza's unfulfilled desires and offering her story as a pedagogically motivated cautionary tale.[136] I see the novel's dividedness another way: through its pedagogical plot, *The Coquette* raises the problem of imagination for readers, including the problem of bringing its deceptive operations to consciousness. Then the novel offers a compensatory solution: readers can exercise a rational surveillance over Eliza as a proxy for surveilling their own imaginations. The novel primes its readers for seeing an equivalence between self-monitoring and monitoring others. In Eliza's letters, the psychic debate be-

135. *Oxford English Dictionary* online, 1st ed. (1895), s.v. "dissipation, *n.*" senses 2–6, http://www.oed.com.proxy.its.virginia.edu/view/Entry/55496?redirectedFrom=dissipation (accessed June 22, 2017).

136. Marion Rust, *Prodigal Daughters: Susanna Rowson's Early American Women* (Chapel Hill: University of North Carolina Press, 2008), 61; Julia Stern, *The Plight of Feeling: Sympathy and Dissent in the Early American Novel* (Chicago: University of Chicago Press, 1997), 84; Davidson, *Revolution and the Word*, 149; Elizabeth Barnes, *States of Sympathy: Seduction and Democracy in the American Novel* (New York: Columbia University Press, 1997), 69–70.

tween her reason and her imagination is often difficult to distinguish from the interpersonal debate between herself and her more prudent friends. Here Eliza recounts a conversation with one virtuous friend, Mrs. Richman, in a letter to another friend, Lucy. At first, Eliza is voicing Mrs. Richman, who warns her not to try to reform the seducer Sanford:

> I cannot conceive that . . . a [virtuous] lady would be willing to risk her all upon the slender prospect of his reformation. I hope the one with whom I am conversing, has no inclination to so hazardous, an experiment. Why, not much. Not much! If you have any, why do you continue to encourage Mr. Boyer's addresses? I am not sufficiently acquainted with either yet, to determine which to take . . . my fancy and my judgment are in scales. Sometimes one preponderates, sometimes the other. Which will finally outweigh, time alone can reveal. O my cousin, beware of the delusions of fancy! Reason must be our guide if we would expect durable happiness. (*C*, 51).

The dialogue runs together until it all seems to be in Eliza's voice—and in a sense, of course, it is; she is the one writing. First she ventriloquizes Mrs. Richman, the voice of Reason; then she ventriloquizes herself, the voice of Imagination. The conversation she recounts mirrors the war between her own "judgment" and "fancy" (the latter a word Foster uses as a synonym for *imagination*). In this world of multiple interlaced battles between reason and imagination, it is easy enough to add one more: the one readers may think is taking place within themselves. Readers can take up the controls, managing Eliza as a surrogate for an analogous, but impossible, labor: that of controlling their own imaginations.

But the more Eliza is required to be a surrogate for one part of the self, the livelier she becomes as a character. Because *The Coquette* is an epistolary novel, Eliza herself has to describe imagination, meaning that the novel winds up making a mechanical process conscious and articulate. No one in the novel is more vivid or more appealing than the character whom readers are being warned not to become. As Jennifer Harris has shown, generations of readers felt deeply attached to Eliza and to the shadowy real figure of Elizabeth Whitman somewhere behind her.[137] The very process of making Eliza into a surrogate for imagination demands that detail upon detail be

---

137. Jennifer Harris, "'Almost Idolatrous Love': Caroline Dall, Sarah Knowles Bolton, Mary C. Crawford and the Case of Elizabeth Whitman," in *Women Writers and the Artifacts of*

added about her. Much like imagination in the Franklin report, imagination in this novel tends to take on a life of its own.

If we see the novel in relation to events like the mesmerism investigation—events that contend with the untimely resurgence of enchantment—then we can think of the novel as aiming at modernity, not as getting
there.[138] In "The Rise of Fictionality," Gallagher stresses "the modernity-
fictionality connection": she wants to explain why modernity would favor
the development of a genre that offers plausible, but nonreferential, narratives. "Modernity," she proposes, "is fiction-friendly because it encour-
ages disbelief, speculation, and credit. The early novel's thematic emphases
on gullibility, innocence deceived, rash promises extracted, and impetuous
emotional and financial investments of all kinds point to the habit of mind
it discourages: faith. . . . Hence, while sympathizing with innocent credulity,
the reader is trained in an attitude of disbelief, which is flattered as superior
discernment."[139] What is modern about the novel, then, is the relation with
credulity into which its readers have to enter. On my view, Gallagher is right
to point to this relation with credulity as essential to the genre. Of the two
acts she has the novel performing with respect to its reader—training in an
attitude of disbelief and flattering superior discernment—I would emphasize, however, the flattery over the training. Flattery means, here, that fiction conspires with its reader to suggest that she has achieved the modern
goal of "superior discernment," or "philosophic doubt," as the *Report* put it:
mastery over credulity. But flattery also means that actual mastery has *not*
been achieved; to flatter is to exaggerate an accomplishment. Similarly, in
reading a mesmerism exposé, one's superior discernment is rather flattered
than trained. Readers get a symbolic control over their own imaginations
by virtue of knowing how the dupes' imaginations work and when they are
active. Setting out to master the imagination, debunker-readers might well
find themselves pursuing a more complex set of pleasures: mastering others' imaginations as a proxy for their own. It may be that the real payoff of
aiming toward modernity is this apparently auxiliary benefit—of feeling,
rather than being, enlightened.

Celebrity in the Long Nineteenth Century, ed. Ann R. Hawkins and Maura Ives (London:
Ashgate Press, 2012), 119–32.

138. See Talal Asad, *Formations of the Secular: Christianity, Islam, Modernity* (Stanford,
CA: Stanford University Press, 2003), 13.

139. Gallagher, "Rise of Fictionality," 345–46.

A FLUID—THAT IS—A FLUID

In that period between the Franklin report and Charles Poyen's first lecture tours in New England, there was one text on animal magnetism that seemed to know about debunking's compensatory pleasures. Elizabeth Inchbald's farce *Animal Magnetism* (1789), first printed in Dublin and steadily performed in the United States between 1794 and 1830, saw that the question about animal magnetism was not how the patients could be so gullible.[140] It was how and why the scientific observers of the process—the debunkers and their readers—had come to believe in belief. *Animal Magnetism* is set in Paris in the aftermath of an investigation into animal magnetism by "the faculty," a reference to the 1784 investigations. An elderly quack, the Doctor, is trying to force his ward Constance to marry him in spite of their difference in age. He has refused on her behalf an offer of marriage from a young Marquis, whom Constance loves. Meanwhile the Marquis's valet also wants to marry Constance's servant Lisette. The Doctor is planning to revive his medical practice by learning the secrets of mesmerism, and the lovers use this desire against him. La Fluer, valet to the Marquis, pretends to be Doctor Mystery, a mesmerist who has promised to initiate the Doctor. His name, "Fluer," means "to flow" in French, and fluidity is the constant focus of his remarks. Asked what animal magnetism is, La Fluer first confirms that the

140. Elizabeth Inchbald, *Animal Magnetism: A Farce, in Three Acts, as Performed at the Theatre Royal* (Dublin: P. Byron, 1789); *Animal Magnetism, a Farce, in Three Acts, as Performed at the New-York Theatre* (New York: Longworth, 1809), the latter of which is hereafter cited in text as *AM*. The earliest advertisement of a performance I have been able to find was in Charleston, South Carolina, in 1794; the farce is regularly advertised in Eastern cities between 1794 and 1830, after which performance falls off, though it does not stop. The following list is selected from the performances advertised in order to show the range of dates and locations: *South-Carolina State-Gazette*, Charlestown, June 19, 1794; *Gazette of the United States*, Philadelphia, December 29, 1796; *Daily Advertiser*, New York, May 28, 1798; *Columbian Centinel*, Boston, January 5, 1799; *Philadelphia Gazette*, December 3, 1801; *L'Oracle and Daily Advertiser*, New York, April 25, 1808; *Alexandria Daily Gazette*, Alexandria, VA, May 2, 1811; *Daily National Intelligencer*, Washington, DC, August 8, 1814; *Boston Gazette*, January 9, 1815; *New-York Courier*, March 19, 1816; *Franklin Gazette*, Philadelphia, July 31, 1819; *The American*, New York, June 24, 1820; *Baltimore Patriot*, January 6, 1823; *Boston Commercial Gazette*, October 20, 1825; *Augusta Chronicle*, Augusta, GA, February 5, 1828; *Providence Patriot*, Providence, RI, July 30, 1828; *Baltimore Patriot*, October 9, 1828; *New-York Morning Herald*, July 20, 1830.

Doctor is "intirely ignorant" of it. "And so am I," La Fluer admits in an aside (*AM*, 11). He then explains that animal magnetism is "a fluid—which is— a—fluid—and you know, doctor, that this fluid—generally called a fluid, is the most subtle of all that is the most subtle . . . it ascends on high, (*looking down*) and descends on low, (*looking up*) penetrates all substances, from the hardest metal, to the softest bosom—you understand me I perceive?" (*AM*, 11).

"Not very well," confesses the Doctor (*AM*, 11). And who can blame him? Yet Inchbald's scene gives us all the essentials: animal magnetism is a subtle fluid, whatever that may be—no one has a very clear idea—with some sort of polarity that is very hard to keep clear in one's head (thus La Fluer looks down for up, and up for down). If the mechanisms are obscure, however, the results are crystal clear: animal magnetism deceives people (here, the Doctor) and it seduces them—as La Fluer says, it "penetrates . . . the softest bosom." La Fluer elaborates with a simile:

> This fluid is like a river, that—that—runs—that—goes—that—gently glides—so—so—so—while there is nothing to stop it. But if it encoun- ters a mound or any other impediment—boo—boo—boo—it bursts forth—it overflows the country round—throws down villages, hamlets, houses, trees, cows, and lambs; but remove obstacles which obstruct its course, and it begins again, softly and sweetly to flow—thus—thus— thus—the fields are again adorned, and every thing goes on as well as it can go on. (*AM*, 11–12)

It's hard not to envision some pretty bawdy business during this speech. There are no stage directions, but all the talk of penetrating bosoms and encountering mounds introduces a certain train of thought. By this point in the play we already know that mesmerists use a "magnet, which is held in the hand of the physician, as a wand of a conjuror is held in his" (*AM*, 10). The smart money is on La Fluer holding the magnet less like a con- jurer's wand than like a dildo, with a pelvic thrust to emphasize each "so" (the crescendo), "boo" (the climax), and "thus" (the *dénouement*). "Thus it is with the *animal fluid*, which fluid obeys the command of my art," La Fluer concludes, quite possibly breathlessly. "Surprising art!" is the lecher- ous Doctor's laugh line (*AM*, 12).

The Doctor, who is alive to the possibilities here, whispers to La Fluer, "Pray, doctor, is it true, what they report that he who is once in posses- sion of your art, can, if he pleases, make every woman who comes near him, in love with him?" (*AM*, 13). La Fluer confirms the suggestion, and from this point forward Constance and her maid Lisette—who overhear the conversation—pretend to fall in love with whoever holds the wand. When the Doctor takes the wand, he gets more than he bargained for. Both women pretend to feel, as Lisette says, "not merely a love—but a rage—a violence." Lisette warns the Doctor, "take care how you turn my affection to hatred" (*AM*, 17–18). Playing voracious sexpots, the two women get the Doctor to pass the wand off to his servant Jeffry, with whom they immediately pretend to be besotted: "Jeffry, will you be deaf to my passion?" cries Lisette (*AM*, 19). The lovers also convince the Doctor that he has killed a patient (played by the Marquis) with his attempts at magnetism; they blackmail him with the threat of taking the case to the Faculty. That prospect, along with a few more passes of the aphrodisiac baton, leaves the Doctor trembling, confused, and imploring Constance to marry the Marquis.

In Inchbald's play, animal magnetism is not a subtle fluid, but a fetish: an apparently magical object whose "powers" are simply what credulous imaginations attribute to it. The commissioners had thought so, too. But there is an important difference between Inchbald's model and the commissioners' model. For Inchbald, the person who attributes chimerical powers to the magnetic wand is not the patient. It is the one who believes the patients are affected. The lovers' plot turns on the *Doctor's* belief in the inert wand's powers. In a more orthodox treatment of fetishism, Constance and Lisette would be the idolaters. They are the ones on whom the fetish-object, the wand, directly works. They spend virtually the whole play falling in love instantly with whoever holds the phallic wand. In the commissioners' farcical experiments, the patients—majority female—are in fact the ones who idolize the wand, going into convulsions when it enters their presence. But in *Animal Magnetism*, when Constance and Lisette convulse with passion, they are only pretending, playing into the Doctor's own idea of potent magnetism and rapacious female sexuality.

It is far from impossible that the original mesmeric patients were acting out a farce, though the commissioners barely consider that idea. In Inchbald's play the possibility that deceit goes the other way is front and center. The credulous person, in the last analysis, is the Doctor, who believes implicitly in the women's credulity. It may seem odd to say that "credulity" is what Constance and Lisette are performing; what they are most obviously performing is lust. But credulity is more than belief: it is the compound of imagination and passion that leads one to attribute power where no power exists. Credulity leads one to construct a chimera out of bits and pieces

Placebo

of one's own internal circulations, whether that chimera is the animal-magnetic fluid or a seducer who suddenly seems to dispose of powers of attraction that are not really his. As is the right of the bawdy dramatist (or of the psychoanalyst—Freud made the same distillation in his use of the primitive fetish), Inchbald has pared away from credulity all but its most laughable element: sex. Even so, her treatment bears on the dynamics of "belief." Her play proposes that the wand is a fetish not for those on whom it apparently acts, Constance and Lisette, but for the one who believes that it acts on those foolish others; namely, the Doctor. The one the wand jerks around is the one who believes that others are so manipulable, so biddable, that the passing of a baton will madden them with love.

"Intirely ignorant" of animal magnetism, and never directly subjected to it, the Doctor is fascinated by the idea of its effects on others. To Inchbald, that fascination is what opens the Doctor up to ridicule: so sure is he that others are ultramanipulable that he becomes easily manipulated himself. Latour tells us that in the scene of idolatry, the one who believes in others' belief is the one who is Modern. That position, not so-called primitive fetishism, is the one requiring explanation. Thus Latour proposes a new great divide, "a new *cogito*, a new fixed point: I believe in belief, therefore I am modern!"[141] What is it like to be the Doctor in Inchbald's play—a believer in belief? On what trajectory does it place one? The Doctor starts out contemptuous and ends up sidelined. He expects to yank Lisette and Constance around like puppets on strings—but he quickly finds that their feints within feints outpace him. Their credulity, at first the object of his contempt, soon becomes too powerful a force for him to handle.

"JUST IMAGINATION"

The position of American readers of the Franklin report between 1784 and 1836 would bear comparison to the Doctor's own. They believed in belief, and therefore they were modern. But the strange outcome of believing in belief was that its power tended to get beyond one. The commission report's reception laid out the three basic steps of a dance that magnetists and their opponents would reprise many times over in the years to come. First, debunking: the phenomenon in question does not exist. Second, invention of

---

141. Latour, *Factish Gods*, 45; *Dieux faitiches*, 95.

an idol-function: people's belief in the nonexistent thing is to be explained by some quality of their minds, whether imagination, credulity, enthusiasm, suggestibility, nervousness, or one of a host of similar possibilities. Third, management: one must make an effort to get a handle on, or at any rate live with, the idol-function just invented, since it turns out to be just as worrying as the enchantment it has been pressed into service to explain. This final step was quite variable. Relations with the idol-function—with credulity—sometimes took the form of attempts at rational control, sometimes of fetishistic compensation for what could not be managed, and sometimes even of enthusiastic embrace.

The unanticipated need to live with idol-functions after inventing them was what allowed the commission report to become part of, rather than an obstacle to, future practice. If idol-functions needed supervision and control, the commissioners themselves had already admitted that the magnetist, the *dépositaire* or trustee of the patient's credulity, had that managerial power. French mesmerists were quick to see the possibilities. Before the commission had even completed its experiments, Deslon prefigured the nimble about-face that practitioners would soon make en masse: he said that magnetism, rather than being a deplorable example of credulity, was actually the science of governing it. As Bailly sardonically recorded, Deslon "declared in our session held at the house of Dr. Franklin the 19th of June, that he thought he might lay it down as a fact, that the imagination had the greatest share in the effects of animal magnetism; he said that this new agent might be no other than the imagination itself, whose power is as extensive as it is little known."[142] Animal magnetism *was* imagination, Deslon proposed in a clever save. Not all of his colleagues would have gone so far as that. But over the early part of the nineteenth century, most French magnetists would retool their practice as a means of explaining how credulity worked and how it could be used. These would become magnetists' questions, as they were the commissioners'. Rather than allowing their practice to be the final example in the long history of false religions, mesmerists would start explaining that history themselves. This was the brand of magnetism that would come to the United States with Charles Poyen in 1836.

Instead of being a problem for animal magnetism's subsequent practitioners, then, credulity turned out to be their greatest prize. The theory that magnetism *did not exist* wound up subsidizing its existence for at least a century and maybe two, depending on how you count. That period includes

142. [Bailly], *Report*, 100; *Rapport*, 58.

the entire history of magnetism in the United States as well as the histories of mesmerism's successor practices in Europe, hypnosis and psychoanalysis. J. M. Charcot, who institutionalized a new form of magnetism—hypnosis—in his hysteria clinic at the Salpêtrière in Paris, was still manipulating credulity in the 1870s and 1880s, much as the commissioners had accused magnetists of doing a century earlier.[143] He treated his hysterical patients in part by making suggestions to them while they were in a hypnotic state, when they followed his commands far more readily than they would normally have done.[144] He also accepted the reality of autosuggestive paralyses, or hysterical paralyses—combinations of paralytic symptoms, that is, that failed to correspond to organic damage to the nerves. Like the Franklin commission, whose theories came to Charcot through the animal magnetism he adapted in his own practice, he insisted that the mind could cause real symptoms in the body.[145] Freud retained Charcot's insight that nonorganic paralysis could exist; hypnotic suggestion he did his best to expunge, though historians such as Mikkel Borch-Jacobsen tell us its shadow still remains in the *transference*, the passionate attachment to the analyst that the patient develops in successful treatments.[146] If Borch-Jacobsen is right, then magnetism recently celebrated its bicentennial: two hundred years of flourishing nullity. Psychoanalysis aside, in France and its former colonies you can still do a *stage*, or internship, in animal magnetism, just as you might in animal husbandry—though the reality of the one is considerably more contested than the reality of the other.[147]

"Theory is well and good," Freud overheard Charcot saying, "but it does not prevent things from existing."[148] In the case of animal magnetism, he was certainly correct. I would take Charcot's declaration one step farther: the theory that proclaims "it does not exist" (or, "it is 'just' imagination") actually permits a certain kind of being to flourish. As Léon Chertok and Isabelle Stengers comment, "the commission's conclusion, 'it's just

143. Gauld, *History of Hypnotism*, 310.

144. Ibid., 310–15.

145. Chertok and Stengers, *Critique of Psychoanalytic Reason*, 30–36; *Le Cœur et la raison*, 40–46.

146. Borch-Jacobsen, *Emotional Tie*, 93.

147. Christiane Bougerol, *Une ethnographie des conflits aux Antilles: Jalousie, commérages, sorcellerie* (Paris: Presses universitaires de France, 1997), 145.

148. Sigmund Freud quoted in Chertok and Stengers, *Le Cœur et la raison*, 41; my translation. For an alternate rendering, see Martha Noel Evans's translation in Chertok and Stengers, *Critique of Psychoanalytic Reason*, 31.

imagination,' would see its significance reversed, and would have the role not of an ending but of a beginning."[149] Whether adventitiously or deliberately, magnetists capitalized on the powers that the Franklin commission and other debunkers were attributing to belief. They recognized, as Adams did, that imagination was something worth controlling if it could really do all that the commissioners said it could. Debunkers had one reason for inciting credulity: as long as they could see it in others, they could feel as though they were controlling it in themselves. Mesmerists thought of another reason: credulity evidently made people easy to manage. Eventually they would come up with a third reason: credulity, properly manipulated, led to extraordinary insight. The benefit of studying enchantment from the perspective of those who are preoccupied with debunking it is that we can then follow all these roads: the road of compensation, of management, and of enthusiastic reuse, all of which start with the story that debunkers tell about the credulity of the mesmeric patient. *Because* mesmerism was debunked, it thrived. Credulity was not to be contained within the original bounds that debunkers or even mesmerists gave it. It would become sophisticated, critical, subtle, and reflective—more than a means of management and control—in and through the attempts to master it.

---

149. Chertok and Stengers, *Le Cœur et la raison*, 37; my translation. As before, for an alternate rendering, see Evans's translation in Chertok and Stengers, *Critique of Psychoanalytic Reason*, 26.

BEYOND RADICAL ENCHANTMENT

Mesmerizing Laborers
in the Americas

O sing me a song of the Factory Girl!
Link not her name with the SLAVES.—
She is brave and free as the old elm tree
That over her homestead waves.

John H. Warland, "Song of the Factory Girl"[1]

MAKING MAGNETISM INTO THE SCIENCE THAT could explain credulity
required, or at any rate fortuitously coincided with, a change in technique.
The Franklin report and the French Revolution conspired to create a lull in
magnetic practice in France. But in the early nineteenth century, under the
leadership of Franz Anton Mesmer's pupil the Marquis A. M. J. Chastenet
de Puységur and Jardin des Plantes librarian J. P. F. Deleuze, French mesmerists regrouped.[2] Practitioners still performed the magnetic passes, thus
communicating an invisible fluid into subjects' bodies. But convulsions

1. John H. Warland, "Song of the Manchester Factory Girl," quoted in Arthur Schlesinger Jr., *The Age of Jackson* (Boston: Little, Brown, 1945), 272. The song is also published
in *New Hampshire Sentinel*, Keene, NH, March 7, 1850, as "Song of the Factory Girl"; song
title varies. The earliest publication date is uncertain; Schlesinger's source would suggest
the 1830s or 1840s.

2. Alan Gauld, *A History of Hypnotism* (Cambridge: Cambridge University Press, 1992),
111–18.

and expectorations became a thing of the past. Instead, the fluid now produced *somnambulism*, a trancelike state in which subjects became credulous toward their mesmerists' suggestions and obedient to their commands, sometimes also developing clairvoyant powers. The relationship between the somnambulist and the mesmerist, the *rapport*, closely resembled the relationship of ~~sorcerer and enchanted victim~~. Yet the rapport was not, or not only, enchantment: like the commissioners' "imagination," it was also a means of *explaining* enchantment. According to Deleuze, "animal magnetism . . . [has] been known throughout history," but past attempts to describe it "have been founded on false physical theories or on superstition."[3] Votaries of primitive religions had used the state of somnambulism to inflate the reputations of their nonexistent gods. But really, somnambulism was just the natural effect of certain uses of the animal-magnetic fluid. Like the Franklin commission, mesmerists were proposing an idol-function: the credulous had mistaken the effects of the animal-magnetic fluid for the work of supernatural powers. But unlike the Franklin commission, they intended to keep up the use of that idol-function. They would continue the practice of the false priests, but openly, and toward enlightened ends. All the miracles of false religion—prophecy, faith healing, and unquestioning obedience—would become powers of which a technician could dispose.

US mesmerism developed from this new strain of the French practice; in that respect, it was the offspring of both Mesmer and Benjamin Franklin. The founder of US mesmerism, Charles Poyen, was a Creole sugar planter who lived an itinerant life; born on his family's plantation in Guadeloupe in 1806, he attended medical school in France in his late teens, where he learned about animal magnetism. He then returned briefly to Guadeloupe, where he discovered his fellow planters practicing mesmerism on enslaved people. Finally he moved to New England, where a branch of his family had taken refuge during the failed slave revolution of the 1790s. There, after a few false starts, he established the practice of mesmerism—first in the factory cities and then in the region as a whole. Mesmerism would thrive in the United States from the time of Poyen's 1836 lecture tour at least until spiritualism eclipsed it in the 1850s.[4] In another sense, though, mesmerism

3. J. P. F. Deleuze, *Histoire critique du magnétisme animal*, 2 vols. (Paris: Mome, 1813), 1:11.

4. Eric T. Carlson, "Charles Poyen Brings Mesmerism to America," *Journal of the History of Medicine and Allied Sciences* 15 (1960): 121–32; Robert C. Fuller, *Mesmerism and the American Cure of Souls* (Philadelphia: University of Pennsylvania Press, 1982); Gauld, *History of Hypnotism*, 179–96; Ann Taves, *Fits, Trances, and Visions: Experiencing Religion and*

had already been thriving. Poyen complained that Franklin's pernicious influence made it difficult for him to gain a foothold: "the public on hearing that lectures were given on the delusion exploded some fifty-three years ago by '*the great Franklin*,' laughed, and denied every thing, without examining," he wrote.[5] But actually Franklin had prepared the ground for him. The impressive powers that the Franklin commission had attributed to credulity made it an important object to master—and this was precisely what Poyen would now offer to do. In 1836, to combat Poyen's growing influence, the *Boston Courier* republished John Adams's letter to Benjamin Waterhouse demanding "some method of managing and controlling" the imagination.[6] Poyen's claim—one that would no doubt have appalled Adams and Waterhouse—was that mesmerism could be this method. There was not as much daylight between those who debunked mesmerism and those who practiced it as either side might have liked to think. Adams thought credulity was primitive, but so did Poyen: he wanted to control it in others, not succumb to it himself. Poyen sought a technique for managing credulity, but so did Adams, or Amariah Brigham: it was only that their solution would probably have involved enlightening the public, not making magnetic passes along people's spines.

Scholars who have mapped occult practice as radical or countercultural have often seemed to envision a pitched battle between those who both practiced enchantment and admired it, and those who neither practiced enchantment nor admired it but hoped instead to see it stamped out.[7] What

Explaining Experience from Wesley to James (Princeton, NJ: Princeton University Press, 1999), 119–65; Sheila O'Brien Quinn, "How Southern New England Became Magnetic North: The Acceptance of Animal Magnetism," *History of Psychology* 10, no. 3 (2007): 231–48; and Russ Castronovo, "The Antislavery Unconscious: Mesmerism, Vodun, and 'Equality,'" *Mississippi Quarterly* 53 (Winter 1999/2000): 41–47. Poyen was not the first to bring mesmerism to the United States, but he was the first to do so with lasting success. On earlier attempts, see Emily Ogden, "*Edgar Huntly* and the Regulation of the Senses," *American Literature* 85, no. 3 (September 2013): 430–34.

5. Charles Poyen, *The Progress of Animal Magnetism in New England* (Boston: Weeks, Jordan, 1837), 44.

6. [John Adams], "Animal Magnetism Alias Medical Witchcraft," *Boston Courier*, December 1, 1836, reprint of John Adams, "Boston, Nov. 29: Extract of a Letter Dated September 8, 1784, Auteuil, near Paris," *American Herald*, Boston, MA, November 29, 1784.

7. I have in mind here the radical enchantment position discussed more fully in the introduction. Representative works include Ann Braude, *Radical Spirits: Spiritualism and Women's Rights in Nineteenth-Century America* (Boston: Beacon Press, 1989); Molly McGarry, *Ghosts of Futures Past: Spiritualism and the Cultural Politics of Nineteenth-Century*

this model makes too little of is the distinction between being the false priest who enchants and the dupe who is enchanted. Like the French commissioners who were in many ways their forebears, nineteenth-century mesmerists reproduced a state of enchantment (renamed the "somnambulistic rapport") in their subjects. But they themselves were not enchanted, nor did they see that state as a particularly dignified or admirable one. Like the French commissioners in their experiments with sham devices, mesmerists imagined themselves performing an enlightened version of the false priest's techniques. One could look down on enchantment and still incite it toward any number of ends: managing the enchanted subject; understanding, as William Godwin had suggested, "ecclesiastical history"; or enjoying the satisfactions of mastering others' credulity when one could not be sure of mastering one's own.[8] The occult was not a safe house where magic could flourish; it was, as John Modern, David Walker, Ann Taves, and others have seen, a place where a secular age worked out what enchantment's uses might be.[9]

At the moment of its US founding, mesmerism offered enchantment as a means by which properly secular moderns could control those who were not modern yet. As a slave owner, Poyen had a compelling reason to be interested in such a practice: his wealth depended on dominating people whom he and his fellow planters saw as savages. He learned in French medical circles that mesmeric techniques worked best on women, uneducated people, and "primitive" races: those usual suspects that the commissioners, too, had considered less likely to approach Mesmer's claims with great incredulity (*une grande incrédulité*). Poyen observed mesmerism being used on nervous patients in French hospitals and on slaves in Guadeloupe before finally introducing it in the United States. With the help of his demonstration partner, the factory worker Cynthia Gleason, Poyen told

---

America (Berkeley: University of California Press, 2008); and Alex Owen, *The Darkened Room: Women, Power, and Spiritualism in Late Victorian England* (Philadelphia: University of Pennsylvania Press, 1990).

8. [William Godwin], introduction to [J. S. Bailly], *Report of Dr. Benjamin Franklin, and Other Commissioners, Charged by the King of France with the Examination of the Animal Magnetism, as Now Practised at Paris,* [trans. William Godwin] (London: J. Johnson, 1785), xviii.

9. Taves, *Fits, Trances, and Visions*; David Walker, "The Humbug in American Religion: Ritual Theories of Nineteenth-Century Spiritualism," *Religion and American Culture* 23, no. 1 (2013): 30–74; John Lardas Modern, *Secularism in Antebellum America* (Chicago: University of Chicago Press, 2011), 43–44.

New England's cotton industrialists that mesmerism could help them with
workforce supervision. Mesmerism was never destined to become institutionalized as a means of factory management. Still, Poyen's impulse to present it in these terms speaks volumes about the way he understood his own
manipulation of the credulous. As we trace the itinerary that mesmerism
followed to reach the United States, from hospital to plantation to factory,
modern enchantment will prove to be neither a vestige nor a refuge. It was
not the signature of a kinder, gentler secularism. Modern enchantment was
delusion employed, credulity profitably directed—at least as long as Poyen
had his way. But Poyen would not have his way forever, and the future of US
mesmerism would bear witness to the variety of practices that could grow
out of these disciplinary beginnings.

THE FACTORY BELL

Success did not crown Charles Poyen's earliest efforts as a mesmeric lecturer.
He began by trying to sell the Boston medical establishment on mesmerism, but after some initial interest, the *Boston Medical and Surgical Journal*
dropped him.[10] By the autumn of 1836, Poyen was in a "very precarious
situation," as he put it in his account of mesmerism's American beginnings,
The Progress of Animal Magnetism in New England (1837).[11] His lectures on
mesmerism had not been profitable, and he was "reduced to the utmost
degree of poverty."[12] So he sent home for money. Home was Guadeloupe,
where, with his mother and siblings, Poyen owned Le Piton, a "large sugar
plantation, with many slaves" located in the far northwest corner of the island.[13] Poyen distances himself from slavery in *The Progress of Animal Magnetism*, merely saying that his "parents" owned a plantation whose name

10. Carlson, "Charles Poyen Brings Mesmerism to America," 124–28. The *Boston Medical
and Surgical Journal (BMSJ)* looked favorably on Poyen in the spring of 1836, publishing
articles by and about him, but it turned against him in June: *BMSJ*, February 3, February 10,
March 23, April 6, April 27, June 22, 1836. See also Poyen's response, *BMSJ*, July 20, 1836.

11. Poyen, *Progress*, 50.

12. Ibid.; Quinn, "How Southern New England Became Magnetic North," 235–36.

13. Poyen, *Progress*, 50.

he does not give.[14] But he can be confidently identified as the joint owner of Le Piton.[15] In 1827, on the death of Charles's father, Mathieu, the notary Alphonse Poirié appraised Le Piton and its slaves as they passed to Mathieu's heirs. Poirié judged the total worth of Poyen's slaves to be just under ninety thousand francs, one-third of Le Piton's value and the single largest part of the inheritance.[16] Poirié did not record how many enslaved people lived at Le Piton. But if he valued the enslaved similarly to the way he had in another case that year, where he listed individuals at an average of one thousand francs each, then Mathieu Poyen had left about ninety enslaved people to his family.[17] The money Charles Poyen received from Le Piton in 1836 allowed him to continue his American tour: had it not been for the "very timely" receipt of "some funds from my country," Poyen declared, "I should have been compelled either to return home, or to engage in some other employment."[18] Had it not been for the proceeds of slavery, American mesmerism might never have gotten off the ground.

Newly flush, Poyen headed for the textile city of Pawtucket, Rhode Island, where the products of another slave system, the cotton plantations of the South, were pouring in at a rate of hundreds of thousands of pounds of raw cotton per year.[19] Poyen's lectures there cost seventy-five cents a ticket,

14. Ibid. "Parents" in English is a false cognate for *parents*, meaning relatives, in French. Poyen may have meant his relatives, and it was true that Poyen's relatives—his mother and siblings—along with Poyen himself owned Le Piton as of 1837. In either case, Poyen is downplaying his own involvement, since he, too, was one of the owners of Le Piton.

15. My identification of the magnetizing Charles Poyen with the Charles Poyen who jointly owned Le Piton is based on, first, date and location of death ("Death of Dr. Poyen," *BMSJ*, September 25, 1844, 166; Philippe Rossignol and Bernadette Rossignol, *La Famille Poyen*, vol. 1, *Généalogie* (Le Pecq, France, 2013), 94); and second, paternal uncle's residence in Newburyport, Massachusetts (Poyen, *Progress*, 41; Rossignol, *La Famille Poyen*, 85–87). On Le Piton's ownership, see Rossignol, *La Famille Poyen*, 94–95, 114–15; Alexis Léger (notary), "Notoriété relative à la succession de M. Neyop de Poyen," February 25, 1864, Guadeloupe, NOT GUA 1722, Archives Nationales d'Outre-Mer (hereafter cited as ANOM).

16. Alphonse Poirié (notary), "Inventaire après le mort de Mathieu Augustin Poyen Montrop," May 29, 1827, Guadeloupe, NOT GUA 2535, ANOM.

17. Alphonse Poirié (notary), "Inventaire après le mort de Jean Baptiste Denis Lambert," March 14, 1827, Guadeloupe, NOT GUA 2535, ANOM.

18. Poyen, *Progress*, 49.

19. US House of Representatives [Secretary of the Treasury Louis McLane], *Documents Relative to the Manufactures in the United States*, 2 vols. (Washington, DC, 1833), 1:170–77 (hereafter cited as McLane Report). The McLane Report's "Schedule of Manufactures" for

between one and two days' wages for a cotton factory worker, so it is likely that his audiences were made up mostly of owners and managers.[20] Owners were in the midst of consolidating their power over workers' time with the help of a new technology, the power loom.[21] Rhode Island's early cotton mills, the first of which Samuel Slater opened in 1790, had employed children to spin by machine, while adult outworkers wove cloth by hand.[22] Though child workers were subject to strict time discipline,[23] outworker-weavers largely controlled their own production rhythms.[24] But conditions for adult workers changed with increasing automation. Between 1813 and 1823, the Boston Associates introduced the power loom in new mills in Waltham and Lowell, Massachusetts.[25] Rhode Island firms adopted the technology throughout the 1820s, with the process of adoption complete by 1830.[26] Power looms gave owners a new level of control over work schedules.[27] The water-powered machines brought weavers into the factory building and subjected them to the pace of the mill wheel. Since children could not operate the new machines and master weavers largely refused to do so, factories began hiring unmarried women, a class managers found more tractable.[28] Weavers now reported to the factory at sunrise to work a twelve-

---

Pawtucket estimates the number of pounds of domestic cotton used by each factory in Pawtucket per annum circa 1829, based on self-reporting by factory owners and managers. The sum of the Pawtucket estimates is more than 660,000 pounds.

20. [Advertisement], *Pawtucket Chronicle*, November 11, 1836. Wages ranged from thirty-eight cents to just over one dollar per day: McLane Report, 1:171, 175, 177.

21. Gary Kulik, "Pawtucket Village and the Strike of 1824: The Origins of Class Conflict in Rhode Island," *Radical History Review* 17 (Spring 1978): 29.

22. Barbara Tucker, "The Merchant, the Manufacturer, and the Factory Manager: The Case of Samuel Slater," *Business History Review* 55, no. 3 (1981): 298–99.

23. Barbara Tucker, *Samuel Slater and the Origins of the American Textile Industry, 1790–1860* (Ithaca, NY: Cornell University Press, 1984), 160.

24. Gail Fowler Mohanty, "Putting Up with Putting-Out: Power-Loom Diffusion and Outwork for Rhode Island Mills, 1821–1829," *Journal of the Early Republic* 9, no. 2 (Summer 1989): 195–97.

25. Thomas Dublin, *Women at Work: The Transformation of Work and Community in Lowell, Massachusetts, 1826–1860*, 2nd ed. (New York: Columbia University Press, 1993), 17–20.

26. Mohanty, "Putting Up," 191–92, 211, 216; Tucker, "The Merchant," 305; Kulik, "Pawtucket Village," 13.

27. Kulik, "Pawtucket Village," 13–14.

28. Tucker, *Samuel Slater*, 218–19; Kulik, "Pawtucket Village," 13–14; James Lawson Conrad Jr., "The Evolution of Industrial Capitalism in Rhode Island, 1790–1830: Almy, the Browns, and the Slaters" (PhD diss., University of Connecticut, 1973), 334; Editha Hadcock,

to fourteen-hour day, six days a week. The factory bell, which tolled for start and stop times that managers alone determined, was both the symbol and the real instrument of the discipline the weavers faced.[29]

Among these weavers was Cynthia Gleason, the first American mesmeric clairvoyant. Gleason was a skilled operator and lifelong textile worker. She did not see Poyen's lectures until she became an exhibit in them.[30] But Niles Manchester, her physician and the part owner of a mill along Sargent's Trench, had attended and had been favorably impressed.[31] Poyen had presented animal magnetism as a means of both curing illness (by rebalancing the body's nervous fluids) and inducing clairvoyant states. Manchester asked Poyen to consult on Gleason's case. Poyen would report on Gleason in the *Providence Daily Journal*. The *Journal*, under the editorship of Thomas Webb, was perhaps the most important among a handful of papers that championed mesmerism in 1836 and 1837.[32] Gleason had worked in Pawtucket's factories for the past decade. For almost as long, she had been "laboring under a complicated nervous and functional disease, which baffled all the skill of physicians." According to Poyen, "the sleep of the patient ha[d] become difficult, short, [and] very much troubled by pains." Gleason felt "a dulness of the mind, and heaviness of the system, for several hours after awaking"—the predictable result of working six fourteen-hour days per week.[33] Gleason's body failed to comply with the factory bell's rhythms, so Poyen used animal magnetism to bring her back into line. The two met at Gleason's lodgings almost daily in that first week, often with a small coterie of mill personnel observing.[34] On an evening when the cotton manufacturer Ruel Richards

---

"Labor Problems in Rhode Island Cotton Mills, 1790–1940," 2 vols. (PhD diss., Brown University, 1945), 1:41.

29. Tucker, *Samuel Slater*, 227; Kulik, "Pawtucket Village," 28.

30. Charles Poyen, "Surprising Phenomena of Animal Magnetism," *New-York Spectator*, November 24, 1836, [2]; reprint of same article from *Providence Daily Journal* (*PDJ*), November 17, 1836.

31. Stephen W. Williams, *American Medical Biography* (Greenfield, MA, 1845), 382; Robert Grieve, *An Illustrated History of Pawtucket, Central Falls, and Vicinity* (Pawtucket, RI, 1897), 111, 139.

32. Quinn, "How Southern New England Became Magnetic North," 243. Other promagnetism papers include the *Nantucket Inquirer*, ed. Samuel Haynes Jenks, and the *New Bedford Mercury*, ed. Benjamin Lindsey; see "Waking Up," *PDJ*, August 5, 1837; "Animal Magnetism," *Connecticut Courant*, Hartford, CT, September 16, 1837.

33. Poyen, "Surprising Phenomena of Animal Magnetism," [2].

34. See Poyen, "Surprising Phenomena of Animal Magnetism," [2]; see also Poyen, "Experiments in Animal Magnetism," *PDJ*, November 23, 1836.

was present, Poyen placed Gleason under his control by magnetizing her.[35] Then he "'*mentally*' requested the somnambulist to go to bed . . . and told her, '*mentally*,' to sleep until eight o'clock exactly." The next morning, efforts to wake Gleason before eight proved "all in vain." But "as the clock was striking *eight* she stretched her hand out of the clothes, rubbed her eyes, and got up."[36] The factory bell in Gleason's soul had begun to ring.

Poyen had used mesmerism to implant his will in Gleason, as though he were demonstrating that magnetism could make workers internalize factory schedules. "The magnetical agent," he explained, "is a fluid existing in every individual, but which is secreted and emanated only by the will of him who wishes to impregnate with it another individual."[37] By "impregnating" Gleason with the magnetic fluid, he could make her actions conform to his desires. Implantation of the managerial will in laborers was also the point of the mills' strict schedules, as Barbara Tucker points out: schedules were meant to inculcate "the so-called habits of industry: regularity, obedience, sobriety, steady intensity, and punctuality."[38] Suffused with Poyen's will, Gleason was preternaturally punctual; she awoke from the magnetic sleep feeling "*as bright as a dollar*" and ready to begin making more bright dollars for her employers.[39]

According to Poyen, the power that had allowed him to possess Gleason with the spirit of the factory timetable was primitive religion, updated for modern use. Animal magnetism, Poyen wrote, had "struck with amazement and admiration the greatest men of antiquity," but these great men, "being not able to account for it, the natural causes being yet unknown, attributed them [*sic*] to the beneficial interposition of the gods, Isis, Osiris, Serapis, Apollo, Vulcan, Jupiter, Esculapius, &c."[40] False priests had always

---

35. See Poyen, "Experiments in Animal Magnetism," *PDJ*, November 23, 1836. On Richards, see Grieve, *Illustrated History of Pawtucket*, 162.

36. Poyen, "Experiments in Animal Magnetism," *PDJ*, November 23, 1836.

37. Charles Poyen, introduction to *Report on the Magnetical Experiments Made by the Commission of the Royal Academy of Medicine of Paris*, by Henri Marie Husson, trans. Charles Poyen (Boston, 1836), lx; translation of Henri Marie Husson, *Rapport sur les expériences magnétiques faites par la commission de l'Académie Royale de Médecine* (Paris, 1831). Like many in the French tradition, Poyen posited such a fluid but did not think the question was settled.

38. Tucker, *Samuel Slater*, 163.

39. Poyen, "Surprising Phenomena of Animal Magnetism," [2]. Dollar coins were in use at the time, thus the reference to a dollar as "bright."

40. Poyen, introduction to Husson, *Report on Magnetical Experiments*, liii.

worked their miracles by manipulating the animal-magnetic fluid—they simply had not realized they were doing it. Now animal magnetism refurbished their enchantments as disciplinary techniques. Poyen had learned about this technical means of wielding primitive religious powers when he was a medical student in France. In Guadeloupe, he had seen his fellow planters use the same methods on their slaves. When he met Gleason in Providence, thus inaugurating not just American mesmerism but a whole strand of the American occult tradition, he carried this education with him.

"ISIS MAGNETIZING HER SON HORUS"

In 1829, Poyen had sailed from his native Guadeloupe to France, where he would spend the next four years studying medicine in Paris.[41] By that time magnetism had become a means of inducing credulous, enchantment-like states, and it was receiving modest attention among the medical faculty.[42] The groundwork had been laid at almost the same moment that the commissioners were investigating Charles Deslon, Mesmer's prominent pupil. In the 1780s the Marquis A. M. J. de Chastenet de Puységur was regularly magnetizing Victor Race, a peasant on his estate in Buzancy, in the hopes of curing Race's chronic illnesses. But Race did not convulse when magnetized. Instead, he would enter a trancelike state in which he could explain to Puységur the origins of his own illness. He seemed tied to his magnetist by the bond Puységur called the "rapport": he was obedient to Puységur's wishes and sometimes seemed to read his mind. Puységur named the state "magnetic somnambulism," by analogy with regular sleepwalking.[43] Over the first few decades of the nineteenth century, convulsive crises faded among magnetic patients, to be replaced by effects ranging from mild sleepiness

NIGHT FAMILY!

41. Supplément to *Journal politique et commercial de la Pointe-à-Pître*, March 26, 1829; Poyen, *Progress*, 41–42.

42. Gauld, *History of Hypnotism*, 128–38. Texts of the medical reception include: Husson, *Rapport sur les expériences magnétiques* (1831 ed.); Léon Rostan, "Magnétisme," in *Dictionnaire de médecine*, 21 vols., ed. N. P. Adelon et al., (Paris: Béchet jeune, 1821–1828), 13: 421–69; E. J. Georget, *De la physiologie du système nerveux et spécialement du cerveau*, 2 vols. (Paris: J. B. Baillière, 1821); *L'Hermès: Journal du magnétisme animal, publié par une société de médecins de la Faculté de Paris* (Paris: Lévi, 1826–1829).

43. Gauld, *History of Hypnotism*, 39–44.

to full-blown somnambulism of Race's sort. Magnetism could still rebalance the body's magnetic fluid, a process of which drowsiness was often the outward sign. But for those capable of somnambulism—which was not every one—it gave the gift of clairvoyance. And it also connected the somnambulist to the mesmerist with the rapport—a bond that, at its strongest, could amount to mind control. This rapport was what permitted Poyen to control Gleason.

With the somnambulistic rapport, magnetists turned the tables on Franklin. Over the early decades of the nineteenth century, French magnetists were to concede the Franklinian point that mesmerism had something to do with false religion. But they rejected the idea that magnetism was merely a reheated old falsehood. On the contrary: they had begun to claim that magnetism was, itself, a means of explaining how it was that primitives had believed in all those nonexistent gods. J. P. F. Deleuze, who knew Puységur but was his junior by many years, and who took over leadership of the Paris-area magnetic circles by the first decades of the nineteenth century, published two major works defining the new practice: *Histoire critique du magnétisme animal* (1813) and *Instruction pratique du magnétisme animal* (1825). The first explained how false religions of the past had been instances of unknowing use of animal magnetism; the second presented these practices as an organized technique.[44] The consensus view among magnetists by the 1820s was that animal magnetism had rationalized false religion, making magical rites into modern techniques that could be used to cure and to control. "Priests of false gods, hiding their proceedings under the veil of sacred mystery, manipulated such nervous patients [*crisiaques*] as prophetesses [*pythonisses*], sibyls, oracles, etc. in their temples," wrote the magnetizer E. F. d'Hénin de Cuvillers. The priests credited their gods, but "all these priests were in effect magnetizers."[45] As they had waved their hands mysteriously, they had accidentally performed the magnetic passes. They had thus created a rapport with their subjects. Like the Franklin commission, magnetists saw priestesses and sibyls as forming part of what Godwin called "the history of the errors of mankind."[46] But now animal mag-

---

44. Deleuze, *Histoire critique du magnétisme animal*; J. P. F. Deleuze, *Instruction pratique sur le magnétisme animal* (Paris: Dentu, 1825).

45. E. F. d'Hénin de Cuvillers, "Conclusion de l'Introduction aux *Archives du magnétisme animal*," *Archives du magnétisme animal* 1, no. 1 (1820): 219–20. Hénin de Cuvillers was unorthodox in that he completely identified magnetism with imagination, rather than presenting it as an alternative explanation for belief; see Gauld, *History of Hypnotism*, 119–20, 131.

46. Godwin, introduction to *Report*, xvii.

netism, not imagination, was the master term that could explain the history of errors.[47]

The rapport was in effect the rational description of spell casting. Hénin de Cuvillers's *Archives du magnétisme animal* (1820–1823)[48] carried frontispieces of world religions reinterpreted as animal magnetism, including one image of "Isis magnetizing her son Horus" (Fig. 2).[49] The *Bibliothèque du magnétisme animal* (1817–1819), issued by the Société du Magnétisme to which both Deleuze and Puységur belonged, discovered mesmerism at work in the miracles of a "pretended devil . . . *Horey*" worshipped by "the blacks living on the banks of the Gambia" and in the trances that Laplanders induced through drum rituals.[50] With respect to the Weberian senses of enchantment and disenchantment, mesmerists straddled the line between the categories. In a disenchanted world, rational actors employ "technical means and calculations" to manipulate nature; in an enchanted world, by contrast, "an American Indian or a Hottentot,"—in short, a "savage"—uses "magical means" to propitiate "mysterious powers."[51] But mesmerists took the spell casting that "savages" such as "blacks living on the banks of the Gambia" might have used to propitiate "*Horey*," subjected it to calculation, and redeployed it as a technique. Thus mesmerism enchanted its subjects in the original sense of the word: it placed them under the spell of the magnetic rapport, deluding and enthralling them. But it was also a Weberian disenchantment, in that it claimed to rationalize the allegedly premodern practices of "savages," *pythonisses*, and false priests. Mesmerism thus had the distinction of being at once an enchantment to its subjects and a disenchantment to its practitioners.

47. See "Recherches historiques sur le magnétisme animal, chez les anciens, etc.," *Bibliothèque du magnétisme animal* 8 (1819): 60–92, 159–76; Hénin de Cuvillers, "Conclusion de l'Introduction," 220.

48. Described in Gauld, *History of Hypnotism*, 120.

49. "Isis magnétisant son fils Horus," frontispiece to *Archives* 7, no. 19 (1823). See also "Le magnétisme animal retrouvé dans l'antiquité," frontispiece to *Archives* 3, no. 7 (1822). On world religions, see Tomoko Masuzawa, *The Invention of World Religions; or, How European Universalism Was Preserved in the Language of Pluralism* (Chicago: University of Chicago Press, 2005).

50. "Recherches historiques sur le magnétisme animal, chez les anciens, etc.," *Bibliothèque du magnétisme animal* 8 (1819): 171–72, 262. On the *Bibliothèque* and the Société du Magnétisme, see Gauld, *History of Hypnotism*, 119–20.

51. Max Weber, "Science as a Vocation," in *From Max Weber: Essays in Sociology*, ed. and trans. H. H. Gerth and C. Wright Mills (New York: Routledge, 1948), 139.

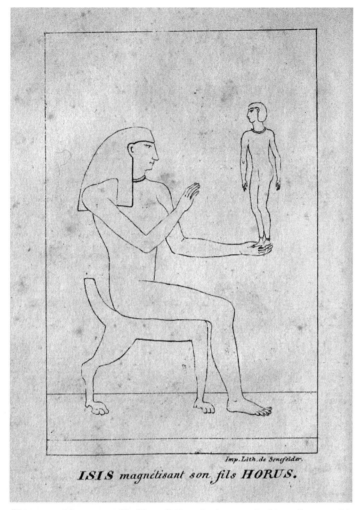

imp. Lith. de Senefelder.

ISIS *magnétisant son fils* **HORUS.**

Fig. 2. "Isis magnétisant son fils Horus." Frontispiece to *Archives du magnétisme animal* 7, no. 19 (1823). Courtesy of Francis A. Countway Library of Medicine, Center for the History of Medicine, Harvard University.

In his *Instruction pratique du magnétisme animal* (*Practical Instruction in Animal Magnetism*), "without question the most popular" magnetizing manual ever published,[52] Deleuze explains in great technical detail how to

52. Adam Crabtree, *From Mesmer to Freud: Magnetic Sleep and the Roots of Psychological Healing* (New Haven, CT: Yale University Press, 1993), 128; Deleuze, *Instruction pratique.* Translations of the *Instruction pratique* are from J. P. F. Deleuze, *Practical Instruction in*

enchant, or rather, mesmerize: "take [the subject's] thumbs between your two fingers, so that the inside of your thumbs may touch the inside of his"; "withdraw your hands . . . waving them so that the interior surface be turned outwards, and raise them to his head"; "descend slowly along the body as far as the knees."[53] These gestures allowed the operator to direct "the vital principle [*le principe qui nous anime et nous fait vivre*]" from his own body into that of the subject.[54] Magnetic somnambulism, the condition this process induced, was a pleasurable combination of delusion, thrall, and inspiration; the subject's will and senses passed into the magnetist's control, but at the same time many somnambulists developed clairvoyant powers.[55] A somnambulist's state was essentially identical to that of a votary entranced by the false priests, but the role of the operator had changed. The magician had become a technician.

In making this about-face, Deleuze and others owed something to the Franklin commission. The commissioners and other antimagnetists of the ancien régime were arguably the first to see the relationship between the magnetist and the patient as enchantment. Rather than taking an interest in the new fluid that Mesmer wanted them to ratify, the commissioners had looked for affect and influence. These, they had wagered, would be the signs that patients' credulity—their imaginations—accounted for the so-called magnetic effects. And they had found an impressive tie between operator and patients: that power of which the magnetist was the *dépositaire*, or trustee. As magnetists themselves recognized, the new magnetic rapport basically retooled the *dépositaire* relationship as a proper effect of mesmerism rather than as the sign of its failure. Magnetists sometimes quoted from the 1784 report on the magnetist as the *dépositaire* of a great power, because they thought the passage went in their favor. In Charles Poyen's own rendering—he quoted the passage in three of his American publications—the commissioners had admitted, "It is impossible not to recognize . . . a great power that agitates the patients, or affects them, and of which the operator seems to dispose as the only possessor [*dépositaire*] of it."[56] As far as Poyen was concerned,

Animal Magnetism, trans. Thomas C. Hartshorn (Providence, RI: B. Cranston, 1837) unless otherwise noted; citations to the *Instruction pratique* that follow include page references for both the 1837 American and the 1825 French editions.

53. Deleuze, *Practical Instruction*, 22–23; *Instruction pratique*, 25–26.

54. Deleuze, *Practical Instruction*, 11; *Instruction pratique*, 9.

55. Deleuze, *Practical Instruction*, 83–84, 101; *Instruction pratique*, 137, 164.

56. Poyen, *Progress*, 32; see also Charles Poyen, "Sketch of the History of Animal Magnetism," *Boston Pearl, a Gazette of Polite Literature*, March 26, 1836, [220–22]; and Poyen,

the commissioners were describing nothing more or less than the rapport. In 1784, such a relationship was not among the phenomena Mesmer claimed to be producing, thus its existence could serve to weaken his claims. But by the 1820s, that had changed. Mesmerists now concerned themselves precisely with the strange sway the magnetist had over the subject.

As interest in animal magnetism grew among the Paris medical faculty in the 1820s, practitioners looked for ways to use the formidable powers of enchantment in the care of patients.[57] Deleuze suggested a use for mind control: "the magnetizer will say to the somnambulist, '*You will return home at such an hour: you will not go this evening to the theatre: . . . you will take your medicines without being obstinate: you will take no liquor: you will drink no coffee: you will occupy yourself no longer in such a thing.*'"[58] Because the rapport made patients obedient, he thought, they would readily comply. As for the gift of prophecy that somnambulists sometimes exhibited, it could be directed toward prescription and the prediction of fits. Paul Villagrand, a magnetic somnambulist and a patient at the Hôpital de la Charité, predicted he would be cured by New Year's Day if doctors followed the bloodletting regimen that had come to him in a magnetism-inspired vision; they did, and he was.[59] Another somnambulist-patient, asked when his next epileptic fit would be, replied, "I shall have one on Monday, the 27th, at twenty minutes past three."[60] So it proved.

Poyen's time as a medical student coincided with this period of magnetic ferment among the medical faculty, but his interest was tepid until he fell ill in 1832 "with a very complicated nervous disease."[61] His Martiniquan friend Alfred Fillassier, who was writing a medical thesis on magnetism,

---

introduction to Husson, *Report on Magnetical Experiments*, lxiv. Poyen loosely translated this passage to make it seem favorable to his position. Godwin's rendering was more exact, as presented in chapter 1 of the present volume.

57. Husson, *Report on Magnetical Experiments*, 76; Henri Marie Husson, *Rapport sur les expériences magnétiques faites par la commission de l'Académie royale de médecine* (1831), reprinted in J. D. Dupotet de Sennevoy, *Cours de magnétisme en sept leçons*, 2nd ed. (Paris: 1840), 442.

58. Deleuze, *Practical Instruction*, 83; *Instruction pratique*, 137.

59. Husson, *Report on Magnetical Experiments*, 129–33; Husson, *Rapport sur les expériences magnétiques* (1840 ed.), 474–76.

60. Husson, *Report on Magnetical Experiments*, 142; Husson, *Rapport sur les expériences magnétiques* (1840 ed.), 481.

61. Poyen, *Progress*, 39. Poyen demonstrates knowledge of the main texts of Paris medical mesmerism in his introduction to Husson, *Report on Magnetical Experiments*, lxvi–lxx; see also Poyen, *Progress*, 40.

introduced him to a clairvoyant we know only as Madame Villetard.[62] Villetard became a clinical prophet when placed in the state of magnetic somnambulism. She had begun her career by diagnosing her own illness and
could now diagnose the illnesses of others.[63] After she had been magnetized
by the physician Pierre-Jean Chapelain, Villetard gave Poyen "a correct and
minute description of the symptoms of [his] disease" and prescribed a cu-
rative regimen.[64] According to Fillassier, Villetard's "dark and piercing eyes
[and] her face that was thin and aged, but full of fire . . . gave her something
of the air of a sorceress [*quelque chose de l'air qu'on prête aux sorcières*]."[65]
The sorceress found employment in a clinic, her powers enclosed within
Chapelain's mesmeric technique. Her case is a classic example of mesmerism's operations: identify an enchanted power; envelop it in natural explanations and transparent, repeatable gestures; and make an instrument of it.

Mesmerism took a domain that seemed to have reference to spirits and
gods—namely, the casting of spells—and redescribed that domain in rational
terms. It was in that sense a disenchantment. But if disenchantment was
supposed to liberate humanity from superstition's spell, mesmerism did not
aspire to set everyone free. No more did it envision a modernity in which
everyone was subject to incantations. Mesmerism's efficacy depended on keeping just certain people—somnambulists—enchanted. The techniques worked
best on those with tendencies toward false religion: primitives, nervous patients, and Christian enthusiasts.[66] Mesmeric histories of false religion glided
easily among these various categories: primitive magicians "were themselves mostly *crisiaques* [nervous patients]," said Hénin de Cuvillers, and
Deleuze pointed out that nervous patients displayed the most "singular phenomena" as somnambulists.[67] Poyen, among others, lumped together recent
Jansenist cults and ancient Egyptian ones.[68] Mesmerism offered the means

62. Alfred Fillassier, "Quelques faits et considérations pour servir à l'histoire du magnétisme animal" (thesis, Faculté de Médecine de Paris, 1832); Poyen, *Progress*, 39.

63. Fillassier, "Quelques faits," 29.

64. Poyen, *Progress*, 40.

65. Fillassier, "Quelques faits," 28.

66. On false religion and these categories, see John Modern, *Secularism in Antebellum
America* (Chicago: University of Chicago Press, 2011), 18n45.

67. Hénin de Cuvillers, "Conclusion de l'Introduction," 220; Deleuze, *Practical Instruction*, 17; *Instruction pratique*, 19.

68. Poyen, introduction to Husson, *Report on Magnetical Experiments*, liii; see also "Recherches historiques sur le magnétisme animal, chez les anciens, etc.," 261–74; Hénin de
Cuvillers, "Conclusion de l'Introduction," 221–32.

by which those who had modernized "already" could manipulate those who had not modernized "yet."[69] Like lab techs extending gloved hands into a box of infectious material, mesmerists could appropriate the enchanted powers that worked so well on premodern subjects without contaminating themselves. In the encounter with someone who was still primitive, the mesmeric impulse was not to liberate that person from superstition (an impulse that would have been problematic in itself). The impulse was to annex that person's enchantment and deploy it toward the mesmerist's own ends.

THE MAGNETIC PLANTATION

Sometime in the late 1820s, Deleuze sent his *Instruction pratique* to a cousin in Guadeloupe, where it circulated among the planters.[70] By the time Poyen returned home in the winter of 1832–33, his fellow colonists were magnetizing their slaves.[71] Poyen "found a great many rich and intelligent planters devoted . . . to the practice of Animal Magnetism."[72] If mesmerism was a way of grasping primitive people by the handle of their own enchantment, no wonder it captured colonists' attention. To the editors of Paris magnetism periodicals, the African worshippers of the "pretended devil . . . *Horey*" may have been theoretical figures. But to planters, the same fetishists appeared instead as the members of an enslaved labor force that outnumbered them three to one and engrossed the better part of their capital.[73] Planters

69. Dipesh Chakrabarty, *Provincializing Europe: Postcolonial Thought and Historical Difference* (Princeton, NJ: Princeton University Press, 2000), 8.

70. G. P. Billot and J. P. F. Deleuze, *Recherches psychologiques sur la cause des phénomènes extraordinaires, observés chez les modernes voyans; ou, Correspondance sur le magnétisme vital, entre un solitaire et M. Deleuze*, 2 vols. (Paris: Albanel et Martin, 1839), 2:23.

71. Poyen spent fourteen months on the island between mid-1832, when he was in Paris (Poyen, *Progress*, 39–41) and May 1834, when he arrived in Maine: "Passenger List for the Brig *Frances Ellen*, May 29, 1834," *Copies of Lists of Passengers Arriving at Miscellaneous Ports on the Atlantic and Gulf Coasts and Ports on the Great Lakes*, microfilm ed. (Washington, DC: National Archives, 1964); Quinn, "How Southern New England Became Magnetic North," 234.

72. Poyen, *Progress*, 41.

73. Manuel Moreno Fraginals and Heather Cateau, "The Crisis of the Plantation," in *General History of the Caribbean*, vol. 4, ed. K. O. Laurence and Jorge Ibarra Cuesta (Paris: UNESCO, 2011), 72; Kevin A. Yelvington et al., "Caribbean Social Structure in the Nineteenth Century," in Laurence and Cuesta, *General History of the Caribbean*, vol. 4, 287.

took an interest in Deleuze's manual because they had an interest, in the other sense, in co-opting enchantment before it could work against them.

Even as planters contemptuously pleaded the impossibility of emancipating "pagans" and "savages" with no better guide to moral behavior than their "African fetishism," they took that "fetishism" seriously as a source of danger to themselves.[74] Guadeloupe's plantations were complex "agricultural, industrial, and commercial operations"[75] whose owners were concerned with technological improvements and with market conditions overseas; with price competition from French beet sugar and with the use of water-powered mills.[76] But enchantment was still a major force in these modern establishments. Doris Garraway writes that before the French Revolution, "colonial authorities both feared and revered African slaves for their knowledge of the spirit world."[77] Records of planters accusing their slaves of malicious magic down to abolition in 1848 suggest that the pattern continued after 1789. Starting in 1827, an ordinance permitted planters to petition the colony's primary governing body, the Conseil privé, for the deportation of "dangerous slaves" without judicial process. The category of dangerous slaves (*esclaves dangereux*) included fomenters of rebellion, arsonists, and runaways (*esclaves marrons*). But almost equally prominent were slaves accused of witchcraft and poisoning.[78] Planters making these accusations did not necessarily believe them. They sometimes used the process to get permission to sell their slaves out of the colony, something that was otherwise prohibited—to Puerto Rico, for example, where they would

74. M. A. Granier de Cassagnac, *Gazette des Deux Mondes*, July 23, 1841.

75. Gabriel Debien, *Les Esclaves aux Antilles Françaises, XVIIe–XVIIIe siècles* (Basse-Terre, Guadeloupe: Société d'Histoire de la Guadeloupe, 1974), 95.

76. [P. S.?] Dupuy, "Copie du rapport à M. le Ministre de la Marine et des Colonies, sur des expériences faites à la Guadeloupe, concernant la fabrication du sucre," *Annales de la Société d'Agriculture et d'Economie Rurale de la Martinique* (Saint-Pierre, Martinique, 1839), 453; H. de Branche et al., "Plantations d'Amérique et papiers de famille, II," *Notes d'histoire coloniale*, no. 60 (1960): 63–65; Fraginals and Cateau, "Crisis of the Plantation," 73–74.

77. Doris Garraway, *The Libertine Colony: Creolization in the Early French Caribbean* (Durham, NC: Duke University Press, 2005), 167.

78. "Mesures de correction ou de précaution prises à l'égard d'esclaves dangereux ou mauvaises sujets, 1827–1848," Série géographique, Guadeloupe, SG GUA 111.770, ANOM (hereafter cited as "Esclaves dangereux," ANOM). The same is true for Martinique: Série géographique, Martinique, SG MAR 42.346–49, ANOM.

fetch a higher price.[79] But whether these petitions represented economic interest, fear of sorcery, or both at once, they make clear that Deleuze's *Instruction pratique* intervened in a society where slave magic played a prominent discursive role. Not unlike the deliberations of the Conseil privé itself, magnetism would allow planters to use Africans' supposed enchanted tendencies against Africans themselves—only in this case, it was not a matter of bringing accusations but of appropriating and directing slaves' magical powers.

Poyen reports that when he returned, he "had the opportunity of witnessing several cases of somnambulism, produced by my friends on some of their colored servants."[80] His friends were orthodox Deleuzians: "the effects I have observed in France coincided perfectly with those I witnessed in the *West Indies*."[81] Poyen would have been well prepared to see the utility of appropriating magic for managerial purposes. He came from a family that had owned sugar plantations in Guadeloupe since the seventeenth century; since the eighteenth century one branch of the family had held the marquisat and plantation of Sainte-Marie.[82] The family's coat of arms, a "marquis' crown, supported by two savages," was the fitting emblem of wealth gained at the cost of the enslaved (Fig. 3).[83] Several Poyens took an interest in industrial improvement; the family plantation of Bois Debout had a newer water mill for fabricating sugar,[84] and Jean Baptiste Poyen de Sainte-Marie, the Marquis de Sainte-Marie and Charles's great-uncle, wrote the lesser Antilles' best known plantation management guide, *De l'exploitation des sucreries* (1792).[85] The extended Poyen family also made two sorcery complaints to the Conseil privé. As a result of one, Catichette, enslaved on the Bois

79. Manuscript transcription from *Le Siècle*, Paris, France, December 11, 1842, in "Esclaves dangereux," ANOM.

80. Poyen, *Progress*, 41.

81. Poyen, "Animal Magnetism," *PDJ*, December 3, 1836.

82. Philippe Rossignol and Bernadette Rossignol, "De Saint-Affrique à Bordeaux en passant par la Guadeloupe: La Famille Poyen," *Bulletin du Centre d'Histoire des Espaces Atlantiques*, n.s., 5 (1990): 142, 152.

83. Sarah Anna Emery, ed., *Reminiscences of a Nonagenarian* (Newburyport, MA: William H. Huse, 1879), 185.

84. On Bois Debout as a Poyen plantation, see Rossignol, *La Famille Poyen*, 111; on its water-powered mill, see Dupuy, "Copie du rapport," 453.

85. Jean Baptiste Poyen de Sainte-Marie, *De l'exploitation des sucreries; ou, Conseils d'un vieux planteur aux jeunes agriculteurs des colonies* (Basse-Terre, Guadeloupe: 1792); Rossignol, *La Famille Poyen*, 43.

The Poyen arms are :

GULES, A CHIEF AZURE, PEACOCK ON TERRACE VERT.
THREE MULLETS PROPER   CREST—MARQUIS'
CROWN, SUPPORTED BY TWO SAVAGES,
DEXTER CLUB AT GROUND, SINIS-
TER CLUB AT SHOULDER.

Fig. 3. The Poyen family coat of arms, according to Sarah Anna Emery, ed., *Reminiscences of a Nonagenarian* (Newburyport, MA: William H. Huse, 1879), 185. Courtesy, American Antiquarian Society.

Debout plantation, was expelled from the colony in 1829 on "suspicion of witchcraft"; when she returned in 1840, "death again began to decimate the plantation's slaves [*atelier*]."[86] The Conseil privé agreed, as they almost invariably did, to expel Catichette a second time—perhaps meaning she was sold at a premium in Puerto Rico.[87] This was the family tradition into which Charles was born in 1806 at Le Piton, his father's plantation at the time and, after 1827, his own.[88]

86. Another case was brought by a Poyen de Belleisle in June 1830; for both cases, see "Esclaves dangereux," ANOM.

87. "Esclaves dangereux," ANOM.

88. Register of births, marriages and deaths (*état civil*), 1806, Sainte Rose, Guadeloupe, ANOM; Poirié (notary), "Inventaire après le mort de Mathieu Augustin Poyen Montrop," ANOM; Rossignol, *La Famille Poyen*, 94.

Poyen never mentions magnetizing his own slaves. Private records survive from only a tiny number of plantations in nineteenth-century Guadeloupe, and Le Piton is not one of them. But Poyen mentions that an acquaintance of his and one of the island's most prominent citizens, the Marquis François-Xavier Eimar de Jabrun, performed magnetic experiments. Jabrun owned two plantations and frequently served in colonial government.[89] Like the Poyens, he mixed industry and sorcery: he supported technical innovations in sugar production,[90] and in 1830 he accused his slave Germain of sorcery before the Conseil privé, based on the evidence that Germain "associat[ed] only with the most infamous poisoners in the neighborhood [*ne fréquentais que les Gens les plus mal famés du quartier et réputés Empoisonneurs*]."[91] Poyen names Jabrun as a fellow magnetizer.[92] Several factors strongly suggest that Jabrun was also the Guadeloupean who reported cases to Deleuze, even though Deleuze's published correspondence (the only version extant) has the name as "Jaboun."[93] In a letter to a third party, Deleuze describes what he has been learning from "the owner of a plantation in Guadeloupe, who had made numerous magnetic experiments on that island, and who has just spent six months in Paris."[94] Whether Jabrun's cases were typical and how extensively Guadeloupeans practiced mesmerism are alike impossible to say, because sources about mesmerism on the island are so limited. It may be that mesmerism was not extensively practiced; or it may be that the way in which it was practiced—privately, by medical amateurs on the people they enslaved, according to the few sources we have—did not leave much of a trace. Planters may have remembered that animal magnetism was practiced in ancien régime Saint-Domingue (present-day Haiti).[95]

89. *Almanach de la Guadeloupe et dépendances* (Basse-Terre, Guadeloupe: Imprimerie du Roi, 1832–1836); Lawrence C. Jennings, *French Anti-Slavery: The Movement for the Abolition of Slavery in France, 1802–1848* (New York: Cambridge University Press, 2000), 112; Nelly Schmidt, *Abolitionnistes de l'esclavage et réformateurs des colonies, 1820–1851: analyse et documents* (Paris: Karthala, 2000), 1091.

90. Dupuy, "Copie du rapport," 446, 451, 454.

91. "Esclaves dangereux," ANOM.

92. Poyen, *Progress*, 41.

93. I find no mention of a "Jaboun" on the island; Deleuze's comments about Paris travel are consistent with Jabrun's habits; Poyen mentions Jabrun as a magnetizer (*Progress*, 41).

94. Billot, *Recherches*, 1:145.

95. François Regourd, "Mesmerism in Saint Domingue: Occult Knowledge and Vodou on the Eve of the Haitian Revolution," in *Science and Empire in the Atlantic World*, ed. James Delbourgo and Nicholas Dew (New York: Routledge, 2008): 311–32.

But two political revolutions, the Haitian and the French, divided the lesser Antillean planters of 1832 from their Saint-Domingue counterparts; and with the advent of somnambulistic prophecy, animal magnetism had undergone a minor revolution, too. Thus Deleuze's report on Guadeloupean magnetism from the 1830s gives us the best itinerary to follow speculatively, as a way of understanding what mesmerism meant to the planter who introduced it in the United States.

One might have expected planters to use magnetic thrall to redouble the control they had over their slaves, but none of the limited evidence proves (or for that matter, disproves) such an expectation. In Jabrun's cases, it is clairvoyance, not thrall, that comes to the fore. He used magnetic enchantment as a surveillance technique. Having read Deleuze's *Instruction pratique*, Jabrun had "tried to magnetize many of his slaves" and had "found some very lucid somnambulists among them."[96] He understood that susceptibility to mesmeric enchantment should be greater the more primitive the subject, and he told Deleuze "that somnambulism is more frequent among negroes [*nègres*] than among whites."[97] One of the somnambulists Jabrun had discovered among his slaves "informed him of everything that happened on his plantation" and had "rendered him some great services," according to Deleuze, a guarded phrase that suggests the detection of rebellion.[98] Somnambulists had the ability to see distant events, and Jabrun's slave availed himself of this power to supervise the plantation.

Poyen de Sainte-Marie's *De l'exploitation* describes the surveillance practices that Jabrun might have reproduced mesmerically. A planter "must look after the work on his plantation with the greatest application," but he ought not "to look constantly over the shoulders of [*rester constamment derrière*] his slaves." Stealth was more effective: a planter should appear "always at different hours and from different directions; before showing himself, he should observe what is happening." Thus his enslaved and free managers, "not suspecting his presence . . . will show him their energy or their negligence."[99] The planter was to become a specter, liable to sudden and unwelcome apparition. "The most energetic surveillance possible" figured in Conseil privé records, too, as the means by which planters detected sorcerers

96. Billot, *Recherches*, 2:23.
97. Ibid., 1:145.
98. Ibid., 2:23.
99. Poyen de Sainte-Marie, *De l'exploitation*, 4. On plantation management, see Debien, *Esclaves*, 96–97.

among their slaves.[100] A somnambulist who could travel invisibly would have been a frighteningly efficient aide-de-camp.

Even on a global scale, mesmeric surveillance could subvert rebellion. Sometime around 1829, Jabrun escorted a Creole somnambulist, evidently a white woman, to France.[101] There, under Pierre-Jean Chapelain's magnetic ministrations, she reported in 1831 that "there had been a slave revolt in Martinique, and that in Guadeloupe they were taking precautions against the same misfortune."[102] Colonial gazettes confirming her prophecy arrived in Paris a month later. Enslaved Martiniquans, marching under a French-Revolutionary flag with the inscription "la liberté ou la more [sic]" (liberty or death) had nearly succeeded in burning the city of Saint-Pierre. Several were killed in combat, and twenty-one were condemned to death.[103] The Creole woman confronted this frightful combination of primitivity and modernity with an untimely combination of her own: mesmerism's technical enchantment. Thanks to the spell Chapelain placed on her, the Paris circle had the earliest colonial intelligence. They appropriated the enchanted powers that might have worked against them.

"MR. DELEWZ" COMES TO AMERICA

In 1834 Charles Poyen sailed from Pointe-à-Pître, Guadeloupe, to Maine, where he listed his occupation as "planter" on his customs entry form.[104] Within a few years, he would begin lecturing on mesmerism in the United States. But first, he visited family. In 1792, Charles Poyen's grandfather had seen trouble coming, even without the benefit of somnambulistic powers. Immediately following the French Revolution, Guadeloupe's enslaved popu-

100. "Esclaves dangereux," ANOM. See also "Police des esclaves, esclaves dangereux, expulsion, décisions du Conseil privé, 1827–1831," Série géographique, Martinique, SG MAR 42.348, ANOM.
101. Billot, *Recherches*, 1:145.
102. Billot, *Recherches*, 2:23. Chapelain is called "M. le docteur Chap.**" throughout the text, but he can be identified by the fact that he is mentioned in the context of *L'Hermes*, a journal Chapelain edited: Billot, *Recherches*, 1:9, and *L'Hermès* 3 (1828); 116, 222–24, 255–64.
103. Bernard Moitt, "Slave Resistance in Guadeloupe and Martinique, 1791–1848," *Journal of Caribbean History* 25 (January 1991): 149–51.
104. "Passenger List for the Brig *Frances Ellen*, May 29, 1834;" Quinn, "How Southern New England Became Magnetic North," 234.

lation had tried to bring liberty, equality, and fraternity to the island in a series of small-scale rebellions.[105] At that time, Charles's grandfather Pierre Robert Poyen Saint-Sauveur had only just purchased the plantation of Le Piton, but he hastily sold it again and fled with Charles's father, aunts, and uncles to Newburyport, Massachusetts.[106] The family bided its time while the French National Assembly abolished slavery in 1794 and while former slaves fought off British efforts to take the island.[107] In 1802, Napoleon recaptured Guadeloupe and reinstated slavery in spite of stiff resistance.[108] Shortly after, Charles's father, Mathieu Augustin Poyen, returned to repurchase Le Piton (where Charles would soon be born),[109] while Charles's uncle Joseph Rochemont Poyen remained in Newburyport.[110] Now, in 1834, Charles traveled to Massachusetts to visit this uncle in exile. Since Joseph's arrival forty years before, the area around Newburyport had changed radically. The factory city of Lowell had sprung up nearby; between 1830 and 1836, its population went from six thousand to eighteen thousand.[111] In the months after he emigrated, Charles tutored in French for Lowell's "very first families," learning the contours of the managerial class to whom he would eventually peddle mesmerism successfully.[112] Via the Poyens' interests on two continents, mesmerism had found a new home: from the hospitals of Paris and the plantations of Guadeloupe, it had come to the textile factories of New England.

Deleuze's technical manual had made this journey as well. First the *Instruction pratique* had guided experimentation in Paris hospitals. Then the Marquis de Jabrun had tried Deleuze's instructions on his slaves. Now Poyen opened a new field to the manual's conquest. By December 1836, just

105. Moitt, "Slave Resistance," 139–40.

106. Rossignol, *La Famille Poyen*, 82, 115; Emery, *Reminiscences of a Nonagenarian*, 184; D. Hamilton Hurd, *History of Essex County, Massachusetts, with Biographical Sketches of Many of Its Pioneers and Prominent Men*, 2 vols. (Philadelphia: J. W. Lewis, 1888), 2:1555. The death of "Poyen St. Sauveur, who was a planter in the Island of Guadeloupe" is recorded on October 14, 1792, in *Vital Records of Newburyport, Massachusetts, to the End of the Year 1849*, 2 vols. (Salem, MA, 1911), 2:779.

107. Moitt, "Slave Resistance," 142–44.

108. Ibid., 145–47.

109. Rossignol, *La Famille Poyen*, 87, 115.

110. Rossignol, *La Famille Poyen*, 85; marriage certificate of Sally Elliot to Joseph Poyen, March 5, 1805, in *Vital Records of Haverhill, Massachusetts, to the End of the Year 1849*, 2 vols. (Topsfield, MA, 1911), 2:106; Emery, *Reminiscences of a Nonagenarian*, 185; Poyen, *Progress*, 41.

111. Dublin, *Women at Work*, 21.

112. Poyen, *Progress*, 42.

Fig. 4. Magnetizing with manual in hand. Frontispiece to Chauncy Hare Townshend, *Facts in Mesmerism, with Reasons for a Dispassionate Inquiry into It* (New York: Harper & Brothers, 1841). Courtesy, Albert and Shirley Small Special Collections Library, University of Virginia.

weeks after Poyen used animal magnetism to make Gleason's sleep schedules as regular as clockwork, enthusiasm was such that Providence's citizens were doing nothing but attending mesmerism lectures, as the *New-Bedford Mercury* joked.[113] To satisfy readers who had heard of "professor Poyen" and "his pupil Miss Charlotte [i.e., Cynthia] Gleason" and were "anxious to know the method of magnetising," the *Mercury* provided the first partial American translation of the "Practical instruction on animal Magnetism" by "a Mr. Delewz." The translation included Deleuze's instructions to "take [the subject's] thumbs between your fingers, in such a manner that his and your thumbs may be applied to each other . . . The hands are then to be placed on the shoulders, and suffered to remain there two or three minutes, and afterwards gently brought down, the arms to the thumbs."[114] The eminently transmissible techniques for casting a spell had found a new set of "primitive" souls on which to work (Fig. 4).

As in France and in Guadeloupe, some New Englanders were more prone to enchantment, and thus to somnambulism, than others. Nervous pa-

113. *New-Bedford Mercury*, December 9, 1836, [1].
114. "Animal Magnetism," *New-Bedford Mercury*, December 30, 1836, [4].

tients had been the paradigmatic somnambulists of France; African slaves had been most susceptible in Guadeloupe. In the United States it would be female factory workers. David Reese declared that "factory girls" were "the chief somnambulists in the country" in his *Humbugs of New-York* (1838).[115] The first famous mesmeric somnambulist, Gleason, was a factory worker, though hardly a girl—she was thirty-seven when Poyen met her, older than Poyen himself. Her successor in somnambulistic fame, Loraina Brackett, reportedly worked in a factory as well.[116] The industrial city of Providence, Pawtucket's close neighbor, became the center of the magnetic movement in its first two years, but on Reese's view the problem went beyond Providence: "Third-rate doctors, merchants, and mechanics . . . providing themselves each with a factory girl who would *rather sleep than work* . . . have scattered themselves abroad in the villages, towns, and cities of the land" to give lectures on animal magnetism.[117]

Factory girls raised the specter of a distinctive kind of enchantment: seduction. Like the false priest, the seducer could cast a delightful and delusive mist over his victim, subverting her will. Factory novels like *Ellen Merton, the Belle of Lowell* (1844) worried about the "inexperienced, artless" women who made up Lowell's largest population of workers.[118] *Ellen Merton's* sensational demography suggested that "nine-tenths of those fallen and degraded females . . . in the metropolis of New England, have been operatives in the Mills at Lowell." Operatives could not be expected to be "proof against the practised and cunning arts of the deliberate, calculating, cold-blooded libertine."[119] The libertine of the factory city replaced the false priest of primitive religion as the charlatan who would delight, delude, and—impregnate, if not inspire—his hapless mark. Sometimes the false priest and the libertine

115. David Reese, *Humbugs of New-York: Being a Remonstrance against Popular Delusion* (Boston: Weeks, Jordan, 1838), 24, 45.

116. Sheila O'Brien Quinn, "Credibility, Respectability, Suggestibility, and Spirit Travel: Lurena Brackett and Animal Magnetism," *History of Psychology* 15, no. 3 (2012): 273–82; Quinn, "How Southern New England Became Magnetic North," 236. On Loraina (also Lurena) Brackett's work history, there are conflicting reports: Charles Durant, *Exposition; or, A New Theory of Animal Magnetism* (New York: Wiley & Putnam, 1837), 163; Charles Negus and Jno. [John] W. Tenney, "Letter to Hartshorn," *PDJ*, November 10, 1837. See also chapter 3 of the present volume.

117. Reese, *Humbugs of New-York*, 35.

118. Introduction to *Ellen Merton, the Belle of Lowell; or, The Confessions of the 'G.F.K.' Club* (Boston: Brainard, 1844), 3. See also Dublin, *Women at Work*, 23–57.

119. Introduction to *Ellen Merton*, 3.

combined. In an 1832 scandal, the unmarried Rhode Island textile operative Sarah Maria Cornell was found hanged to death and pregnant; suspected in both crimes was Ephraim Avery, a Methodist camp meeting leader.[120] Mary Clarke's dramatic adaptation, *Sarah Maria Cornell* (1833), made Cornell's seduction an enchantment. In the play, Sarah foresees her doom in a prophetic dream: "were I inclined to superstition, I should fancy I was to be murdered!" At a camp meeting where "moonbeams sporting through [the] branches . . . impel each heart to the love of God" and to "the love of his creatures," "Averio" carries Sarah off while "girls cry; men shout; [and] all is a scene of confusion."[121] Pregnancy; death; exit all. The revivalist Lothario combined the ensorcelling powers of sex and the Spirit.

Textile operatives of managers' imaginations lived in a world more primitive than the managers' own, just as Guadeloupean slaves had done in the eyes of their enslavers. And workers' susceptibility to seduction was a disciplinary liability for factory owners, just as slaves' alleged magical abilities were for planters. In Clarke's play, the first crack in the virgin vessel is Sarah's disregard of the factory bell: the morning after her prophetic dream, the usually punctual Sarah, a "good, virtuous, and industrious" girl, arrives late.[122] Discipline and sex-magic stood on opposite sides in writing surrounding the factories.[123] Management apologists such as Henry Miles, author of *Lowell, As It Was* (1845), countered the charge that Lowell was a "hotbed of corruption, tainting and polluting the whole land" by describing Lowell's stringent "moral police," including company-run boardinghouses and supervised factory floors.[124] "The only access [to the factory] is through the counting room, in full view of those whose business it is to see that no improper persons intrude themselves upon the premises," Miles assured his readers.[125]

120. Catherine Read Williams, *Fall River: An Authentic Narrative* (Boston: Lilly, Wait, 1834); David Kasserman, *Fall River Outrage: Life, Murder, and Justice in Early Industrial New England* (Philadelphia: University of Pennsylvania Press, 1986), 1–28.

121. Mary Clarke, *Sarah Maria Cornell, or, The Fall River Murder: A Domestic Drama in Three Acts* (New York, 1833), 4, 8, 24, 29.

122. Ibid., 4.

123. Hannah Josephson, *The Golden Threads: New England's Mill Girls and Magnates* (New York: Duell, Sloan, & Pearce, 1949), 4; Dublin, *Women at Work*, 77.

124. Henry Miles, *Lowell, As It Was, and As It Is* (Lowell, MA, 1845), 62, 128. See also Carl Gersuny, "'A Devil in Petticoats' and Just Cause: Patterns of Punishment in Two New England Factories," *Business History Review* 50, no. 2 (Summer 1976): 137–38.

125. Miles, *Lowell, As It Was*, 64.

As in Guadeloupe, part of animal magnetism's appeal was that it could bring enchantment over to the cause of management. Just as Poyen had used animal magnetism to "impregnate" Gleason with his will and thus wake her at 8:00 a.m., factory agents could in theory avail themselves of the "magnetical agent."[126] They could see their employees heavy not with productivity-destroying children but with the managers' own—wills. "The spring of numberless superstitions" in earlier times, animal-magnetic power now rested in the hands of specialists, who could use it to counter the wiles of camp-meeting demagogues.[127] The *Providence Daily Journal* got the message, referring to "the manner of healing diseases by the Indian powows [*sic*]" as "Animal Magnetism."[128] The *Daily Intelligencer* of Washington, DC, envisioned magnetism shedding light on "many other things which need not be enumerated, including even the case of demoniacs, the gift of prophecy, the frenzy of a mob, and the *esprit du corps*."[129] In a March experiment in Lowell, at the home of Lowell Carpet Manufactory agent Alexander Wright, Poyen and Gleason even tumbled into questioning the miracles of the New Testament. Poyen handed Gleason a glass of water "in willing that the water should be *Rum* for her." Gleason resourcefully exclaimed, "Wine! will it make me dizzy?"[130] The hydraulic force of Gospel miracles, the two collaborators implied, could be diverted into modern channels. Poyen and Gleason offered manufacturers a religious power that would turn their water wheels rather than luring their workers to the enchanted and lurid precincts of camp meetings.

Magnetism never became institutionalized in the factories. But through Poyen's lectures, the dream of a perfect coercion beguiled the leisure hours of industrial towns. He and Gleason spent a few months doing demonstrations in the Pawtucket–Providence area before going on a tour in 1837 that took in the factory cities of Nashua and Lowell. From the first public demonstrations in Pawtucket, Poyen took pains to show that the magnetic rapport gave him a degree of control over Gleason that lay beyond the grasp of her factory superiors. A few days after they met, Gleason and Poyen performed before an

126. Poyen, introduction to Husson, *Report on Magnetical Experiments*, lx.

127. Ibid., liii–liv.

128. "Animal Magnetism," *PDJ*, January 4, 1837.

129. "Communications: Theory of Animal Magnetism," *Daily National Intelligencer*, Washington, DC, December 15, 1836, [2].

130. Poyen, *Progress*, 166–67. On Wright, see Frederick William Coburn, *History of Lowell and Its People*, 3 vols. (New York: Lewis Historical Publishing, 1920), 2:131–33; *Massachusetts, Town and Vital Records, 1620–1988*, accessed June 24, 2017, http://search.ancestry.com/search/db.aspx?dbid=2495.

audience of 170 people at the Pawtucket Hotel, according to Poyen's account in the *Providence Daily Journal*.[131] Having magnetized Gleason, he called Edward Walcott to the platform. Gleason probably worked for a company like Walcott's, under the supervision of someone like him. Walcott was the part-owner and agent, or manager, of the Walcott Manufacturing Company, a firm that produced cotton cloth by power loom.[132] "At my request," Poyen wrote, "Edward Walcott Esq. asked the somnambulist to drink of the water that he presented to her . . . but she took no notice of it." Poyen then "*mentally* asked Gleason whether she wished for some water"—that is, he thought it at her—and she instantly responded "that she '*did not feel thirsty.*'" Poyen now mentally urged Gleason to drink some water anyway, and "she opened her lips, grasped at the tumbler, and drank two or three swallows of the liquid."[133]

Walcott's spoken commands had not been heard, let alone heeded; Poyen's silent ones convinced Gleason to act against her own inclinations. On another occasion, Poyen made the same point with a Brown University professor, Gleason's physician Manchester, and the Reverend E. B. Hall in succession. Gleason ignored all three when they addressed her; when Poyen spoke, she attended and obeyed.[134] Poyen could also transfer this power to others when he chose. If, while Gleason was magnetized, he wished for the rapport to pass from him to someone else, then that person would suddenly become audible to Gleason. In some cases she would also obey her new partner, who effectively occupied the position of the magnetist. In November, a physician observing their experiments had the same experience as so many others: he "spoke to [Gleason] several times, but obtained no answer." He then asked Poyen "to establish communication between him and her," meaning to put them in rapport. Poyen did so: "I requested her '*mentally,*' without a word spoken by any one present, to hear this gentleman—and immediately she gave him her hand, in a friendly manner, and began to hold conversation with him. I signified that I would cause the communication to cease; I merely *wished* that it would be so; and immediately the somnambulist pushed away [his] hand, and ceased to hear him."[135] Not only

131. Poyen, "Surprising Phenomena of Animal Magnetism," [2].

132. William Bagnall, *The Textile Industries of the United States* (Cambridge, MA: Riverside Press, 1893), 255–57. On the labor management responsibilities of an agent, see Bagnall, *Textile Industries*, 257; Tucker, "Merchant," 307–8; Dublin, *Women at Work*, 21–22.

133. Poyen, "Surprising Phenomena of Animal Magnetism," [2].

134. Poyen, "Experiments in Animal Magnetism," *New York Commercial Advertiser*, November 23, 1836, reprint of article originally published in *PDJ*, November 19, 1836.

135. Poyen, "Experiments in Animal Magnetism," *PDJ*, November 23, 1836.

did Poyen's magnetism trump the magnetism of the upper classes, but he could give his own power to them and take it away at will.

Gleason developed clairvoyant gifts similar to Madame Villetard's within a few months.[136] If Poyen placed Gleason in rapport with an audience member who was sick, Gleason could *"feel* the disease" within her own body as though she herself were "affected with it."[137] Sometimes she also directly saw the state of the internal organs, as when she said of the ailing W. J. Winsor, "he has scarcely any spleen. It is very small and shrunk, and light colored."[138] Her clairvoyance allowed her to diagnose diseases and prescribe remedies; for Winsor, according to Poyen's article in the *Providence Daily Journal*, she prescribed the rheumatic drops of "Mr. Brown of Providence," who was himself a frequent advertiser in the *Journal,* including in the issue in which Poyen's account of the Winsor experiment appeared.[139] Gleason even diagnosed Poyen, who had never fully recovered from the troubles Villetard had discerned four years before; Gleason "seized," he said, with "much accuracy and minuteness, the various symptoms of the nervous disorders with which I have been affected for nearly five years." Gleason gave Poyen a prescription, and in a reversal of roles, he obeyed it—though not unquestioningly. First he judged whether the treatment was "rational."[140] Diagnosis hinted at the reciprocity that could emerge within the rapport. In the case of Gleason's diagnoses of Poyen, who controlled whom? Perhaps he was imposing on her, in that he constrained her to feel the painful symptoms of his own disease. Then again, was she not possessing his body, invading it, "seizing" his symptoms? The two were caught up in feeling together, and this kind of sympathy would complicate the operator's sovereignty as mesmerism developed.

But even clairvoyance, which held out the promise of a more equal footing for Gleason, still bore the imprint of factory life. Her powers of vision turned out to adapt her ever more perfectly to the work of supervising a power loom. Power loom technologies varied somewhat, but a weaver's primary tasks were to retie broken web yarns and to replace empty shuttle

---

136. Poyen, "Animal Magnetism: Pawtucket, 20th Dec., 1836," *PDJ*, December 31, 1836.

137. Poyen, *Progress*, 145.

138. Poyen, "Animal Magnetism: Pawtucket, 20th Dec., 1836," *PDJ*, December 31, 1836.

139. Poyen, "Animal Magnetism (concluded): Pawtucket, 20th Dec. 1836," *PDJ*, January 2, 1837; and advertisements for "Brown's Universal Medicine" and "Brown's Stomach Restorer," *PDJ*, January 2, 1837. See also Emily Ogden, "Pointing the Finger," *J19* 1, no. 1 (2013): 166–72.

140. Poyen, "Animal Magnetism: Pawtucket, 20th Dec. 1836," *PDJ*, December 31, 1836.

bobbins with full ones; the latter process itself involved seven steps. In 1836, a skilled weaver ordinarily attended two looms at once.[141] In the 1844 *Lowell Offering*, a workers' magazine, "Susan" reported her difficulties in managing even one loom: "I could take care of two if only I had eyes in the back part of my head, but I have not got used to 'looking two ways of a Sunday' yet."[142] Gleason could do just this. The director of Providence's Greene Street School, Hiram Fuller, saw Poyen will "that [Gleason's] mind would leave the brain, would come out of the body, and see what should be held over or behind her." Gleason more or less successfully identified a watch key, a book, a bunch of peacock feathers, and a large pencil.[143] In the state of somnambulism, Gleason did have eyes in the back of her head. She was a weaving prodigy as well as a mesmeric one, and it was not unusual for her questioners to be as interested in the magic of industry as in the magic of mesmerism. Gleason told Brown University president Francis Wayland that she could handle five looms at a time, though three or four was her usual load.[144] Supervising three or four looms would have been exceptional in the mid-1830s; five was almost preternatural.[145] Gleason gave her audience two marvels at once: her somnambulism and her technical skills as a weaver. As the New Hampshire *Sentinel* put it, "the Pawtucket subject works *wonders*."[146]

In January 1837, Gleason left her factory post to tour New England with Poyen in exchange for room, board, and a small cash salary.[147] This decision is a possible mark of her preference for work as a somnambulist over work as a weaver: perhaps, to adopt David Reese's remark but without the contempt, Gleason decided she would *rather sleep than work*. (Actually her clairvoyance *was* work, as her salary testified.) Another possibility is that she lost her factory post. Her experiments with Poyen often took place during work hours, which raises the question of whether her illness might have

141. Dublin, *Women at Work*, 67.

142. "Letters from Susan: Letter Second," *Lowell Offering*, June 1, 1844, 170.

143. [Hiram Fuller], "Remarkable Phenomena of Animal Magnetism," *New Hampshire Sentinel*, December 8, 1836, [1], reprint of article originally published in *PDJ*, November 24, 1836.

144. See Poyen, "Experiments in Animal Magnetism," *PDJ*, November 23, 1836; and Poyen, "Experiments in Animal Magnetism," *New York Commercial Advertiser*, November 23, 1836; reprint of article originally published in *PDJ*, November 19, 1836.

145. Dublin, *Women at Work*, 101–2; "Letters from Susan," 169.

146. Editorial introduction to [H. Fuller], "Remarkable Phenomena of Animal Magnetism," [1].

147. Poyen, *Progress*, 118.

forced her to give up her position as a weaver. If so, she might have had difficulty finding another—the climactic event of the 1837 depression, the Panic
of 1837, was just a few months away. Gleason and Poyen traveled on and
off for two years, spreading the fame of animal magnetism throughout the
East, before they went their separate ways.[148] Gleason continued occasional
work as a clairvoyant; she died in 1847.[149] The two left Deleuze's techniques
of enchantment lastingly established in New England.

"DEATH-BLOW"

As Deleuze's *Instruction pratique* traveled from France to Guadeloupe to
New England, each new group of readers adapted its enchantment techniques to local needs. In Paris, the powers that magnetism had borrowed
from the world's false religions made some patients compliant and helped
diagnose others. In Guadeloupe, mesmerism warded off rebellion. And in
the United States, it made a more tractable weaver out of the first American
somnambulist. Poyen claimed that seeing mesmerism in all these places
had proved to him that "the human soul was gifted with the same primitive
and essential faculties, under every climate, among every nation, and under
whatever skin, black, red, or white."[150] This sense of universal brotherhood
stopped him neither from owning slaves in Guadeloupe nor from apparently advocating the transportation of American slaves back to Africa.[151]
Poyen left for France around 1839, and when he died in Bordeaux in 1843, he

148. "From the N. Y. *Daily Express*: Animal Magnetism in Massachusetts," *Connecticut
Courant*, December 15, 1838.

149. Quinn, "How Southern New England Became Magnetic North," 246.

150. Poyen, *Progress*, 41.

151. In fall 1837, Poyen claimed that the *Literary and Theological Review* (he called it the
"*Theological and Literary Review*") would soon be publishing an essay of his, entitled "Phil-
osophical and Historical Essay on Slavery, followed by the Exposition of a New System of
Measures for the Civilization of Africa, and the Abolition of Slavery in the United States"
(*Progress*, 42–43). But no essay ever appeared in that journal under his name. Russ Castronovo has proposed that the anonymously published "Slavery and Abolitionism," *Literary and Theological Review* (March 1839) is the missing essay; see Castronovo, "Antislavery
Unconscious," 46n10. But this seems unlikely; "Slavery and Abolitionism" does not concern colonization as Poyen had promised, and its dense allusiveness to the King James
Bible is out of keeping with Poyen's usual range of reference—and probably beyond his
capacities. Poyen never demonstrated any knowledge of the Bible elsewhere, whether in

was still in possession of his share of Le Piton.[152] But read against the grain, Poyen's declaration may serve as a good description of what made mesmerism appealing. By framing itself as having capitalized on superstition—on what had not yet been calculated—mesmerism could seem to be most useful precisely where the most modernization had yet to be done. If all souls had the same "primitive" faculties, then mesmerism taught an eminently transferrable technique for manipulating any population. Enchant them to manage them. Take hold of their unvarying primitive souls.

Before he left for France, Poyen encouraged the translation of Deleuze's *Instruction pratique* as *Practical Instruction in Animal Magnetism* (1837); it became perhaps the most influential magnetizing manual in the United States, as it had been in France and Guadeloupe.[153] The manual's translator, the schoolteacher Thomas C. Hartshorn, effectively took over as Providence's mesmerism coordinator during Poyen's tour, promoting the practice in the *Daily Journal* and arranging appointments for visitors.[154] As they traveled, Poyen and Gleason gained "hundreds of converts from among the most scientific and respectable families in the country," but Providence was the nerve center: in that city alone, wrote Charles Durant, author of the antimesmeric *Exposition* (1837), "there are six professors of the science; they studied under professor Poyen, and are now equally or better [*sic*] magnetizers than their instructor."[155] Providence became, as James Freeman Clarke put it, the "head quarters" of mesmerism in America.[156]

French or in English, and his English-language ability seems to have been limited. More probably, Poyen's essay on African colonization was never published.

152. On Poyen's death and succession, see Léger (notary), "Notoriété relative à la succession de M. Neyop de Poyen," ANOM; "Death of Dr. Poyen," 166; "Décès et inhumations," *Lloyd Bordelais: Feuille maritime et commerciale*, May 10, 1843; Rossignol, *La Famille Poyen*, 94. See "Animal Magnetism," New Orleans *Daily Picayune*, February 20, 1839, [2], for an advertisement of one of Poyen's last appearances, and *Massachusetts Barre Gazette*, March 6, 1840, [2], on his departure.

153. Thomas C. Hartshorn, "Appendix" to *Practical Instruction in Animal Magnetism*, by J. P. F. Deleuze, trans. Thomas C. Hartshorn (Providence, RI: B. Cranston, 1837), 8–9, (hereafter cited in text as *PIA*).

154. Durant, *Exposition*, 160; Thomas C. Hartshorn, "The Magnetizer" series, *PDJ*, April to August 1837. The series was published anonymously, but Hartshorn later identified himself as the author in his "Appendix" to *Practical Instruction in Animal Magnetism*, by J. P. F. Deleuze, trans. Thomas C. Hartshorn, rev. ed. (New York: Appleton, 1843), 251.

155. Durant, *Exposition*, 46–47.

156. James Freeman Clarke Journal, September–October 1837, Perry-Clarke Collection, Massachusetts Historical Society, Boston.

Hartshorn's translation of the *Instruction pratique* is a fitting emblem of how the practice developed in the United States: first a footnote to the Deleuzian French tradition, it soon took on a life of its own. Hartshorn issued his Deleuze translation in three parts throughout the fall of 1837, including with each installment a compendium of local cases sent to him by practicing correspondents.[157] This "Appendix," original to the American edition, expanded with each installment. By the time all three parts were published together in late fall of 1837, the appendix amounted to two hundred pages of close-set type. It had dozens of authors (these being Hartshorn's correspondents); it was almost as long as the manual itself; and it was at odds with Deleuze's recommendations at many points (*PIA*). New England mesmerism was beginning to outgrow its origins. The experiments Hartshorn compiled soon took directions Poyen had not conceived and did not approve. Hartshorn declared that "somnambulism will probably give the death-blow to superstition" right before launching into the lengthy appendix of cases, each of them an instance of "superstition," or primitive religion, retooled as animal magnetism, and allegedly brought to heel (*PIA*, 70). The manual Poyen had carried to the United States was more of a lightning strike to "superstition" than a deathblow: it animated enchantment in a new shape. And like many a creature, animal magnetism outran the expectations of its creator. Mesmerism's enchantments did not long remain under the ideal control that Poyen had envisioned.

157. The *PDJ* announced the first installment on August 24, 1837, the second installment on October 20, 1837, and the final installment on November 10, 1837. As each volume of the *Practical Instruction* appeared over the fall, the publisher reprinted the previous volume or volumes with it. The different editions are difficult to distinguish from each other. The best way to ensure that one has a copy with the complete translation and appendix is by checking the pagination: the complete edition, published after November 10, has a 262-page translation of Deleuze, a separately paginated 204-page appendix (including table of contents), and a separately paginated four-page "Notice" following the appendix.

IN IMAGINATION

Traveling Clairvoyance and the Suspension of Disbelief

Thus our "sturdy unbeliever" was prepared *to bolt* anything. Was there ever such an instance of headlong, unhesitating credulity?

Quarterly Christian Spectator on William Leete Stone (1837)[1]

You mos pe pigger vool as de goose, vor to dispelief vat iz print in de print. 'Tiz de troof—dat it iz—eberry vord ob it.

Edgar Allan Poe, "The Angel of the Odd" (1844)[2]

CREDULITY GOT OUT FROM UNDER CHARLES Poyen's thumb when a distinct form of clairvoyance developed in Providence during the summer of 1837. Thomas C. Hartshorn, who was compiling cases for his appendix to J. P. F. Deleuze's *Practical Instruction* at the time, called it "travelling somnambulis[m]."[3]

1. "Stone's *Letter on Animal Magnetism*," review of *Letter to Doctor A. Brigham, on Animal Magnetism*, by William Leete Stone, *Quarterly Christian Spectator* 9, no. 4 (1837): 652.
2. Edgar Allan Poe, "The Angel of the Odd," in *Collected Works of Edgar Allan Poe*, 3 vols., ed. Thomas Ollive Mabbott (Cambridge, MA: Harvard University Press, 1969-1978), 3:1103 (collection hereafter cited in text as *CW*).
3. Thomas C. Hartshorn, "Appendix" to *Practical Instruction in Animal Magnetism*, by J. P. F. Deleuze, trans. Thomas C. Hartshorn (Providence, RI: B. Cranston, 1837), 57. References to this appendix are hereafter abbreviated *PIA* and cited parenthetically in text ex-

While under the mesmeric influence, some subjects were able to "travel (in spirit)" to distant places, where they could stroll around, see local sights, and enter houses.[4] Clairvoyants had demonstrated far vision before: the Creole somnambulist who scooped the colonial gazettes with news of rebellion in Martinique had done so, for example. But the new form of prophecy was, as one of the letter writers in Hartshorn's appendix explained, less a matter of vision than of "locomotion" in that somnambulists experienced actual movement to a destination.[5] They had the faculty, as mesmeric skeptic Charles Durant put it, of "annihilating distance, which they travel in spirit, although thousands of miles distant from the body, and tell in one minute what is being transacted in the harem of the Sultan, while the somnambulist's body may be in Providence or France."[6] In actuality, travel to exotic locations was rare; somnambulists mostly confined themselves to the Eastern Seaboard. There were about a half dozen well-known traveling somnambulists in Providence, many of them praised in Hartshorn's appendix and criticized in Durant's *Exposition; or, a New Theory of Animal Magnetism* (1837). Somnambulists often flew, describing their itineraries by reference to new forms of travel, such as steamboat routes and railway lines.[7] After they arrived at their destinations, their experiences remained kinetic and in many cases leisurely: they would stroll about, acting either as tourists or as genteel visitors, admiring parlor furnishings or the landmarks of the Capitol in Washington, DC (*L*, 14).[8] Providence visitors meanwhile watched a dreamy woman—nearly always a woman—walking in circles through a house, miming contact with invisible objects.[9]

This form of clairvoyance had a new emphasis: storytelling. Somnambulists could transport themselves in imagination to other cities only if

---

cept where there is other information to be conveyed that necessitates a note. In the present volume, see chapter 2, note 157, for a description of the publication history of this text.

4. Charles Ferson Durant, *Exposition; or, a New Theory of Animal Magnetism* (New York: Wiley & Putnam, 1837), 44.

5. G[eorge] Capron (GC) to Thomas C. Hartshorn (TH), Providence, RI, August 31, 1837, *PIA*, 32.

6. Durant, *Exposition*, 19.

7. GC to TH, Providence, RI, August 31, 1837, *PIA*, 32; E. L. Frothingham to TH, Boston, October 3, 1837, *PIA*, 116; William Leete Stone, *Letter to Doctor A. Brigham, on Animal Magnetism: Being an Account of a Remarkable Interview between the Author and Miss Loraina Brackett, While in a State of Somnambulism* (New York: Dearborn, 1837), 20 (hereafter cited in text as *L*).

8. Benjamin Kent (BK) to TH, Roxbury, MA, November 27, 1837, *PIA*, 138–42.

9. BK to TH, Roxbury, MA, November 27, 1837, *PIA*, 139.

those in rapport with them first convinced them, through narrative, that they were really traveling. A mesmerist sometimes kept control of the traveling somnambulist via the rapport, but more often the rapport was transferred to some visitor who wanted to question the clairvoyant more closely. Thus a skeptical visitor could be placed in an odd position: he had to narrate, and sometimes even act out, the very travel in whose existence he did not believe. As Hartshorn instructed in his note on "Travelling Somnambulists," "if you wish to carry a somnambulist to your own house or to the house of a friend . . . take his hand, and ask him if he will go with you to your house . . . and if he says he does not know the way, tell him you will go with him." Then, Hartshorn tells the skeptical visitor, "carry your mind home, and he will soon be there with you. Bid him to let you know when he arrives" (*PIA*, 59–60). When Benjamin Kent visited the blind clairvoyant Loraina Brackett, for example, it was necessary to make her flight vivid for her and to guide her to Roxbury in such a way that she would "avoid the steeples and trees that will be in our way."[10] Brackett could travel only if she believed the story she was told. In other words, the vehicle of her clairvoyance was her credulity. That credulity appeared to be prodigious, but it was not unlimited. When Kent was too vague about claiming to catch up with her rapid flight either "in the cars" or "in the stage," she chastised him: "*your stories do not seem to hang together.*"[11] If the story of travel was ably told, on the other hand, then—in an alchemy that recalls the imagination-induced convulsions of Mesmer's patients—her imagined travel would become real travel. Brackett would be able to report facts about the destination that she had not known before.

The knot of beliefs, pretenses, and delusions quickly became impossible to untangle. In theory, the handlers of the rapport were supposed to enchant somnambulists while remaining detached themselves, but in practice there was no detached position available. Telling an interactive story meant regularly following the somnambulist's suggestions and negotiating with her sense of the plausible, as Kent learned when Brackett challenged him. "My feelings," he confessed, "very much resembled those of an oratorical tyro, who has lost the place in his manuscript, and stands before an audience . . . utterly at fault!"[12] Engaging the credulity of a clairvoyant required more narrative ability than Kent had. It also required a willingness

10. BK to TH, Roxbury, MA, November 27, 1837, *PIA*, 134.
11. Ibid., 137.
12. Ibid.

to credit—that is, be credulous toward—the clairvoyant's own representations, such as Brackett's statement that she could fly faster than any terrestrial form of locomotion. In traveling somnambulism, credulity tended to become mutual.

There was no more striking—or more infamous—instance of mutual credit than Brackett's conversion of the well-known skeptic William Leete Stone to the mesmeric cause. Through a scene of mutual storytelling much like the one she acted out with Kent, Brackett elicited from Stone the "headlong, unhesitating credulity" that the *Quarterly Christian Spectator* review of my epigraph deplored. Stone was familiar with the Franklinian arguments against mesmerism and had visited Providence prepared to set the practice down "as the work, if not of credulity and imposture, at least of mental excitement, sympathy, and delusion," as he put it (*L*, 8). But in the account he wrote of his encounter with Brackett, the *Letter to Doctor A. Brigham on Animal Magnetism* (1837), he showed how the rapport could become reciprocal in spite of a skeptic's best efforts. Stone's progress from Franklinian skeptic to believer is a good illustration of what happened to magnetism in general as it proliferated beyond Poyen's lectures. The Franklin commission had understood magnetism as a manifestation of credulity's power to affect the body.[13] Then Poyen and Cynthia Gleason introduced the practice as a tool for *manipulating* credulity. But in Stone's untutored account—Poyen actually chastised him for his heresy, in his *Letter to Col. Wm. L. Stone* (1837)—a third meaning contends with both of these.[14] Enchanting someone else, however couched in technical terms, rebounded on the enchanter. Stone's beliefs were also affected; his imagination, too, was activated. In his experiments and in the controversy surrounding them, mesmerism seems in practice to be a technique of reciprocal credulity between operator and somnambulist—though Stone struggles with how to articulate that fact and even with whether to admit it.

Mutual delusion was a hard sell then, and it is a hard sell now. Group fanaticism was the very thing that had worried the Franklin commission when it described how convulsions became contagious in Mesmer's public process: one credulous patient started convulsing, thus egging the others

---

13. The addressee of Stone's *Letter*, Amariah Brigham, had himself been one of the popularizers of this view in the United States, as described in chapter 1.

14. Charles Poyen, *A Letter to Col. Wm. L. Stone, of New York, on the Facts Related in his "Letter to Dr. Brigham," and a Plain Refutation of Durant's "Exposition of Animal Magnetism"* (Boston: Weeks, Jordan, 1837), 6.

on, and soon the whole room was in an uproar over nothing. *Folie à deux*—
that is, a shared belief in a delusional memory, story, or reality—remains a
recognized mental illness.[15] It is not much easier now than it was in 1837 to
tolerate the shared credulity and indifference to truth that Stone and Brackett elaborated. The secular agent's question, Talal Asad writes, is, "what
should human beings do to realize their freedom, empower themselves,
and choose pleasure?"[16] Freedom and empowerment surely cannot be accomplished—or so it appeared to the *Quarterly Christian Spectator* and others taking the same dim view of Stone and Brackett—while one is mired in
a group delusion. And yet there are unmistakably moments when a mutual
indifference to truth permits us to rethink rigid or limiting assumptions.
Magnetism permitted Brackett, for example, to expand the limits that others placed on her because of her blindness.

Could credulity—vulnerability to deception, tendency toward thrall,
indifference to truth—have something to be said in its favor? That is the
question Stone's conversion raised, and it is the question of this chapter.
Poets and fiction writers have been obliged to defend the falsehoods with
which they captivate their readers at least since Plato's *Republic* put them
on the defensive, and so imaginative literature is a natural place to turn.
Brackett and Stone might be described as having *suspended their disbelief*—
but only if that phrase, widely disseminated since Samuel Taylor Coleridge
first used it, is divested of its tendency to sanitize delusion and to protect
the reader of imaginative literature from the charge of credulity. Critics
have sometimes tried to rescue fiction from this taint—treating it as enchantment without the nasty bits—but in so doing have cleansed it of one
of the more important modes of thinking that it offers us: how to tolerate
error without paranoid overreaction. Edgar Allan Poe's relationship to fiction and delusion is complicated—he hoaxed, and he created the unhoax-
able detective Auguste Dupin—but I follow a thread through his oeuvre
that shows him asking his readers to be more tolerant of the possibility
of deception and not to sacrifice all other goods simply to avoid it. "A Tale
of the Ragged Mountains" (1844) finds resources for that line of thinking
in traveling somnambulism. And "The Angel of the Odd" (1844) makes tol-
erance of delusion into a humorous credo. Poe's Angel demands exactly

15. Alistair Munro, *Delusional Disorder: Paranoia and Related Illnesses* (Cambridge:
Cambridge University Press, 1999), 186–91.

16. Talal Asad, *Formations of the Secular: Christianity, Islam, Modernity* (Stanford, CA:
Stanford University Press, 2003), 71.

the conversion that Stone made—and that the *Quarterly Christian Specta-tor* bemoaned: from "sturdy unbeliever" to credulous dupe. All of what is printed is *not* true, but behaving as though it were—being ready to "*bolt* anything"—nonetheless has the advantage of detaching one from the pride of skepticism and leaving one open to the attractions of new truths. The Angel's credo is this chapter's as well, offered with all the humor and all the seriousness of the original: believe what is print in the print; 'tis the truth, every word.

THE CONVERSION OF A SKEPTIC

Lurena Brackett, later known as Loraina in the period of her animal-magnetic fame, was born circa 1818 in Dudley, Massachusetts, to a family of limited means.[17] At the age of sixteen, she lost her vision in an accident: "an iron weight, weighing two or three pounds, f[e]ll from a height upon the top of her head."[18] Accounts differ about where the injury happened: either at the private home where Brackett was boarding while attending school or in a textile factory where she worked.[19] She succumbed to a nervous ill-ness, perhaps of a "uterine" character, soon after.[20] She was deprived of her "reason," too, "for a number of months, during which time she was subject

17. On the Brackett family, see Sheila O'Brien Quinn, "Credibility, Respectability, Sug-gestibility, and Spirit Travel: Lurena Brackett and Animal Magnetism," *History of Psychol-ogy* 15, no. 3 (2012): 276; Charles Negus and Jno. [John] W. Tenney, "Letter to Hartshorn," *Providence Daily Journal (PDJ)*, November 10, 1837. There is doubt about Brackett's date of birth. Hartshorn gives her birth date as May 1818, in a separately paginated addendum to *PIA*: "Notice," 2. This notice appeared first in *PDJ*, November 10, 1837. Later records com-port with the 1818 birthdate, including the record of Brackett's entry at the New-England Institution for the Blind in Boston (Perkins School for the Blind Archives, Boston, MA, Pupil Register no. 2, 1832–1894, s. v. "105") and the record of her marriage (Quinn, "Cred-ibility," 279). Quinn nonetheless gives Brackett's birthdate as September 1816 based on the *Vital Records* of Dudley, Massachusetts ("Credibility," 276, 279). Subsequent references to the Perkins School for the Blind Archives are abbreviated PS.

18. GC to TH, Providence, RI, August 31, 1837, *PIA*, 29; corroborated in Hartshorn, "No-tice," 2. See also Quinn, "Credibility," 5; *L*, 10.

19. Hartshorn ("Notice," 2) claims the accident happened at a school; Durant says it hap-pened at a textile factory: *Exposition*, 163.

20. Capron links the illness to the injury: GC to TH, Providence, RI, August 31, 1837, *PIA*, 29-30. Brackett's physicians at the time, John Tenney and Charles Negus, trace it instead

to the most violent spasms, and other serious derangements of her nervous system."[21] For a time she was mute. Painful treatments, including cupping, blistering, and strychnine, did little to help her.[22] Her reason and her voice returned. Her vision did not.[23] Eventually Brackett was accepted as a ward of Massachusetts at the New-England Institution for the Education of the Blind in Boston (called the Perkins Institution starting in 1840), where everything but her clothing allowance would be paid by the state. She was to be trained as a teacher for the blind.[24] She set out from Dudley for Boston in the spring of 1837.[25]

On her way, Brackett stopped to see friends in Providence. It was a fateful decision. In Providence, it would have been a truth universally acknowledged, that a hysterical young woman must be in want of a mesmerist. Brackett's friends put her in touch with George Capron, a physician who had learned the Deleuzian techniques from Poyen. Capron hoped to restore Brackett's vision with magnetism, and in that he had no permanent

---

to an "obstruction in the uterine function," thus making the suggestion that Brackett was hysterical: Negus and Tenney, "Letter," *PDJ*, November 10, 1837.

21. GC to TH, Providence, RI, August 31, 1837, *PIA*, 29–30.

22. Negus and Tenney, "Letter," *PDJ*, November 10, 1837.

23. GC to TH, Providence, RI, August 31, 1837, *PIA*, 34.

24. On plans for Brackett's education, see GC to TH, Providence, RI, August 31, 1837, *PIA*, 30. On her status as a state beneficiary upon her admission in 1838, see PS, Pupil Register no. 2. On the expectations of state beneficiaries, see Samuel G. Howe, *Annual Report* 4 (Boston, 1836), 16. The name of the school changed to the Perkins Institution and Massachusetts Asylum for the Blind in the 1840 *Annual Report*: Samuel G. Howe, *Annual Report* 8 (Boston, 1840), [1]; on the history of the school's name, see Frances A. Koestler, *The Unseen Minority: A Social History of Blindness in the United States* (New York: David McKay Co. and American Foundation for the Blind, 1976), 399. At present the institution is known as the Perkins School for the Blind, and its archives, extending over the whole period of the school's existence, are called the Perkins School for the Blind Archives. To avoid confusion, I call the school the Perkins Institution wherever possible, even though some of the events this chapter describes took place before the name change.

25. Capron says that Brackett arrived in Providence in mid-May 1837: GC to TH, Providence, RI, August 31, 1837, *PIA*, 34. The first mention of her magnetic gifts in print is on May 31, 1837: [Thomas C. Hartshorn], "The Magnetizer, No. 11," *PDJ*, May 31, 1837. She is not mentioned by name but can be identified on the basis of the context and her future relationship with Hartshorn. "The Magnetizer" papers were originally published anonymously, but Hartshorn later claimed authorship: Thomas C. Hartshorn, "Appendix," in J. P. F. Deleuze, *Practical Instruction in Animal Magnetism*, rev. ed., trans. Thomas C. Hartshorn (New York: Appleton, 1843), 251.

success.[26] But Brackett proved to be as skilled a somnambulist as Gleason had been. While in the magnetic state, Brackett regained her sight. Even when she was blindfolded as an extra precaution against fraud, she seemed to see the room around her. Capron reported that while magnetized, "she walked about the house, drank her tea, &c. with as much ease and confidence as she could have done, had she been in the full possession of her sight, and in a waking state."[27] Gradually her vision expanded: while magnetized she could travel in spirit to other cities. She visited Washington, where she viewed the monuments; she toured Saratoga Springs, where she sipped the bitter mineral water and "dashed it from her on tasting, and said she disliked it" (*L*, 14). Capron estimated that she was magnetized well over one hundred times in the summer of 1837, often in front of visitors who spread her fame back home.[28] Animal magnetism waylaid Brackett in Providence for more than a year, after which she went on to matriculate at the New-England Institution for the Blind (Perkins Institution) as she had planned.

Traveling somnambulism probably started in Providence late in the spring of 1837, right around the time Brackett arrived.[29] Hartshorn suggests that it was not uncommon in Providence "to send a somnambulist in

26. At the time of Brackett's admission at the Perkins Institution (then the New-England Institution for the Blind) in July 1838, her blindness was "Total": PS, Pupil Register no. 2. Capron later maintained that her treatment had been progressing well but that she suffered setbacks when it was abruptly discontinued early in 1838: GC to TH, Providence, RI, August 1, 1843; Thomas C. Hartshorn, "New Appendix" to *Practical Instruction in Animal Magnetism*, rev. ed., by J. P. F. Deleuze, trans. Thomas C. Hartshorn (New York: Appleton, 1843), 370–71.

27. GC to TH, Providence, RI, August 31, 1837, *PIA*, 31.

28. Ibid. Accounts written by Brackett's visitors include Frederick A. Farley to TH, Boston, October 3, 1837, *PIA*, 62-64; John Flint to TH, Boston, October 1, 1837, *PIA*, 64-67; E. L. Frothingham to TH, Boston, October 3, 1837, *PIA*, 115-19; BK to TH, Roxbury, MA, November 27, 1837, *PIA*, 129-47; Durant, *Exposition*, 161–72.

29. Poyen believed there were precedents for seeing at a distance, but not for traveling mentally to places where the somnambulist had never been: *Letter to Stone*, 8, 12. Alan Gauld's international study corroborates Poyen's view; Gauld mentions a handful of earlier instances resembling the travel of Providence clairvoyants. Caroline Ramer, a German clairvoyant working with J. C. Valentin, on one occasion in 1819 looked into the distant home of a visitor and described a piano she saw there. It is unlikely Ramer was known in the United States. Gauld sees Ramer's case and a few others like hers as anomalous, among "perhaps the oddest cases of ostensible paranormal cognition" from Europe in the early nineteenth century: *A History of Hypnotism* (Cambridge: Cambridge University Press, 1992), 149.

spirit to examine the sick," so it may be that remote diagnosis was a transitional form that eventually gave way to travel for its own sake.[30] Hartshorn was traveling somnambulism's most devoted chronicler, and he often arranged for visitors from other regional cities to see practitioners in action (*PIA*, 50). His humorous accounts of the travels of "Somnambulus" in the "Magnetizer" series in the *Providence Daily Journal* in April and May 1837, roughly contemporary with Brackett's arrival, are some of the earliest references to traveling somnambulism in print.[31] Besides Brackett, other traveling clairvoyants included Mary Ayres, whose social class is unknown and who visited Jersey City with Charles Durant;[32] Amelia Andros, who was the daughter of cotton factory owner George R. A. Olney and the wife of varnish manufacturer William Andros;[33] and Miss Parker (born c. 1810), a friend of Brackett's who was well known for having diagnosed an enlarged spleen in a patient at a quarter mile's distance.[34] Women's names were often withheld from print, and some of the anonymous cases recorded by Hartshorn probably represent practitioners beyond these four (*PIA*, 50–51).

30. *PIA*, 56; Charles Poyen, *The Progress of Animal Magnetism in New England* (Boston: Weeks, Jordan, 1837), 150–51. Capron, Brackett's magnetist, had worked with a somnambulist who mentally visited her family in the country in February, before he met Brackett: Poyen, *Progress*, 100, 105; letter from GC, first printed in the *Boston Courier*, February 25, 1837. Capron, however, specifies that he does not believe this somnambulist actually gained her information from imaginative travel; he believes her knowledge was instead her response to the action of his will—that is, to suggestion (Poyen, *Progress*, 105). Hartshorn also recounts a case from December 1836 in which a somnambulist seemed to follow his magnetizer mentally as the latter moved through the city: *PIA*, 46.

31. [Thomas C. Hartshorn], "The Magnetizer, No. 3," *PDJ*, April 25, 1837; "The Magnetizer, No. 4," *PDJ*, May 1, 1837; "The Magnetizer, No. 7," *PDJ*, May 9, 1837; "The Magnetizer, No. 10," *PDJ*, May 23, 1837.

32. Durant, *Exposition*, 210–12, including a corroborating letter, David Reese to Charles Durant, New York, September 29, 1837. Ayres's mesmerist was William Grant; Isaac Hartshorn records traveling somnambulism to Newport with an unnamed clairvoyant and Grant as the mesmerist in Isaac Hartshorn to TH, Providence, RI, September 1, 1837, *PIA*, 62.

33. Durant, *Exposition*, 56-57. On Andros's husband, William Noice Andros, see *Exposition*, 56; *1850 United States Federal Census*, accessed June 24, 2017, http://search.ancestry .com/search/db.aspx?dbid=8054. On her father, George R. A. Olney, see *Exposition*, 57.

34. Durant, *Exposition*, 48–50, 173–79; Durant estimates Parker's age at twenty-seven in 1837 (173), and he also attests to her friendship with Brackett (179). Parker's remote diagnosis was widely reported, though not usually under her name: see *PIA*, 14–18, extracted from *Salem Gazette*, August 11, 1837. William Leete Stone also reprinted this account of the case, taken from *PIA*, as an appendix to his *Letter*, 63–66.

Cases from both Hartshorn's "Appendix" to Deleuze's *Practical Instruction in Animal Magnetism* and Durant's *Exposition* usually show clairvoyants being sent to nearby cities. Longer-distance travel seems only to have happened when a visitor present could verify details: for example, a visitor recently returned from Cuba sent one anonymous woman there, asking her to navigate by going "along the sea coast in a southwesterly direction, until she came to the peninsula of Florida."[35] A friend of Charles Durant's also sent Amelia Andros to visit "his former residence in Calcutta,"[36] and Hartshorn describes "sending several somnambulists far to the west," probably meaning in the neighborhood of Ohio, and having them look at the clocks there, to find out whether they would read the local time correctly.[37] More commonly, though, the cities somnambulists visited were the ones their visitors came from, within a day's stagecoach, rail, or steamboat journey from Providence: "Boston, Salem, Newport, Taunton, New-Bedford, New-York, and other places," as Hartshorn summarizes (*PIA*, 50).

Initially there were indications that traveling somnambulism would fit with the model of enchantment managed toward useful ends. Some observers envisioned the practice joining newspapers and rapidly improving transportation infrastructure as a means of transmitting information quickly. One paper suggested that a somnambulist could function as "a sort of telegraph," helping editors "to obtain the earliest intelligence of the price of cotton, and other important items of news, commercial or political."[38] In Hartshorn's "Magnetizer" series, the fictitious "Somnambulus" passes "into . . . the sanctum sanctorum of secret deposit—the iron safe of the tottering merchant—whose balance sheets speak of the ruinous effects of the experiment made upon the currency of the Country."[39] Hartshorn showed some prophetic flair of his own here. He published these words on May 9, 1837. On May 10, the New York banks suspended specie payment on their notes, precipitating the Panic of 1837.[40] Using somnambulists in such

35. Frederick S. Church to TH, Providence, RI, September 1, 1837, *PIA*, 148. The experiment took place in May 1837.

36. Durant, *Exposition*, 93.

37. *PIA*, 120n. Hartshorn had sent somnambulist Amelia Andros to Cincinnati: Durant, *Exposition*, 58.

38. "Animal Magnetism," *Charleston Courier*, November 13, 1837.

39. [Thomas C. Hartshorn], "The Magnetizer, No. 7," *PDJ*, May 9, 1837.

40. Reginald Charles McGrane, *The Panic of 1837: Some Financial Problems of the Jacksonian Era* (Chicago: University of Chicago Press, 1924), 93; Edwin G. Burrows and Mike Wallace, *Gotham: A History of New York City to 1898* (New York: Oxford University Press,

a situation would have had an analogous logic to using a somnambulist to get early news of rebellion. Slave revolts and financial panics struck fearful observers as eruptions of unreason. The clairvoyant was like a native informant from these irrational domains. But such uses belonged to a speculative future. In practice, visitors were more likely to fantasize with clairvoyants about their beloved home cities than to exploit the relationship to gain time-sensitive knowledge.

By August 1837 the praise of Brackett and other traveling clairvoyants had grown so loud that William Leete Stone felt obliged to do something about it. Stone was the editor of the *New York Commercial Advertiser* and a well-known skeptic; his "whole course as editor" had been "opposed, in every way and on every occasion, to all sorts of humbug and imposture," according to the *Boston Courier*.[41] Stone had the impression that "destiny" had "cast upon his shoulders the task of showing up impostures."[42] He came to town to investigate Brackett, fully expecting to expose her as a fraud. He had satirized Poyen, whom he considered a "strolling dealer . . . in somnambulism," within weeks of the latter's first meeting with Gleason (L, 6).[43] He had published on other humbugs, too; his extensively researched *Matthias and his Imposture* (1835) had called the career of the Prophet Matthias, the messiah who induced his followers to hand over their savings and follow him to Sing Sing, "one of the most singular and extraordinary delusions that have [sic] ever appeared."[44] As for Maria Monk's *Awful Disclosures* (1836), in which a writer purporting to be a former nun accuses a Montreal abbess of running a prostitution ring, it was "A TISSUE OF CALUMNIES" from start

---

1999), 611–14. A great many people were prophesying bank failure in the spring of 1837, as Jessica M. Lepler shows in *The Many Panics of 1837: People, Politics, and the Creation of a Transatlantic Financial Crisis* (New York: Cambridge University Press, 2013), 94–156.

41. "Col. Stone's Letter to Dr. Brigham," *Boston Courier*, October 5, 1837; William L. Stone II, *The Family of John Stone, One of the First Settlers of Guilford, Conn.* (Albany, NY: J. Musell's Sons, 1888), 56, 81.

42. William L. Stone, *Maria Monk and the Nunnery of the Hôtel Dieu* (New York: Howe & Bates, 1836), iii.

43. For the *Commercial's* coverage of animal magnetism, see Poyen, "Experiments in Animal Magnetism," *New York Commercial Advertiser*, November 23, 1836, reprint of same article from *PDJ*, November 19, 1836; "Animal Magnetism," *New York Commercial Advertiser*, December 5, 1836.

44. William L. Stone, *Matthias and his Impostures; or, The Progress of Fanaticism*, 3rd ed. (New York: Harper and Bros., 1835), 3–4.

to finish, according to Stone's exposé on the topic.[45] His Franklinian bona
fides was impeccable; he had compared the Matthias cult to the standard
list of fanaticisms, including the Salem witch trials, the South Sea bubble,
Kentucky revivalism, and animal magnetism itself, than which there was
"no greater absurdity."[46]

During his visit, Stone told the magnetized Brackett a story designed
to convince her that they were traveling to New York. Exactly how Brackett was affected is a complicated question; Brackett left no writings on the
topic, and so we have only others' accounts of her experiences. But one
thing is certain: the story had a profound effect on Stone himself. He wound
up converting to Brackett's cause. Stone announced his change of heart in
the *Commercial* at the beginning of September, and within a week or so the
full account of his visit with Brackett, an open *Letter to Doctor A. Brigham
on Animal Magnetism*, appeared before a flabbergasted public. "We have
had our time and times of laughing at animal magnetism," Stone declared
in the *Commercial*. "We shall laugh at it no more."[47] His readers were very
far from making the same resolution. "Such an exhibition of credulity we
did not expect to see any where," wrote the *Hampshire Gazette*.[48] Stone had
"been successful in catching and *nailing to the counter* two monstrous humbugs (Matthias and Maria Monk)," only to be "caught by a third (animal
magnetism)," lamented another paper.[49] (The expression "nail to the counter" alludes to what merchants did with counterfeit bills or coins—so animal magnetism figured as a debased currency in the years of the Panic.)[50]
"We have not yet recovered from our amazement sufficiently to hazard an
opinion," confessed the editors of the *Albany Evening Journal*. "Can he be
serious?"[51] they genuinely wondered. He was.

45. W. Stone, *Maria Monk*, 33; Maria Monk, *Awful Disclosures* (New York: M. Monk,
1836). On Maria Monk, see Jenny Franchot, *Roads to Rome: The Antebellum Protestant
Encounter with Catholicism* (Berkeley: University of California Press, 1994), 154–61.

46. W. Stone, *Matthias*, 305–6, 312.

47. "Animal Magnetism," *New York Commercial Advertiser*, September 4, 1837.

48. "Col. Stone on Animal Magnetism," *Hampshire Gazette*, October 4, 1837.

49. *New Hampshire Sentinel*, November 2, 1837.

50. *Oxford English Dictionary* online, 3rd ed. (2011), s. v. "nail, *v.*" phrase 2, http://www.oed
.com.proxy.its.virginia.edu/view/Entry/124845?rskey=qieySv&result=2 (accessed June 22,
2017).

51. "A Letter on Animal Magnetism, by W. L. Stone," *Albany Evening Journal*, September 29, 1837.

Though some leapt into the fray to defend "the Colonel," as Stone was familiarly known, many more attacked him afresh. Widely noticed, reviewed, and mocked, Stone's *Letter* quite literally stopped the presses: a small crowd of animal magnetism authors, their treatises halfway or all the way printed, scrambled to insert appendixes. Texts altered at the eleventh hour include the first American edition of the *Report of Dr. Franklin and Other Commissioners* (1837), whose editors squeezed in a series of "Remarks on Col. Stone's Pamphlet." While Charles Durant was putting the finishing touches on his *Exposition*, he heard rumors of Stone's impending publication and went to his office to remonstrate with him.[52] That effort had no effect, and so he added some vehement "Strictures on Col. Wm. L. Stone's *Letter*" to his *Exposition*, in which he accused Stone of "*weakness, infatuation*, and *idiocy*" and decried Stone's "reprehensible conduct, in raising a false beacon on your high name and character, to strand the weak minds of a credulous world."[53]

Storytelling was Stone's undoing. He had arranged to see Brackett at the home of Henry Hopkins, where she was staying. There, he and a small group of other inquirers watched George Capron place her in the somnambulistic state by making a few quick magnetic passes. Though Brackett's sightless eyes were blindfolded, she described engravings and portraits that hung on the parlor wall, turning her back to the images in order to see them (*L*, 15–19). These preliminaries completed, Capron transferred his rapport with Brackett to Stone so that he could question Brackett directly: Capron "clothed me with the power of enjoying her exclusive company," in Stone's

---

52. Durant, *Exposition*, 220–22.

53. Several texts had appendixes on Stone added when printing was evidently already under way. The *Report of Dr. Franklin and Other Commissioners, Charged by the King of France with the Examination of the Animal Magnetism as Practised at Paris* (Philadelphia: H. Perkins, 1837) has a few paragraphs of "Remarks on Col. Stone's Pamphlet" appended to the text. The first seventy-five pages of the pseudonymously published *Philosophy of Animal Magnetism: Together with the System of Manipulating Adopted to Produce Ecstacy and Somnambulism—the Effects and the Rationale* (Philadelphia: Merrihew and Gunn, 1837), attributed to "A Gentleman of Philadelphia," had been printed when Stone's *Letter* came out, prompting the author to take account of the *Letter* in his remaining text and "recommend . . . Colonel STONE's pamphlet as a work of surpassing interest" (76). Durant added "Strictures on Col. Wm. L. Stone's *Letter to Doctor A. Brigham, on Animal Magnetism*" to his *Exposition*, 216–25 (quotations at 217). And Laughton Osborn's *The Vision of Rubeta* (Boston: Weeks, Jordan 1838), a mock epic about Stone, rushed to press unfinished (389–90n) with a new canto about Brackett (Canto Fourth; see pp. 235–59) and a few footnotes added to earlier cantos (e.g., 157n, 178n, 179n.).

genteel description (*L*, 19). Like most of Brackett's visitors, Stone wanted to see her touring another city with her feet still firmly planted in Providence. He wanted, in his own words, to test her power "of transporting herself in imagination from one place to another, no matter how distant" (*L*, 13). Stone said "imagination" advisedly: he was perfectly aware that the Franklin commission had used it to dismiss Mesmer's claims, just as he intended to dismiss Capron's and Brackett's (*L*, 7).

Stone's job, as the visiting skeptic, was to humor Brackett in the belief that she was traveling to New York, while remaining aloof from that fantasy. But he spun such an appealing fiction that he became caught up in it himself. He followed Brackett's lead as much as she followed his. After Stone was in rapport with Brackett, he proposed a journey to New York via "the steamboat *Narragansett*," then lying at dock in Providence, according to his account in the *Letter*. "It is a very fine boat," he tells Brackett, probably from personal experience; he may even have taken the *Narragansett* to Providence to see her. Brackett replies that she prefers "to go through the air" (*L*, 20). Stone readily accedes to this request, adding a suggestion of his own:

> "Very well," I replied,—"we will step into a balloon. That will be a pleasant mode of travelling."
>
> She did not, however, seem to comprehend what was meant by a balloon, and repeated her desire to go through the air. I assured her that I would as gladly accompany her that way as any other. (*L*, 20)

Stone here starts to lose control of the narrative. He cannot be sure what Brackett means by going through the air, balloon-free, but he assents anyway. He is humoring her, but he is also accepting direction from her. He fabricates a history of expertise: "I am used to that way of travelling," he next assures her, though obviously this is not the case, since he is not even sure what way of traveling she is talking about, "and will bear you up in perfect safety." Brackett then shows him the way by pantomiming flight: "she grasped my right hand more firmly—took my left hand—and pressed upon both, tremulously, as if buoying herself up." Yet again, to humor Brackett, Stone has to follow her lead by "bearing her up in perfect safety" according to the means she has indicated: "I raised my hands some ten or twelve inches, very slowly, favoring the idea that she was ascending" (*L*, 20).

When Stone and Brackett touch down in New York, Stone becomes more responsive still. This is a city Stone knows and loves; the New York he builds for and with Brackett is finely drawn. No longer blandly assenting that they will "go through the air," he now does generous counterfactual labor on behalf of Brackett's vision. First, Stone applies himself to the task of working out where people who had "gone through the air" would have to land, were such a thing possible. The Battery is a logical conclusion, since it is the place "where the Providence steam-boat comes in" (*L*, 21). The Battery had also been the standard point of departure for balloon launches in New York throughout the 1830s—Charles Durant, who later accused Stone of credulity, was perhaps the most famous of the balloonists to fly from the Battery, attracting tens of thousands of spectators.[54] Durant's intolerance of Stone and Brackett may have stemmed from professional rivalry; he reserved Stone's claim that he was "used to that mode of travelling" for particular ridicule in his *Exposition*.[55] It was, after all, a claim Durant himself was quite a bit more qualified to make. In any case, though Stone has not been able to entice Brackett into an imaginary balloon basket, he still brings them down in the Battery, New York's unofficial ballooning terminal. "Here we are at New-York," he announces to Brackett after a decent interval of flight; "come, we will descend at the north end of the Battery" (*L*, 21).

From here they tour the southern tip of the island before walking up Broadway like many a promenader before them. Frequently, Brackett offers images she has glimpsed, Stone sharpens them with his immense local knowledge, and Brackett then repackages a word or two of his into a new observation. Skeptics were amazed that Stone fell for this routine. Stone's questions are, as David Reese noted in *Humbugs of New-York* (1838), "*leading*" in their character, almost without an exception."[56] As they enter the Castle Garden pleasure grounds with the use of his season ticket, Brackett protests, "I don't like the looks of that man by the gate." This, he reassures her, must be "a constable or police officer—they always had somebody of that character by the gate—but he knew me very well, and would open the gate as soon as we should come up" (*L*, 22). Soon she sees a man "with [a] large round hat, like a Quaker's" and a "round jacket." Stone excitedly observes, "it instantly occurred to me that she had described the dress of the Castle-Garden Boat Club, whose boat-house stands at the farther end

54. "Balloon," *Workingman's Advocate*, September 11, 1830; Charles Ferson Durant, *Grand Aerostatic Ascension, of Charles F. Durant, the First Native Citizen of the United States That Ever Attempted an Ascension in a Balloon, on Thursday, September 9, 1830* (New York: J. C. Spear, 1830).

55. Durant, *Exposition*, 199.

56. David Reese, *Humbugs of New-York: Being a Remonstrance against Popular Delusion* (Boston: Weeks, Jordan, 1838), 40–41.

of the bridge, where, also, their boat is moored." He later confirmed with a member of the club "that such was their dress, and he believed that one of their members must have been there at the time" (*L*, 23). When, riffing on the name, she tells him "it does not seem much like a garden," he instantly supplies the history of the place as an old fort (*L*, 22). The gates of the pleasure grounds open to some combination of his knowledge, her belief, and his belief in her belief.

Even more obviously collaborative than their joint conjuring of the Castle Garden boatman is what happens at the home of Mr. Ray, which Stone points out to Brackett as they pass. Asked what she sees at the house, Brackett begins, "Why—they are" and then stops. "They are what?" Stone eagerly questions her. "Why, I am trying to see," she replies. Stone's own clairvision does not permit him to bear with Brackett any longer, and he bursts out, "What do they look like? Do they resemble lions?" She agrees that they do; "*bronzed* lions." Stone regrets having "spoken the word lions too hastily." But still he considers her "unaided discovery" that the lions were "*bronze*" and "*dormant*" to be "the most striking development in the case, thus far" (*L*, 25). At the end of their walk, when Stone escorts Brackett into what he supposes to be the basement kitchen of his New York residence, she misidentifies all the servants. But by this time he is so persuaded of Brackett's abilities that he can only assume that she has "made a mistake, and gone into a wrong house" (*L*, 32–33). He then shepherds her across the street and into his own basement.

"JUGLARESA"

Stone's credulity astounded skeptics. The lions of Mr. Ray in particular had them rolling in the aisles. Anyone who would defend Stone, cracked a paper in Buffalo, "must, in our opinion, have more brass in his face than is contained in Mr. Ray's bronze lions."[57] According to the *American Quarterly Review*'s retelling of the lion episode, Stone "first points out Mr. Ray's house, and asks, 'How do you like that?' and Miss Brackett was sharp enough to see that such a question would not have been asked, unless there were

57. Clipping from unidentified evening newspaper, Buffalo, NY, October 23, 1837, in Charles Ferson Durant Biographical File, Institute of Aerospace Sciences Archives, Library of Congress, Washington, DC (hereafter cited as Durant Biographical File).

something remarkable to distinguish Mr. Ray's from other houses. She, therefore, answered, 'it is a splendid house.' Any fool might have guessed as much." When she sees sculptures at the door, "he very wisely asks if they are *lions*, to which she with astonishing sagacity answers, 'Yes.' She then observes, 'they are *bronzed* lions,' which luckily happens to be the fact, showing that people will guess correctly sometimes." It was "really too absurd to be seriously treated," the *Review* protested.[58]

Stone was supposed to tell Brackett a noble lie about travel to New York, in order to activate her powers. But in Laughton Osborn's estimation, what had happened instead was that Brackett had told Stone an *ignoble* one. "Did you indeed deceive me?" the Stone character asks the Brackett character in a short farce Osborn composed on the occasion of Stone's *Letter*, his *Critique of the Vision of Rubeta* (1838). "Be sure I did, and should be happy to do it again," answers Brackett, a.k.a. "Juglaresa."[59] Osborn's objection was not to deceit per se. He was silent on the subject of mesmerists and visitors deceiving somnambulists, even though he squawked when trickery went the other way. Practitioners routinely deceived somnambulists about the nature of the objects around them to show the strength of the rapport: as Hartshorn explains, "A peach may . . . be transformed into an apple, a pear, an iron ball, &c. A handkerchief folded, may be changed into a child, a cat, or a dog, and thrown into the lap" (*PIA*, 19). Capron, for example, demonstrated that if he willed Brackett's glass of water to be ice cream, she would promptly ask for a spoon.[60] Subterfuge had also been a key part of skeptical efforts to discredit mesmerism ever since the Franklin commissioners had deliberately misled their experimental subjects. Durant's *Exposition*, lavishly praised by skeptics, involved an elaborate gaslighting campaign in which Durant represented himself as a fellow demonstrator and lecture promoter to another Providence clairvoyant, Amelia Andros, over many months.[61] Deception was not a scandal in itself.

But when the mark was a powerful white man and the deceiver a working-class blind woman, skeptics strenuously objected to the loss of their prerogatives. Stone, lamented David Reese, had been "magnetized out of his

58. "Animal Magnetism," *American Quarterly Review* 22 (December 1837): 405.
59. Laughton Osborn, *The Critique of the Vision of Rubeta: A Dramatic Sketch in One Act* (Philadelphia, 1838), 22.
60. BK to TH, Roxbury, MA, November 27, 1837, *PIA*, 132–33.
61. Durant, *Exposition*, 72.

usual self-possession."[62] To be "magnetized," for the skeptics, was to be enchanted and fooled—and that was the woman's place. In Osborn's *Critique
of the Vision of Rubeta*, Juglaresa tries to violate the Stone character, Rubeta.
"You are mad—you're—you're—would you ravish me? . . . Rape! murder!
fire! rape!" Rubeta cries.[63] Both of the two possible jokes here feminize Stone
as a means of humiliating him and Brackett both: either he is hysterically
crying "rape" when no rape is likely, or he has really let himself be violated by
a woman. Osborn could not forgive Stone for a wounding review of his first
novel, and the *Critique* was actually the *second* satire of Stone that he had
published. The first was a learned and very obscene mock epic, *The Vision of
Rubeta* (1838), in which Stone (a.k.a. Rubeta) is "High-Priest of Hypocrites
and King of Fools" (as portrayed in a satiric family crest; Fig. 5).[64] Brackett, a
divine changeling, learns from the goddess Impudence "To see men's bowels
through their button'd hose, / Use priest and layman for her pliant tools, /
And make dull Capons [in other words, Caprons; in other words, gelded
turkey-cocks] of a score of fools."[65] Brackett's destiny was to castrate the men
who would believe in her. The more Brackett seemed to have any say over
what happened in the rapport, the more Osborn seethed with misogyny and
resentment.

How should Brackett's discretion, her creativity, and even her fugitive
control in the rapport be interpreted? One tempting possibility is simply to
reverse Osborn's discourse, agreeing with his assessment of her sovereignty
but not with his paranoid reaction to it. Then I would agree that yes, Brackett *did* have power in the rapport; she *did* have the means to violate Stone.
I would celebrate the rapport as the instrument of a blind, working-class
woman's resistance. There would be some truth to such a reading. Brackett
certainly had more discretion over their journey than Stone had expected.
But here would be the disadvantage: making him the "fitful credulous creature," as he had once called Maria Monk,[66] and herself the confidence man
would not really alter the framework in which being enchanted is being
bent over. We would still remain in a secular mode where, as Asad writes, "in
the final analysis there are only two mutually exclusive options available:

62. Reese, *Humbugs of New-York*, 39.
63. Osborn, *Critique of the Vision of Rubeta*, 22–23.
64. Osborn, *Vision of Rubeta*, 3.
65. Ibid., 236.
66. W. Stone, *Maria Monk*, 48.

Fig. 5. William Leete Stone's family crest as satirically imagined by Laughton Osborn. Frontispiece to Osborn, *The Vision of Rubeta* (Boston: Weeks, Jordan, 1838). The crest features toads, because Stone's alias, Rubeta, means "poisonous hedge toad"; Stone in a nun's costume with a chamber pot on his head, in honor of his adventures at the Hôtel Dieu; an ass with Stone's head, representing charlatanry; and, crowning it all, another ass with a pamphlet in its mouth whose cover reads "ANIMAL MAGNETISM." Stone's motto according to Osborn is "PSITTACUS, MURES, RANA, ASINUS, MATULA, EN MEA SIGNA!" meaning, "Parrot, mice, frog, ass, chamber pot: behold my standard!" Courtesy, Albert and Shirley Small Special Collections Library, University of Virginia.

either an agent (representing and asserting himself or herself) or a victim (the passive object of chance or cruelty)."[67]

A more meaningful advance would be to refuse to boil down Stone and Brackett's journey to a story of one of them (the agent) duping the other (the victim). Bruno Latour describes a cartoon of a father whose daughter discovers him smoking. "What are you doing?" she asks him. He tells her he is smoking a cigarette. "Oh," she replies. "I thought the cigarette was smoking you."[68] The father begins frantically putting the cigarette out. As Latour remarks, "From the active form, 'I smoke a cigarette,' to the passive form, 'you are smoked by a cigarette,' nothing has changed other than the apportionment of master and instrument. The father alternates too drastically from one position to the other: too comfortable in the first image, too panicked in the last."[69] This could have been a description of the way Stone's interlocutors saw his *Letter*. Too comfortable when they think Stone is in control, they are too panicked when they think Brackett is. Reversing the skeptics' affects—panicking when Stone smokes Brackett, and rejoicing when she smokes him—would only compound the skeptics' error. That critical move would leave unexamined the law of the excluded middle, in which one is either enchanter or enchanted, agent or patient, man or rape victim. It would not be a very dramatic advance in gender politics, either, since taking would remain the contemptible position. Superficially, a woman would be in charge; structurally, the abject position would still be the feminized one.

And anyway, neither of those polarized descriptions (Stone is in charge! No, Brackett is!) seems quite right. Stone does not fully control Brackett; no more does Brackett fully control Stone. Latour suggests the metaphor of a puppeteer who controls her puppets but is always also "slightly outstripped" by them: they lead her, they suggest things that surprise her. She, the puppeteer, may also be strung up by what Latour calls "second-level puppeteer[s]:" "texts; language; the spirit of the times; the habitus; society; paradigms; epistemes; styles."[70] But these do not control the puppeteer any more completely than she controls her puppets. Brackett and Stone, too,

67. Asad, *Formations of the Secular*, 79.

68. Quoted in Bruno Latour, *On the Modern Cult of the Factish Gods*, chapter 1, "On the Cult of the Factish Gods," trans. Catherine Porter and Heather MacLean (Durham, NC: Duke University Press, 2010), 54–55; translation of *Sur le culte moderne des dieux* faitiches, *suivi de* Iconoclash, rev. ed. (Paris: La Découverte, 2009), 115.

69. Latour, *Factish Gods*, 55–56; *Dieux faitiches*, 116–17.

70. Latour, *Factish Gods*, 62–63; *Dieux faitiches*, 130.

were subject to such second-level puppeteers; notably, the very real discrepancy between them in terms of gender, class, and disability. Surpassed by these structures, still, they slightly surpassed them in their moment of collaboration. Latour asks, "What if the question rested instead on the absence of mastery, on the incapacity—either in the active or passive form—to define our attachments? How can we speak with precision of . . . 'the middle voice,' the verb form that is neither active nor passive?"[71] Rather than simply handing over to Brackett the controls that Stone had seemed to operate, I want to think about their journey as an action in the middle voice. In the middle voice of the verb "to enchant," we would no longer see one confidence man pulling the strings and one credulous dupe being jerked about, but rather two people playing cat's cradle.

During this moment of mutual indifference to truth, Brackett's abilities as a blind woman may have been reconstructed. Brackett was subject to some limiting "truths" about blind women: they could not move about confidently, could not work, and could not read. Yet the scene of mesmeric experimentation demanded that even skeptics like Stone actively entertain the possibility that Brackett *could* do all those things. Both Brackett and her visitors had to believe, or pretend to believe, that her abilities might expand in impossible ways. These abilities centrally included things that neither Brackett nor her visitors expected her to be capable of: imaginative travel to New York, yes, but also looking at engravings on a wall, reading text, and even moving freely. In that middle zone between her interlocutors casting a spell on her, and her casting one on them, Brackett may have found a space in which she could renegotiate her abilities as a blind person.

The *Annual Reports* of the Perkins Institution, where Brackett was headed when she stopped in Providence, give some sense of the limited expectations the blind faced.[72] Reformer Samuel G. Howe started his term as director of the institution determined to disprove the belief that the blind were innately dull-witted and torpid. Any such appearance, he said, was simply an example of how expectations became self-fulfilling prophecies.[73]

71. Latour, *Factish Gods*, 56; *Dieux faitiches*, 117.

72. Howe, *Annual Reports* (1834–1852).

73. Howe, *Annual Report* 9 (1841), 4–6; Ernest Freeberg, *The Education of Laura Bridgman: First Deaf and Blind Person to Learn Language* (Cambridge, MA: Harvard University Press, 2001), 10–13. Howe would later adjust his expectations downward: see Freeberg, *Laura Bridgman*, 197–202. See also James W. Trent Jr., *The Manliest Man: Samuel G. Howe and the Contours of Nineteenth-Century American Reform* (Amherst: University of Massachusetts Press, 2012), 59–64.

Howe advised parents of the blind, "never check the motions of the child; follow him, and watch him to prevent any serious accident, but do not interfere unnecessarily; do not even remove obstacles which he would learn to avoid by tumbling over them a few times . . . and if you should see him clambering in the branches of a tree, be sure he is less likely to fall than if he had eyes."[74] If the expectation is that the blind boy can climb a tree, Howe urged, then he will be able to do so. If not, then he will not.

But even Howe did not imagine a blind *girl* climbing a tree. "Let a boy saw wood, take care of cattle, do jobs about the house . . . let him learn to ride, to swim, to row, to skate, &c," he urged. For a blind girl, on the other hand, the program is both less ambitious and less painstakingly envisioned: "bring up a girl to be active about the house; to do every possible kind of work which requires motion of the body; and do not confine her too much to knitting, sewing, &c.," he advised.[75] That "&c" is so much less promising than the one that follows "to ride, to swim, to row, to skate." If Howe found it a stretch to envision confident activity on the part of a blind woman, think what it must have been like for Brackett's average interlocutor: first for her magnetist Capron and then, as her fame grew, for her other visitors. It was hardly less remarkable to them that she could walk safely around Providence unaccompanied than that she could spiritually stroll on Broadway. It is possible that Brackett herself felt the same way.

But the animal-magnetic experiment specifically required both Brackett and her interlocutors to entertain what they knew to be impossible. They had to believe, or pretend to believe, in sure-footed movement around Providence just as they had to humor Brackett in her spiritual travels to New York. E. L. Frothingham went to see Brackett in August 1837, as he reports in Hartshorn's "Appendix" to Deleuze's *Practical Instruction*. Like Stone, he would see her travel in imagination back to his own home, Boston.[76] But first he watched as Capron magnetized Brackett and then asked her to walk to a nearby house in Providence. Brackett promptly "rose from her chair, to which she had been previously led in a helpless state, walked through the room with the greatest confidence, avoiding the chair which stood in her way, and passed into the next room." She put on her coat as the magnetic experimenters rushed to follow, and she beat them to the house where Capron had told her to go. There "we found this blind young lady,

74. Howe, *Annual Report* 9 (1841), 8.
75. Ibid.
76. E. L. Frothingham to TH, Boston, October 3, 1837, *PIA*, 115–19.

now endowed with more than natural sight, running through the house like a young girl let loose from school on a holiday."⁷⁷ Benjamin Kent reported much the same thing to Hartshorn: though Brackett had to be led to a chair "in the perfect attitudes of blindness" when in her ordinary state, she sprang up with a "sure step" to leave the room just as soon as she was magnetized.⁷⁸ Stone, too, had heard of her being "sent to a fancy dry goods store to select various articles of merchandize" where "she performed the service as well as a lady of perfect sight would have done it" (*L*, 9). This looked like seeing. But was it? What if magnetism restored not Brackett's sight but Brackett's confidence in her movements—and Capron's, too, for that matter? What if it was a confidence game that freed its players rather than enthralling them? Magnetism made both Brackett and her interlocutors credulous about her abilities, and "sight" was then the name they gave to the confident activity Brackett manifested under those conditions. Magnetism created a space in which whatever extensions of her abilities were possible, and however they came to be possible, others were ready to entertain these extensions. Stone's credulity was, under another description, simply his openness to her self-redefinition.

Stone made a promising attempt at describing the mutual confidence he found with Brackett. At the moment of their departure for New York, as he is lifting Brackett's hands with his to "favor the idea that she was ascending," he sums up their flight: "And away, in imagination, we sailed" (*L*, 20–21). That phrase can run the gamut of Stone's progress from skepticism to credulity. Called on to describe Brackett's powers, Capron said she had "the ability to see objects not present—in a distant city, for instance."⁷⁹ Just this ability to call up objects not present had allowed imagination to deceive the mesmeric patients of 1784; now it was a way to describe Brackett's prodigious abilities. When Stone arrived in Providence as a skeptic, he might have said that he sailed in imagination in that he pretended to take the journey, telling Brackett a story in service of the mesmeric experiment. Brackett, on the other hand, sailed in imagination in the Franklinian sense of being self-deceived. She was like Mesmer's patients, who were "affected, if at all, only through the workings of their own imaginations" (*L*, 7).

But as their journey gets under way, the "we" appears to become a more genuine "we," and these two versions of the imagination seem to melt

77. Ibid., 116.

78. BK to TH, Roxbury, MA, November 27, 1837, *PIA*, 130.

79. GC to TH, Providence, RI, August 31, 1837, *PIA*, 32.

into one. Stone says he is "favoring" Brackett's idea of ascent by pressing on Brackett's hands. But why should the cycle of "favoring" stop there? As far as we know, it is just as accurate to say that when she pressed his hands, *she* was favoring *his* idea of her belief—or that all this favoring was going on at once. "In imagination" permits the polarity that Stone believed existed when he first came to Providence. But it also permits the symmetry he and Brackett actually practice when he arrives on the scene. Both parties to the rapport narrate, and both respond credulously to the suggestions of the other. At Mr. Ray's house, home of the infamous lions, Brackett reaches out as if to touch the foundation wall. Stone asks her what it is made of, and her answer, to which he largely leads her, convinces him that she sees the truth: it is "Eastern granite" (*L*, 25–26). In one way, Stone led Brackett to an answer. But from another perspective, she led him to one: her empty gesture of touching the air in front of her in Henry Hopkins's Providence parlor prompted Stone to supply something—Eastern granite—that she could touch. Stone's intimacy with New York became Brackett's intimacy with it. Neither of them, alone, could touch Eastern granite in New York while standing in Providence, but they could manage it together. That touch of Eastern granite happens in the middle voice, located in no one person's skin.

SUSPENDED

In Stone and Brackett's joint flight "in imagination," both participants hold their beliefs lightly. They do not constantly interrogate themselves about what kind of imagination they are "in"—a fiction, a fraud, a delusion, or a mesmeric migration of souls. They float among these possibilities as though suspended from something that may, or may not, be a balloon. They treat as momentarily unimportant the questions of whether or not the objects of their belief are real and whether or not they are being played for fools. That lightness may have permitted Brackett a confident locomotion that was otherwise inaccessible to her—that was contrary to what those around her believed the blind could do.

After Stone's experience with Brackett, the very word *belief* stopped making sense to him, so loosely had he held his convictions. "Allow me to correct a misapprehension," Stone wrote to Brigham, in response to the latter's request that he describe what had made him a "believer." "The inference from your letter is, that I have suddenly become a convert to Animal

Magnetism. . . . This is an error. I am not a positive believer in the system, because I know not what to believe" (*L*, 5). He felt "compelled, if not to relinquish, at least very essentially to modify, my disbelief" (*L*, 6). The experiments Stone had seen "have brought me from the position of a positive sceptic to a dead pause" (*L*, 5). The vast majority of papers ignored this distinction, reporting Stone's "conversion" nonetheless.[80] Stone's "narrative was accompanied by so many evidences, that he confided in [Brackett's] miracles . . . that every reader is constrained to regard the Colonel as a convert to the new science," Reese wrote.[81] But Stone's *Letter* does show evidence of his having abandoned the whole framework in which he had to be either a dupe or a manipulator of one. A dead pause between skepticism and conversion describes well the middle ground he and Brackett find together, where each partly tells a story to the other. That middle ground is "credulity" without the overlay of humiliation that Osborn and Reese (not to mention Stone himself, before this meeting) wanted to give it.

Might Stone's state be described as a "willing suspension of disbelief"? The well-known phrase comes from Samuel Taylor Coleridge's description in the *Biographia Literaria* (1817) of how he and William Wordsworth conceived the plan of their *Lyrical Ballads*. Coleridge's half of the project was to compose poetry on "persons and characters supernatural, or at least romantic; yet so as to transfer from our inward nature a human interest and a semblance of truth sufficient to procure for these shadows of imagination that *willing suspension of disbelief for the moment*, which constitutes poetic faith."[82] The dead pause of the rapport and Coleridge's poetic faith bear comparison with each other: both are intermediate states between belief and disbelief, and both are attempts at remediation or recuperation of enchantment within a disenchanted context.

Coleridge's formulation is a promising way to understand the mesmeric rapport as it developed in the United States. But the suspension of disbelief

80. Some papers called Stone a "convert": "For the *National Intelligencer*," *Daily National Intelligencer*, Washington, DC, September 13, 1837; "Animal Magnetism," *Boston Courier*, September 7, 1837; "Animal Magnetism," *Rhode-Island Republican*, September 20, 1837. Others simply saw him as a believer: "Animal Magnetism," *Alexandria Gazette*, October 5, 1837, extracted from the New York *Express*; "Animal Magnetism," *Connecticut Courant*, September 16, 1837.

81. Reese, *Humbugs of New-York*, 39.

82. Samuel Taylor Coleridge, *Biographia Literaria*, ed. James Engell and W. Jackson Bate, vol. 7 (2 vols. in 1) of *The Collected Works of Samuel Taylor Coleridge*, ed. Kathleen Coburn (Princeton, NJ: Princeton University Press, 1983), 2:6. My emphasis.

would first need to be disentangled from a purpose it has frequently served: as the slogan of a secularist view of literature. Fiction readers can look suspiciously like credulous people—they are passionately moved by characters who do not exist—and one use of the suspension-of-disbelief thesis has been to protect them from that disgraceful imputation. Is the reader that dread thing, a dupe? Certainly not. She is still clearheaded, still empowered. It is just that the reader has, as Catherine Gallagher emphasizes, *willingly* and momentarily suspended disbelief.[83] The double negative of Coleridge's phrase here becomes euphemistic. The reader is not a believer, just *not* a *dis*believer. Thus she takes "small, controlled doses" of belief, as Jane Bennett reminds us we must do in fiction and other modern pursuits; she has her "delight without delusion," as Michael Saler recommends.[84] Deployed in this way, the suspension of disbelief proves to be a fig leaf for credulity to wear in the company of secular moderns.

Coleridge showed some fig-leaf tendencies himself. For one thing, he took a Franklinian view of mesmerism. As Tim Fulford has shown, Coleridge compared the demagoguery of William Pitt to the demagoguery of Mesmer—but not because he thought any invisible fluid transfer occurred in either case. Instead, "Mesmerism . . . was a matter of superstition, and superstition sprang from powerlessness—from 'having placed our *summum bonum* (what we think so, I mean,) in an absolute Dependence on Powers and Events over which we have no Controll.'"[85] In describing poetic faith, Coleridge was equally sensitive to protecting the dignity of the secular agent from dependence on chimerical powers. His aim in the *Lyrical Ballads* was to "interest . . . the affections by the dramatic truth of such emotions, as would naturally accompany such [supernatural] situations,

83. Catherine Gallagher, "The Rise of Fictionality," in *The Novel*, vol. 1, *History, Geography, and Culture*, ed. Franco Moretti (Princeton, NJ: Princeton University Press, 2006), 347.

84. Jane Bennett, *The Enchantment of Modern Life: Attachments, Crossings, and Ethics* (Princeton, NJ: Princeton University Press, 2001), 10; Michael Saler, "Delight without Delusion," chapter 2 in *As If: Modern Enchantment and the Literary Prehistory of Virtual Reality* (New York: Oxford University Press, 2012), 57–104. For a critique of the strain of criticism that sees literary reading as enlightened enchantment, see Tracy Fessenden, "The Problem of the Postsecular," in "American Literatures/American Religions," ed. Jonathan Ebel and Justine S. Murison, special issue, *American Literary History* 26, no. 1 (2014): 154–67.

85. Coleridge quoted in Tim Fulford, "Conducting the Vital Fluid: The Politics and Poetics of Mesmerism in the 1790s," *Studies in Romanticism* 43, no. 1 (2004): 72; see also Fulford's discussion of Coleridge and mesmerism, 57–78.

supposing them real. And real in *this* sense they have been to every human being who, from whatever source of delusion, has at any time believed himself under supernatural agency."[86]

Coleridge sharply distinguishes poetic faith from superstition even at the very moment of creating an analogy between the two. Poetic "Illusion" is partial and willing; religious "Delusion" is total and unwilling.[87] He also, as Gallagher points out, offers reassurance that poetic faith is a brightly bordered experience, not just unlikely but constitutively unable to bleed into real life. We need not worry for our empowerment. In the *Lectures on Literature*, Coleridge compares reading to a dream: "It is laxly said, that during Sleep we take our Dreams for Realities; but this is irreconcilable with the nature of Sleep, which consists in a suspension of the voluntary and therefore of the comparative power. The fact is, that we pass no judgement either way—we simply do *not* judge them to be <un> real. . . . Our state while we are dreaming differs from that in which we are in the perusal of a deeply interesting Novel, in the degree rather than in the Kind."[88] Gallagher summarizes the secular ideal Coleridge is appealing to here: one can say of the reader that "she had the enjoyment of deep immersion in illusion *because* she was protected from delusion by the voluntary framework of disbelief."[89] The fiction reader's enjoyment of illusion is only a temporary injunction, happening in a "controlled situation";[90] soon she will return to her ordinary state of judging and willing.

It may be true that fiction has, for the most part, these bright borders, and that readers of fiction generally do know that it is fiction. But I part company from Coleridge when he assumes that "pass[ing] no judgment either way" is contrary to our usual state. Here I suspect that, in the process of distinguishing fiction, something else is also being accomplished: protection for the idea that human beings are normally empowered, self-conscious, and free. *Is* judging and willing our ordinary state? Or is this characterization a secular prescription for how ordinary life *ought* to be, not a description of how it is? Among the problems with the secular view that a

86. Coleridge, *Biographia Literaria*, 2:6.

87. Samuel Taylor Coleridge, *Lectures 1808–1819 on Literature*, ed. R. A. Foakes, vol. 5 (2 vols. in 1) of *The Collected Works of Samuel Taylor Coleridge*, ed. Kathleen Coburn (Princeton, NJ: Princeton University Press, 1987), 2:265–66.

88. Ibid., 2:266. Quoted (from a different edition) in Gallagher, "Rise of Fictionality," 348. Gallagher's text does not have the bracketed "<un>."

89. Gallagher, "Rise of Fictionality," 349.

90. Ibid., 348.

person must be an empowered agent intervening in history is that it is not a good representation of daily life: "Because behavior depends on unconscious routine and habit, because emotions render the ownership of actions a matter of conflicting descriptions," Asad observes, "we should not assume that every act is the act of a competent agent with a clear intention."[91] Poetic faith, I want to suggest, might be said to suspend not disbelief but the *demand* to disbelieve. It might be the temporary lifting of the imperative that one must be a secular agent—an imperative, in any case, that it is probably impossible for us to satisfy. Poetic faith would then permit us to own up to the state we really do inhabit a lot of the time: that of "pass[ing] no judgment either way." Literature might be a chance to practice tolerating the suspended states that are, in fact, fairly characteristic of us.

Edgar Allan Poe's fiction tends toward theorizing literary reading in this way: as a suspension of the demand to disbelieve. Here is Poe revising Coleridge's more famous formulation in that direction: "You mos pe pigger vool as de goose, vor to dispelief vat iz print in de print. 'Tiz de troof—dat it iz—eberry vord ob it;" or, in free translation, "you must be a bigger fool than a goose, to disbelieve what is printed. Every word of it is true" (*CW*, 3:1103). This motto comes from Poe's "The Angel of the Odd," a swift dream sequence that has wrongly been classed with Poe's minor tales. Thomas Mabbott calls it "a bit of good-natured buffoonery," but "The Angel of the Odd" is also a think piece that can bear the weight of theorizing Poe's approach to fiction (*CW*, 3:1098).[92] The story begins with the narrator reading something in the paper that smacks of humbug. Exasperated, he makes a terrible oath: "I intend to believe nothing henceforward that has anything of the 'singular' about it" (*CW*, 3:1102). The narrator's rash vow brings down on his head the wrath of the Angel of the Odd, a grouchy German made of rum barrels who is tutelary spirit to "the *odd accidents* which are continually astonishing the skeptic" (*CW*, 3:1104). The Angel considers that the skeptical narrator has blasphemed against him by refusing to believe in the improbable events he sponsors. He demands, in an accent as odd as his accidents, that the skeptic treat every word that is printed as the truth.

91. Asad, *Formations of the Secular*, 72.

92. As Lara Cohen writes, critics have found it to be "one of Poe's most baffling comic tales": *The Fabrication of American Literature: Fraudulence and Antebellum Print Culture* (Philadelphia: University of Pennsylvania Press, 2012), 58. Cohen profitably reads the story as a meditation on puffery in literary review culture.

I understand the suspension of the demand to disbelieve as being something like the Angel's position. Those who scorn to disbelieve—who refuse to take an attitude of reflexive skepticism—thereby signal that they no longer take seriously any humiliations they might allegedly sustain by being fooled, whether these be wounds to pride, masculinity, secular agency, modernity, or whiteness. Acolytes of the Angel decline to see power in that way. The solution the narrator tries first, of believing nothing, does not have this advantage. As long as the narrator attempts to keep himself uncontaminated by credulity, he is buying into a system where being duped is a wound. In "The Angel of the Odd," what injures the narrator is not credulity but parsimonious belief. As insulted gods often do, the Angel scourges the blaspheming narrator, subjecting him to the trials of Barnum. Through a series of odd accidents of just the kind he had refused to believe in, the narrator loses his house, his wife, his hair, his pants, and his footing. Before long he is in free fall after tumbling off a cliff. He grabs the guide rope of a passing balloon—piloted by none other than the Angel. In exchange for saving him, the Angel demands a catechism: "Und you pelief, ten . . . at te last? You pelief, ten, in te possibility of te odd?" (*CW*, 3:1109). The narrator assents, but, because of a technicality, the Angel drops him anyway—whereupon he falls through his own chimney and wakes up from the dream sequence. In its play on the story of the god smiting the unbeliever, "The Angel of the Odd" offers a thesis about antebellum modernity. Doubt of newspaper hoaxes is only a special case of a general, and overticklish, modern rejection of belief. Sure that they are thereby escaping humiliation, moderns identify something called "credulity": they humble others by accusing them of it and puff themselves up by avoiding it. But in "The Angel of the Odd," the path out of humiliation is the opposite. If the skeptic wants to avoid being "a bigger fool than the goose," then he will adopt the Angel's credo: "I believe everything printed."

To suspend, or at any rate hopelessly to confound, the demand to disbelieve was one of the most sustained projects of Poe's career, and so he is a better guide than Coleridge in these waters. Meredith McGill and Jonathan Elmer have reoriented our study of Poe in recent years around the body of his periodical publishing, rather than around the body (ailing, drunken, Byronic, and gutter-bound) of the author himself.[93] Both in their individual ways give us an author whose statements tend to dismantle themselves

---

93. Meredith McGill, *American Literature and the Culture of Reprinting, 1834–1853* (Philadelphia: University of Pennsylvania Press, 2003); Jonathan Elmer, *Reading at the Social*

even as they are made. McGill's Poe is an author who uses and relates to the reprintings of his work; Elmer's is one who speaks to a desire for an insincere and deceptive, not an authentic, literary voice. (In Elmer's terms, Poe responds to the "readerly and cultural desire which *resists* having to believe rather than merely entertain its ideas.")[94] Both critics bring into relief Poe's relation to an antebellum print culture that routinely exposed its readers to hoaxes and lies.[95] They show us that Poe's hoaxing need not be seen as having the humiliation of the reader as its end goal; it need not be seen, as Elmer puts it, in the light of a "character flaw."[96] Poe permits us neither the fantasy of his forthright authorship nor of our shrewd readership.

I read Poe's hoaxing as a means of calling for a hiatus in disbelief's prestige. Rather than using fiction to inoculate his readers against credulity, Poe used it to infect them permanently with it. He asked them to consider how they were so sure credulity was a bad thing or an exceptional thing. No great respecter of the difference between fraud and fiction, Poe hoaxed, in "The Balloon Hoax" (1844) and in two stories about mesmerizing someone at the point of death: "The Facts in the Case of M. Valdemar" (1845) and the "Mesmeric Revelation" (1844).[97] As Mabbott quips with respect to those who believed Poe's "Mesmeric Revelation" was a true account, "the credulous were many" (*CW*, 3:1026). Poe also theorized about hoaxing, in "Raising the Wind; or, Diddling Considered as One of the Exact Sciences" (1843). And he advocated belief, humorously, in "The Angel of the Odd." Fooling people, though a gratifying side effect, was not the ultimate goal of all this activity. The goal instead was to blur the lines between fiction and reality: to create precisely the effect that Coleridge wanted to rule out, of the reader being actually deluded by fiction.[98] Poe's occasional hoaxing limited the degree to which readers could use his works to indulge in imaginative

---

Limit: Affect, Mass Culture, and Edgar Allan Poe (Stanford, CA: Stanford University Press, 1995).

94. Elmer, *Reading at the Social Limit*, 175.

95. McGill, *American Literature and the Culture of Reprinting*, 169-70; Elmer, *Reading at the Social Limit*, 174–223; see also Cohen, *Fabrication of American Literature*, 56–64.

96. Elmer, *Reading at the Social Limit*, 174.

97. On Poe's hoaxes, see John Tresch, "'The Potent Magic of Verisimilitude': Edgar Allan Poe within the Mechanical Age," *British Journal of the History of Science* 30, no. 3 (1997): 275–90; Stefan Andriopoulos, *Ghostly Apparitions: German Idealism, the Gothic Novel, and Optical Media* (New York: Zone Books, 2013), 128–37; and Elmer, *Reading at the Social Limit*, 174–223.

98. Coleridge, *Lectures 1808–1819 on Literature*, 2:265.

play that left their secular sense of dignity intact. Genre bending mitigated what for him was a liability of imaginative literature, not its saving grace: its tendency to be recognizable as fiction.

Unlike Poe's other two mesmerism stories, "A Tale of the Ragged Mountains" was never taken for a true account; the generic marker of its title, "Tale," clearly points the reader toward fiction. But its subject is the suspension of the demand to disbelieve, and Poe turned to traveling somnambulism to imagine this possibility. The "Tale" depicts a scene of storytelling in which fiction, delusion, and reality cannot be distinguished from one another. The "Tale" recounts the relationship of a mesmerist, Doctor Templeton, and his patient, Bedlo, between whom "there had grown up, little by little, a very distinct and strongly marked *rapport*, or magnetic relation" (*CW*, 3:941). Bedlo proves to be a traveling somnambulist, and one whose relation to his mesmerist is a lot like Brackett's own: he is as much the teller as the auditor of transformative stories. As with Stone and Brackett, Bedlo and Templeton each tell a story that becomes real for the other, sharing the positions of author and credulous reader. Stone's *Letter* was widely distributed and well known, so there would be nothing surprising in Poe's having read it. As a follower of New York literary scenes, Poe could have heard something about the *Commercial* editor's surprising "conversion" to animal magnetism through any number of sources. He certainly knew about Stone's *Letter* by 1846, when he referred to Stone in his review of Osborn's *Vision of Rubeta* in the "Literati of New York."[99]

In Poe's "Tale," Templeton's act of writing his memoirs in his study triggers his somnambulist, Bedlo, to experience the same events. The dynamic resembles the one Stone expected to create with Brackett: he would tell a story of a journey to New York, and she would experience that story via spiritual travel. The "Tale" uses traveling somnambulism to invert the Coleridgean idea that fiction, like a dream, stands apart from reality, making no call on our judgment one way or the other. Dreams in the "Tale" become real, as do stories. Mesmerism's attractiveness to Poe lay partly in its tendency to treat dreams as a source of real knowledge. The very term *somnambulist* expressed this apparent paradox: like a sleepwalker, the magnetic somnambulist both dreamed and lived out a real experience. Templeton, a former British colonial officer in India, recalls the events of the Cheyte Sing rebellion against

99. Edgar Allan Poe, "The Literati of New York, No. II," *Godey's Lady's Book* 32 (June 1846): 271–72. On Poe's other sources on mesmerism, see Sidney E. Lind, "Poe and Mesmerism," *PMLA* 62, no. 4 (1947):1085–94.

Warren Hastings's administration in 1780, in which his friend Oldeb was killed (*CW*, 3:949).[100] In the story's present, 1827 Charlottesville, Virginia, Bedlo lives through the story as Templeton writes it down—though neither he nor Templeton at first realizes what is happening or even that they are in magnetic rapport. Bedlo takes a somnambulistic voyage to Benares in 1780, occupies Oldeb's body, and feels what Oldeb sees and feels. When Oldeb dies, he returns in spirit to his Charlottesville coordinates, where he recounts what has happened to his mesmerist and to the narrator.

Bedlo's account is the shadow of a shadow: a retelling of his reexperiencing of Templeton's remembering of Oldeb's experience. Yet Poe will not have it dismissed as a dream: during his somnambulistic voyage, Bedlo performs "a series of tests," as he puts it, to wake himself: pinching his arms, calling aloud, and splashing water on his face. None of the "tests" manages to wake him (*CW*, 3:944, 46). He implausibly walks out of the Charlottesville woods into a teeming Eastern bazaar; but "all was rigorously self-consistent," and so this cannot be a dream, either, as his mesmerist Templeton confirms (*CW*, 3:946). Not only are Bedlo's somnambulistic experiences real, but his recounting of them has narrative priority in Poe's "Tale." Oldeb's story is never directly narrated; it mainly appears in Bedlo's retelling. Templeton's memoir, too, makes up only a small part of the story and follows Bedlo's account. Thus the primary moment of storytelling belongs here to the somnambulist, not the mesmerist.

Bedlo's story also has an efficaciousness to match Templeton's. Templeton is so moved by Bedlo's narration that it engenders actual experiences for him, just as his memoir had done for Bedlo. A few days after Bedlo tells Templeton about his own death in India as Oldeb, Templeton fulfills the story in Charlottesville by accidentally killing his patient. In the rebellion in India, Oldeb had been killed by one of the "remarkable" arrows of the "Bengalee," which were "made to imitate the body of a creeping serpent, and were long and black, with a poisoned barb" (*CW*, 3:947, 949). Templeton kills Bedlo by accidentally introducing a poisonous leech among the medicinal ones he is using to bleed his patient. The "poisonous sangsue," reports the local paper, "may always be distinguished from the medicinal leech by its blackness, and

100. On the story's colonial context, see Mukhtar Isani, "Some Sources for Poe's 'Tale of the Ragged Mountains,'" *Poe Studies* 5, no. 2 (1972): 38–40; Christopher Rollason, "Poe's 'A Tale of the Ragged Mountains,' Macaulay and Warren Hastings: From Orientalism to Globalisation?" in *India in the World*, ed. Cristina Gámez-Fernández and Antonia Navarro-Tejero (Newcastle upon Tyne, UK: Cambridge Scholars, 2011), 109–20.

especially by its writing or vermicular motions, which very nearly resemble those of a snake" (*CW*, 3:950). With the poisonous leech, Templeton acts out the ending of the story Bedlo has told him—originally his own story but now subsisting in the middle voice between them.

We might think of the "Tale" as a palindromic fiction: one in which authors read, and readers write, without any preference for moving in one direction or the other between the two. The names of the two doubled characters, Oldeb and Bedlo, form a palindrome: OLDEBEDLO (Fig. 6). Their names run indifferently backward and forward, each at once the original to and the copy of the other. The whole "Tale" also has a palindromic structure. If we place its events along a time line, they run from Oldeb to Bedlo, just as I have placed the names in the diagram: from Oldeb's death, to Templeton's retelling, to Bedlo's somnambulistic reexperiencing, to Bedlo's oral retelling, and finally to Bedlo's death. But the point about a palindrome is that you can read it in whatever direction you want, backwards or forwards. Poe's "Tale" starts in the middle, roughly at the B, with Bedlo's retelling. Then it runs back and forth indifferently: back to Bedlo's somnambulistic voyage, forward through the voyage itself, back to Templeton's memoir and Oldeb's historical death, forward to the newspaper article that will announce Bedlo's demise.

As Poe's story zigzags along time's arrow, it upsets more than the forward direction of history. It upsets the hierarchy of original event and derivative tale; of mesmerist's thought and somnambulist's automatic repetition. To look at the narrative structure of the "Tale," one would think there was no reason to have a preference for moving from event to tale, rather than from tale to event. Nor is there any decay of vividness as you move from event to derivative experience. If anything, the decay moves in the opposite direction: Bedlo's somnambulistic voyage and his retelling of it are the most vivid and the most complete. The death of Oldeb and the memoir, arguably the precipitating events, are briefer and sketchier. So too is the dry newspaper account of Bedlo's "real" death in Charlottesville. The derivative experience is the one Poe prioritizes. Adam Frank has recognized Poe's mesmeric tales as meditations on, or fantasies of, authorial influence: "the mesmeric method," Frank writes, "may have more to do with Poe's intense desire for successful written material than with anything else."[101] Frank sees mesmeric authorship as a fantasy of control, so that "a mesmeric scene of writing" combines with "manipulative control over a male body."[102] But the

---

101. Adam Frank, "Valdemar's Tongue, Poe's Telegraphy," *ELH* 72, no. 3 (2005): 645.
102. Ibid., 647.

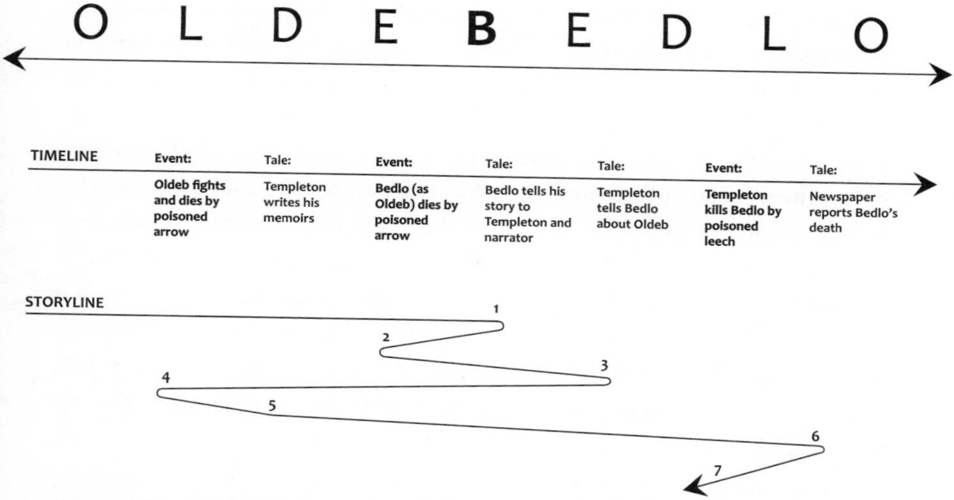

$$\text{O} \quad \text{L} \quad \text{D} \quad \text{E} \quad \textbf{B} \quad \text{E} \quad \text{D} \quad \text{L} \quad \text{O}$$

TIMELINE

Event:	Tale:	Event:	Tale:	Tale:	Event:	Tale:
Oldeb fights and dies by poisoned arrow	Templeton writes his memoirs	Bedlo (as Oldeb) dies by poisoned arrow	Bedlo tells his story to Templeton and narrator	Templeton tells Bedlo about Oldeb	Templeton kills Bedlo by poisoned leech	Newspaper reports Bedlo's death

STORYLINE

1
2
3
4
5
6
7

Fig. 6. Diagram of Edgar Allan Poe's "A Tale of the Ragged Mountains" (1844). Graphic design by Amelia Saul.

"Tale" does not involve a writer monopolizing authorship; instead, it is the somnambulist-reader, Bedlo, whose account gets top billing. And as McGill reminds us, manipulation is not, in any case, a magisterial form of authority. "Poe's association of authorial control with duplicity defines authorship not as origination but as manipulation," she writes, "a practice defined by interruption, inconsistency, and uncertainty, not mastery."[103] Poe's manipulative designs leave room for—even ensure, McGill shows—second, third, and fourth acts in which reprintings of Poe's work speak back to him.

The palindromic form of the "Tale" similarly demotes and distributes authorship. It demotes authorship, in that the storyteller's purchase on reality is no higher and no more immediate than the auditor's. And it distributes authorship, in that both the mesmerist and the somnambulist wind up as tale-tellers. So it is fitting that the central figure for this demotion and distribution, the palindromic name, does not have an author, either. Though I have spelled the name "Bedlo" throughout, Poe spells it "Bedloe" until the very end, when a newspaper obituary for Bedlo introduces the palindromic spelling. The narrator remarks to the paper's editor: "I presume . . . you have authority for this spelling." "Authority?—no," replies the editor; "it is a mere typographical error" (*CW*, 3:950). The palindrome structuring the whole

103. McGill, *American Literature and the Culture of Reprinting*, 186.

"Tale" turns out to be the chance outgrowth of a compositor's inattentiveness; a collaboration between a faltering hand and a prolific machine. One might readily think, here, of McGill's "unauthorized Poe"[104]—or of a figure resonant with her literary-market-surfing author, the Latourian actor. "Really?" Latour says to the idea of the creator as a sole and sovereign agent. "Is an engineer master of his machine? Was Pasteur master of his lactic acid? Is a programmer master of his program, a creator, of his creation, an author, of his text? No one who has ever truly acted could utter such impieties."[105] The Latourian actor is also acted upon and reacts with indifference to the suggestion that this position is an ignominious one. As though to dispatch once and for all the heroic model of authorial agency, Poe's story ends with an unmastered press producing an unmastered text—a typographical error that "slightly outstrip[s]" both reader and author.[106]

The palindromic operation of stories in Poe's "Tale" is not instructing us to believe per se but to relinquish our sense that disbelieving stories is a more prestigious position than believing them. We are to credit what is printed, including when the text is the product of error: not because it is true but because we thereby avoid laying claim to the position of the powerful and proud skeptic. Rather than reassure his readers that their sovereignty would be secure, Poe did his best to deprive them of it. He imagined a new regulative ideal for fiction—an ideal, that is to say, that fiction mostly could not meet, but that it could strive toward. Fiction would be as poorly distinguished from delusion as possible. Readers would believe what was printed. They would court the humiliation of being hoaxed in order to take away credulity's power to wound them. In the end, what would be suspended was not disbelief but rather disbelief's prestige.

"THE GALLING CHAINS OF DEPENDENCE"

Poe used mesmerism to question our intolerance of mutual deception, jointly constructed stories, and unlocatable truths. Credulity as practiced by

---

104. Ibid., 141.

105. Latour, *Factish Gods*, 64; *Dieux faitiches*, 132. McGill notes that we seem to be "uncomfortable" with "the fact of an author's subjection to market forces": McGill, *American Literature and the Culture of Reprinting*, 186.

106. Latour, *Factish Gods*, 62; *Dieux faitiches*, 130.

Stone and Brackett presented analogous challenges. In the mesmeric rapport, the two were relatively indifferent to truth and relatively willing to risk being practiced on, each by the other, to claim the vision that might be gained thereby. They leaned flamboyantly into belief while also retaining some sense that the pitch they had given themselves was a performance. The journey Stone describes in his *Letter* differs from imaginative literature in precisely the ways Poe pushed fiction to differ from itself: there is no strict boundary between dream and reality, since the journey to New York starts out as a fiction in Stone's mind but becomes a reality. And there is a distribution of the roles of author and reader, with both Brackett and Stone improvising and responding to each other's improvisations.

But economic realities were not suspended, and there were substantial obstacles to a full realization of the coauthorship that Stone's text evidences at many points. One of the two authors in this rapport had a printing press at his command; the other did not. Stone was a newspaper editor, while Brackett never published about her mesmerism experiences—and if she wrote about them, the manuscripts do not survive (though letters from her later life do, among the papers conserved by the Perkins School for the Blind Archives). Here is a small but telling example of the evidentiary problems we face in reconstructing Brackett's experience of her mesmeric fame. We know that Brackett learned of Stone's vindication of her gifts in early September, when she received the September 4 issue of the *Commercial Advertiser* in which Stone announced his change of heart.[107] Brackett called on fellow somnambulist Miss Parker to discuss the article.[108] What did the two of them think of it? What might Brackett and Parker have said? We have no idea. The only reason we know the two women met at all is that Durant, Brackett's worst enemy, was trying to prove collusion between them. His account: Brackett "was indolent, and preferred idleness to work; the only way to accomplish her desires, was to feign disability to labor," so she "feigned blind."[109] Brackett and Parker were "great cronies," he said; "they come together almost every day, and tell each other what has transpired."[110] His implication is that they were conferring on how to delude the public.

107. "Animal Magnetism," *New York Commercial Advertiser*, September 4, 1837. Durant reports that he saw Brackett discussing the article (*Exposition*, 179), and he was in Providence approximately September 4 to September 7 (*Exposition*, 153, 185).

108. Durant, *Exposition*, 179.

109. Ibid., 163.

110. Ibid., 174n.

The evidence is, of course, open to a simpler interpretation: Miss Parker was Brackett's friend. Durant's vitriol is extreme, but his lack of interest in Brackett's perspective is typical even of many of her well-wishers. Each person who wrote about Brackett had his or her own, often hostile, agenda; even when friendly, the agenda seldom included recording Brackett's views.

There was no mysterious compositor who had his or her way with Stone's *Letter*, dropping the *E*—as the newspaper of Poe's "Tale" did with Bedlo(e)'s name in his obituary—and reversing the word, thus inventing a palindromic Nots who would negate and entangle each of Ston(e)'s acts: STONOTS, like OLDEBEDLO. Or was Brackett, in a certain sense, that reversed author? In this final section I want to read this imagined and plural figure on the other side of Stone's *Letter*: Brackett, in a way, but not exactly the historical Brackett, or not with the degree of certainty we can call Stone Stone. (And any writer's identity with himself or herself is already a wobbly proposition.) I attempt to think from some of the positions the historical Brackett may have occupied, based on some of the things she wrote or reportedly said. Between the many accounts given of experiments with Brackett in Hartshorn's appendix to Deleuze, and the manuscripts of hers that the Perkins Archives preserved from the period after her enrollment there in 1838—including letters Brackett wrote to director Samuel G. Howe about her struggles in the decade after she left the school in 1844—one can construct a partial and speculative perspective.[111] There is material enough to describe the context in which Brackett might have evaluated somnambulism's pleasures, privileges, and costs.

111. PS, Incoming and Outgoing Correspondence, 1828–1932. According to PS, Pupil Register no. 2, Brackett left Perkins in June 1844. Brackett's departure can also be dated to summer 1844 based on her disappearance from her friend Laura Bridgman's journal at that time. Bridgman records on June 15, 1844, that Brackett had gone to stay two months at Providence: PS, Laura Bridgman journal, June 6–July 17, 1844. Brackett is also included on lists of beneficiaries of the school's Trustees until April 1, 1844, as reported quarterly by Samuel Gridley Howe (SGH) to the Massachusetts Secretary of State. Beneficiary lists cease to be recorded after this point: PS, Register of Correspondence Sent, 1842–1844 (repurposed ledger book). Bridgman's journal suggests that Brackett may have returned to live in Boston, however, until March or April 1847, since Bridgman notes in July 1849 that she had not seen Brackett for two years and three months: PS, Laura Bridgman journal, July 23, 1849. Between 1844, when Bridgman's entries on Brackett cease, and May 16, 1847, when SGH and Brackett began to correspond, I have been able to learn little about her life. Howe's letter of May 16 does not survive but is referenced in PS, Incoming Correspondence, 1846–1847, Loraina Brackett (LB) to SGH, Southbridge, MA, July 1, 1847.

Although the record of her journey to New York with Stone is what gives us the clearest sense of Brackett's collaborative narration with her interlocutors, her more quotidian abilities make it clearest what magnetism might have offered her. Some of her "supernatural" powers seem to amount mainly to access to simple enjoyments. Her clairvoyance freed her from others' expectations that blindness would constrain her. In the summer of 1837, Brackett may have spent as much as half her time in the magnetic state, to some extent by her own choice. She was not always willing to be magnetized when asked, and occasionally she found her visitors tedious and invasive. "I don't like to be looked at in this way by strangers," she protested in Stone's hearing (*L*, 16). But on the other hand, she also sometimes chose to stay in the magnetic state when demonstrations were over. Jesse Metcalf, with whose family Brackett lived for a time, told Hartshorn that Brackett was magnetized every day at his house, and that "she would sometimes remain in the magnetized state ten or twelve hours, during which she would walk about the house as well as any other person; but when she was awake, she would have to grope about, and feel her way" (*PIA*, 35). According to Metcalf, while magnetized, she could often be found "looking at objects with great pleasure, especially pictures, portraits, &c. This makes her delight in being in that state" (*PIA*, 35). She would also describe what she saw "very accurately" (*PIA*, 35). Depending on one's perspective, magnetism either afforded her the possibility of seeing, or it afforded her an opportunity for an imaginative exercise of taste before a rapt audience. Either way, these were capacities that she and her circle believed she did not have at other times.

While magnetized, Brackett read. On one occasion when she remained magnetized overnight, she read and partly memorized a book that had been published since she had become blind—Hannah More's *Book of Private Devotions* (1836).[112] Reading was reportedly something Brackett keenly missed. Boredom and confinement were especially galling to her by temperament: "the natural activity of her mind makes it difficult for her to sit idle," said Hartshorn. The ability to read, Hartshorn thought, was probably "one cause of her being so fond of remaining magnetized" (*PIA*, 87). As with the confident excursions around Providence that such observers as Stone, Frothingham, and Kent concluded were "sight," her "reading" may or may not have been reading with the eyes. It may be that whatever sensory link with printed text Brackett had remaining to her, magnetism allowed her to capitalize on it.

---

112. *PIA*, 87; Hannah More, *The Book of Private Devotion: A Series of Prayers and Meditations, with an Introductory Essay on Prayer* (New York: Leavitt, Lord, 1836).

There are a few imaginable avenues of sensory contact where reading is concerned. One of the most interesting is the possibility that even
before going to Perkins, Brackett had been exposed to some of the new
techniques for tactile reading that Howe was developing there. Howe had
his own printing press and was producing books in what would come to be
called Boston line type, an embossed type using angular versions of Latin
characters (Fig. 7).[113] Unlike Braille, which has its own character set, Boston
line type uses the Latin alphabet. A literate and formerly sighted person like
Brackett could have taught herself to read it. She may even have been taught
to do so by a Perkins pupil. One of Howe's first students, Lydia Davis, lived
in Brackett's hometown of Dudley. Davis had enrolled at Perkins in 1833, a
year after the school opened.[114] By 1837 she was preparing to be a teacher
there herself.[115] Home on vacation in 1837, Davis wrote to Howe on May 23
that she had been teaching his methods to a woman in Dudley whose "facil-
ities of communicating with the world both by sight & voice, are cut-off," as
Howe put it in his reply to Davis.[116] This description fits Brackett, who had
lost her voice temporarily and her sight permanently in her accident, and
Brackett was in Dudley until she left for Providence in mid-May. If Brackett
was Davis's pupil, then she already knew about reading by touch by the time
she arrived in Providence. Even if she was not Davis's pupil, she may still
have known about the techniques she would be taught at Howe's school, her
ultimate destination. More's *Private Devotions* was not available in Boston
line type, or in any tactile-type format as far as I have been able to determine. But knowledge of Boston line type could have suggested to Brackett the experiment of tactile reading. Brackett might have been able to feel
the slight embossing left on the reverse side of a paper by ordinary printing.[117] Or she may have reconstructed the text by other means, including

113. Howe, *Annual Report* 2 (1835), 13–15; Elisabeth Gitter, *The Imprisoned Guest: Samuel
Howe and Laura Bridgman, the Original Deaf-Blind Girl* (New York: Farrar, Straus, & Giroux, 2001), 39; Koestler, *Unseen Minority*, 95, 399.

114. PS, Perkins Institutional Records, Enrollment and Biographies, 1832–1839.

115. PS, Register of Correspondence Sent, April 6, 1841–June 5, 1845, SGH to Lydia Davis,
April 18, 1843. See also PS, Register of Correspondence Sent, September 26, 1836-December 26,
1838, SGH to Lydia Davis, Dudley, MA, June 9, 1837.

116. PS, Register of Correspondence Sent, September 26, 1836–December 26, 1838, SGH
to Lydia Davis, Dudley, MA, June 9, 1837. Howe refers to a letter from Davis, May 23, 1837;
the letter is not extant.

117. I am indebted to Jennifer Arnott, librarian at the Perkins School for the Blind Archives, for this suggestion. See also Koestler, *Unseen Minority*, 397–98, on the accidental

Fig. 7. Sample of Boston line type. Title page of Samuel G. Howe's edition of Lindley Murray, *Murray's Grammar of the English Language, Altered and Abridged* ([Boston]: Printed at the New England Institution for the Education of the Blind, 1835). Courtesy of Houghton Library, Harvard University, Typ 899 35.57.

hearing it read aloud or distinguishing shapes. There was always debate about her degree of blindness, though the school register at the time of her admission describes it as "Total."[118]

But the degrees of capacity for movement and reading that Brackett showed need not be viewed as Brackett's attackers and defenders alike generally did: under the rubric of the genuine as opposed to the feigned. Brackett's blindness may have been something she performed in concert with and in negotiation with others, not unlike her animal-magnetic gifts. Tobin Siebers describes a spectrum of possible performances, from passing, or concealing a disability, to what he calls "the masquerade": an exaggerated performance of disability used for a variety of purposes, including managing the reactions and behavior of those around one.[119] Siebers, who had postpolio syndrome, has recounted how he was challenged by a gate attendant when he boarded an airplane early, "so that I [did] not have to navigate crowded aisles on wobbly legs." After that experience, he writes, "I . . . adopted the habit of exaggerating my limp whenever I board planes."[120] Those around Brackett apparently expected her presentation of her blindness to be uniform. They did not, however, expect that her behavior when magnetized and her behavior when awake would be continuous with each other. So animal magnetism may have allowed her more freedom to range between the various possibilities of playing up a disability (masquerade) and playing one down (passing). Perhaps magnetism let Brackett pass as sighted, temporarily. Or, an even more interesting possibility, perhaps magnetism let her give up an onerous masquerade of blindness that she had to keep up in her ordinary life if she was to secure the help she needed from those around her. Maybe she could always move confidently, but outside of animal magnetism, the cost of doing so was losing the recognition of her disability on which she depended. In that case, the animal-magnetic trance—which we might assume was the most theatrical part of her day—may have been the least so.

It is reported, at any rate, that Brackett routinely lived in the magnetic trance for the benefit of no audience other than herself, as when she

---

discovery (in late eighteenth-century France) by Valentin Haüy and François Lesueur that Lesueur, who was blind, could discern letters by touch on the reverse side of printed pages.

118. PS, Pupil Register no. 2.

119. Tobin Siebers, *Disability Theory* (Ann Arbor: University of Michigan Press, 2008), 96–119.

120. Ibid., 96.

returned nocturnally to places she had visited during the day's experiments. Benjamin Kent of Roxbury had taken her on an imaginative journey to his home, where she was delighted by his private "Museum," a collection of natural history curios that contained some four thousand specimens by the time Brackett saw it.[121] She was so taken with the collection, in fact, that she made a private visit after her public one was complete, asking to be magnetized overnight, then imagining herself back to his house while he was sleeping. There she strolled about like a ghost of refined tastes, admiring his "shells" and "Chinese rice paper flowers" at her leisure.[122] Whether you understand her journey in imagination as a transportation of the soul or as an artistic transport, it is not hard to see why such a state might have appealed to a woman of active mind otherwise thought to be incapable of moving about on her own, exercising her aesthetic perceptions, or acquiring new knowledge from books. The indifference to truth that Brackett and Stone showed when they saw Mr. Ray's lions together was the same indifference that permitted Brackett to evade the alleged truth about blindness. Magnetism gave Brackett an audience expecting she might be able to fly to New York, rather than one convinced she could not find her way around a parlor. She lived for a time in a wider world because they—and she—found a way to be open to these possibilities. That openness was what went under the name "credulity." The magnetic state, then, may have done Brackett a fairly simple good, in spite of the irritations to which it exposed her in the way of poking and prodding visitors. It may have given her things to do with her mind: reading, visiting, imagining, admiring. If Brackett did not "ride, swim, row, skate, &c," like the blind boy of Howe's imagination, she did take steamboats and balloons; she strolled and flew.

As for the trade-offs—magnetism's ills—Brackett was exposed to them already, with or without magnetism. From the perspective of a powerful *Commercial Advertiser* editor, dependence on others and belief in their false accounts might have seemed like exceptional humiliations that could be avoided through good sense. But whether Brackett liked those experiences or not, they were pervasive occurrences in her life. Being duped or clearheaded; being a dependent or seizing unexpected power; these seem

---

121. BK to TH, Roxbury, MA, November 27, 1837, *PIA*, 146. On Kent's museum, see Justin Winsor, *History of the Town of Duxbury, Massachusetts: With Genealogical Registers* (Boston: Crosby & Nichols, 1849), 53n. Winsor suggests that Kent's cabinet had four thousand specimens by 1833, when he resigned his ministry in Duxbury (see 53n, 210).

122. BK to TH, Roxbury, MA, November 27, 1837, *PIA*, 141, 145–46.

like the concerns of a wishful thinker when placed beside the picture that emerges from her papers in the Perkins Archives. Brackett's choices were always among a range of possible dependencies. Would she be a traveling clairvoyant or a state beneficiary at Perkins (then the New-England Institution for the Blind) in 1837? Would she stay at Perkins, or would she return to Providence as a guest of her friends the Metcalfs (1841)?[123] Would she live by sewing purses and other fine goods or by charity (1848)?[124] Would she go—literally—to the poorhouse, or would she marry her doctor, Samuel Carpenter (1849)?[125] Never, in any of the recorded turning points in Brackett's adult life, was autonomy on the table. It makes little sense to measure her position as a mesmeric clairvoyant against that possibility, which might have seemed to her even more incredible than spiritual travel. Instead, the question is to what extent these dependent positions gave Brackett room for invention and enjoyment.

David A. Gerber has written eloquently of the problems involved in making a moral evaluation of nineteenth-century performances by people with disabilities.[126] Gerber's subject is the freak show: the Barnumesque display of racialized and extraordinary bodies. Brackett shared with freaks the possibility of making a life by performing disability; still, freak shows differed from Brackett's performances in important ways. The antebellum freak show was highly public, whereas Brackett's séances were semiprivate, always taking place in the homes of people known to her. And the freak show involved, as Elizabeth Grosz puts it, "the most severe and gross physical disorders," rather than more common or more assimilable disabilities.[127] Gerber raises the problem of consent with respect to the freak show.

123. PS, Register of Correspondence Sent, April 6, 1841–June 5, 1845, SGH to Miss Metcalf, Providence, RI, May 18, 1841; SGH to Mr. Bartlet [Brackett], Dudley, MA, May 20, 1841; SGH to LB, Dudley, MA, May 20, 1841.

124. PS, Incoming Correspondence, 1848–1849, LB to SGH, Dudley, MA, January 1, 1848.

125. PS, Incoming Correspondence, 1848–1849, LB to SGH, Wilkersons, CT, December 31, 1848. The date of the letter as written appears to be 1848, but it has been amended by an early archivist to 1849, and the letter is filed under 1849 in the bound volume of correspondence. Given that Brackett was married to Samuel Carpenter in March 1849 (see Quinn, "Credibility," 279) and that she is not yet married to Samuel Carpenter at the time of writing, 1848 is likely the correct date.

126. David A. Gerber, "The 'Careers' of People Exhibited in Freak Shows: The Problem of Volition and Valorization," in *Freakery: Cultural Spectacles of the Extraordinary Body*, ed. Rosemarie Garland Thomson (New York: New York University Press, 1996), 38–54.

127. Elizabeth Grosz, "Intolerable Ambiguity: Freaks as/at the Limit," in Thomson, *Freakery*, 55.

If a performer claims to consent, "how are we to evaluate the quality of that consent—especially in light of the extent to which people with physical anomalies have experienced broad and abiding social oppression and marginalization?" And does consent bear on our own "judgment about the morality of such a display?"[128] To some extent we can infer that Brackett chose her role as a mesmeric performer, though it was not—as what choice is?—from among an unlimited set of options. Still, for Gerber, "beyond the question, 'Is this choice voluntary?' or the surmise, 'This choice is so bad, it could not be voluntary,' there are situations where we might say, 'This choice is so bad, I don't care if it is voluntary.' "[129]

If I enter into the world Gerber's resonant questions sketch for me, there are many pitfalls: in fact, it begins to seem that Brackett must be either an agent or a victim; either a puppet or someone cynically pulling the strings. Before Gerber will agree that there has been "consent," he seeks individual autonomy and an ability to resist.[130] One could look for resistance of this kind in Brackett's performances, but to do so would be to set aside the other lesson she has to teach: that narrowly defined resistance may be more a regulative ideal than a real possibility. Neither her performances with Stone nor her other negotiations of dependency fit neatly into the agent-or-victim paradigm. Viewed through the lens of her life, a white-knuckled grasp on truth and independence seems like the posture of a paranoid visionary—the act of an Osborn, perhaps, or a Reese.[131] As Eva Kittay has written, "the encounter with dependency is . . . rarely welcome to those fed an ideological diet of freedom, self-sufficiency, *and* equality."[132] That rich diet was a luxury that Brackett for the most part could not afford. Skeptics were scandalized at the idea of being taken in. But Brackett had to *hope* to be taken in: into the self-descriptions and the houses of those who could shelter her. She had to collaborate with the narratives her benefactors told about themselves. She had to adapt to the terms they set for her and to the conditions of their homes. She could not privilege truth above all else, and even if she prized independence, it was never in her grasp. Considering animal magnetism from within the limitations she faced is one way to answer

---

128. Gerber, "Problem of Volition," 38.

129. Ibid., 40.

130. Ibid. On resistance, see Asad, *Formations of the Secular*, 70–73.

131. Cf. Osborn, *Vision of Rubeta*, 178n; Reese, *Humbugs of New-York*.

132. Eva Feder Kittay, *Love's Labor: Essays on Women, Equality, and Dependency* (New York: Routledge, 1999), 5.

Kittay's provocation: "Rather than joining the able on a quixotic quest for a nonexistent independence, we might take the occasion of thinking about disability to suggest better ways to manage depedency."[133] Topically, Brackett's post-1838 letters do not deal with animal magnetism. But they offer the perspective of someone whom hard experience had taught to think in terms of the choice between dependencies, not the absolute freedom from them. That may be the appropriate perspective from which to approach Brackett's animal-magnetic experience.

In July 1838, Brackett arrived at the New-England Institution for the Blind (Perkins Institution) and became pupil number 105 in its student register.[134] According to Capron, she felt driven out of Providence by skeptical attacks.[135] Durant's *Exposition* in particular had created a sensation there; some booksellers refused to carry it, and there were rumors that someone—perhaps Brackett herself—was planning to sue Durant for libel.[136] In the relative calm of the school, Brackett's education included half a day of needlework but also half a day of music and liberal education, including arithmetic, grammar, and philosophy.[137] Brackett would have learned to read Boston line type now if Lydia Davis had not already taught her. Books, maps, and images in tactile type would have been available to her in quantities that were uncommon anywhere in the world.[138] That meant a great deal; much later, after leaving the school, she would write to ask Howe for an embossed-type copy of the "*Cyclopedia Natural Histor[y]*" and a devotional guide. "I left all my books in Providence—and have had no opportunity to send for them—I miss them more than [I can say] for I . . . have not any friends to come in and read to me," she told Howe.[139]

133. Eva Feder Kittay, "Dependency," in *Keywords for Disability Studies*, ed. Rachel Adams, Benjamin Reiss, and David Serlin (New York: New York University Press, 2015), 54–58, quotation at 57.

134. PS, Pupil Register no. 2.

135. GC to TH, Providence, RI, August 1, 1843, in Hartshorn, "New Appendix" to *Practical Instruction* (1843), 369–70.

136. Clippings from the New York *Sun*, October 30 and November 6, 1837, Durant Biographical File.

137. PS, Perkins Institutional Records, School Journal, General Abstracts, June and July 1839.

138. Howe, *Annual Report* 2 (1835), 14; Freeberg, *Laura Bridgman*, 16–17, 129; Gitter, *Imprisoned Guest*, 39; Trent, *Manliest Man*, 98–99.

139. PS, Incoming Correspondence, 1846–1847, LB to SGH, Southbridge, MA, July 1, 1847. See also Howe, *Annual Report* 13 (1845), 18.

The school's deportment chart from 1839 records Brackett's behavior as "Correct Attentive Industrious," a description dittoed down the line for five female pupils. She was "Very exemplary; faithful and well behaved."[140] That praise is an indirect mark of what it cost Brackett to be at the Perkins Institution. Her tuition was free, but she had to stay in the school's good graces, and in Howe's. After spending a short time as a Massachusetts state beneficiary, Brackett became a beneficiary of the school's trustees—meaning that her tuition was paid at Howe's discretion.[141] He was capable of sending away pupils who disappointed him. Sullivan Anthony was the first black pupil at the Perkins Institution, admitted after an initial refusal on Howe's part. After a time as a trustees' beneficiary at the school, Anthony went back to his sponsors in Providence with a note warning that he was "very indolent" and "much addicted to the solitary vice."[142] In the year Brackett arrived, star music student Sarah Clough was virtually imprisoned in the school because of what Howe viewed as sexual misbehavior. Clough, a congenitally blind woman, had been secretly planning to marry the congenitally blind Charles Morrill, a former pupil and teacher. Howe was violently opposed because of the likelihood, as he thought, that they would have blind children. He wrote a vitriolic letter to Morrill, telling him that "there can be little difference, morally, between your bringing sightless individuals into the world & taking children of your neighbours & putting their eyes out."[143] This affair took place right around the time Brackett arrived, and Howe was still dealing with its aftermath a year later when Brackett earned the marks "Correct Attentive Industrious" in the school journal.[144] Howe wrote personally to her

140. PS, Perkins Institutional Records, School Journal, General Abstracts, June and August, 1839.

141. Howe had influence over the choice of state beneficiaries as well. As of September 1, 1840, Brackett became a beneficiary of the Perkins trustees. See PS, Register of Correspondence Sent, April 6, 1841–June 5, 1845, SGH to Massachusetts Secretary of State, September 30, 1841; March 31, 1842; April 1, 1843; and SGH to Mr. Bartlet [Brackett], Dudley, MA, May 20, 1841. See also PS, Register of Correspondence Sent, 1842–1844 (repurposed ledger book), SGH to Massachusetts Secretary of State, October 1, 1843; January 1, 1844; and April 1, 1844.

142. PS, Register of Correspondence Sent, April 6, 1841–June 5, 1845, SGH to Mr. Capron, Providence, RI, April 23, 1841. On Sullivan Anthony, see Trent, *Manliest Man*, 105–7.

143. PS, Register of Correspondence Sent, September 26, 1836–December 26, 1838, SGH to Charles Morrill, n.d. [July–August 1838].

144. PS, Register of Correspondence Sent, January 1, 1839–March 31, 1841, SGH to Miss Goto[?], October 12, 1839; *PS*, Perkins Institutional Records, School Journal, General Abstracts, June 1839. On this affair, see Trent, *Manliest Man*, 63.

brother that "Lurena has been as welcome here as she could be in her own father's house . . . her meek resignation to the dispensations of Providence, her truly Christian Spirit, and her amiable and exemplary deportment, endeared her to us all."[145] (Howe used here the birth spelling of Loraina's name, Lurena.) Howe's vehement reaction to Morrill and Clough's attempted marriage gives some context for his mildness to Brackett. Here was the carrot, but Brackett no doubt knew about the stick.

Illness soon prevented Brackett from continuing her studies, though she stayed on at Perkins. Her health was never good, and at some point— possibly in the winter of 1839–1840—she had an accident that left her mobility limited for the rest of her life. From that point forward she was not strong enough to participate in school, and at times she could not walk.[146] Laura Bridgman's diary gives a vivid sense of Brackett's trials. Bridgman came to Howe's school not long before Brackett did, in 1837. Deaf and blind from a young age, Bridgman had nonetheless learned language with the help of Howe and a series of teachers. Bridgman became Howe's celebrity pupil and his advertisement for the school. In the 1840s, crowds came to see her on the Perkins Institution's exhibition days.[147] Though Bridgman was just a child of eight when Brackett arrived, the two became lifelong friends. Perhaps they found common ground in their celebrity. Bridgman's diary frequently mentions her friend "Lurena." The diary of 1841 testifies to the monotony and pain of Brackett's illness and its cure, with cupping and bleeding administered by an employee at the institution:

> [day one:] "harrington did burnt lurenas back much lurena did cry because it did hurt sores"
> [day two:] "harrington did burn but lurena did cry"
> [day three:] "harrington burnt lurenas back to make sores"

145. PS, Register of Correspondence Sent, April 6, 1841–June 5, 1845, SGH to Mr. Bartlet [Brackett], Dudley, MA, May 20, 1841.

146. PS, Perkins Institutional Records, School Journal, General Abstracts, December 1839–March 1840. On the accident, see Quinn, "Credibility," 278–79, though my complete reading of Laura Bridgman's journals did not turn up the undated fragment from c. 1848 that is Quinn's source on this event. The Perkins Archives have been substantially reorganized since Quinn consulted them (conversation with librarian Jennifer Arnott, June 2015), and this fragment may have been recataloged in such a way that Quinn's original citation cannot be traced.

147. On Bridgman's early life and education, see Gitter, *Imprisoned Guest*, 3–6, 45–101; and Freeberg, *Laura Bridgman*, 2, 26–65.

[soon after:] "harrington did cut lurenas back it make water run much harrington did burn lurenas back"[148]

Brackett would endure painful treatments repeatedly for the rest of her life.[149] "I have mad[e] use of Dr J B Smith's Torpedo Electro Magnetic Machine and in some respects I can truly say I have received more benefit from it than from all other remedies combined for the last ten years," Brackett wrote to Howe in 1848, when she had an inflamed spinal column and weakness of the heart, and could not walk.[150] "The last ten years" meant she was comparing it to everything she had tried since being Capron's magnetic patient in Providence. Magnetism had at least the virtue of not being physically painful.

Brackett considered leaving Perkins in 1841 for unknown reasons; she would have gone to live with her friends the Metcalfs in Providence. But Howe convinced her to stay.[151] In 1844 she left for good, and from that point until her marriage in 1849 she faced the virtually impossible task of earning a living.[152] Sewing was the only way she could make money, but she was often incapacitated by illness. She lived precariously, sometimes with family, sometimes with a series of friends who took her in temporarily.[153] She corresponded with Howe throughout this period, telling him in detail about her plight. Howe did not abandon Brackett to her fate after she left Perkins, even though it might have been easier to turn away from struggles that made a mockery of his hopes of blind independence. Over the years, Howe watched the labor market grind his pupils down. By 1843 he was adjusting his expectations. He wrote in the *Annual Report* for that year, "with

148. PS, Laura Bridgman's journal, n.d. [September–November 1841].

149. She was also magnetized by Howe at Perkins until 1842, though there is little information about the nature of these treatments. GC to TH, Providence, RI, August 1, 1843, in Hartshorn, "New Appendix" to *Practical Instruction* (1843), 370; see also Quinn, "Credibility," 278; Freeberg, *Laura Bridgman*, 71–72.

150. PS, Incoming Correspondence, 1848–1849, LB to SGH, Wilkerson's, CT, April 19, 1848.

151. PS, Register of Correspondence Sent, April 6, 1841–June 5, 1845, SGH to Miss Metcalf, Providence, RI, May 18, 1841; SGH to Mr. Bartlet [Brackett,] Dudley, MA, May 20, 1841; SGH to LB, Dudley, MA, May 20, 1841.

152. On the date of departure, see PS, Pupil Register no. 2. On the date of marriage, see Quinn, "Credibility," 279.

153. PS, Incoming Correspondence, 1848–1849, LB to SGH, Wilkerson's, CT, April 19, 1848; December 31, 1848.

an enlightened mind, with a due sense of self respect, and a determination not to be a burden upon others, the blind person will grapple resolutely with the difficulties which . . . must ever oppose his progress to independence. These difficulties, it must be admitted, are numerous and great; more so than we ourselves formerly supposed."[154] Committed to the ideal of self-sufficiency for his students, Howe had to admit that the obstacles they faced were almost insurmountable. They could not all secure the intellectual and musical work—such as being church organists or choirmasters—to which he thought they were best suited.[155] He resigned himself to the necessity that the blind should do manual labor, and he started a small factory where men and a few women worked to make mattresses and cushions.[156] He ran the shop at a loss. He also sold work sent back by pupils who lived at a distance, including Brackett.[157]

Brackett knew better than Howe did how dim her prospects of earning a living really were. But she kept making the attempt. She wrote to him in July 1847 to thank him for selling a dollar's worth of her handmade things: "baskets, pin cusheons, pinballs, needle books, one watch guard, and one tidy." "I have stock for another dozzen baskets but though[t] I had better not make them till I know whether they sell pretty well—do you find ready sale for the tidy?" she asked him. She commented on the problem of competition:

[you say] your wife [Julia Ward Howe] thinks I put my articles very low—I think so too—but there is so much competition in every thing I have ever found it useless for people the blind especially to expect a fair compensation for their labor[.] If you can find any who are willing to give a little more than I have put them at I shall be very thankful[.] If I do not get more I think I must fall considerably short of ear[ning] fifty dollars this year—I do not wish you to ask more than they are really worth because of my being blind and destitute[.] I shall make every effort to

154. Howe, *Annual Report* 11 (1843), 12. See also Trent, *Manliest Man,* 64–65.
155. Freeberg, *Education of Laura Bridgman,* 13; Howe, *Annual Report* 13 (1845), 6.
156. Howe, *Annual Report* 13 (1845), 4, 12-13; *Annual Report* 16 (1848), 59. On Howe's changing views and the establishment of the workshop, see Trent, *Manliest Man,* 63–66.
157. Howe, *Annual Report* 14 (1846), 14–15; *Annual Report* 15 (1847), 16; *Annual Report* 16 (1848), 56-57; PS, Incoming Correspondence, 1846–1847, LB to SGH, Southbridge, MA, July 1, 1847.

earn my own living—if I find I cannot I suppose I shall have to submit to
the galling chains of dependence[.][158]

That closing line—"I suppose I shall have to submit to the galling chains of
dependence"—is both painful to read and difficult to interpret. One could
take the line straight. It must have been galling indeed to live on the edges
of other people's lives, with barely the right even to ask for a tolerable place
to work. While living with her brother six months later, Brackett told Howe,
"I am doubtful about being able to se[w] much. . . . [T]he stiffness remains
in my fingers, and I labor under the disadvantage of being obliged to sit
either in a cold room or in a room with half a dozzen children all of which
are great hinderances,—especially to blind persons."[159] Or one could take
the line as a strategic concession to Howe's dreams of self-sufficiency for
the blind. It may be that in talking about the galling chains of dependence,
Brackett was performing the proud wish for independence she knew Howe
wanted to see. She may have needed to do that precisely because she did
depend on him: most of her needlework sales were transacted through him.

Brackett's prediction that she would fall short of earning the fifty dollars necessary to balance her books for 1847 proved all too accurate. For
Brackett, each new year brought not celebration but the annual reckoning of
her disastrous accounts. In a letter she sent Howe on New Year's Day 1848,
it is almost as though she is training him to understand that dependence
is not an abstract moral failing but an unavoidable fact—as indisputable
as the arithmetic his school had taught her. She patiently shows him what
is plain to her: she cannot make ends meet. Brackett recapitulates her 1847
revenues and expenditures, calculating to the cent the cost of her board,
medical care, and supplies for her needlework, and then setting these against
her income from her work:

> I find in looking over my accounts the proceeds of my labour has fallen
> considerably short of what I thought it would amount to when we talked
> affairs over last winter[.] The articles I have sent to you—even if the bas-
> kets were sold at [unintelligible] and the rest at the lowest price—would
> amount to 34,80—I have received ten dollars in money and stock to the
> amount of 3,62ct—which would leave a balance of 21,18ct[.] I have sold

158. PS, Incoming Correspondence, 1846–1847, LB to SGH, Southbridge, MA, July 1, 1847.
159. PS, Incoming Correspondence, 1848–1849, LB to SGH, Dudley, MA, January 1, 1848.

articles, in this vicinity to the amount of 15,00$ and received an annuity
of three dollars on a bag basket and needle book—which I sent to the
fair in Worcester making in all 52,80[.] my stock has cost me 16,49[.][160]

Her profit from her work, she told Howe, was $36.31 for the year. But Brack-
ett's board cost $104 a year. Half of that could be forgiven if she took care
of her hosts' children, completing her needlework in the evenings. But she
did not have the stamina to sleep only four hours a night, as she would then
have to do: "this constant application was more than I could bear, and my
health gave way under it." Meanwhile her medical expenses for her most
recent illnesses came to $20. The $36.31 she cleared for the year was less than
a third of what she needed. As she told Howe, "the prospect of extricating
myself from this embarrassment looks dubious enough." Still, she kept on.
"I should like to know what success you have had in selling my work, if
you have any upon your hands now . . . and if you will take the trouble to
sell more . . . and what I had better make mostly," Brackett concluded this
dismal letter.[161]

    In 1848 Brackett would be shunted from grudging relative to chari-
table friend and back again. At the end of the year she faced the choice of
either "the pauper house" or marriage to her doctor, Samuel Carpenter.[162]
She chose marriage. She wrote to Howe again on the eve of the New Year,
December 31, 1848, to tell him of her dire predicament, and of the financial
and medical help Carpenter had given her (he was paying for her board
and waiving his fee).[163] That date speaks volumes: it was one day before her
next annual balancing of the books, and as usual the books were not going
to balance. Was the marriage, which took place three months later, the
solution?[164] The letter announcing Brackett's marriage, alone among all the
ones the Perkins Institution kept from her, was not in her distinctive round
hand. Brackett always wrote in pencil, as the Perkins pupils were evidently
taught, judging from the body of their correspondence with the school.
This letter was instead in the tiny angular ink writing of the sighted. Car-

    160. Ibid.
    161. Ibid.
    162. PS, Incoming Correspondence, 1848–1849, LB to SGH, Wilkerson's, CT, December 31,
1848.
    163. Ibid.
    164. Quinn, "Credibility," 279.

penter, her only friend at the time, may have written the letter—in which Carpenter, if it was indeed he, puffs himself for having "the deep sympathies of his soul . . . stirred up" by Brackett's plight. Brackett's amanuensis, whoever it was, thanks Howe on her behalf for ten dollars he has sent as a gift.[165] Brackett may have been holding up her end of a tacit bargain by making introductions between Carpenter and her wealthy benefactor. The Brackett–Carpenter marriage is a closed book; she never tots up the debits and credits as she scrupulously did with her currency accounts. For all I can determine, the marriage may have been a happy one for Brackett. But one thing is sure. When she reached out to grasp Carpenter's hand, she was not a free partner shaking on a contract. She was a castaway saving herself from going down for the third time in the waves.

Brackett's marriage did confer one important benefit: it gave her the resources to pursue her friendship with Laura Bridgman. After her marriage, Brackett made a honeymoon visit with Carpenter to the Perkins Institution that became, in reality, a short honeymoon between her and Bridgman. Bridgman, elated, recorded the visit at unusual length in her diary for July 23, 1849, where she notes with precision that the two friends had not been in each other's company for "2 years & almost 3 months."[166] She lovingly describes the fine clothes that made up Brackett's bridal wardrobe—including the colors that she could not see but that she must have asked a teacher to describe to her. As Bridgman's teachers sometimes did with special visitors, including her mother, they left it to their pupil to identify her surprise guest at first. Here is Bridgman's description of that moment:

> It appears a verry long time since I wrote in my Journal. I have a great number of details to relate. The 1st of June I did not ascertain that my very dear friend Mrs. Carpenter had been here all the P. M. . . . As we entered the room I met a lady whose hand I took. I did not recognise her at first. In a few minutes I was so very rightly delighted to see her although it was 2 years & almost 3 months since she left me. I caught hold of her waist so that she could rise from a comfortable rocking chair. She instantly jumped up with me & danced along with me so very merrily.

---

165. PS, Incoming Correspondence, 1848–1849, LB to SGH, Wilkerson's, CT, December 31, 1848. For examples of correspondence from the blind, see PS, Incoming Correspondence, bound volumes, 1836–1849.

166. PS, Laura Bridgman journal, July 23, 1849.

I was struck with great astonishment to find out how very well & steady
Mrs. C could stand or walk. It added to my happiness to see her restored
to her condition or state.[167]

Bridgman would have remembered Brackett in a wheelchair, which is the
reason for her attempt to help Brackett stand up from her rocking chair
and for her surprise when it proves unnecessary. Brackett was evidently
going through a period of better health—but she was also galvanized by
Bridgman's presence. As in the 1837 experiments in Providence with Stone,
Frothingham, and Kent, she leapt up from her rocking chair in a moment
of joy and possibility.

   Brackett's marriage to Carpenter permitted both this honeymoon visit
and another visit later from Bridgman to Brackett's new home in Providence—where, she proudly told Howe, she had a housekeeper.[168] Brackett wrote
to Howe about the sympathetic bond she and Bridgman shared: "Between
us, there is a congeniality, a love and friendship, an intuitive perception of
each others thoughts and fe[elings] which rarely exists between to [sic] human beings—To me all unrestrained Laura poured out her *whole heart*, all
her joys, her secret thoughts, sorrows, and trials."[169] But Howe called Bridgman back to Perkins early, a cruel blow to Brackett. Even then she duly reassured Howe about his generosity: "I know that you are always *just* and *kind*,
in your *decisions* and have good reason for not desiring her to return to me—
that you permitted her to remain with me as long as she did—is a *favour* for
which *above* all *others*, I can never cease to feel grateful to you," she wrote to
him.[170] Howe's letter to her was perfunctory, assuring her that while Bridgman had been disappointed to leave her at first, she now agreed it had been
for the best. Howe invited Brackett to visit her friend in Boston, something
that Brackett's health would not permit her to do.[171] That may be what Howe
was counting on. Brackett died five years later, and there is no sign that she
ever spent time with her friend in person again.

   Durant, Reese, and Osborn were shocked at the inroads magnetism
allegedly made on empowerment and freedom. But Brackett did not shop

167. Ibid.
168. PS, Incoming Correspondence, 1852–1853, LB (now Lurena B. Carpenter) to SGH,
Providence, RI, n. d. [May 1852]; see also LB to SGH, Providence, RI, March 29, 1852.
169. PS, Incoming Correspondence, 1852–1853, LB to SGH, Providence, RI, May 11, 1852.
170. Ibid.; see also LB to SGH, Providence, RI, n. d. [May 1852].
171. PS, Register of Correspondence Sent, November 15, 1848–May 19, 1853, SGH to LB,
May 5, 1852. Brackett declined the invitation in her May 11 letter on account of her health.

in the fancy stores where they sold those luxury goods. She was, if anything, the laborer who manufactured them by hand in cold rooms, painful stitch after tiny silver bugle bead after painful stitch. She had to perform meekness or self-reliance for Howe, based on her best guess as to what would please him. When it came to disempowerment, lying, and dependence, life taught Brackett not to be overly ticklish. Blindness and invalidism had been her lot for three years before she met the personnel of Providence animal magnetism, and they were to be her lot thereafter. What animal magnetism did was to introduce her visitors into a world of interdependency and playing along that was probably much more familiar to her than it was to them. She may have been better able than they were to appreciate the flexibility that went along with the particular mesmeric form of dependence, one in which accepted truths—about, for example, blindness—were not automatically to be believed. She may also have been, by the necessity she faced throughout her life, more skilled than they were at the kind of diplomacy that permits others' conflicting narratives to subsist alongside our own. Magnetism permitted her some room to find out which alleged necessities she could lift with a change of narrative—though many, such as her economic want, were intractable. It is not saying much—but magnetism was probably among the more flexible dependencies that Brackett faced.

"CRAZZY"

In 1843, Laura Bridgman's teacher Mary Swift wrote an entry in the Perkins Institution teachers' journal. She reported that Bridgman, using finger spelling, "asked me if I knew any *crazzy* persons then altered it to craxy & finally to crazy—asked her who told her the new word crazy—She said, 'Lurena told me about crazy persons and said she was crazy.'"[172] The account contains what may be Loraina/Lurena Brackett's ghostly signature in the form of a "typographical" error: she would have finger-spelled the word to her friend to teach it to her, and Brackett had a tendency to double her Zs, as Bridgman does on her first spelling attempt. *Dozen* was generally "dozzen"

172. PS, Teacher Journals for the Deafblind Department, Journal for January 4, 1843–April 1, 1843, Mary Swift, February 27, 1843. On finger spelling, see Gitter, *Imprisoned Guest*, 83–87.

in Brackett's letters.[173] Director Samuel G. Howe often combed the teachers' journal for passages to include in the institute's *Annual Reports*, where he offered a running narrative on Bridgman's progress, and this passage is among those he included. But first he either copyedited it, or bowdlerized it, depending on your perspective: Loraina, according to Howe, "*said she was* [once] *crazy*" (Howe's brackets).[174] Perhaps Brackett had meant to refer to the period after her accident at the age of sixteen, when she lost her reason temporarily. But it is also possible that she meant to tell Bridgman about some current trouble of mind; some sense of being out of step with those around her. In that case, Howe's emendation was for propriety, not clarity. He would have been loath to discomfit his subscribers, who patronized Bridgman and might not have liked to see her keeping company with a madwoman.

A skeptic wrote in the *Philadelphia Gazette* in October 1837 that "it seems indispensable that every practical expositor of [mesmerism's] mysteries must possess an impaired and broken intellect. From the brain of a nervous invalid, shattered by casualty or disease, given to hallucination, and erratic in its images, must flow those disclosures which kill both time and distance; which annul the laws of vision; which refute all existing theories as to the organization of the senses or of the mind. . . . If these be true [i.e., mesmerism's claims] then the greatest wisdom, and the clearest sighted citizens of our republic, are on sick beds, and in the wards of lunatic hospitals."[175] This is meant to be a reductio ad absurdum. But is it really so absurd? Whether she was mad or not, Brackett certainly had the wisdom born of institutions and sickbeds. She was somewhat less beset than the humbug hunters were with the illusion of self-sufficiency. A lifelong dependent, she knew what it meant to navigate foreign parlors and asylums with deportment charts.

And *that* madness might be divinest sense. I began this book with an encounter on exhibition day at the Perkins Institution between two invalids, one a visitor and one an inmate. Margaret Fuller, a lifelong sufferer from spinal disease, came unexpectedly face-to-face with Loraina Brackett—probably in the early 1840s, when Brackett was in a wheelchair after her

173. PS, Incoming Correspondence, 1846–1847, LB to SGH, Southbridge, MA, July 1, 1847; Incoming Correspondence, 1848–1849, LB to SGH, Dudley, MA, January 1, 1848.

174. Howe, *Annual Report* 11 (1843), 29.

175. Clipping from the *Philadelphia Gazette*, October 16, 1837, Durant Biographical File.

accident and possibly *crazzy, craxy,* or *crazy.*[176] Brackett passed Fuller a note that the recipient viewed as a "talisman" of credulity, credenciveness, or a mysterious "affinity" that permitted "more rapid and complete modes of intercourse between mind and mind." Here is what that note said:

> The ills that Heaven decrees
> The brave with courage bear.[177]

One could call Brackett's message of passive endurance a platitude, but it did not strike Fuller that way; she kept the "pencilled lines, written in the stiff, round character proper to the blind" as a reminder of "the blind girl . . . [who] saw my true state more clearly than any other person did."[178] Credulity, physical suffering, and even the ritualistic utterance of set phrases share one thing in common: they have little of that self-originating and freedom-seeking quality that we validate as agency.[179] And yet it was bearing and suffering, believing and humoring, that Brackett did well; these were the dispositions that made up her clairvoyant powers, and they were the dispositions into which she initiated her visitors.

Brackett's work as a clairvoyant was to accustom those around her to the possibility of playing along. In William Leete Stone's *Letter to Doctor A. Brigham, on Animal Magnetism,* he and Brackett conclude their visit as they began, with a joint flight—in this case back from New York to Providence. "We will fly," Brackett tells him. And Stone, as before, replies, "Very well—I am used to that way of travelling" (*L,* 49). Once more they clasp hands, and "she went through the same process of ascending into the air by my assistance, as before." Once again, they enjoy the sights from the air; "lingering a moment, as if hovering over the town, I directed her attention to several objects," including an asylum, the Bellevue Alms House. They admire New Haven and New London, Connecticut, before finally descending

---

176. On an earlier meeting between Fuller and Brackett, see Deborah Manson, "'The Trance of the Ecstatica': Margaret Fuller, Animal Magnetism, and the Transcendent Female Body," *Literature and Medicine* 25, no. 2 (2006): 305–7.

177. Margaret Fuller, "The New Science, or the Philosophy of Mesmerism or Animal Magnetism," review of *Etherology; or, The Philosophy of Mesmerism and Phrenology,* by J. Stanley Grimes, *New York Tribune,* February 17, 1845, reprinted in *Life Without and Life Within; or, Reviews, Narratives, Essays, and Poems,* ed. Arthur B. Fuller (Boston: Brown, Taggard, & Chase, 1859), 173.

178. Ibid.

179. Asad, *Formations of the Secular,* 79.

in Providence again, "as from the first flight" (*L*, 48). Was it, however, quite the same? Was the cooperative lie, "I am used to that way of travelling" quite as much of a lie as it had been at the beginning? Was the Stone who pointed out the Bellevue Alms House quite as ignorant of the lessons of madness and dependence as he had been when he started? Brackett initiated visitors like Stone into a game of give-and-take in which belief in her limitations as a blind woman, and even belief itself, temporarily fell away. She and her visitors caught at the balloon strings of a humorous indifference like the one Poe's odd angel advocated: believe what is printed. 'Tis the truth, every word.

4

OUT OF CHARACTER

Phrenomesmerism and the Secular Agent

What is our meter of man, our anthropometer[?]

Ralph Waldo Emerson, Journal (1841)[1]

LORAINA BRACKETT'S CLAIRVOYANCE CONSISTED IN THE ability to make other people's worlds more vivid. For William Leete Stone, she conjured the New York of his imagination. For Margaret Fuller, she conjured a mirror image of Fuller herself; she made her visitor feel that Brackett "saw [Fuller's] true state more clearly than any other person did."[2] These acts of recognition came at the price of self-effacement. Momentarily indifferent to what she knew to be true, Brackett lent her belief to the narratives of others. Credulity here was a generous disempowerment of the self in support of the projects of her interlocutors. Like earlier forms of credulity in the mesmeric scene, this capacity for self-disempowerment would follow the path of instrumentalization. In the early 1840s, a new form of mesmeric

1. Ralph Waldo Emerson, *Journals and Miscellaneous Notebooks of Ralph Waldo Emerson*, 16 vols., ed. William H. Gilman et al. (Cambridge, MA: Harvard University Press, 1970), 8:108. The quotation appears in "Journal H" (1841).

2. Margaret Fuller, "The New Science, or the Philosophy of Mesmerism or Animal Magnetism," review of *Etherology; or, The Philosophy of Mesmerism and Phrenology*, by J. Stanley Grimes, *New York Tribune*, February 17, 1845, reprinted in *Life Without and Life Within; or, Reviews, Narratives, Essays, and Poems*, ed. Arthur B. Fuller (Boston: Brown, Taggard, & Chase, 1859), 173. See also chapter 3 of the present volume.

practice arose. Known as *phrenomesmerism*, it redirected the abilities of clairvoyants toward the reading and validation of character. Its subjects first showed the ability to act out the characteristics associated with whichever of their phrenological organs the operator touched with a finger. Setting aside their usual personalities, they would perform mirth or despair, pride or humility, violence or tenderness. Some subjects could read the characters of individual people, too. Either by touching a person's skull or by holding an object belonging to him or her, these clairvoyants would find themselves possessed—or rather, mesmerized—by the personality they encountered. Based on this experience of possession, they would then produce a reading of relative strengths and weaknesses and distinctive characteristics. Credulity was pressed into the service of validating others' characters, of clarifying others' outlines, of telling others who they were. Mesmeric subjects had a novel use, or perhaps it was more a crystallization of a purpose they had served before, most clearly in the Franklin commission experiments: they made others feel like secular agents.

"OUR ANTHROPOMETER"

The *secular agent*, Talal Asad writes, is the actor understood "within the framework of a secular history of freedom from all coercive control, a history in which everything can be made, and pleasure always innocently enjoyed." The secular agent's freedom is defined "as its ability to create its self." But is self-creation actually compatible with the absence of coercion? As Asad observes, "the paradox inadequately appreciated here is that the self to be liberated from external control must be subjected to the control of a liberating self already and always free, aware, and in control of its own desires."[3] The paradox cuts a few ways. For one thing, in the pursuit of "freedom from all coercive control," the agent subjects himself to the coercive power of his own ego ideal. He is not free from his freedom. He is controlled as much as controlling. Impressibility (the capacity to be molded) is just as necessary to secular agency as impressiveness (the will to mold) may be. For another thing, this controlling self is more spectral, more difficult to locate, than the controlled self is. At best, it is an imaginary friend made in

---

3. Talal Asad, *Formations of the Secular: Christianity, Islam, Modernity* (Stanford, CA: Stanford University Press, 2003), 72–73.

the image of still-unrealized plans for improvement, a hologram of future perfection.

The elusive controlling self can only be encountered in the impact it has on the controlled self. It exists in what it effects. To aspire to self-control is thus to have a motive for self-measurement: one sees how well the project is going by assessing the results. Ralph Waldo Emerson wished in an 1841 journal entry for a new kind of instrument to be exhibited "in our Mechanics Fair," one that would take the measure of men. "Quicksilver is our guage [*sic*] of temperature of air & water, clay is our pyrometer, silver our photometer, feathers our electrometer, catgut our hygrometer, but what is our meter of man, our anthropometer[?]" he asked.[4] The anthropometer, whatever it might be, would provide that steady diet of information about the process of self-molding that alone makes the process seem real. If Emerson is expressing a wish here, one shared by many in an age of men on the make, he is also expressing a doubt. I suspect there is more doubt than wish. Can Emerson really be hoping that the man-measuring equivalent of dirt, feathers, and catgut will present itself? It may be that his analogy is a reductio ad absurdum. When anthropometers appear, despair: the late, decadent phase of self-knowledge will have arrived.

Emerson did not have long to wait for the end. By 1844 Joseph Rodes Buchanan—mesmerist, phrenologist, and can-do Kentuckian—would be lecturing in Boston on the practice he called "psychometry," a term that, as he explained years later, "literally signifies *soul-measuring*."[5] Psychometry was "analogous to the words, thermometry, barometry, electrometry, and similar terms, which signify special measurements," Buchanan explained. "The thermometer measures caloric (*thermo*, temperature)," he went on; "the barometer measures the weight (*baro*, weight) of the atmosphere; the electrometer measures electric conditions; the psychometer measures the soul (*psyche*)."[6] Psychometers, unlike the other instruments Buchanan lists, were human beings: they were mesmeric clairvoyants. That which would measure man, was man—or more often, woman. To perform psychometry on a person, clairvoyants only needed an autograph letter from him or her. Buchanan's theory was that the relative strength of the writer's

---

4. Emerson, "Journal H" (1841), in *Journals*, 8:108, 118. Both entries are indexed by Emerson under "Anthropometer" (8:596).

5. Joseph Rodes Buchanan, *Manual of Psychometry: The Dawn of a New Civilization* (Boston: Holman Brothers, Press of the *Roxbury Advocate*, 1885), 3.

6. Ibid.

phrenological lobes left a signature on the page, a residual imprint of the character preserved in "nervaura" (Buchanan's new name for animal magnetism). Clairvoyants registered this fluidic signature either by touching letters, still sealed, with their hands—in which case the "impression . . . gradually passes up the arm . . . and reaches the brain"—or by placing letters in the center of their foreheads, so that the *sillage* of soul could pass directly into the "mental organs."[7] Just as Buchanan was gaining traction in Boston, Emerson would write in "Experience" (1844) about the "impudent knowingness" of the phrenologists who "esteem each man the victim of another, who winds him round his finger by knowing the law of his being, and by such cheap signboards as the color of his beard, or the slope of his occiput, reads the inventory of his fortunes and character."[8] Buchanan, undaunted, performed just such readings with the help of his clairvoyants. "Our anthropometer" was the mesmeric subject.

While psychometers registered the distinctive characters of those they read, they temporarily lost their own characters. Like many mesmeric subjects before them, they purchased their clairvoyant powers at the expense of their self-command. The Franklin commission had described how Franz Anton Mesmer's patients in France made him the trustee, or *dépositaire*, of the powers of their own imaginations, ceding to him the control they ought to have kept in their own hands. Their credulity and their manipulability were of a piece. Charles Poyen and his successor mesmerists in Providence, Rhode Island, tried to make use of this ceded control in management and in communication. Skeptic David Reese had said that William Leete Stone was "magnetized out of his usual self-possession" by a story; being transported in that way was also the source of Brackett's traveling powers.[9] Psychometers were magnetized out of *their* self-possession, too, in order to be "possessed," as Buchanan said, by the letter writer to the extent of "los[ing] all self-control." A "very delicate" lady, while touching a letter written by Henry Clay, "became so possessed of its spirit" that "she replied haughtily

7. Joseph Rodes Buchanan, "Psychometry," *Buchanan's Journal of Man* 1, no. 2 (February 1849): 59–60. *Buchanan's Journal of Man*, which was edited by Joseph Rodes Buchanan and published in Cincinnati, 1849–1856, is hereafter cited as *BJM*.

8. Ralph Waldo Emerson, "Experience," in *Essays: Second Series*, ed. Joseph Slater, et al., vol. 3 of *The Collected Works of Ralph Waldo Emerson*, ed. Joseph Slater et al. (Cambridge, MA: Harvard University Press, 1983), 31.

9. David Reese, *Humbugs of New-York: Being a Remonstrance against Popular Delusion* (Boston: Weeks, Jordan, 1838), 39. The story of Stone and Brackett is recounted in chapter 3 of the present volume.

to the questions which [Buchanan] proposed, as though she considered them quite impertinent or insulting."[10] Psychometers often recognized writers' characters by feeling the deformation of their own personalities: if the writer was haughty, the psychometer momentarily became so. These readers had the same tendency to lose self-command long associated with the mesmeric subject, but Buchanan gave this tendency a new name and a new use: subjects were not credulous, but "impressible," and their impressibility permitted them to reflect others' characters accurately.[11]

In psychometry, the transaction in which the enchantment of one person ensured the modernity of another became breathtakingly direct. The clairvoyant was to reflect back to others their characters, by momentarily losing her own. Psychometry offered the inquirer a "mirror in which to scan his own countenance."[12] Being read by a psychometer meant being recognized. It meant, often, being validated as an empowered agent choosing freedom and making history. For example, Buchanan's signature—a loopy, violet-inked affair—inspired the psychometrically gifted "Rev. Mr. G." with visions of potency (Fig. 8).[13] Mr. G. saw "the scene of a leader or adventurer, marching on toward a distant height, while a multitude behind were looking upon his progress." This hero wore "a species of Roman helmet" and seemed to have "some connection with a locality on Lower Market street," Buchanan's childhood residence.[14] Potency, futuristic vision, and middle-class coordinates: seldom has the secular ideal been so trenchantly summarized.

A psychometer such as Mr. G. could play a complex supplemental role in assuring the object of his reading—here, Buchanan—of his strong character. For one thing, he confirmed for Buchanan the reality of his self-image. Buchanan was in the scientific avant-garde. He was, to use another phrase from Mr. G.'s reading, looking back as he "paused to wait until the foremost could overtake him."[15] In Mr. G.'s vision, Buchanan is already the fully realized agent he hopes to become. Mr. G. also eases the discomfort of the logical consequence of self-control, that the agent must be he who is acted upon as well as he who acts, both the unfree subject of himself

10. Joseph Rodes Buchanan, "Psychometry—(Continued)," *BJM* 1, no. 4 (April 1849): 154.
11. Buchanan, "Psychometry," *BJM* 1, no. 2 (February 1849): 56.
12. Buchanan, "Psychometry—(Continued)," *BJM* 1, no. 4 (April 1849): 155.
13. Ibid., 145–46; Letter from Joseph Rodes Buchanan to James Freeman Clarke, April 24, [n. d.], in the Perry-Clarke Collection, Massachusetts Historical Society.
14. Buchanan, "Psychometry—(Continued)," *BJM* 1, no. 4 (April 1849): 146.
15. Ibid.

Fig. 8. Joseph Rodes Buchanan's autograph, from an April 24 [no year, circa 1840s] letter to James Freeman Clarke. Perry-Clarke Collection, Massachusetts Historical Society.

and the free ruler of himself. Mr. G. temporarily relieves Buchanan of the
need to be his own subject, since for the moment *Mr. G.* is that subject:
possessed by Buchanan, he engrosses the role of impressibility to himself.
Credulity, insofar as it meant having a too-easily-impressible character, too
ready to believe or be molded by the claims of others, was not the opposite
of self-control. It was the internal necessity of self-control. Psychometry
told an important truth: it showed that the relationship between fixity and
impressibility, between agency and credulity, was more like symbiosis than
like opposition. And it placed the impressible side of the pair at center stage.

"ENTIRE CONTROL OF THEIR CHARACTER"

Buchanan's invention of autograph psychometry was unique to him, but
it grew out of a variation on mesmerism that originated simultaneously
with several practitioners. In 1841, three mesmerists in the United States—
Buchanan, La Roy Sunderland, and Robert Collyer—began to direct the
animal-magnetic fluid at phrenological organs to stimulate their activity.[16]

16. Alan Gauld, *A History of Hypnotism* (Cambridge: Cambridge University Press, 1992),
185. For an account of the career of Sunderland, who quickly moved on from phrenomesmerism to a suggestion-like theory he called "pathetism," see Ann Taves, *Fits, Trances, and
Visions: Experiencing Religion and Explaining Experience from Wesley to James* (Princeton,
NJ: Princeton University Press, 1999), 128–38. Representative early works from these three
practitioners are Joseph Rodes Buchanan, *Sketches of Buchanan's Discoveries in Neurology* (Louisville: J. Eliot & Co.'s Power Press, 1842); Robert Collyer, *Psychography; or, The
Embodiment of Thought* (Philadelphia, 1843); and the *Magnet*, which was edited and mostly
written by La Roy Sunderland. See "Phreno-Magnetism," *Magnet* 1, no. 1 (June 1842): 20–21;
"Phreno-Magnetism," *Magnet* 1, no. 2 (July 1842): 37–38; and "Phreno-Magnetism," *Magnet* 1,
no. 3 (August 1842): 55–56.

If their fellow mesmerist J. Stanley Grimes is right, there was also a fourth contender for priority in Britain, Spencer T. Hall.[17] (Historian Alison Winter, however, places the development of phrenomesmerism in Britain one or two years later and does not consider Hall a leader in the field.)[18] The US phrenomesmerists aimed to use mesmerism to map the phrenological organs more accurately, thus furnishing a tool for self-culture and education. Rather than the clairvoyant reading the character of another person, the technique that would later develop in psychometry, the mesmerist would directly manipulate the clairvoyant's character by touching her skull. Prodding any one of a subject's organs artificially amplified its function, so that a small organ would temporarily act with the strength of a larger one. "I find that I have been able to assume the entire control of their character," Buchanan said of the most impressible subjects, "and operate upon their minds or bodies in the most fantastic manner that caprice could suggest."[19] He boasted, "It is in my power to excite . . . any portion of the brain, either large or small; to put that portion into full and vigorous action as an efficient portion of the character of the person upon whom I operate, and then, at will, suspend its action. . . . The individual subjected to the experiment becomes conscious of a sudden development of new traits in his character, by the increased strength of the emotions, passions, and intellectual faculties which are excited, or in the sudden diminution of powers which he has been accustomed to exercise."[20] William Cullen Bryant reported to his friend in Paris the advent of "a Dr. Buchanan at Louisville" who "makes the choleric man imperturbably good-natured, the funny man as stupid as an oyster, etc."[21]

Buchanan's experiments in Louisville, where he began his career, were so popular that one performance at the city's Medical Institute caused a stampede on the stairs.[22] In a typical 1842 demonstration there, Buchanan

17. J. Stanley Grimes, *Etherology; or, The Philosophy of Mesmerism and Phrenology* (New York: Saxton & Miles, 1845), 250n.

18. Alison Winter, *Mesmerized: Powers of Mind in Victorian Britain* (Chicago: University of Chicago Press, 1998), 113–14, 117.

19. Buchanan, *Sketches*, 10, reprinted from the *Louisville Public Advertiser*, August 25, 1841.

20. Buchanan, *Sketches*, 6, reprinted from the *Louisville Public Advertiser*, August 25, 1841.

21. William Cullen Bryant to Orville Dewey, January 11, 1842, in *Letters of William Cullen Bryant*, 6 vols., ed. William Cullen Bryant II and Thomas G. Voss (New York: Fordham University Press, 1975–1992), 2:167.

22. "Louisville: Correspondence of the *Herald*," *New York Herald*, January 24, 1842.

first induced a "Mesmeric sleep" in his subject by placing "his right hand on the forehead," while "with his left [he] grasped the hand of the patient." After the patient was magnetized, Buchanan exhibited a cranium cast marked with the phrenological organs to his audience and then touched matching organs on the subject's head in succession. The patient manifested "in the strongest and most unequivocal manner, the various feelings, tastes, and emotions which phrenologists contend are indicated by protuberances."[23] While one unidentified organ—destructiveness, perhaps—"caused so fearful a paroxysm of despair, that the subject drew a knife from his pocket and would have used it, had it not been taken instantly from him," others had "droll" effects. Stimulation of "acquisitiveness" left "the subject evidently taking and concealing imaginary objects"; under the spell of "the love of children," sometimes called *philoprogenitiveness*, he mimed "nursing and caressing imaginary children, dandling them on his knee, and hushing them to sleep in the real nursery-maid style." The delusional performances ceased as soon as "the operator . . . with a few passes of his hand, dispelled the Mesmeric influence—the patient gradually unclosed his eyes, and reason at once resumed her empire."[24] Personality resumed her empire, too. So long as the performance continued, the subject's real character—the real relative strength of his organs—was in abeyance.

The period of phrenomesmerism's rise was one of increasing influence and geographic spread for US mesmerism. All three of the major practitioners started magazines: Sunderland had the *Magnet* (Fig. 9);[25] Collyer started up a one-issue wonder, the *Mesmeric Magazine*;[26] and Buchanan's *Journal of Man* ran for six years starting in 1849—an eternity in the world of magnetic publishing.[27] All three gave mesmerism new names, though Sunderland's pathetism, Collyer's psychography, and Buchanan's neurology were arguably

23. "Experiments in Phreno-Magnetism," *Madisonian*, May 26, 1842. Reprinted from the Philadelphia *Inquirer*.

24. Ibid.

25. *Magnet* (New York, 1842–1844). Sunderland was the editor from June 1842 to November 1843; on the end of his tenure, see "Theory of Pathetism," *Magnet* 2, no. 6 (November 1843): 126. There was no December 1843 issue, and Peter P. Good became editor in January 1844.

26. *Mesmeric Magazine* (Boston), ed. Robert Collyer, 1, no. 1 (July 1842).

27. *Buchanan's Journal of Man* (Cincinnati), ed. Joseph Rodes Buchanan, 1849–1855 (*BJM*). The magazine also had a later run under the same title (1887–1890).

just "animal magnetism in disguise."[28] The three men's controversies over priority of discovery bear witness to mesmerism's growing reach and prestige. These three practitioners were sufficiently dispersed that they could be in doubt as to whether the others had read their own publications and plagiarized them, or whether they had all made independent discoveries. Sunderland's magnetic career centered on New York,[29] Collyer's on Boston and New York, though he had previously studied with the mesmerist John Elliotson in London.[30] Buchanan got his start in Little Rock and Louisville.[31] Buchanan suspected the others of cribbing from him, since he doubted that something could be published in "a paper of so wide a circulation as the *Louisville Journal*" and yet not be read throughout the known world.[32]

The suspicious attitude was mutual. Buchanan's rivals were especially annoyed when he got the imprimatur of two prominent editors, William Cullen Bryant of the *New York Evening Post* and John O'Sullivan of the *Democratic Review*. Bryant and O'Sullivan took part in a committee formed in the fall of 1842 to investigate Buchanan, who by that time had moved east and was lecturing in New York City. Bryant and O'Sullivan proved powerful allies for him; the committee bore out Buchanan's claims, and the favorable "Report of the Sub-Committee" appeared that winter both in the *Evening Post* and, in slightly abridged form, in the *United States Magazine and Democratic Review*.[33] (I refer to this investigation as the "*Democratic Review* experiments" hereafter.) Collyer and Sunderland redoubled their attacks on Buchanan when the *Democratic Review* reached them, showing that we do

28. "Animal Magnetism In Disguise," *New York Herald*, November 3, 1842. See also La Roy Sunderland, "Dr. Buchanan's Lectures," *Magnet* 1, no. 7 (December 1842): 154, where the identical phrase appears; and Grimes, *Etherology*, 263.

29. Taves, *Fits, Trances, and Visions*, 135.

30. Collyer, *Psychography*, 10–11; Gauld, *History of Hypnotism*, 183–84. On Elliotson, see Winter, *Mesmerized*, 46–100.

31. Buchanan, *Sketches*, 7, 22.

32. Buchanan, "Letter to the Editor of the New York *Watchman*," February 22, 1842, reprinted in *Sketches*, 41. Buchanan's published letter responded to an article in the January 15, 1842, issue of *Zion's Watchman*. Neither issue is extant. Sunderland counterattacked: see "Dr. Buchanan's Lectures," *Magnet* 1, no. 7 (December 1842): 154n; "New Discoveries," *Magnet* 1, no. 1 (June 1842): 13.

33. "Neurology," *United States Magazine and Democratic Review* 55 (January 1843): 79–93. For the excerpt from the "Report of the Sub-Committee," *New York Evening Post*, December 6, 1841, see "Neurology," 81–91. For an alternate reprint, see "Neurology; Report of the Sub-Committee," *Wisconsin Democrat*, January 3, 1843.

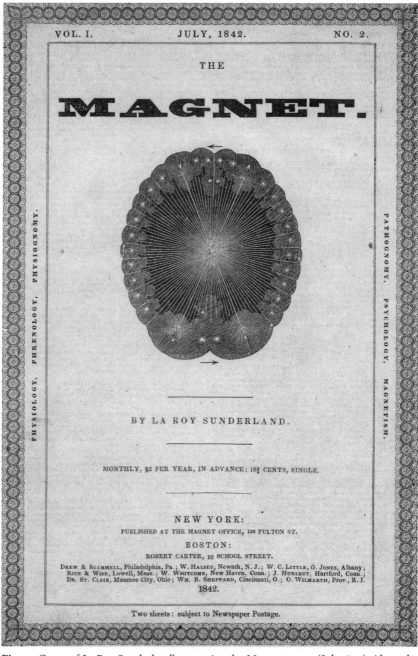

Fig. 9. Cover of La Roy Sunderland's magazine the *Magnet* 1, no. 2 (July 1842). Along the left and right margins run the words "PHYSIOLOGY, PHRENOLOGY, PHYSIOGNOMY, PATHOGNOMY, PSYCHOLOGY, MESMERISM." Widener Library, Harvard University, WID_Phil22.9.

indeed hate it when our friends become successful.[34] Whoever may have been phrenomesmerism's alpha, Buchanan was the omega. Within a few years, he had won ascendancy among his competitors. His was the name to be enduringly associated with the practice.[35]

Phrenomesmerism's initial goal was to facilitate self-culture and education by producing a more accurate map of the organs than skull palpation or dissection could do. Phrenology had already offered such a map, but phrenomesmerism was a faster and more precise method of confirming that the location of organs was correct[36]—just as some might say today that functional magnetic resonance imaging (fMRI) is an improvement over autopsy. Rather than pawing blindly at a living skull or examining a dead one, the phrenomesmerist simply magnetized the organs and saw immediately, through the subject's performance, which traits were amplified as a result. "In the course of a single month, I have been able to ascertain more of [the brain's] true physiology than has heretofore been acquired by all the labors of all the Physiologists and Pathologists," Buchanan wrote while in a grandiose mood—a frequent occurrence for him.[37] Phrenomesmerism was an "immense power . . . for the purposes of *Education*—for promoting the *general social happiness*, by a due regulation of the passions—for the *reformation of criminals*—and for the *philosophical re-organization of the science of medicine.*"[38] Like older phrenological maps, the new one could be used by parents tailoring a program of education to their children or by adults deciding on the right careers for themselves. As John Modern points out, the *American Phrenological Journal* suggested that phrenomesmerism could also directly redress "mental imbalance" among the phrenological organs: "again, enchantment serving disenchanted ends."[39] C. Townshend offered a telling simile in his introduction to a manual of phrenological reading according to Grimes's system: just as the mechanic confronted with a Lowell mill could see that "a collection of cogs, wheels, spokes, braces, beams, and

34. Collyer, *Psychography*, 9–10; Sunderland, "Neurology: To the Editor of the *Democratic Review*," *United States Magazine and Democratic Review* 59 (May 1843): 544–45, and the editorial response, 545.

35. Grimes, *Etherology*, 223–24, 239.

36. See John Lardas Modern, *Secularism in Antebellum America* (Chicago: University of Chicago Press, 2011), 159–60.

37. Buchanan, *Sketches*, 4, reprinted from the *Louisville Public Advertiser*, August 25, 1841.

38. Ibid., 21.

39. Modern, *Secularism in Antebellum America*, 159.

polished wires" was actually "the most extensive and valuable manufactory ever erected on the banks of the Merrimac," so the skilled examiner could tell a "father" that his son's "massive" brain and large "Self-Esteem, Combativeness, [and] Destructiveness" meant that he had "all the talent for a superior mechanic, artist, physician, lawyer, or clergyman."[40] Phrenomesmeric expertise abetted the formation of character.

The aspirations to read, rationalize, and control could not have been more avid. And yet phrenomesmerism's tendencies were complicated by an element entirely missing from phrenology. Feeling bumps on the skull in no way entailed changing the character; magnetizing them did. In phrenomesmerism, studying human character—presumably a fixed and knowable property—required manipulating it, and thus rendering it unfixed, in the subject. New phrenological charts could be issued only at the expense of making an experimental subject lose his or her character. Modern notes that "the possibility of 'self-losing' was integral to the metaphysics of phrenology," because the delicate balance of the many faculties seemed poised to fall apart.[41] Phrenomesmerism, unlike phrenology proper, temporarily *made* its subjects fall apart. The phrenomesmeric subject would act in ways that neither his previous behavior nor the slope of his occiput would have predicted. Buchanan's magnetic touch would change the subject into someone or something he had never been and might never be again: a murderer, an orator, a nursemaid. In this way the locations of, respectively, combativeness, self-esteem, and philoprogenitiveness could be confirmed. Thus phrenomesmeric performance had the effect, almost certainly unintended, of emphasizing the interdependence between the kind of agent that took impressions and the kind of agent that made them.

TO READ IS TO BE OVERPOWERED

Within a year of phrenomesmerism's beginnings, starting in the fall of 1842, Buchanan developed his technique of psychometry. Rather than magnetize his subjects directly with his own hands, Buchanan asked them to place

40. C. Townshend, *Improved Phreno-Chart . . . According to Grimes's New System of Phrenology* (Boston: White and Potter, 1853), iii–iv.

41. Modern, *Secularism in Antebellum America*, 158.

their hands on particular phrenological organs on other people's skulls.[42] The influence of the organ touched would pass through the subject's hand, thus "magnetizing" him or her. Whatever quality was associated with the organ would suddenly be manifested in the subject's own personality. If a clairvoyant stroked another person's organ of amativeness, for example, loving feelings would arise in the clairvoyant's own mind. Not only that, but the strength of these feelings would be governed by the strength of the organ being palpated. Thus phrenomesmeric readers could judge the relative prominence of various personality traits in the skull they were examining based on the strength of the sentiments aroused in themselves. Sunderland developed a similar technique at the same time or a bit before and reported on his experiments with it in fall issues of the *Magnet*.[43] Buchanan tried the new method with Mrs. R., one of the subjects of the *Democratic Review* experiments in November 1842. When she touched Buchanan's skull "on the front portion," she suddenly felt "*disposed to regard every body with kindness.*" That reaction permitted Buchanan to deduce that his own "moral organs" were well developed.[44]

Psychometry reinterpreted the elements of the phrenomesmeric rapport. In phrenomesmerism, the partner of the rapport, usually the mesmerist, manipulated the clairvoyant's character by pressing on her phrenological organs. In psychometry, the mesmerist effectively transferred his rapport to another person—the one whose skull the clairvoyant touched. Now, instead of being controlled by a mesmerist's hands, the clairvoyant was controlled by this new subject's skull. She could sympathetically read the character that lay beneath the skull's distinctive surface—she might even become possessed by that character, acting it out and temporarily experiencing it as her own.[45] Where she had formerly been governed by a mesmerist, now she was governed by the object of her reading. Reading, then, was genealogically linked with being overpowered. Hegel's conclusion to the master and slave dialectic in the *Phenomenology of Spirit* (1807) is that "the *truth* of the independent consciousness is accordingly the servile consciousness."[46] The

42. Buchanan, "Psychometry," *BJM* 1, no. 2 (February 1849): 57.

43. "Magnetic Examinations," *Magnet* 1, no. 4 (September 1842): 84.

44. "Neurology; Report of the Sub-committee," *Wisconsin Democrat*, January 3, 1843.

45. On psychometry, see Dana Luciano, "Sacred Theories of Earth: Matters of Spirit in *The Soul of Things*," *American Literature* 86, no. 4 (December 2014): 713–36; Modern, *Secularism in Antebellum America*, 223–24.

46. G. W. F. Hegel, *Phenomenology of Spirit*, trans. A. V. Miller (New York: Oxford University Press, 1977), 117 [§193].

same proved to be the case in psychometry's historical development out of phrenomesmerism. To obey someone else—to be constrained to obey that person—turned out to entail having insight into that person's desires.

The psychometric rapport permitted the person whose skull was being read not just to exert control over the clairvoyant but also to compel recognition from the clairvoyant. There was already a quotidian form of the person whose impressibility allowed her both to be easily managed and to reassure the powerful of their power: the wife. "The constant culture and shelter which [women] have enjoyed," Buchanan explained, "have diminished that hardy force of character which might enable them to impress their own will upon others; but they have also given a delicate pliability, a genius for adaptation which is more important to conjugal happiness than any force of character." Men, he thought, would prefer that their wives be "impressible and yielding in . . . domestic life."[47] Kyla Schuller calls the married pair "the two-bodied subject," the culture's means of finessing the problems of impressibility by tying them to white women. The concept of *impressibility* "bifurcated the civilized body into a two-part unit" with "the Anglo-Saxon female absorb[ing] the instability of impressibility and its tendency to excess."[48] Buchanan saw how phrenomesmeric impressibility might serve to adjust a wife's docility to the proper level. With her combativeness excited, one Louisville woman told him "she felt as if born to command." Concerned, Buchanan asked her whether "the influence she seemed to be under was favorable to obedience." It would, on the contrary, "produce disobedience," she replied. In response, her husband "jocosely remarked to the Doctor, 'that he must stop that: it was a fault he did not wish to see increased in her.'"[49] Buchanan accordingly altered his manipulations to favor obedience instead.[50] He would modify another wife to suit her husband's needs in New York, where the husband of Mrs. R., a subject in the *Democratic Review* experiments, asked Buchanan to point out the organ of "*levity*" to him. That way, he explained, "he might excite it whenever it became desirable to enliven her."[51] Mr. R. then extracted such an excess of affective labor from his wife that she "could not contain herself" and seemed "under the influence

47. Buchanan, "Sympathetic Impressibility," *BJM* 1, no. 8 (October 1849): 357.

48. Kyla Schuller, "Taxonomies of Feeling: The Epistemology of Sentimentalism in Late-Nineteenth-Century Racial and Sexual Science," *American Quarterly* 64, no. 2 (June 2012): 278, 293.

49. Buchanan, *Sketches*, 48, reprinted from the *Louisville Journal*, December 1, 1841.

50. Ibid., 49.

51. "Neurology," *United States Magazine and Democratic Review* 55 (January 1843): 88.

of exhilarating gas." Buchanan had to perform remedial passes to restore her equilibrium.[52]

If impressibility subjugated the wife to her husband, it also gave her the capacity to interpret him and those around him. As a "safe and quiet monitor to her husband," she could assist him by detecting "lurking vices" in those who might be trying to swindle him.[53] By her insights, she could help her children undertake "self-education, guided by self-study . . . the great duty of human life."[54] She also offered her husband existential recognition. The study of one's own character, as Buchanan put it, involved seeing oneself as a "rude block of marble, which represents the character of an uncultivated human being." It involved seeing oneself as not-yet-existent. The psychometer-wife could see the "beautiful statue" that was not yet there.[55] She recognized, even made real, a character that was still in the process of becoming itself. Thus psychometry involved some surprising transfers of power. On the one hand, the psychometer's reading ability was descended from the phrenomesmeric subject's absolute obedience. Theoretically speaking—that is, in terms of the transfer of neurvauric fluid that happened between members of the rapport—the two were identical. To read was to be overpowered. And yet, the overpowered reader also seemed to be the one capable of offering reassurance to the object of her reading that he was real; that his character did, or could, exist. It was as though the object of the reading were a ghost whose existence could be validated only in the psychometer's special vision.

The next form psychometry assumed underscored the ghostliness of the read character even more emphatically. Reading skulls proved to be a transitional mode. Buchanan's psychometers soon moved on to autograph manuscripts, which they would use almost exclusively from 1843 forward.[56] One of his New York subjects had seemed to have "the power of recognizing a mental influence in any autograph that he might touch."[57] This anonymous man held four letters in succession without reading their contents, and with each "his description [of the writers' characters] would not have been more correct if he had described the individuals from familiar

52. Ibid.

53. Buchanan, "Sympathetic Impressibility," 357.

54. Buchanan, "Psychometry—(Continued)," *BJM* 1, no. 4 (April 1849): 156.

55. Ibid.

56. Some of his students, however, would use a variety of other objects: see Luciano, "Sacred Theories of Earth."

57. Buchanan, "Psychometry," *BJM* 1, no. 2 (February 1849): 57.

personal knowledge!"[58] "Does it not appear," Buchanan asked rhetorically, "that something emitted from the person or mind of the writer, has become attached to, or connected with, the paper, as if the mental and the physical were capable of entering into a psycho-material combination?"[59] What is writing itself but a psycho-material combination? Letters, though remarkable when you stop to think about them, are also common; Buchanan's readers could readily "select from your letters the one which was written with the greatest intensity of feeling and force of thought," as he instructed them to do.[60] Some even had famous signatures at their disposal because autograph collecting was in vogue.[61] The assumption behind collecting, that the autograph furnished "an almost mystical encounter" with the writer, as Tamara Plakins Thornton observes in her history of handwriting, may also have fueled Buchanan's invention.[62] The psychometer who conjured, and sometimes physically imitated, the character of the letter writer was a clairvoyant version of the ordinary collector, who, according to Thornton, "savor[ed] the greatness that emanated from the handwriting of remarkable individuals."[63]

It appears that Buchanan decamped to Boston in the winter of 1843 and 1844, not long after hitting on the idea of reading character via manuscript emanations. In Boston, William Lloyd Garrison's abolitionist *Liberator* backed him,[64] and his lectures were successful enough to support a spin-off business by the spring: Bela Marsh advertised the sale of "marked busts, neatly made, adapted to Buchanan's Neurology."[65] One of Buchanan's Boston psychometers, probably drawn from his classes, was the unidentified "Rev. Mr. K."[66] Mr. K. offers a glimpse into what it felt like to be a psy-

58. Ibid.

59. Ibid., 60.

60. Ibid., 59.

61. Tamara Plakins Thornton, *Handwriting in America: A Cultural History* (New Haven, CT: Yale University Press, 1996), 86–88.

62. Ibid., 87.

63. Ibid., 87.

64. "Dr. Buchanan's Lectures (From the *Boston Post*)," *Liberator*, February 9, 1844; "Report of Neurological Experiments, From the *Boston Courier*," *Liberator*, June 28, 1844.

65. [Advertisement by Bela Marsh], *Liberator*, May 3, 1844.

66. Mr. K. is identified as the member of a "Neurological Society" in Joseph Rodes Buchanan, "Psychometry—(Continued)," *BJM* 1, no. 3 (March 1849): 111–12; and experiments with him are dated to 1844 in Joseph Rodes Buchanan, "Psychometry—(Continued)," *BJM* 1, no. 5 (May 1849): 209.

chometer. He describes his own character temporarily sharing a body with
the letter writer's, with the latter being generally the more obtrusive of the
two. Mr. K. recalls that while touching a particular letter whose writer he
aimed to identify, he felt "sensations" passing up his arm from his fingers.
Next, he recounts, "my whole arm became violently agitated, and I yielded
to an irresistible impulse, to give utterance to my thoughts and feelings. A
determined, self-confident, daring and triumphant feeling, suggested the
language I used, and it seemed to me, that I could have gone on triumph-
antly to the accomplishment of any purpose, however subtile or strong
might be the opposition to be overcome."[67] While touching the letter, Mr. K.
expressed the feelings emanating from the letter as though they were his
own: "Let it come!—let it come!—LET IT COME!" he exclaimed. As soon
as Mr. K. took his hand off the letter, he analyzed his own sensations: "It
seemed to me when my hand was on it, I could go through everything—I
had the feeling—*I* AM *sufficient for it*."[68] He hazarded, "it seems from some
foreign, furious spirit, or from *such a man as Gen. Jackson*."[69] Mr. K. was
correct: the letter was from Andrew Jackson. Buchanan quotes a portion
of the letter, where Jackson worries that "the people, shaken in their confidence and divided in their action, shall loose [*sic*] both their advocates
and their cause," should his political enemies triumph over him.[70] Jackson
wrote these words in a September 1826 letter to Buchanan's father-in-law,
the Kentucky senator John Rowan; Buchanan had apparently borrowed the
manuscript for his own purposes.[71]

On Buchanan's view, psychometric reading followed seamlessly from
the phrenomesmerist's ascendancy over the subjects he manipulated. Like
Buchanan himself, Jackson had the habit of command, and here his letter
commanded the submissive Rev. Mr. K. "Never did [Jackson] succeed more
fully in infusing his spirit into his subordinates, on the field of battle, than it

67. Quoted in Buchanan, "Psychometry—(Continued)," *BJM* 1, no. 3 (March 1849):
100–101.
68. Ibid., 102.
69. Ibid., 103.
70. Ibid., 101.
71. Andrew Jackson to John Rowan, September 5, 1826, in *The Papers of Andrew Jackson*,
vol. 6, *1825–1828*, ed. Harold D. Moser and J. Clint Clifft (Knoxville: University of Tennessee Press, 2002), 206–7. With the exception of a postscript and the signature, the letter is
not in Jackson's hand but in that of his secretary—a fact whose psychometric implications
may be considerable! Was Mr. K. sharing a body not only with Jackson but also with his
secretary?

was infused, on this occasion, into the meek and spiritual clergyman, at the distance of more than a thousand miles, by the agency of that thrilling letter," Buchanan declared.[72] Yet as an image of subordination, Mr. K.'s acting out of Jackson's personality was deeply strange. While the impressible clairvoyant was actually present, standing right before the eyes of the audience and speaking to them, the position of controller was merely theoretical, occupied by a scrap of handwriting. Jackson would not have been present at all had it not been for Mr. K.'s deliberate self-disempowerment in favor of the letter.

Psychometry tended to derealize the read character, while the reader remained a person of flesh and blood. Control may have been on the letter's side, but vividness was on the psychometer's. Jackson's moral character became Mr. K.'s theatrical role. It was not uncommon for the subjects of Buchanan's experiments to be compared to actors. Of his subjects' delineations of phrenological traits, the *Philadelphia Inquirer* commented, "we never saw them surpassed on the stage."[73] At the New Harmony community, Robert Dale Owen saw one of Buchanan's subjects recite a speech "from the play of Damon and Pythias . . . with a tone, and look, and gesture, that [the actor Edmund] Kean himself might have envied."[74] Buchanan understood psychometry as reading by disempowerment. I would suggest that it was disempowerment in the special sense that Asad describes in theatrical acting. When an actor plays a role, "the actor's agency consists not in the actions of the role she performs but in her ability to *disempower* one self for the sake of another."[75] Jackson's character in Mr. K.'s experiment was more like the fictional character an actor portrays than like the moral character a person possesses.

In that they disempowered themselves to endow an absent agent with being, psychometers resembled early mesmeric patients. According to the Franklin commission, those patients' imaginations cobbled together Mesmer's nonexistent fluid for him out of the effects of their imaginations. Similarly, psychometers imagined and acted out characters for the objects of their readings. Jackson existed, yes; but he was not likely to appear in the average citizen's parlor by anything less than psychometric means. The Franklin

---

72. Buchanan, "Psychometry—(Continued)," *BJM* 1, no. 3 (March 1849): 101.

73. "Experiments in Phreno-Magnetism."

74. Robert Dale Owen, *Neurology: An Account of Some Experiments in Cerebral Physiology, by Dr. Buchanan, of Louisville, Communicated to an American Newspaper, at Dr. Buchanan's Request* (London: J. Watson, 1842), 5.

75. Asad, *Formations of the Secular*, 75.

commission, struggling to define the power that acted in the magnetic scene, said that the subjects made the magnetist the *dépositaire*, or trustee, of the power of their own imaginations. If, that is, the magnetist appeared to have the potency of a magician, it was the patients themselves who had deposited that potency with him. Similarly, Mr. K. deposited his own potency in Jackson. Psychometry placed the letter writer in the position of the false priest: the magic of his character appeared only because of the impressibility of the psychometer. In spite of Buchanan's ambitions to make character transparent, psychometry moved in the opposite direction. It made the real character a chimerical power that appeared only thanks to the work that the psychometer did in patching that character together from impressions. And maybe a real character *was* a chimerical power. The paradox at the heart of secular agency—that the self, to be free from external control, must already be subject to the control of a self fully free and aware—means that the agent can never quite pin down that part of itself that is fulfilled and in control. That part is elsewhere. Mastery's existence can be ratified only by the stamp it seems to be making—on "oneself," yes, but also on one's subordinates. The latter mark is easier to see. The work of the psychometer was to ratify—to be a fetishistic proxy for—the agent that might not exist.

HUSBANDS AND MAGICIANS

Buchanan lingered long enough in the Boston area to inspire *The Blithedale Romance* (1852), Nathaniel Hawthorne's novel of psychometry. Written after the rise of spiritualism, *Blithedale* is nonetheless set in mesmerism's early days and makes particular reference to Buchanan's practices. *Blithedale* reflects both on the Brook Farm socialist community, defunct by 1852, and on the mesmeric techniques that had been practiced there. During his time in Boston, Buchanan had the good fortune to fall in with some people who had particularly easy access to prominent autographs: the Brook Farmers. As Emerson quipped of the community, "the art of letter-writing, it is said, was immensely cultivated. Letters were always flying not only from house to house, but from room to room."[76] Brook Farm, and the reformist circles

76. Ralph Waldo Emerson, "Historic Notes of Life and Letters in New England," in *The Complete Works of Ralph Waldo Emerson*, 12 vols. (Boston: Houghton, Mifflin, 1903–1904), 10:364.

surrounding it, richly provided Buchanan with raw materials: autograph letters and strong characters. Several residents and regulars were gifted psychometers, mesmerists, or mesmeric clairvoyants, including Anna Quincy Thaxter Parsons, John Orvis, Fred Cabot, and Cornelia Park. Hawthorne had briefly been a resident himself, though before Buchanan's arrival in Boston. Buchanan told Hawthorne's friend James Freeman Clarke, who hosted some of his experiments, that "the venerable Elizabeth Peabody [was] one of the most zealous and punctual" of the students in an advanced psychometry class that met for three hours daily.[77] Peabody was Hawthorne's sister-in-law. John O'Sullivan, a member of the pro-Buchanan *Democratic Review* investigating committee, was Hawthorne's patron.[78] The necromancer from Kentucky would have been difficult for Hawthorne to escape.

Hawthorne clearly did not like Buchanan, or any mesmerist, very much. Nonetheless, he found phrenomesmerism to be a fruitful thought experiment. In *Blithedale*, self-control, history-making, and freely chosen pleasure are mirages that can be conjured up only with the collusion, willing or unwilling, of an impressible person: usually an actress, a wife, or a mesmeric clairvoyant. Reality-making power is all on the side of these subordinates, while the husbands or magicians who extract service from them are humbugs at bottom. Independence of character, like mesmerism itself, is a sham as far as this romance is concerned. *Blithedale* tells the stories of two interwoven events: first, the failure of a utopian community, Blithedale (based on Brook Farm), whose collective plan to make history and choose pleasure comes to nothing; and second, the less-than-victorious flight of a psychometer, Priscilla, out of captivity to a humbug mesmerist and into marriage with a monomaniacal husband, Hollingsworth. Priscilla's marriage breaks the heart of her sister, Zenobia, a women's rights advocate and frustrated tragic actress. The narrator, Miles Coverdale, observes and half participates in the love triangle of the other three, which plays out mostly at the Blithedale community. Hawthorne's romance asks how life can be both tolerated and narrated from the position in which, Hawthorne was convinced, everyone ultimately winds up: that of being molded by the world, rather than molding it. How to live as an impressible subject, inevitably under someone's—or something's—control?

77. Joseph Rodes Buchanan to James Freeman Clarke, April 24, [n.d.], Perry-Clarke Collection, Massachusetts Historical Society.

78. Edwin Haviland Miller, *Salem Is My Dwelling Place: A Life of Nathaniel Hawthorne* (Iowa City: University of Iowa Press, 1991), 149–50, 240.

The plainest example of an impressible character in *Blithedale* is Priscilla, who arrives at the socialist community in flight from her stage career as the Veiled Lady. The wan Priscilla is a natural clairvoyant: from an early age, "hidden things were visible to her . . . and silence was audible"; she seemed to travel to "distant places and splendid rooms" without ever leaving her father's house.[79] At Blithedale, Priscilla inadvertently reveals psychometric gifts when she brings the narrator, Coverdale, a sealed letter from the post office. Like Buchanan's subject Mr. K., Priscilla intuits the character of the letter writer by touch and acts it out so accurately that, without a word passing between them, Coverdale realizes whom she resembles. Priscilla does not know the letter was written by Margaret Fuller and has never met the famous reformer (*BR*, 52), but nonetheless she adopts "a certain curve of the shoulders, and a partial closing of the eyes" that together make her a dead ringer for Fuller. Watching Priscilla, Coverdale comments, "it forcibly struck me that her air, though not her figure, and the expression of her face, but not its features, had a resemblance" to the letter writer (*BR*, 51). Unconsciously, even against her will, Priscilla makes another person's character real.

Both a husband and a mesmerist try to lay claim to Priscilla in *Blithedale*. Hollingsworth, the husband, and Westervelt, the mesmerist, depend on her to make their chimerical powers appear to be genuine, just as she conjured Fuller out of absence. What Hollingsworth wants Priscilla to make real is complicated—ultimately, it is himself. Westervelt's desire to be known for his mesmeric powers, on the other hand, is simple in its crudity. Westervelt has little magic of his own; what few powers he does have amount to the charlatan's tools, deception and manipulation, covered with a thin glamour. Hawthorne's description of Westervelt's alleged abilities could have been drawn from one of Buchanan's boasts: "Human character was but soft wax in his hands; and guilt, or virtue, only the forms into which he should see fit to mould it." If Westervelt so willed, "the maiden, with her lover's kiss still burning on her lips, would turn from him with icy indifference; the newly made widow would dig up her buried heart out of her young husband's grave, before the sod had taken root upon it; a mother, with her babe's milk in her bosom, would thrust away her child" (*BR*, 198). We never know quite how Westervelt presses Priscilla into his service; perhaps it is through a magical body-snatching or perhaps through

---

79. Nathaniel Hawthorne, *The Blithedale Romance and Fanshawe*, ed. Fredson Bowers, vol. 3 of *The Centenary Edition of the Works of Nathaniel Hawthorne*, ed. William Charvat et al. (Columbus: Ohio State University Press, 1964), 187 (hereafter cited in text as *BR*).

a quotidian seduction. While he has charisma enough for these low manipulations, Westervelt has nothing to do with producing Priscilla's higher
powers, such as prophecy and the knowledge of a hidden world. These are
her native abilities, and Westervelt only displays what he has caged. As for
the mesmerist himself, "the whole man [is] a moral and physical humbug"
(BR, 95). His reality as a magician is as much borrowed from Priscilla as is
Margaret Fuller's momentary appearance.

Hollingsworth, the would-be prison reformer and Priscilla's eventual
husband, depends on her for his reality, too. He says as much when he gath-
ers with Priscilla and her sister Zenobia at the rock called Eliot's Pulpit; the
scene effectively decides which of the two women will win his love. Hollingsworth articulates an anti–women's rights position that amounts to the
plea that women should devote themselves to reassuring him that he exists.
Woman's "office," he declares, is "that of the Sympathizer; the unreserved,
unquestioning Believer; the Recognition, withheld in every other manner,
but given, in pity, through woman's heart, lest man should utterly lose faith
in himself" (BR, 122). The naked will to power in this speech—and the patent
weakness, too—are so blinding that it is hard to look directly at the words.
They say, however, that Hollingsworth requires that his wife should idolize
his purpose as a primitive fetishist would idolize a wooden god. Without
such a "Believer," Hollingsworth can have no "faith in himself." Under an
enlightenment conspectus, an idol has no animation except for that which
the imagination of the credulous believer lends it; its lifelike qualities are in
fact the *believer's* qualities, projected onto the object. Hollingsworth fears
he is much the same: not just fraudulent but lifeless until Priscilla lends him
her "Recognition." Hollingsworth's character, like Westervelt's magic, would
clatter inanimate to the floor without her support.

What Priscilla is to shore up in Hollingsworth is at once his aspira-
tional identity and his project for life: his scheme of prison reform. As with
Westervelt's magical powers, there is something fraudulent and unreal about
Hollingsworth's "philanthropic theory." "Hollingsworth," Coverdale observes,
"had a closer friend than ever you could be. And this friend was the cold,
spectral monster which he had himself conjured up, and on which he was
wasting all the warmth of his heart, and of which, at last—as these men of a
mighty purpose so invariably do—he had grown to be the bond-slave. It was
his philanthropic theory!" (BR, 55). The "cold, spectral monster which he had
himself conjured up" is the idol he needs Priscilla, the wifely "Believer," to
worship. It is the humbug he needs her, with her real powers of impressibility, to breathe into life. He will be, as a man should be, "her acknowledged

principal"—making her his agent in the older nineteenth-century sense, the one who disempowers herself to carry out the acts of another (*BR*, 123). Wholly dedicated to his "philanthropic theory," Hollingsworth fits the ideal of secular agency: he is self-controlled and self-identical; he is empowered; and he has every intention of making history. And yet Hollingsworth's overweening purpose is not fully real without Priscilla to manifest, by her impressibility, the dent it has made in her.

An autobiographical shadow lies behind the romance's comparison of mesmerist and husband: Hawthorne encountered mesmerism mostly through the enthusiasm of his wife's family for the practice. The Peabodys' interest in mesmerism dated back to Poyen's arrival in 1836, before Hawthorne met them.[80] Sophia Peabody, later Sophia Hawthorne, had been the beneficiary of a long-standing treatment regimen at the hands of Joseph Fiske, who was both Poyen's acolyte and her father's dental assistant.[81] It seems likely that the biographical entanglement of mesmerism and dentistry helped inspire the trait Hawthorne called "the devil's signet" on Westervelt in *Blithedale*, his chimerical smile: "every one of his brilliant grinders and incisors was a sham" (*BR*, 95, 198). Hawthorne first objected to Sophia's use of magnetism when he learned that she was undergoing treatment from her friend Cornelia Park during their courtship.[82] Hawthorne, who was decidedly the indoor type, was living rather unhappily at Brook Farm at the time; he tolerated the rustic life with an ill grace, keeping up a steady drizzle of complaints about the weather.[83] From Brook Farm, he wrote in October 1841 to warn Sophia against mesmerism: "there would be an intrusion into thy holy of holies—and the intruder would not be thy husband!"[84] Within a few weeks, he left the Roxbury community and set the wheels in motion to

80. Taylor Stoehr, *Hawthorne's Mad Scientists: Pseudoscience and Social Science in Nineteenth-Century Life and Letters* (Hamden, CT: Archon Books, 1978), 38.

81. Ibid., 39–40. As Stoehr points out, Fiske wrote to Poyen: see Charles Poyen, *Progress of Animal Magnetism in New England* (Boston: Weeks, Jordan, 1837), 200–201.

82. On Cornelia Park's relationship with Sophia, see Megan Marshall, *The Peabody Sisters: Three Women Who Ignited American Romanticism* (Boston: Houghton Mifflin, 2005), 257–58, 433; on Park's biography and on Nathaniel's objections to her mesmerizing Sophia, see also Nathaniel Hawthorne, *The Letters, 1813–1843*, ed. Thomas Woodson et al., vol. 15 of *The Centenary Edition of the Works of Nathaniel Hawthorne*, ed. Thomas Woodson (Columbus: Ohio State University Press, 1984), 383n2, 588.

83. Miller, *Salem Is My Dwelling Place*, 187, 195–98.

84. Hawthorne, *Letters, 1813–1843*, 588.

make good his possession of Sophia through marriage.[85] Even then he was never quite free of mesmeric inroads. When Buchanan came to town in 1843–44, Hawthorne was surrounded on all sides by the phrenomesmerist's advocates, and years later, his sister-in-law Elizabeth would try to press his daughter Una into service as a spiritualist medium, much to his horror.[86]

In Hawthorne's romance treatments of mesmerism, then, he synthesized a long experience of domestic nuisance. Mesmerism had in effect competed with him for his wife's allegiance. But *Blithedale* does not simply vindicate the husband against the mesmerist. In his other mesmeric novel, *The House of the Seven Gables* (1851), Hawthorne contrasts husbandly claims with mesmeric ones: the former are legitimate, the latter tyrannical. That novel has the daguerreotypist Holgrave as a countercultural version of the husband Hollingsworth, and Phoebe as a sunnier counterpart to Priscilla. While recounting a tale of mesmerism, Holgrave accidentally mesmerizes Phoebe with his storytelling power. Rather than consolidate "his mastery over Phoebe's yet free and virgin spirit," as he is sorely tempted to do, Holgrave holds back.[87] Hawthorne's narrator praises him: "Let us, therefore . . . concede to the Daguerreotypist the rare and high quality of reverence for another's individuality."[88] This is almost neoliberal in its smug contortions: Holgrave's empire as both author and husband ensures Phoebe's liberty. "If I possessed such a power over thee, I should not dare to exercise it," the young Nathaniel assured the young Sophia in the 1841 letter.[89] In *Blithedale*, by contrast to the self-justifications of the letter and the earlier novel, every use of an impressible person to shore up one's own sham smile is at least dark, and perhaps diabolical. There is little to choose between Hollingsworth's demand for a "Believer" and Westervelt's demand for a clairvoyant.

The House of the Seven Gables believes in husbandly agency and wonders how to assert it in a properly circumscribed manner. *Blithedale*, by contrast, is suspicious of husbands and treats the problem of their power as one of kind, not degree. For the latter novel, the husband's self-determination is like the magician's power: a chimera, and specifically a "cold, spectral

85. Miller, *Salem Is My Dwelling Place*, 199.

86. Bruce A. Ronda, *Elizabeth Palmer Peabody: A Reformer on Her Own Terms* (Cambridge, MA: Harvard University Press, 1999), 248–49.

87. Nathaniel Hawthorne, *The House of the Seven Gables*, vol. 2 of *The Centenary Edition of the Works of Nathaniel Hawthorne*, ed. William Charvat et al. (Columbus: Ohio State University Press, 1965), 212.

88. Ibid., 212.

89. Hawthorne, *Letters, 1813–1843*, 588.

monster" parasitic for its existence on someone else. The only honest position is impressibility, and *Blithedale* is narrated from that position. Coverdale compares himself to a "mesmerical clairvoyant" in his ability to be "impressed" by others' "spheres" (*BR*, 46–47). Arriving at Blithedale, he comes down with a bad fever whose ravages make him even more sensitive than he normally is. Priscilla performs her Fuller impression in his sickroom, as though to offer a graphic illustration of how Coverdale will interpret other characters by being absorbed in them, sometimes against his inclinations. Coverdale is terrible at choosing pleasure and even worse at making history. He impresses himself on no one, while anyone can reshape him. His definitive feature is "that quality of the intellect and the heart, which impelled me (often against my own will, and to the detriment of my own comfort) to live in other lives, and to endeavor . . . by bringing my human spirit into manifold accordance with the companions whom God assigned me—to learn the secret which was hidden even from themselves" (*BR*, 160). Thus, he represents an unusual attempt to narrate from what looks, from a secular perspective, like failed agency. Instead, I want to insist, it is an experiment in a kind of selfhood that neither veils nor enslaves others.

"HATING MILES COVERDALE"

Critics have not taken kindly to this experiment. If any character in American literature has inspired greater animosity than Coverdale has, I don't know who it is. "Hating Miles Coverdale" is so popular a pastime that Michael Borgstrom has devoted an entire article of that title to the task of documenting it. Attacks on the narrator are "unusually hostile" and "ad hominem," Borgstrom notes.[90] "Coverdale bashing is great sport," remarks David Leverenz, pleasantly tired after a lengthy bout in the ring.[91] What do people hate in Coverdale? They claim to hate his voyeurism. He is "self-absorbed and heartless, cloyingly malicious and intrusive," Leverenz says.[92] That is not quite the whole story. They hate that instead of acting on his erotic impulses

90. Michael Borgstrom, "Hating Miles Coverdale," *ESQ: A Journal of the American Renaissance* 56, no. 4 (2011): 363.

91. David Leverenz, *Manhood and the American Renaissance* (Ithaca, NY: Cornell University Press, 1989), 253.

92. Ibid., 248.

and working for a political future, he watches passively while others do both. They hate him, I think, not for watching per se but for raising the uncomfortable suggestion that any one of us might be ineffectual, and that sexual liberation and political utopia may not be in our grasp. Coverdale's inability to maximize freedom and choose pleasure calls into question whether any of us will manage to do those things. The energy with which critics want to dispel such a doubt is at the root of much of the animosity Coverdale inspires. But to dispel this doubt is only to react symptomatically to Hawthorne's unsettling provocation: empowerment might not be possible.

There are two principal complaints about Coverdale: he is not much of a revolutionary, and he is not much of a lover. The two complaints have a common element: Coverdale is not much of an agent. As for the charge of failure as a revolutionary, here is some of the evidence against the prisoner. Coverdale flees the utopian community and belittles it in his recollections. He "relentlessly devalues Blithedale's idealism," as Christopher Newfield puts it.[93] Newfield, describing a view that he partly takes but of which he is also critical, writes, "One of Blithedale's biggest problems . . . is the presence of people like him."[94] That is to say, the socialist utopia fails because some of its members lack commitment. A critic as distant from Newfield in time and in sensibility as Richard Chase can say something recognizably similar: "Coverdale . . . is too timid and cold to live the emotional life which his intellect perceives."[95] A political charge against Hawthorne sometimes lies behind the critiques of Coverdale. In 1852 Hawthorne published both *Blithedale* and a campaign biography of Franklin Pierce featuring his suggestion that slavery is "one of those evils which divine Providence does not leave to be remedied by human contrivances, but which, in it[s] own good time, by some means impossible to be anticipated . . . it causes to vanish like a dream."[96] As Eric

93. Christopher Newfield and Melissa Solomon, "'Few of Our Seeds Ever Came Up at All': A Dialogue on Hawthorne, Delany, and the Work of Affect in Visionary Utopias," in *No More Separate Spheres! A Next Wave American Studies Reader*, ed. Cathy N. Davidson and Jessamyn Hatcher (Durham, NC: Duke University Press, 2002), 384. Newfield and Solomon's piece is a conversation, with portions of the article appearing under each of their individual names. I follow the article's own attributions by crediting each quote either to Newfield or to Solomon.

94. Ibid., 383–84.

95. Richard Chase, *The American Novel and Its Tradition* (Garden City, NY: Doubleday, 1957), 84.

96. Nathaniel Hawthorne, *Life of Franklin Pierce* (Boston: Ticknor, Reed, & Fields, 1852), 113.

Cheyfitz has said, these are "the easy remarks of a comfortable, middle-class, white, Protestant male who feels no need to envision forms of transformative social action in a time of crisis."[97] While Cheyfitz's critique of Hawthorne is unassailable on its own terms, there is another way to understand Coverdale's ineffectiveness. Quietism and the frank acknowledgement of our limited powers can look a lot alike. "Where [Hawthorne's] heretical prophecies tend is toward a vision of a systematic disjunction between human intention and historical consequence, between the purpose of social action and action's effect," Richard Brodhead has suggested; "the course men plot for history and the course history actually takes are simply two separate things."[98] Hating Coverdale may be a way of defending against Hawthorne's defeatism. But a little defeatism is a reasonable reaction to the sunny conviction that everyone is on schedule to make his or her mark on history, sooner or later.

As objectionable as Coverdale's political cowardice has been his erotic pusillanimity. Critique of the latter has taken two forms over the years: either homophobic reaction or irritation at a missed opportunity for liberation. In either case, Coverdale is queer. Some critics have found queerness itself to be a failure of potency, while others think Coverdale does not pursue his forbidden desires vigorously enough. To Richard Poirier, for whom Coverdale is a "Dandy-Child,"[99] there is "a somewhat sickly, somewhat even masturbatory quality in Coverdale's self-regarding retreat."[100] The retreat Poirier means is the nest in the branches from which Coverdale spies on members of the community in the "Hermitage" chapter. Poirier is activating what Melissa Solomon has described as a "(homophobic) reading grid."[101] Gale Temple, by contrast with Poirier, calls the same nest of branches a "tree-closet."[102] She takes Coverdale to task not for having homoerotic desires but for repressing them. He flees to his hermitage instead of "engaging

97. Eric Cheyfitz, "The Irresistibleness of Great Literature: Reconstructing Hawthorne's Politics," *American Literary History* 6, no. 3 (Fall 1994): 545.

98. Richard Brodhead, "Hawthorne and the Fate of Politics," *Essays in Literature* 11, no. 1 (Spring 1984): 99.

99. Richard Poirier, *A World Elsewhere: The Place of Style in American Literature* (New York: Oxford University Press, 1966), 121.

100. Ibid., 120.

101. Newfield and Solomon, "'Few of Our Seeds,'" 384.

102. Gale Temple, "'Ineffable Socialities': Melville, Hawthorne, and Masculine Ambivalence in the Antebellum Marketplace," in *Hawthorne and Melville: Writing a Relationship*, ed. Jana L. Argersinger and Leland S. Person (Athens: University of Georgia Press, 2008), 124.

in a form of sexual or soul-sharing consummation with Hollingsworth," a phrase that would be at home in the ghastliest of couples therapy sessions.[103] Pretty much no one believes in "Miles Coverdale's [Hetero-] Confession," where Hawthorne tries to tidy things up by making Coverdale admit to a passion for Priscilla (*BR*, 245–47). Lauren Berlant's rewriting—"he—he himself—was in love—with—Hollingsworth"—would sit more easily with most readers.[104] Coverdale's refusal of Hollingsworth's proposal of partnership in prison reform sums up all his evasions (*BR*, 133, 135). Where he could have been Hollingsworth's work wife, thus satisfying both the pleasure-taking and the history-making imperatives, he sidles off to Boston for coal fires and room service (*BR*, 145, 150). Thus he is sickly or closeted, masturbatory or evasive. But is it necessary to point out how ruthless—not to mention pre-psychoanalytic—is this demand that a character act valiantly and immediately on his every sexual wish?

The best readings of Coverdale come from queer studies: Solomon values "his brave refusal to be shamed by a world in which he finds it difficult to extract sustenance," and Jordan Stein finds in Coverdale a queerness that has less to do with homosexuality per se than with an inability to accommodate oneself to the world and its ways of speaking.[105] In this merciful spirit, let me propose an alternate reading of the "tree-closet" scene that has inspired so much healthy-minded erotic coaching. Coverdale says it himself: the "Hermitage" chapter is not about evading action, an independent agent's problem. It is about being acted upon, a psychometer's problem. Coverdale claims the scene as an illustration of his "impressibility"; he was temporarily "degrad[ed]" and "deform[ed]" by Westervelt's "sphere," as the magician walked under his nest of branches (*BR*, 101). Coverdale quickly disowns his cynicism as a spell that Westervelt's near presence cast on him. Westervelt laughs, and the sound clues Coverdale in: he "recognize[s], as chiefly due to this man's influence, the sceptical and sneering view" that had impressed him (*BR*, 101). All of his accusations—Hollingsworth yokes mankind like oxen, Zenobia is treacherous, and the utopian dream is "ridiculous"—actually result from being "possessed" by the magician's out-

---

103. Ibid., 124.

104. Lauren Berlant, "Fantasies of Utopia in *The Blithedale Romance*," *American Literary History* 1, no. 1 (Spring 1989): 36.

105. Newfield and Solomon, "'Few of Our Seeds,'" 390; Jordan Alexander Stein, "*The Blithedale Romance*'s Queer Style," *ESQ: A Journal of the American Renaissance*, 55, no. 3–4 (2009): 212–13.

look (*BR*, 100–101). This momentary rapport is an illustration of the problem with impressibility. To leave oneself open to the inroads others might make is also to leave oneself open to consequences that range in seriousness from compromised judgment to social embarrassment to rape. Impressibility exposes us to diabolical attachments, and so one needs to shield oneself with dependencies that are more livable.

PSEUDONYMS

In *Blithedale*, these tolerable dependencies are often fictions, or at any rate, feints: costumes, nicknames, noms de guerre, and theatrical roles adopted by the characters in the romance. Such roles are not entirely about self-concealment. If the actor embodies a distinctive kind of agency in which one's actions consist in disempowering oneself in favor of the role, then acting can be an antidote to the view that it's a puppet-eat-puppet world. Rather than face a stark choice between pulling the strings or having their strings pulled, these characters hand their strings over to a fiction—which, being a fiction, cannot help but partly hand the strings back. Nearly every character has a handle rather than a name; a label that points to, but never allows us to reach, the real name that is elsewhere. Pseudonyms are rife. Priscilla becomes the Veiled Lady when she goes on stage as a "phenomenon in the mesmeric line" (*BR*, 5). And anyway, is she really Priscilla? "Pray do not ask me my other name—at least, not yet," she pleads when introducing herself at Blithedale—an ambiguous demand that may mean, do not ask me my family name, do not ask me my real name, or do not ask me my stage name (*BR*, 29). "She goes among you by the name of Priscilla," is the most Westervelt will say when asking after her (*BR*, 96).

While the Veiled Lady is a stage name, Zenobia is a literary incognito, used by the writer in print and as a nickname among her private friends but disowned by her "in general society" (*BR*, 93). Asked by Westervelt about "Zenobia," Coverdale refuses to answer; he will only discuss her under "Zenobia's real name" (*BR*, 93). That cognomen is one the reader never learns; Zenobia's realities keep entirely to the rear. Priscilla and Zenobia's father, Moodie, is Fauntleroy in his encrypted account of their past; Moodie itself might well be an alias, since its bearer is in flight from a mysterious disgrace (*BR*, 183). Westervelt holds an honorific title, "Professor," that is almost certainly phony, like everything else about the man. Miles Coverdale is the only person in the novel with both a first and a last name, but he borrows both from someone else, a sixteenth-century translator of the Bible into English—giving his title the same air of unreality as might cling to "John Wayne" signed in a hotel register by a man planning to do some extramarital soul-sharing consummation. Not even Blithedale escapes christening troubles; the "old Indian name of the premises" was unfortunately "harsh, ill-connected, and interminable," and Zenobia's suggestion of "Sunny Glimpse" and Coverdale's of "Utopia" are too sentimental and too satirical, respectively. The community settles finally on Blithedale, as being "neither good nor bad" (*BR*, 37).

In their relation to real referents—that is to say, to historical personages known to Hawthorne—the characters have a similar tendency to put roles on and off, escaping from one costume into another. *The Blithedale Romance* is a sham roman à clef: Hawthorne pretends that his characters refer to real people, but by doing so, he only sends us into a hall of mirrors, where we will never be sure who is standing in for whom. In a true roman à clef, where each character is a thinly disguised version of a real person, one might say that each character is controlled by its historical referent as a psychometer is controlled by the letter she reads. To take an example contemporary with Hawthorne, Thomas Dunn English's roman à clef *1844* (1847) attacks Poe under the name of Marmaduke Hammerhead. Hammerhead is unmistakably Poe, as we can tell by "the broad, low, receding, and deformed forehead," "his manner, in laying down some proposition, which he conceives it would be madness to doubt, yet believes it to be known only by himself," and his authorship of "a poem, called the 'Black Crow.'"[106] It's too easy.

Blithedale never delivers anything remotely approaching that level of certainty. The "Preface" disowns any connection between the characters of the novel and the inhabitants of Brook Farm, but in a manner that raises rather than allays suspicions. Naming the four main characters in terms of their types—the "self-concentrated Philanthropist" (Hollingsworth), the "high-spirited Woman" (Zenobia), "the weakly Maiden" (Priscilla), and "the Minor Poet" (Coverdale)—Hawthorne archly remarks, "all these might have been looked for, at BROOK FARM, but, by some accident, never made their appearance there" (*BR*, 2–3). His narrator then goes on to behave as though the reader knows that the novel is a roman à clef anyway. Some might remember

---

106. Thomas Dunn English, *1844; or, The Power of the 'S. F.'* (New York: Burgess, Stringer, 1847), 121. Previously serialized in the *Weekly Mirror* (New York), July 25, 1846–November 7, 1846: see Dwight Thomas and David K. Jackson, eds., *The Poe Log: A Documentary Life of Edgar Allan Poe, 1809–1849* (Boston: G. K. Hall, 1987), 659, 670.

the Veiled Lady's period of activity a dozen years before, Coverdale remarks, but "it may not be amiss to mention, for the benefit of such of my readers as are unacquainted with her now forgotten celebrity, that she was a phenomenon in the mesmeric line" (*BR*, 5). Zenobia's appearance merits a similar reference to a shared history: "This (as the reader, if at all acquainted with our literary biography, need scarcely be told) was not her real name" (*BR*, 13). So does Hollingsworth's: "His figure was not tall, but massive and brawny, and well befitting his original occupation, which—as the reader probably knows—was that of a blacksmith" (*BR*, 28). These asides have spurred many a speculation over whom the characters represent, with argument on the question of whether Zenobia is Margaret Fuller being especially heated.[107] But the debates have never yielded the level of certainty with which Marmaduke Hammerhead can be identified with Poe—and they never will. *Blithedale* tempts its readers to look for correspondences so that they will have the experience of not finding any. The impression remains far more vivid than the absent stamp, suggesting that these possible historical controls matter less—are in a sense less real—than the fictional characters they purportedly underwrite. Their spectral control leaves the characters in relative freedom.

Sentiments and thoughts, like characters, need a false identity in *Blithedale*: they need a way of being expressed under the rose of irony or frivolity, so that the speaker is not too enmeshed in the necessity of standing by them. Coverdale is king of the trivial, a quality of his that has wrongly been interpreted as cynicism. Quite the opposite: like Oscar Wilde, Coverdale is serious only when he is joking. His motif is the "grandly meditative take on modern life . . . undone by the introduction of a sherry-cobbler," as Stein puts it.[108] "I wish you would see fit to comprehend," Coverdale says to Hollingsworth, "that the profoundest wisdom must be mingled with nine-tenths of nonsense; else it is not worth the breath that utters it" (*BR*, 129). Hollingsworth of course will not see fit to comprehend; always serious, Hollingsworth is also always himself. He is the one monstrous exception to the general rule of pseudonyms. He has neither pen name nor stage name nor alter ego. He does not appear in either of the two romans à clef within the novel,

107. Emerson, "Historic Notes of Life and Letters in New England," 10:364; Georgiana Bruce Kirby, *Years of Experience: An Autobiographical Narrative* (New York: G. P. Putnam's Sons, 1887; repr., New York: AMS Press, 1971), 103. Citation for Kirby refers to the AMS Press edition. See also Louise D. Cary, "Margaret Fuller as Hawthorne's Zenobia: The Problem of Moral Accountability in Fictional Biography," *ATQ* 4, no. 1 (March 1990): 31–48.

108. Stein, "*Blithedale Romance*'s Queer Style," 221.

"Zenobia's Legend,"—her story of Coverdale and the Veiled Lady, where Coverdale goes by Theodore—or "Fauntleroy," Moodie's account of Priscilla's childhood. When the Blithedalers hold a masquerade, complete with goddesses, witches, Puritans, and "gay Cavaliers," Hollingsworth appears "in his ordinary working-dress" (BR, 209–10, 213). Hollingsworth is Hollingsworth is Hollingsworth is Hollingsworth. "Such prolonged fiddling upon one string; such multiform presentation of one idea!" Coverdale says of him, not admiringly (BR, 56).

Authentic prophecy, like authentic sentiments or thoughts, bears the stamp of nonsense. At the opening of the novel, Coverdale is returning from an exhibition of the Veiled Lady, whom he has asked about "the success of our Blithedale enterprise. The response, by-the-by, was of the true Sibylline stamp, nonsensical in its first aspect, yet, on closer study, unfolding a variety of interpretations, one of which has certainly accorded with the event" (BR, 6). This is the sign of truth in Blithedale: solicited on a whim, mentioned "by-the-by," scorned as nonsensical, perceived through a haze of conjecture, and finally fulfilled by events. Prophecies in the novel require not just interpretation but affective decoding, a reversal of the signs of triviality and uselessness with which they are marked. Just after Priscilla's arrival at the farm, Zenobia jokes to Coverdale, "you had better turn the affair into a ballad. It is a grand subject, and worthy of supernatural machinery. The storm, the startling knock at the door, the entrance of the sable knight Hollingsworth and this shadowy snow-maiden, who, precisely at the stroke of midnight, shall melt away at my feet, in a pool of ice-cold water, and give me my death with a pair of wet slippers!" (BR, 33). Zenobia's joke precisely indexes her real death. In a chapter called "Midnight," Zenobia drowns herself in a pool of ice-cold water. Priscilla is her innocent murderer. Zenobia's "wet slipper" betokens her fate when Coverdale, Hollingsworth, and the hired hand Silas Foster find it in the mud of the riverbank (BR, 231). The purple verse Zenobia imagines and ridicules turns out to tell the truth.

Given the general reality of disempowerment—of being impressed upon by others—the achievement may be to engage the battle with humiliation on the field of frivolity, rather than that of tragic capture. The sexes have unequal access to that possibility in Blithedale, despite Zenobia's valiant attempts to claim triviality as her own. For the impressible Coverdale, the worst consequence of being ineffective and subordinate is social embarrassment: "the greatest obstacle to being heroic, is the doubt whether one may not be going to prove one's self a fool," he reflects when recalling the moment of his youth when he was willing to lend himself to Blithedale's socialist enterprise (*BR*, 10). For his female counterpart, the impressible Priscilla, the worst-case scenario is sexual violation. As Priscilla leaves Westervelt's embrace for Hollingsworth's, Coverdale declares that he "religiously believe[s]" that she maintained "her virgin reserve and sanctity of soul, throughout it all" (*BR*, 203). Coverdale can brazen out his foolishness; Priscilla could not have brazened out her rape. Hawthorne lets nonsense and humbug master women in a way that they do not master Coverdale. Zenobia, too, succumbs to the literalization of her own joke: death by a pair of wet slippers. Still, she has her wasteful daily greenhouse flower, shoved into her hair. Of all Zenobia's gifts—her skill as a tragedian, her eloquence— her insouciance is not the least of her achievements.

Zenobia is the narrator of the tale-within-a-tale that is *Blithedale's* mirror for itself: "a wild, spectral legend" that Zenobia "trump[s] up . . . on the spur of the moment" reflecting, in true roman à clef style, the story of the Blithedale community. Tired of parlor theatricals one evening, Zenobia offers to tell the community a legend that is "not exactly a ghost-story . . . but something so nearly like it that you shall hardly tell the difference" (*BR*, 107). Character itself is a ghost story in this novel: the more it seems to point to a definite location, the source of the will that exerts self-control, the less there seems to be anyone there. Zenobia's legend is a parable about two ways of handling character. According to one view, character is something solid at the bottom of a person, beneath the veils of transitory behavior. Someone with a good character has a firm foundation that can be glimpsed in between his or her performances. That view of character is the one with which her tale begins, when the story's Coverdale figure, called Theodore, is speculating with his drinking companions about the identity of the Veiled Lady. On their view, to know her character would be to know what is *under* the veil, what is *behind* her performances. Young men who gather to discuss her have nothing to say about the future age she foretells, and every interest in speculating about whose sister she is. One identifies her with "'a young lady'—and here he mentioned her name—'the daughter of one of our most distinguished families!'" (*BR*, 109). Why would the brother of "the young lady in question" not "defend her character" unless the rumors were true? (*BR*, 109). The interest of the Veiled Lady's exhibitions is in large part "the enigma of her character," which "instead of being solved, presented itself more mystically at every exhibition" (*BR*, 108). The enchantment the men want to discover is the honor of a young woman.

But this view of character comes to no good in Zenobia's legend. Theodore goes on a discovery mission, determined to solve the mystery of the "lady in question." Ignoring the lady's warnings, he lifts her veil, and the lovely face beneath the gauze disappears into a deeper bondage forever. The moral threatens to be something rather commonplace: have faith in those you love. There is a more interesting possibility: leave people their incognitos. Interact with others in the full knowledge that the character you confront is a "spectral illusion." This second view of character may be the one Zenobia's legend teaches. As the young men speculate about the Veiled Lady's possible identity with a certain woman, someone points out that this woman was present at one of the Veiled Lady's exhibitions. "Oh, it was a spectral illusion that you saw!" the others say. "The Veiled Lady is quite up to such a thing" (BR, 109). In this legend, all character—including on the prosaic level of a respectable young woman's sexual purity—is a spectral illusion. To lift the veil on a mission of discovery is to presume that character is what's underneath. But character is, instead, the illusion itself. Character is the veil, which Zenobia describes as "so impalpable, so ethereal, so without substance, as the texture seemed, yet hiding her every outline in an impenetrability like that of midnight" (BR, 111). It is at once the instrument of the Veiled Lady's "bondage," but also her only possible freedom (BR, 112). The magician, it is clear, used the veil to capture her. And yet, had Theodore only permitted her to retain it, she would have been free. The characters that control us are both locked doors, if they belong to others like husbands and magicians, and open doors, if they are fictions or realities belonging to no one in particular.

TALVJ

The sustained preoccupation of Hawthorne's *Blithedale Romance* is the relationship between two modes of impressibility. One of these modes is obedience, as when the docile wife obeys the husband or when the enthralled clairvoyant obeys the magician. Obedience is the form of impressibility that seems to be demanded by secular agency as its supplementary term. Self-control can never be fully realized, but its substitute, control of another person, perhaps can be. The other mode of impressibility that appears in *Blithedale* is interpretation, as when the actor interprets the role, the psychometer interprets the letter, or the narrator Coverdale interprets the impressions he receives of others' characters into a narrative. These two modes of impressibility seem very different, but in fact they are just different ways of describing the same disposition. To obey is also to construe or interpret. In psychometry's native terms, to be capable of reading others' skulls is also to be sensitive to having your own skull manipulated. This close relationship between obeying and acting a theatrical role does a certain mischief to the bond of obedience. The one who obeys is also the one who can, perhaps who must, interpret the will of the one who demands obedience. That interpretation may always turn out to be displeasing to the control. Or the interpretation may even turn out to be not an interpretation but a fabrication: an invented control who, having been created, becomes an alibi and an ally, a pseudonym or veil beyond which one's own actions have a degree of free play. So-and-so (who does not exist!) made me do it.

There is such a thing as *mischievous obedience*: the obedience that misconstrues; the obedience that pledges fealty to a fiction of its own invention. Psychometry was particularly ripe for an obedience that misconstrues; the reader of an absent letter writer's character had free rein to utter all sorts of calumnies against him or her—even, as we saw with Priscilla's reading of Fuller in *Blithedale*, to imitate an unflattering stoop or squint—without the inert autograph manuscript having much opportunity of rebuttal. Brook Farm's chief psychometrist, Anna Quincy Thaxter Parsons, made lavish use of this privilege. Psychometry as actually practiced at Brook Farm was less sexually melodramatic than Hawthorne imagined, and less focused on the character of the letter writer than Buchanan had hoped. Parsons worked independently, without the aid of a mesmerist. For her, the psychometric trick was not just to read another's character but to acquire it as a costume for her wardrobe. She resembled Zenobia or Coverdale more than she did Priscilla: she improvised with others' identities as though they were shawls used in parlor theatricals or fictional characters in her own drama.

Parsons was a lifelong sympathizer with reform causes and with Brook Farm's aspirations. Prevented by ill health and the opposition of her family from living at the community, she visited often.[109] She also corresponded steadily with resident Marianne Dwight from 1844 to 1847, the years when the Brook Farmers became engrossed in Buchanan's psychometry. Few of

109. Helen Dwight Orvis, "Note on Anna Q. T. Parsons," in Marianne Dwight, *Letters from Brook Farm, 1844–1847*, by Marianne Dwight, ed. Amy L. Reed (Poughkeepsie, NY: Vassar College, 1928), xiii–xv (*Letters from Brook Farm* hereafter cited in text as *LBF*); "Union of Women for Association," *Harbinger* 5, no. 1, June 12, 1847: 14; "The Golden Chronicle" (Note on the Will of Anna Quincy Thaxter Parsons), *Massachusetts Ploughman and New England Journal of Agriculture*, November 10, 1906.

Parsons's letters have survived, but Dwight's side of the correspondence offers a window into psychometry as practiced by an impressible subject without a mesmerist on the scene. Dwight at times enclosed specimens of writing for Parsons to read; other times, she took notes on Parsons's readings during visits and passed them around the community. For the two friends, Anna's impressibility was easily integrated into everyday life. "Did you have a good time and some good readings? Do tell me about them," Dwight wrote in an 1844 letter collected in her *Letters from Brook Farm, 1844–1847* (*LBF*, 6). When Dwight described a community dispute in January 1845, she included a header: "(*Place your hand on the bottom of this, and the top of the next page and tell me what impression you get)*" (*LBF*, 61). These were the portions of the letter in which Dwight recounted the conflict (*LBF*, 62n1). Psychometry expressed the friends' sense that even though Anna's family would not permit her to be part of the community in body, she was "a part of its directing spirit," as Dwight told her in May 1845 (*LBF*, 102).

There is no mention of anyone magnetizing Parsons in Dwight's published letters, although several Brook Farm residents had magnetizing ability. Cornelia Park, formerly Sophia Peabody's mesmerist, was a Brook Farm boarder.[110] And when John Orvis, former resident of the Skaneateles community and future husband to Marianne Dwight, came to Brook Farm in April 1844, Fred Cabot magnetized him (*LBF*, 10n2, 13). Orvis, like Parsons, was "*very* impressible, [and] reads characters thro' letters, or by coming into contact with a person" (*LBF*, 13). Dwight told Parsons that Cabot "put him to sleep in a few moments," after which Orvis "read Abby Foord's character finely by putting his hand on her head" (*LBF*, 13–14). Either Parsons, unlike Orvis, entered the state of impressibility without magnetic aid, or the fact that someone mesmerized her did not strike Dwight as a significant part of the process, because it never comes up. Parsons was also an active interpreter of her own readings. Buchanan said that the psychometer should "yield passively to the impression, and follow the natural current of his ideas or feelings."[111] But as Luciano has pointed out, "psychometers' narratives . . . outline something closer to an affective and sensory mingling or embodied duality."[112] In other words, the psychometer retained the capacity to judge and reflect even during the reading. Parsons and Dwight saw no inconsistency

---

110. Kirby, *Years of Experience*, 144–45. Kirby calls her "Cornelia H.," after her maiden name, Hall.

111. Buchanan, "Psychometry," *BJM* 1, no. 2 (February 1849): 59.

112. Luciano, "Sacred Theories of Earth," 725.

in Parsons exerting creative control over her readings after the fact. She looked over and sometimes amended Dwight's transcripts. Dwight then used these corrected copies when she distributed Parsons's readings to friends (see *LBF*, 110).

Parsons had apparently learned psychometry at Buchanan's hands. The earliest trace we have of her involvement in the practice is a January 1844 experiment that took place at James Freeman Clarke and Sarah Huidekoper Clarke's house in the Boston area. It is clear from the account of this experiment, a letter Margaret Fuller wrote to Emerson shortly afterward, that Parsons was already known to have psychometric ability before the experiment took place. James Clarke at one point refers to her earlier reading of a letter by the recently deceased William Ellery Channing.[113] But her expertise had to have been of recent date; Buchanan had not been in Boston long. Present at the experiment were the Clarkes, Parsons, Buchanan, and Buchanan's wife, Anne Rowan Buchanan. Lidian Emerson, Emerson's wife, later heard about the experiment from the participants, and so did Fuller (*LMF*, 3:175–77). Both Fuller and James Clarke were familiar with mesmerism before Joseph Buchanan's advent, having seen Brackett perform in Providence. While under the "Mesmeric influence," Parsons "was tried with five or six autograph letters," including manuscripts from the painter Washington Allston, the minister J. S. Buckminster, the writer Harriet Martineau, and Ralph Waldo Emerson (*LMF*, 3:177).

The group was best satisfied with what they heard about Emerson. Parsons was reluctant to admit to any "fault," but she acknowledged there was a "defect—it is underdevelopment; it puts me in mind of a circle with a dent in it." Buchanan magnetized Parsons's organ of self-esteem so that she could "overlook [i.e., look down on]" Emerson, and under that treatment, she hazarded, "If he could sympathize with himself, he could with every one." Fuller considered her identification of this "defect" to be "a most refined expression of the truth" (*LMF*, 3:178). Sarah Clarke, too, thought "that in all she said about [Emerson], . . . she assumed a tone and emphasis that reminded [Clarke]" of the original (quoted in *LMF*, 3:177). In criticizing Emerson, Parsons was also channeling him: she adopted the indescribable mannerisms by which his friends recognized his character. Emerson appeared—not exactly in spirit, but in the anthropometric combination of his autograph and Parsons's body.

113. Margaret Fuller, *The Letters of Margaret Fuller*, 6 vols., ed. Robert N. Hudspeth (Ithaca, NY: Cornell University Press, 1983–1984), 3:177 (hereafter cited in text as *LMF*).

If we view this experiment under the aspect of mesmerism's long history, then "Emerson" occupied the position of puppeteer. As false priests had controlled their credulous victims; as mesmerists had controlled their somnambulists; as phrenomesmerists had controlled their subjects; so autographs controlled psychometrists. And yet as a matter of fact, Emerson was quite a bit more like a puppet in Parsons's hands. Imaginary Emerson was probably the only version of the essayist who could have been convinced to attend a séance. As Fuller knew, her friend who made "light, so wittily" of mesmerism was hardly likely to show up in person (*LMF*, 3:177). Fuller and Huidekoper Clarke considered inviting him to later experiments with Parsons, but they decided against it because they hesitated to expose Parsons to his withering skepticism (*LMF*, 3:181–82).[114] So having Emerson participate in a mesmeric experiment against his will was really a case of Parsons and her coconspirators pulling *his* strings (as Fuller gently pulls his leg in her letter). In spite of the melodramas of control to which mesmerists and their opponents were both given in theory, puppeteering proved quite reversible. In the case of psychometry, where the read subject usually was not present, this reversibility could not yield the give-and-take that Stone and Brackett performed. Instead the "control," will he or nill he, became involved in a joke at his own expense.

The humorless and the morbidly sensitive were capable of taking Parsons's readings rather hard. Emerson belonged to neither of those categories, and he was broad-minded enough to call on Parsons; she missed him (see *LBF*, 84–85). She and Dwight managed to inspire serious unease, however, in another of their subjects, Charles King Newcomb. This poet and Brook Farm resident seemed destined for great things, but he was not. The twenty-something whom Emerson praised as "one of the most penetrating of men" ("Montaigne") and the "subtlest observer and diviner of character I ever met" ("Historic Notes of Life and Letters in New England") ended his life homeless and obsessed with the task of writing pornographic poems, of which he produced more than a thousand.[115] In 1844, well before Newcomb's star began to fall, Parsons read his character to the evident satisfaction of everyone except for Newcomb himself. The result passed from hand to hand over the summer of 1844. Newcomb gave the reading to Fuller, who told him that it was "in

114. On Emerson's skepticism, see Deborah Manson, "'The Trance of the Ecstatica': Margaret Fuller, Animal Magnetism, and the Transcendent Female Body," *Literature and Medicine* 25, no. 2 (2006): 298.

115. Quoted in Miller, *Salem Is My Dwelling Place*, 193; see also 192–95.

many respects excellent, of [*sic*] the 'eastern magician,' the gleams of sunlight across the dark pine woods, and trailing the little switch. She has seized with force several leading traits, and went much deeper than she did with mine" (*LMF*, 3:201; see also *LBF*, 19–21). (Fuller disliked Parsons's reading of herself.) Fuller asked for her own copy of the Newcomb reading, but its subject dragged his feet (*LMF*, 3:207). He tried to quash the circulation of the reading as quickly as possible; he was reluctant even to return Dwight's copy to her. At last he permitted Dwight to read the notes over once more on the condition that she destroy them afterward (see *LBF*, 19–21).

"Controlling" Parsons with his autograph manuscript really meant giving her the power to define him through her impressions and imitations, and Newcomb did not relish the experience. His power was clearly not comprehensive enough for his own tastes. One might reframe Parsons's accounts of others' characters as being only in a tertiary or secondary sense about the referent (Emerson, Newcomb, Fuller). Newcomb and Fuller complained that they had not been the true objects of Parsons's interest; they may have been right. Psychometry let Parsons act out parts. The fact that these parts carried the names of real people may not have been of the first importance with her. It may have been the sheer throwing of herself over into other, basically imaginary characters that was the source of her enjoyment, and even of her sense of freedom. Her psychometric subjects may have been, for her, like noms de plume: characters under whose auspices she could act differently from the way she acted as Anna Parsons—looking down on Emerson, for example. Parsons made free use of her prerogative to construe her controls as she saw fit, right up to the point where interpretation crossed over into invention.

One of Parsons's fellow phrenomesmeric clairvoyants may actually have invented an alter ego, outside of the context of psychometry, that would allow her into worlds that she could not easily enter under her own name. Mrs. R.—the star of the *Democratic Review* experiments in New York—was not named in print (so in fact we know her *only* by a pseudonym, Mrs. R.). I have not been able to identify Mrs. R. definitively, but there is a strong candidate among Bryant's circle of acquaintance: the philologist Therese von Jakob Robinson, wife of the Union Theological Seminary professor Edward Robinson and intimate friend of Bryant's.[116] Von Jakob Robinson

---

116. William Cullen Bryant, *Letters of William Cullen Bryant*, 2:144, 3:397; Irma Elizabeth Voigt, "The Life and Works of Mrs. Therese Robinson (Talvj)" (PhD thesis, University of Illinois, 1913), 38 (hereafter cited in text as "TR").

appears to be unique among the milieux of the committee members in being a married woman who had scholarly knowledge of the Bible and could speak five or six languages—attributes of Mrs. R.'s, according to the "Report of the Sub-committee."[117] There cannot have been many women in all of New York who could have lived up to that description. Under the pseudonym Talvj (the acronym of her birth name, Therese Albertine Luise von Jakob), von Jakob Robinson published two major works on folklore ("TR," 75, 81): *Charakteristik de Volkslieder* (1840) and *The Literature of the Slavic Nations* (1852; as an article in the *Biblical Repository*, 1834). Born in 1797, the daughter of a professor at the University of Halle, she published translations from English and Serbian while still in her twenties ("TR," 29, 32). Her work attracted the attention of Jakob Grimm (see "TR," 37) and also of Johann Wolfgang von Goethe, who said she had "the heart of a woman, but the brain of a man" (quoted in "TR," 42). When Buchanan stimulated Mrs. R.'s organs of self-esteem, combativeness, and firmness, she chose to "vindicate in an eloquent manner the rights of her sex."[118] She suggested "the good she might do, if placed in her proper sphere," and when reminded by Buchanan that she was both "feeble" and "delicate," "she replied in a proud and energetic manner,—'But the mind can overcome the body's weakness.'"[119] If Talvj was speaking, she knew from experience that this was true. By November 1842, the date of the *Democratic Review* experiments, Talvj's work for the *Biblical Repository* had already been received with lavish praise, including from Bryant's *Evening Post* ("TR," 80–81). There had been time for her earlier publications to be hailed as the first-rate work of—as many assumed—some unknown man ("TR," 32). Talvj was in fact capable of a great deal, when placed in the "proper sphere."

It was obvious to von Jakob from an early age how difficult it would be to pursue a scholarly career as a woman, and she employed a mixed strategy. She gave herself a number of actorly roles, both through marriage to Edward Robinson and through the adoption of pseudonyms. She evacuated Von Jakob Robinson in favor of Talvj, writing in a letter to a relative ("TR," 32) that "the fact, that I had never written under my own name, justified me, I felt, in separating all that pertained to Therese Robinson, formerly Therese von Jakob, entirely from Talvj." Talvj was not Von Jakob Robinson's first

---

117. "Neurology," *United States Magazine and Democratic Review* 55 (January 1843): 89; "TR," 29, 31, 37.

118. "Neurology," *United States Magazine and Democratic Review* 55 (January 1843): 85–86.

119. Ibid., 86.

or last pseudonym. She had gone under her single name and her married name, and in her early years she had published as Ernst Berthold and as "Reseda" ("TR," 32). Marriage, like the adoption of male and androgynous names, was a strategy by which to enter the scholarly world with some of the prerogatives of a man: her husband's name may have been one pseudonym under which she wrote. When Edward Robinson came to study at Halle, she decided to marry him in 1828 after what she called, in a letter to Grimm, "a long and bitter struggle" ("TR," 35). But she judged that her best chance of an intellectual life lay in being his amanuensis, a role in which she served long and faithfully. She translated from German for his scholarly magazine, the *Biblical Repository*, and her biographer suspects that much of the work in the journal "may be attributed to her either directly or indirectly" ("TR," 34–35, 41). Von Jakob Robinson's approach to her scholarly career involved two strategies of disempowerment. She disempowered herself in favor of the pseudonym Talvj; she made her labors and her name the property of her husband. And yet each of these forms of would-be passivity was actually a sophisticated kind of parasitism, in which, always apparently obeying, she in fact occupied her hollowed-out host, directing its actions from within.

Dépositaire, that word the 1784 commissioners used to describe Charles Deslon's borrowed potency, returns as perhaps the best way to express the mischief that appears in mesmeric obedience. The commissioners used the word to debunk the power allegedly acting in magnetic séances. Deslon only *apparently* had control over the fluid of animal magnetism, whereas *in fact* patients had made him the *dépositaire* of the productions of their own imaginations. To recall their exact phrasing: "it is impossible not to recognize in these regular effects an extraordinary influence, acting upon the patients, making itself master of them, and of which he who superintends the process [*celui qui magnétise*], appears to be the depository" [*dépositaire*]."[120] Even if one's intention in addressing the magnetic scene is not to debunk— and debunking is certainly not my own intention—it is still inescapable that the obedient member of the rapport must deposit some power with the controlling member. It is inescapable because credulity is always an

120. [J.-S. Bailly], *Report of Dr. Benjamin Franklin, and Other Commissioners, Charged by the King of France with the Examination of the Animal Magnetism, as Now Practised at Paris*, [trans. William Godwin] (London: J. Johnson, 1785), 28. The original reads: "On ne peut s'empêcher de reconnoître, à ces effets constans, une grand puissance qui agite les malades, les maîtrise, & dont celui qui magnétise semble être le dépositaire": [J.-S. Bailly], *Rapport des commissaires chargés par le roi de l'examen du magnétisme animal* (Paris: Imprimerie du Roi, 1784), 7.

aptitude, not merely a lack of common sense, in the magnetic scene. Not just anyone can be magnetized, and so those who are susceptible have a capacity that others lack.

We have seen a number of different answers to the question of what this aptitude may be. Parsons could realize others' characters (or, in some cases, reinvent them). Brackett could assent to, and add to, others' narratives. Gleason could sense others' illnesses. The clairvoyants of the Hôpital de la Charité, and, based on the limited evidence we have, perhaps also the slaves of the Marquis de Jabrun's Guadeloupe plantation, could convey their knowledge-from-below of the workings of the institutions to which they were subject (how and when fits, crises, and rebellions would manifest themselves in plantations and in hospitals). There is no animal-magnetic power that does not depend to a certain extent on the obedient person providing content and creating a scene. He or she must interpret—or even invent—what the control wants. This interpretation must go beyond the controller's expressed will (or else where would be the miracle?), and the controller who wants things to go well always has an incentive to play along with amplifications, even violations, of the will he understood himself to have. Even when we do not take a debunker's view of the mesmeric scene, the controlled person deposits the controller's will in him; the clairvoyant lends her imagination to the elucidation of the mesmerist's projects. Obedience always involves interpretation—and thus there is a mischief in it. Benjamin Franklin played no small part in the articulation of this relationship at the dawn of US mesmerism. In mesmerism's twilight, as we will see in the next chapter, he was to have his own powers amplified in dubious—perhaps even scandalous—ways. Benjamin Franklin was dead; long live Benjamin Franklin.

THE SPIRIT OF
BENJAMIN FRANKLIN

I feel better; my head is clearer; I can see plainer.

Mesmeric clairvoyant Rachael Draper under the influence of
the spirit of Benjamin Franklin (1850)[1]

PHRENOMESMERISM WAS IN DECLINE BY 1845. Of its principal boosters, only Joseph Buchanan continued to manipulate mental organs; La Roy Sunderland and Robert Collyer had moved on to new pet theories.[2] The practice had lasted long enough, however, to have a transformative impact on mesmeric performance generally. Just as the convulsions and expectorations of Franz Anton Mesmer's subjects had given way to the lucid somnambulism of J. P. F. Deleuze's and Charles Poyen's subjects, now somnambulism gave way to character transformation. Buchanan's 1842 boast became the template for his successors: "I have made [subjects] laugh or weep; walk or be still; fight or apologise for quarrelling; talk or be silent; steal or surrender stolen articles; lie pertinaciously, or confess sincerely every thing that might be asked; believe in Mormonism, ghosts, and all absurd superstitions, or deny every thing supernatural, and even the contents of the Bible."[3] After Buchanan, mesmerists of all stripes offered similar litanies of manipulation.

---

1. Quoted in Emma Hardinge Britten, *Modern American Spiritualism: A Twenty Years' Record of the Communion between Earth and the World of Spirits* (New York, 1870), 53.

2. Alan Gauld, *A History of Hypnotism* (Cambridge: Cambridge University Press, 1992), 185.

3. Joseph Rodes Buchanan, *Sketches of Buchanan's Discoveries in Neurology* (Louisville: J. Eliot & Co.'s Power Press, 1842), 81–82.

Alan Gauld has proposed that audiences expected performers to match the drama of phrenomesmerism—and they largely got what they expected.[4] Some mesmeric subjects acted out a wild oscillation between personalities and beliefs; others, following in the footsteps of psychometers, inhabited single characters with a fidelity unmatched even in the theater (so observers exclaimed). The question was what these performances now meant, in the absence of the old phrenomesmeric theories. If the agent was neither the mesmerist working on the subject's phrenological organs nor the character of a letter writer making an impression—those being Buchanan's two explanations—then what was it? As J. Stanley Grimes wrote in his mesmeric treatise *Etherology* (1845), "at the present time, scarcely two Phrenologians nor Mesmerologists can be found who agree."[5]

Mesmerism would enjoy its final period of robust practice in the United States over the fifteen years following Grimes's remark. That period was marked by a steady and multisided debate over what agent explained mesmeric subjects' performances of character. Just as the 1784 commission had argued with Charles Deslon about what accounted for patients' convulsions—imagination, or animal magnetism—now practitioners criticized one another's explanations of character transformation. Thus mesmerism in the United States ended much as it had begun: with debunking. Only this time, the debunking was mostly an inside job. Sunderland and Buchanan kept objecting to each other; meanwhile, Grimes and a new brigade of successful stage performers joined the fray. The 1850s saw mesmeric lecture series arranged for the express purpose of denouncing other mesmeric lecture series.[6] This being a public fight that anyone could join, séance spiritualism also offered its own proposal starting in 1848: the agents transforming the characters of clairvoyants were spirits of the dead. Mediums channeled departed souls, much as psychometers transmitted the personalities of absent letter writers. Mesmerists maintained their relevancy in part by drafting off the much more popular spiritualism: either they attracted audiences by attacking it, or they collaborated with it, benefiting

---

4. Gauld, *History of Hypnotism*, 189.

5. J. Stanley Grimes, *Etherology; or, The Philosophy of Mesmerism and Phrenology* (New York: Saxton & Miles, 1845), xvi (hereafter cited in text as *E*).

6. J. Stanley Grimes, *The Mysteries of Human Nature, Explained by a New System of Nervous Physiology: To Which Is Added, a Review of the Errors of Spiritualism, and Instructions for Developing or Resisting the Influence by Which Subjects and Mediums Are Made* (Buffalo: R. M. Wanzer, 1857), 344–45 (hereafter cited in text as *MHN*). See also "City Intelligence," *Boston Courier*, January 7, 1850; [Advertisements], *Boston Daily Atlas*, January 19, 1850.

from the new movement's extensive publication and correspondence networks. Meanwhile spiritualism, like mesmerism before it, proposed new uses for the credulous person. Mesmeric clairvoyants had conveyed information about distant events, diagnoses of diseases, and characters. Now spirit mediums' credulity would make them into portals between this world and the next.

In the bewildering diversity of opinion, there was one continuity: each of the competing practices made an invisible agent—whether an absent letter writer, a spirit, or a subtle fluid—appear in the credulous person's behavior. The disagreements over this agent's nature matter less than the agreement that there *was* an agent, of particular importance and prestige, to be apprehended solely through the effects it had on an impressible subject. Like mesmerists, and indeed like debunkers of mesmerism, spiritualists continued to see credulity as an attribute that had been misunderstood by the purveyors of primitive enchantments but that could now be harnessed and redirected into technical channels. The period in which US mesmerism all but ended and worldwide spiritualism began saw credulity employed in each of the ways we have seen it used throughout this history: as the target of debunkings that would reassure the debunker of his own enlightenment; as a tool to deploy toward a variety of modern ends; as an aptitude that could supplement, by its projections, a felt absence of self-control and self-knowledge. In some respects spiritualism represented a distinct break from mesmerism: it was closely tied to women's rights and other progressive movements, as mesmerism was not; and it was considerably more popular and somewhat more securely institutionalized. But in one important respect, there was continuity. Spiritualists, too, believed in belief and thought it could be put to use. They belonged to a tradition that went all the way back to Benjamin Franklin. Thanks to the wonders of the spiritual telegraph, they would hear from their founding father once again.

"I CAN SEE PLAINER"

The Summerland (the spiritualist heaven) held few communicators more prolific than the chair of the 1784 commission. "One of the most frequent names spelled out in the Rochester, New York, manifestations was that of 'Benjamin Franklin,'" wrote practitioner and historian Emma Hardinge Britten, recalling spirits' first communications with mediums from 1848 to 1850. Spirit-Franklin "claimed to be actively interested in promoting" the manifestations, Hardinge Britten observed, "a claim not at all at variance with the pursuits of this renowned philosopher whilst an inhabitant of earth."[7] Franklin had been one of "the spirits chiefly concerned in the inauguration of this telegraphy," among whom were other "philosophic and scientific minds." Like Franklin, these avid communicators had made "the study of electricity and other imponderables a specialty in the earth-life."[8] Franklin, in short, had invented the spiritual telegraph as a continuation of his electrical researches while on earth. The 1784 commission chair's sponsorship of spiritualism is at once a good joke and one of spiritualism's most astute analyses of itself. It was certainly a stretch to say, as Hardinge Britten did, that spiritualism was "not at all at variance" with Franklin's lifework. And yet spiritualists had taken up the commission's charge to manage and control credulity, just as mesmerists did before them. Spiritualists too wanted to turn impressibility to a new use: focalizing the messages of the garrulous dead. The profitable control of credulity was an ambition shared by all the commission's inheritors to one degree or another.

In winter 1850, Franklin appeared to mesmeric clairvoyant Rachael Draper in Rochester, by then a center of spirit activity. As her husband, magnetist, and fellow spiritualist investigator Nathaniel Draper explained in a letter printed in the Rochester *Daily Magnet*, Rachael was capable of clairvoyance and communication with the dead when magnetized.[9] When Franklin first appeared, Rachael asked for proof of identity at Nathaniel's suggestion. After a pause of a few minutes, Nathaniel saw "a violent shock of her person." Worried that Rachael was "waking up," he asked for information. "You wanted a signal and I told him if it was Dr. Franklin he might electrize me, and he did it," Rachael replied. To the question of whether she was injured, she responded, "No; I feel better; my head is clearer; I can see plainer."[10] Franklin had magnetized her, as it were; he had shocked her with electricity from his own system, thus curing her body and clarifying her mind. On another occasion the spirit of Franklin repeated one of Poyen's earliest

7. Hardinge Britten, *Modern American Spiritualism*, 51–52.

8. Ibid., 39. See also Werner Sollors, "Dr. Benjamin Franklin's Celestial Telegraph, or Indian Blessings to Gas-Lit American Drawing Rooms," *American Quarterly* 35, no. 5 (Winter 1983), 459–80.

9. Hardinge Britten, *Modern American Spiritualism*, 52–53.

10. Quoted in ibid., 53.

experiments with Cynthia Gleason: waking his subject at a preappointed time. "At the *precise* time" the spirit rapped, then woke Draper "with an apparent electric shock."[11] Spirit-Franklin synthesized the achievements of the tradition that Earth-Franklin had inaugurated: clarifying heads, unveiling eyes, and regulating bodies, all through the profitable manipulation of an impressible clairvoyant.

It must be admitted that the ghostly Franklin had a sad tendency to garble the electrical discoveries his fleshly counterpart had made. Still, the two shared a great deal, including an interest in scientific experimentation on credulous people. The Franklin of 1848 was said to magnetize the mediums with whom he communicated; Draper more than once saw him working on the battery he was going to use to shock her.[12] Similarly, the Franklin of 1784 (or his commissioners on his behalf) had "magnetized" volunteer patients with fake mesmeric passes, as a way to show that even sham versions of Mesmer's techniques affected the ignorant members of society's lower tiers.[13] In his way, Franklin of 1784 had wanted to clarify minds by magnetizing (though his magnetism was a ruse, designed to enlighten the public about Mesmer's charlatanry and thus stamp out the earnest practice). The Franklins of 1848 and 1784 also shared a penchant for propping up their own agency through the manipulation of mediums. As I argued in the first chapter, one pleasure that debunking affords its practitioners is the relief of controlling others' imaginations and thus receiving the only reassurance possible that one is among the manipulators of this world, and not among the dupes. That pleasure, I suggested, was one of the payoffs of the 1784 debunking. Franklin of 1848 was even more dependent on the credulous than his predecessor had been: without Draper to mediate, he could not appear as an agent at all. The pleasure and utility of controlling the credulous has taken many forms in this book, but a common dynamic remains discernable: agents have controlled impressible people in order to secure evidence of their own power and existence, both of which were otherwise in doubt. In Draper's experiments, that dynamic returned: the power and existence of

11. Quoted in ibid.

12. Quoted in ibid., 52–53. Franklin also was known to magnetize other spirits: see Josiah Brigham, *Twelve Messages from the Spirit John Quincy Adams through Joseph D. Stiles, Medium, to Josiah Brigham* (Boston: Bela Marsh, 1859), 422.

13. As far as we know, Franklin did not magnetize personally; he left that work to his subordinates on the committee, who performed many of their experiments at his house in Passy. See chapter 1.

und themselves confirmed in the performances of mediums. The Benjamin Franklin was more in the spirit of Benjamin Franklin ight at first appear.

"YOU CANNOT OPEN YOUR EYES"

Spiritualists were not the only ones channeling Franklin at the tail end of US mesmeric practice. J. Stanley Grimes was a mesmerist; nonetheless, he devoted much of his career to debunking other mesmerists. In that respect he was Franklin's devotee. His *Etherology* (1845) aimed to stop Buchanan in his tracks and put "a quietus upon the head-touching folly" (*MHN*, 344). Grimes argued that the phrenomesmerists owed the rich variety of character traits they elicited not to a similarly varied set of organs but to a single organ: "Credenciveness." Credenciveness appears only in Grimes's unique map of the skull, first articulated in his *New System of Phrenology* (1839).[14] One of a group of organs that he called the "conforming socials," credenciveness governed the tendency "to act on the testimony of others, and especially those whom we respect." In excess it led to "superstition, credulity"; in deficit it led to "skepticism, and want of what is sometimes called *imagination*" (*E*, 168–69). When overstimulated or overdeveloped, credenciveness made subjects so gullible that they would believe themselves affected in whatever way their mesmerists hinted they should be. As imagination was a faculty that deposited its own powers with chimerical forces, thus creating the false impression that those forces existed, so credenciveness was a depositing organ. It lent its own power to social influences.

Credenciveness could thus explain away the power that any magnetic or religious technique might appear to have. "*Touching* [the phrenological organs], according to the method of Dr. Buchanan, is all a farce" (*E*, 188), Grimes declared, and that method is nothing but "a most egregious tissue of moonshine" (*E*, 239). Buchanan's practice was "begotten by the union of Animal

14. J. Stanley Grimes, *A New System of Phrenology* (New York: Wiley & Putnam, 1839). An illustration showing the organ of credenciveness appears in the introduction to the present volume, reproduced from J. Stanley Grimes, *The Mysteries of the Head and Heart Explained: Including an Improved System of Phrenology; A New Theory of the Emotions; and an Explanation of the Mysteries of Mesmerism, Trance, Mind-reading, and the Spirit Delusion* (Chicago: W. B. Keen, Cooke, 1875), p. [1] (hereafter cited in text as *MHH*).

Magnetism with credulity" (*E*, 263). The effects Buchanan achieved by touching individual organs depended not on direct stimulation of those organs but on the collaboration of credenciveness, which caused subjects to do whatever they thought Buchanan wanted. The action of credenciveness could explain demonic possession and Salem witchcraft (*E*, 31); "the celebrated [D]elphian oracle" and the wonders performed by the Egyptian magicians of Exodus (*E*, 40–41); the "fantastic tricks and evolutions" of the "medicine man" among American Indians (*E*, 41); and "the effects produced in our own day, by the exciting modes of religious worship . . . such as 'falling down in a trance,' 'losing their strength,' . . . &c" (*E*, 43). Buchanan's version of mesmerism, no less than these other forms, needed to "be wrested"—yet again!—"from the hands of superstition, mystery, and quackery, and moulded into symmetrical forms of scientific beauty."[15] Grimes would do that work.[16] His performances often consisted in reproducing Buchanan's dramatic character transformations without touching the heads of his subjects, simply to show that magnetizing individual organs had nothing to do with these changes.

Grimes believed that the organ of credenciveness communicated with the outside world and with the other phrenological organs by means of an invisible fluid diffused through nature and our bodies. He named this fluid "etherium" and loosely modeled its operations on electromagnetic induction. Under normal circumstances, the "organ of consciousness" coordinated the waves of etherium; it was a clearinghouse for the impulses of the other organs, governing and uniting them (*E*, 21, 136). But other organs could easily usurp consciousness's natural place as the dominant organ, producing what Grimes called a "monomania" of their own qualities (*E*, 34). Mesmeric states took place when the organ of credenciveness usurped the executive powers, whether spontaneously or in response to waves of etherium—often produced by mesmeric manipulations—that had reached it from outside (see *E*, 34–36, 188–89). When credenciveness took over, it brought organs under its own control, again by the medium of etherium. This state was called credencive "induction." A person who was inducted would be "generally disposed to oblige, to submit, to imitate, and sympathize; and to believe anything, however absurd, even

15. J. Stanley Grimes, *Etherology and the Phreno-Philosophy of Mesmerism and Magic Eloquence; Including a New Philosophy of Sleep and of Consciousness, with a Review of the Pretensions of Phreno-Magnetism, Electro-Biology, &c* (Boston: James Munroe, 1850), 8–9.

16. La Roy Sunderland was also invested in explaining the history of religion at this moment, as Ann Taves has shown; see Taves, *Fits, Trances, and Visions: Experiencing Religion and Explaining Experience from Wesley to James* (Princeton, NJ: Princeton University Press, 1999), 139–41.

against the evidence of his senses" (*E*, 36). The mesmeric state was a mania of credulity—what Grimes would later call a "credo-mania" (*MHN*, 399).

The technique *Etherology* espoused was the application of "a very simple stimulus which every one has always at hand. . . . Do you ask me what this simple and powerful stimulus is? I answer, that it is AN ASSERTION" (*E*, 186). Assertions played a double role in Grimes's form of mesmerism. First, they induced the trance state, taking the place of the gestures that previous practitioners had thought necessary. An assertion—accompanied, apparently, by a wave of etherium, though Grimes was unclear on this point—would induct credenciveness, causing it to induct the other organs. After a person was inducted (that is, mesmerized), assertions were the means by which the practitioner demonstrated his continuing control throughout the duration of the state. Grimes's favorite opening gambit was to say, "*You cannot open your eyes*" to a group of audience members (*E*, 186). Whoever could not was in the mesmeric state. Susceptible people could then be tried with further assertions, each one more spectacular than the last. Because an "assertion" was the "specific stimulus which naturally influences Credenciveness . . . when a subject is inducted, an assertion has an influence upon him which is almost incredible" (*E*, 36). The subject would behave as though whatever the mesmerist asserted were true: "Tell him that he cannot move or speak, and he cannot; tell him that ice will burn him, and it will do so" (*E*, 36). Grimes still envisioned uses for the manipulation of credulity. He thought character, and perhaps bodily health or disease, could indeed be read through "a species of clairvoyant sympathy" (*E*, 232). And he proposed the cure of diseases by suggestion: "if you find that you have Credencive control over the patient, *assert* that his disease is cured . . . make local passes and applications, and assert that they will certainly be efficacious, and they generally will be so" (*E*, 319–20). But these uses fell mostly into the background in Grimes's writing. He was preoccupied with explaining away all theories that claimed to discern any agent behind mesmeric effects other than credenciveness.

Grimes's attack on Buchanan was similar to the Franklin commission's attack on Mesmer. As Mesmer had depended on imagination to cobble together the effects of the so-called animal magnetism, Buchanan had depended on credenciveness to manufacture for him the alleged effects of touching the various phrenological organs. Without realizing it, Buchanan had been inducting credenciveness through the assertions he made: "let the subject suppose that you are going to excite the organs of his brain—let him believe that you expect when you touch a certain part of his head, that he will be affected in a particular way, and he will generally use all his ingenuity to learn

THE SPIRIT OF BENJAMIN FRANKLIN

your wishes, and make his utmost endeavors to oblige you and accomplish your expectations" (*E*, 187). But these changes were actually accomplished by assertion, "by simply saying to the subject, '*you are Macbeth;*' or, '*you are Queen Victoria;*' or, '*you are a saw-mill*[;]' . . . [t]he subjects will generally assume the character, and act the part according to their conceptions of it, much more perfectly than they could enact the same when in the ordinary state" (*E*, 283). Touching organs had nothing to do with it.

Unfortunately for Grimes, his debunking merely had the effect of freeing phrenomesmeric performance from phrenomesmeric explanation. By underscoring mesmerism's long-standing relationship to credulity, Grimes made available to his successors the rhetorical move that Poyen had employed some time ago, of claiming to harness credulity and put it to use. With the phrenomesmeric explanations out of the way, a variety of new practitioners could offer their own variations on what the performance of character meant. Grimes's debunking of phrenomesmerism, as he lamented, "created, in its place, a still more monstrous error, which has been known under the names of electrobiology, and psychology" (*MHN*, 344). The electrobiologists (also, in early days, called the electrical psychologists) performed before audiences in the thousands starting in 1849; they offered supercharged character transformation à la Buchanan, while cribbing bits and pieces of Grimes's theoretical apparatus. On their view, electricity, not credenciveness, was the agent that could turn lions to lambs and back again. Spiritualists, too, would owe a debt to Grimes's efforts in making character transformation a loose-fish, ready to be harpooned by new explanations. Like many a would-be giver of quietus before him, the Franklin commission included, Grimes was destined to be disappointed by the posthumous productivity of the idol he had smashed.

"YOU CAN MAKE HIM SEE A RIVER"

Electrobiology's beginnings lay in the moment, sometime toward the end of 1848, when Grimes's *Etherology* came to the attention of two mesmeric practitioners, John Bovee Dods and Theophilus Fiske. Fiske's prior career is obscure, except that he had published a lecture on the fraudulence of paper money during the Panic of 1837.[17] Dods, a Universalist minister, had

17. Theophilus Fiske, *Labor the Only True Source of Wealth* (Charleston, SC: Office of the *Examiner*, 1837).

been lecturing on mesmerism since 1841.[18] His *Six Lectures* (1843) describes animal magnetism as a living electricity that cures disease, but the text says little about his techniques.[19] Newspaper reports suggest that in the early days, he offered a potpourri of Poyen and Buchanan: he expected his subjects to show clairvoyance, subjection to his will, and character transformation in response to pressure on the skull.[20] He also shocked people with a galvanic battery.[21] While Buchanan was riding to fame on his success with the *Democratic Review* committee, Dods was recovering from an unfavorable investigation of his practices by David Reese in Baltimore.[22] He did not become a major player until he teamed up with Fiske in 1848.

Dods and Fiske achieved national renown by adopting two major elements of the technique elaborated in *Etherology*. Like Grimes, they induced the mesmeric state with the command, *"You can not open your eyes!"*[23] And like him, too, they made the mesmeric state into a theater of deception. Their subjects would believe anything and act on their beliefs by performing protracted scenes. As Dods wrote, strongly recalling Grimes's descriptions of his own demonstrations, "If [a subject] is entirely in the state, you can make him see that a cane is a living snake or eel; that a hat is a halibut or flounder; a handkerchief is a bird, child, or rabbit; or that the moon or a star falls on a person in the audience, and sets him on fire, and you can make him hasten to extinguish it." Perception was first affected, then action, with the subject willing to pantomime scenes with which he was inspired: "You can make him see a river, and on it a steamboat crowded with human beings. You can make him see the boiler burst, and the boat blow up, with his father or mother, brother or sister, or wife or child on board. You can lay out the lifeless corpse before him in state, cause him to kneel at its side, and to freely

---

18. John Bovee Dods, *Six Lectures on the Philosophy of Mesmerism, Delivered in the Marlboro' Chapel, January 23–28, 1843* (Boston: W. A. Hall, 1843), 6; "Report of the Committee," *Daily National Intelligencer*, Washington, DC, May 29, 1843; Taves, *Fits, Trances, and Visions*, 131.

19. Dods, *Six Lectures*, 12–15.

20. "Report of the Committee;" "Investigation on Mesmerism at Baltimore," *Daily National Intelligencer*, May 29, 1843.

21. "Investigation on Mesmerism at Baltimore."

22. Ibid.

23. John Bovee Dods, *The Philosophy of Electrical Psychology, in a Course of Twelve Lectures* (New York: Fowlers & Wells, 1850; reprinted (stereotype edition) as *The Philosophy of Electrical Psychology, in a Course of Twelve Lectures* (New York: Fowlers & Wells, 1851), 209. Citation refers to the 1851 edition.

shed over it the tears of affection and bereavement." It was possible, too, to "change his own personal identity, and make him believe that he is a child two or three years old, and inspire him with the artless feelings of that age; or that he is an aged man, or even a woman, or a negro, or some renowned statesman or hero."[24] Dods offered the spectacle of seeing someone lose himself. Unlike mesmeric subjects of the past, however, whose losses in this regard had generally entailed a gain—of clairvoyance, of docility, of character-reading ability—electrobiological subjects simply misbehaved.

Electrobiologists claimed, like most mesmerists since 1784, to be manipulating an invisible fluid—electricity in its biological form. Unlike their predecessors among American mesmeric practitioners, they rarely tried to pass their subjects off as capable of some useful contribution by virtue of their credulity—clairvoyance, for example. Nor did they describe their subjects as gifted. Instead their goal was to show that as many people as possible were susceptible to deception, even humiliation, at the hands of the practitioner. They often emphasized that they perpetrated their deceptions on subjects "of well known character and standing in society" who were in a "perfectly wakeful state."[25] This latter claim strictly meant that the subject was not in the state of magnetic somnambulism; what it portended, though, was that anyone could be deceived at any time, without necessarily realizing it. In their insistence on the ease of deception, electrobiologists had the spirit of debunking in them. Some fifty years before, John Haygarth and his conspirators had been hard pressed to contain their laughter as they pretended to "tractorize" gullible patients with wooden rods; the patients' responses showed that any effect Elisha Perkins's metallic "tractors" appeared to have was due only to the imagination.[26] Now, the laughter Haygarth had suppressed burst freely from electrobiologists' audiences, who often found the performances "ludicrous."[27] The target of debunking, this time, was the subject himself. One had to doubt the value of his "perfectly wakeful state" and his "well established character" while he insisted that his hat was a halibut.[28]

24. Dods, *Philosophy of Electrical Psychology . . . Twelve Lectures*, 214.

25. "Electro-Biology," *Mississippi Free Trader and Natchez Gazette*, Natchez, MS, April 13, 1850.

26. See chapter 1 of the present volume.

27. [Annie Denton Cridge], "Mr. Stone's Biological Lectures," *Vanguard*, Dayton, OH, May 23, 1857, 93.

28. "Electro-Biology," *Mississippi Free Trader and Natchez Gazette*, Natchez, MS, April 13, 1850; Dods, *Philosophy of Electrical Psychology . . . Twelve Lectures*, 214.

Grimes was irritated by the electrobiologists, and no wonder: his imitators were badly upstaging him. He recalled the 1850 eruption of electrobiology in Boston (the unnamed lecturer here is probably Fiske): "I went to one of his public exhibitions, and, behold! his biology consisted in merely performing the same experiments, and in precisely the same manner, as I had described and explained in my work on Etherology, under the name of credencive induction" (*MHN*, 344). One of Fiske's successors, G. W. Stone, would go so far as to plagiarize part of Grimes's preface from the reissued version of *Etherology* (1850), the second edition that Grimes intended as a rebuttal to "the pretensions of . . . electro-biology."[29] Both Grimes and Sunderland went head-to-head with Fiske in 1850. Sunderland spoke at the Masonic Temple while Fiske held forth at the Melodeon; the *Boston Courier* carried ads for them both on the same day.[30] Grimes, meanwhile, was lobbing denunciations right and left at the Tremont Temple; his advertisement in the *Boston Daily Atlas*, which was printed adjacent to Fiske's own, promised that he would give both Sunderland's pathetism and Fiske's electrobiology the lie.[31] Grimes also reissued *Etherology* with new strictures on electrobiology.[32] He was still on the attack in November,[33] but by that time electrobiology had become virtually synonymous with mesmerism. The *Boston Daily Atlas*, where Grimes had been a paying advertiser, outraged his dignity by praising him for "Biological experiments [that] surpassed any we have seen before."[34] Competent puffery can be hard to come by.

In the year and a half or so before they came to Grimes's attention in early 1850, Dods and Fiske operated a kind of sleeper cell. They had not yet hit on the name "electrobiology," and they referred to their practice as "electrical psychology" instead. Then, after the phrenological publishers Fowlers & Wells republished the British surgeon Alfred Smee's "Lecture on Electro-Biology," they adopted the name.[35] They lectured on a mix of physiology and

29. Grimes, *Etherology and the Phreno-Philosophy of Mesmerism and Magic Eloquence* (1850), [1]. For the plagiarized passage, compare pp. 8–9 with G. W. Stone, *Electro-Biology; or, The Electrical Science of Life* (Liverpool: Willmer & Smith, 1850), [3].

30. "City Intelligence," *Boston Courier*, January 7, 1850.

31. [Advertisements], *Boston Daily Atlas*, January 19, 1850.

32. Grimes, *Etherology and the Phreno-Philosophy of Mesmerism and Magic Eloquence* (1850).

33. "Human Nature," *Boston Investigator*, November 20, 1850.

34. "Professor Grimes," *Boston Daily Atlas*, November 12, 1850.

35. Alfred Smee, *Principles of the Human Mind, Deduced from Physical Laws, Together with a Lecture on Electro-Biology, or The Voltaic Mechanism of Man* (New York: Fowlers &

mesmeric theory to large audiences, but they withheld information on mesmeric techniques. To get practical advice on how to "biologize," students had to pay ten dollars (five for women) to join a private class. They also had to sign an agreement promising they would not impart the secret to others for any less.[36] This Ponzi scheme collapsed when some of the students—and apparently also Fiske himself—disobeyed the terms. In the first few months of 1850, at least ten individuals simultaneously began advertising lectures on electrobiology in major cities all over the country, as if at a prearranged signal. These lecturers demonstrated technique at rock-bottom prices to large, packed houses. Dods seems not to have started the price war, but he quickly joined in. Besides Fiske,[37] Dods, and B. B. Williams, who sometimes worked as Dods's demonstrator,[38] there were C. Chauncey Burr, in Ohio, who lectured with the help of a Mr. Everett;[39] G. W. Stone, who lectured in Vermont and in Liverpool, England, in 1850, before moving to the American West later in the decade;[40] H. G. Darling, who got his start in Maine and would eventually lecture in Scotland;[41] Dr. Prevost, who appeared in Maine;[42] Professor Sharp, in Milwaukee, Wisconsin;[43] and Oliver Shaw, who first surfaced in Mississippi.[44] Within a month, Fiske would follow Shaw to

Wells, 1850). Before Smee's advent, Fiske and Dods had called their practice "electrical psychology"; they took nothing from Smee to speak of but the name. See [Advertisement], *Baltimore Sun*, December 12, 1848, [2]; "Our Baltimore Correspondence," *New York Herald*, June 19, 1849; "Our Philadelphia Correspondence," *New York Herald*, May 17, 1849.

36. Dods, *Philosophy of Electrical Psychology . . . Twelve Lectures*, 14.

37. "Credit to Whom Credit Is Due," *Boston Investigator*, February 27, 1850.

38. Dods, *Philosophy of Electrical Psychology . . . Twelve Lectures*, [3]; [Advertisement], *Baltimore Sun*, December 12, 1848, [2].

39. [Advertisement], *Daily Ohio Statesman*, Columbus, OH, January 2, 1850; "Electro-Biology," *Daily Ohio Statesman*, January 2, 1850; "Electro-Biology," *Daily Ohio Statesman*, January 4, 1850.

40. "Electro-Biology," *Vermont Watchman and State Journal*, Montpelier, VT, February 7, 1850; [Advertisement], *Vanguard*, Dayton, OH, May 16, 1857, 85; [Cridge], "Mr. Stone's Biological Lectures," 93; G. W. Stone, *Electro-Biology*, 7.

41. [Advertisement], *Bangor Daily Whig & Courier*, Bangor, ME, May 7, 1850; William Gregory, *Letters to a Candid Inquirer on Animal Magnetism* (Philadelphia: Blanchard & Lea, 1851), 153-57; H. G. Darling, ed., *Electrical-Psychology; or, The Electrical Philosophy of Mental Impressions . . . from the Works of Rev. J. B. Dods and Prof. J. S. Grimes* (London: John J. Griffin, 1851), 5-9.

42. [Dr. Prevost], *Bangor Daily Whig & Courier*, Bangor, ME, March 18, 1850.

43. [Advertisement], *Milwaukee Sentinel and Gazette*, February 26, 1850.

44. [Prof. Oliver A. Shaw], *Natchez Semi-Weekly Courier*, Natchez, MS, April 12, 1850.

Mississippi, though not before swinging through New Orleans.[45] The country had broken out in a rash of electrobiologists.

In their lecturing to American and, later, British audiences, these mesmerists "had, perhaps, a wider impact than any others had done before them."[46]
But it can be difficult to get a sense of that influence from the relatively small
number of publications the electrobiologists left. Unlike Poyen or Buchanan,
both of whom were eager to get cases and techniques into print, Fiske never
published at all, and Dods was vague about technique until 1850, by which
time his pupils had already let the cat out of the bag.[47] When their successor Darling wanted to publicize electrobiology's methods, he made a compendium of Dods's lectures and the sections on technique from Grimes's
Etherology; that treatise, as he noted, had "a more *practical* bearing upon the
production of the phenomena . . . in Electrical-Psychology, than any thing
contained in the work of Dods."[48] Lectures, however, spread electrobiology
far and wide.[49] Grimes claimed that an unnamed electrobiologist, probably
Fiske, was pulling in six thousand dollars a week in 1850 (*MHN*, 344). With
tickets at twelve and a half to twenty-five cents a head, Fiske would have
needed to sell a minimum of twenty thousand tickets total for his five lectures per week to bring in those sums—possibly as much as double that.[50]

45. [Advertisement], *Mississippi Free Trader and Natchez Gazette*, Natchez, MS, May 1,
1850; "Communications," *Mississippi Free Trader and Natchez Gazette*, Natchez, MS, April 6,
1850.

46. Gauld, *History of Hypnotism*, 187; see also Alison Winter, *Mesmerized: Powers of Mind
in Victorian Britain* (Chicago: University of Chicago Press, 1998), 281–85.

47. Dods, *Philosophy of Electrical Psychology . . . Twelve Lectures*, 14, 209–18.

48. Darling, *Electrical Psychology*, vi.

49. Dods, *Six Lectures*, 3–4.

50. It is difficult to know how large Fiske's lecture audiences would have needed to be
to earn him six thousand dollars a week (roughly $180,000 a week in 2017 dollars), both
because he was probably teaching small classes at the same time as he was lecturing—and
these fees may or may not be included in the total Grimes reports—and because Fiske sold
lecture tickets for anywhere from twelve and a half to twenty-five cents a head depending
on whether or not one took advantage of his special deals. Fiske did not advertise classes in
the *Boston Daily Atlas*, but judging by evidence elsewhere, his practice seems to have been
to form classes out of the lecture audiences, charging ten dollars per student: see "Communications," *Mississippi Free Trader and Natchez Gazette*, Natchez, MS, April 6, 1850; and
"Electro-Biology," *Hinds County Gazette*, Raymond, MS, June 21, 1850. Classes were probably small, on the order of a dozen students each, given that Dods estimated in 1850 that
he and Fiske had taught their methods to thousands in the private classes over the past
year and a half or so: see Dods, *Philosophy of Electrical Psychology . . . Twelve Lectures*, 14,

Grimes was probably exaggerating. Still, much evidence points to the conclusion that thousands of people heard electrobiology lectures in Boston in
the first few months of 1850. As electrobiologists traveled—and quickly—
throughout the United States, their practice became widely known.

Electrobiologists' well-attended performances emphasized the everyday
nature of deception. Dods and Fiske made two novel additions to Grimes's
technique: you could mesmerize a person by pressure on the ulnar nerve—
possible when shaking someone's hand, Dods said—or by making the subject
stare at a coin, usually with one zinc and one silver side and a copper wire
passing through, reminiscent of the parts of the galvanic batteries Dods had
previously used.[51] Thus at quotidian moments of shaking on contracts or ex-
changing money, credulity could take over. H. E. Lewis, an African American
electrobiologist who achieved considerable success lecturing in Edinburgh
in 1850, once gave a subject an apple while telling him it was an orange: "At
first he denied this, but by degrees he began to feel doubtful. At last he said,
'It is certainly very yellow,' (it was dark brown). He then took a sly glance
round the company, each of whom had an apple, but found them all yellow
too. He next cut out a piece with his finger, looked at the inside, smelt and
tasted it, and concluded with, 'Well, it *is* an orange, but yet I know I took an
apple into my hand.'"[52] Most of our knowledge of Lewis comes from William
Gregory, whose *Letters to a Candid Inquirer* (1851) admiringly chronicles his
lectures on mesmerism in Edinburgh. Gregory found it unsurprising that
a person of African descent would possess magnetic power, since he knew
that "the natives of India generally, are more uniformly susceptible," and that
the practice of "obi [i.e., obeah or vodou] of the West Indies and of Africa

---

in an introduction dated 1850. Prices and frequency (five times a week) of Fiske's lectures
are given in his advertisement in the *Boston Daily Atlas*, January 19, 1850. My estimate that
Fiske would have needed to lecture to around twenty thousand people a week is intentionally on the low end. If we assume he taught thirty people in classes at ten dollars a head in
a given week, he would have needed to sell 22,800 tickets at face price (twenty-five cents)
over his five lectures per week to make six thousand dollars.

51. Dods, *Philosophy of Electrical Psychology . . . Twelve Lectures*, 210, 216–17.

52. Gregory, *Letters to a Candid Inquirer*, 262. Lewis lectured in the United States as well,
though those lectures are not as well documented as the Edinburgh ones that Gregory
records. It was likely Lewis who was reported as lecturing on phrenology in Ohio in 1846
and whose 1848 lectures on "phrenology, mesmerism, and other interesting branches of
science" the African American newspaper the *North Star* praised: "W. C. N." [William
Cooper Nell], "Henry E. Lewis," *North Star*, December 22, 1848; Nathan Falor, "Phrenology
in Ohio," *American Phrenological Journal* 8, no. 6 (June 1846): 194.

depends for its influence on their ["negroes'"] susceptibility."[53] Under Lewis's influence, however, the European subject of the Edinburgh demonstrations became as gullible as an obi practitioner. Lewis's performances called into question the division Gregory tried to make between primitive "negroes" and cultivated Scotsmen. Lewis had the power to elicit credulity from his subjects, even when they were white. In his hands, electrobiology taught enlightenment a lesson about the limits of its achievements.

Electrobiology was faithful to the Franklinian origins of the US mesmeric tradition at the expense of the tradition's other major element, its commitment to making credulity a source of insight. Since Poyen, US mesmerists had generally been dialectical in their relationship to credulity. With the spectacular errors of the mesmeric subject came her spectacular insight, or his prodigious docility: credulity, in other words, had a purpose; it could be employed. Electrobiologists hardly mentioned the possibility of clairvoyance. Instead, they resembled the Franklin commissioners and other debunkers in that the primary use they envisioned for credulity was to bring out in relief the debunker's clear-sightedness. They promised that their deluded subjects would be "amusing" to those in the audience who remained in their right minds.[54] The electrobiologists' commitment to demonstrating pure deception went farther, but not much farther, than Grimes's own. Grimes acknowledged the validity of some uses of the mesmeric state, such as diagnosing clairvoyance, and he considered credenciveness a virtue when practiced in moderation: social cohesiveness, and our respect for "history and tradition," depended on it (E, 189–90). But his best blood went into demonstrating how easily his subjects could be deceived. Like the 1784 commissioners, Grimes and the electrobiologists used credulity primarily as a foil for their own enlightenment. It would be up to spiritualism to revive the suggestion that credulity gave access to special knowledge: knowledge, in this case, of the dead.

"I DID OPEN MY EYES WITH PERFECT EASE"

Not long before electrobiology took off in Boston, etherology had spawned something even more objectionable to Grimes: mediumship, which he saw as another of his own wayward children. "Modern spiritualism originated at

---

53. Gregory, *Letters to a Candid Inquirer*, 96.
54. [Advertisements], *Boston Daily Atlas*, January 19, 1850.

my lectures in Poughkeepsie, N.Y., in 1843," he asserted in 1857 (*MHN*, 346). This claim is overblown, but it has something in common with the truth. Two points of origin are conventionally given for the spiritualist movement: the publication of Andrew Jackson Davis's *The Principles of Nature* (1847), which recorded his mystical prophecies while in a state of mesmeric trance, and the rappings of the sisters Kate and Margaret Fox in the summer of 1848. Both moments are well chosen, since the 1848 manifestations touched off the national movement, and the 1847 prophecies furnished many of its philosophical warp-strings.[55] Grimes had a hand in Davis's apotheosis. Davis himself, who was a young shoemaker's apprentice, and his first mesmerist, local tailor William Levingston, saw Grimes's 1843 demonstrations in Poughkeepsie and began their mesmeric experimentations immediately afterward. Davis was not, however, successfully mesmerized by Grimes, nor did his subsequent trance experience with Levingston particularly resemble anything Grimes would have endorsed: Davis started out as a diagnosing clairvoyant and then began visiting the spirit land.[56] As he recalled his encounter with Grimes in *The Magic Staff* (1857), "the professor went through a series of motions—resembling the 'presto change' [*sic*] of legerdemain performers—and then imperiously said, '*You can't open your eyes!*' He was mistaken. I did open my eyes with perfect ease."[57] Davis's eyes opened wider and wider from then on, first seeing disease, then the history of humankind and the cosmos, then the levels of the spirit world.

Spiritualism had manifold ties to mesmerism, far exceeding the laying on of hands that linked Grimes and Davis. Historians beginning with spiritualism's first chronicler, Emma Hardinge Britten, have recognized this entanglement. Hardinge Britten emphasized "the influence which . . . the magnetic idea exercised upon minds prepared to receive Spiritualism and [upon] organisms already imbued with the necessary force to develop mediumship."[58] Magnetism, in other words, laid the groundwork for spiritualism both in theory and in practice. When the Fox sisters heard rappings

55. Ann Braude, *Radical Spirits: Spiritualism and Women's Rights in Nineteenth-Century America* (Boston: Beacon Press, 1989), 34. See also Robert S. Cox, *Body and Soul: A Sympathetic History of American Spiritualism* (Charlottesville, VA: University of Virginia Press, 2003), 7.

56. Taves, *Fits, Trances, and Visions*, 168-69; Andrew Jackson Davis, *The Magic Staff: An Autobiography of Andrew Jackson Davis* (New York: J. S. Brown, 1857), 12.

57. Davis, *Magic Staff*, 201-2.

58. Hardinge Britten, *Modern American Spiritualism*, 23.

in Hydesville, they initially interpreted the experience without reference to mesmerism. They believed that the sounds were the attempts of an unquiet murder victim to speak to the residents of a house where he had once stayed.[59] But it was not long before the radical Quakers Amy and Isaac Post reinterpreted the manifestations in light of both mesmeric practices and loftier theories of the land of the dead.[60] Thousands of spiritualist practitioners, and "many of the best mediums," got their start in mesmerism, according to Hardinge Britten.[61] As Ann Taves has shown, the link between mesmerism and spiritualism was widely acknowledged.[62]

Somewhat less widely recognized is the fact that spirits got their start in mesmerism, too. As Robert Cox points out, "neither spirits nor specters were a rarity" in upstate New York before the beginning of spiritualism proper.[63] Many years before the Fox sisters heard poltergeists in upstate New York, orthodox mesmerists were already warning their flocks against the heresy of spirit communication. In the July 1842 *Magnet*, only the second issue of that phrenomesmeric journal, Sunderland had to issue a "caution . . . against believing these stories of visits to the moon, and conversations in unknown tongues, and even with spirits of the dead!"[64] In 1845, Grimes listed spirit communication among the erroneous interpretations of mesmeric phenomena: it was a "delusion into which [practitioners] have been led by their own credulity, and the peculiar condition and superstition of the subjects" (*E*, 304). These protests only show that it was a very short step from acting out the characters of phrenological organs or letter writers to performing the characters of the dead.

Anna Parsons, the Brook Farm psychometrist, made the leap almost without noticing it. During an 1845 reading of a letter written by Charles Fourier, the founder of the socialist doctrine of associationism, Parsons had a vision of Fourier's spirit. He appeared just as Parsons made a negative comment on his character: "he was more intellectual than spiritual." Marianne Dwight recounts that "*the moment she said this Fourier came to her,—so mournful he looked almost reprovingly at her. She asked him, Isn't*

59. David Chapin, *Exploring Other Worlds: Margaret Fox, Elisha Kent Kane, and the Antebellum Culture of Curiosity* (Amherst: University of Massachusetts Press, 2004), 40–41.

60. See Braude, *Radical Spirits*, 10–12; Chapin, *Exploring Other Worlds*, 40–44.

61. Hardinge Britten, *Modern American Spiritualism*, 23.

62. Taves, *Fits, Trances, and Visions*, 167–68.

63. Cox, *Body and Soul*, 6.

64. "Caution," *Magnet* 1, no. 2 (July 1842): 34.

it so? and he acknowledged it."[65] Spirit-Fourier reluctantly had to acknowledge living Fourier's shortcomings. "He is sadder now at this moment than he ever was when living," Parsons reported; "knows he was more intellectual than spiritual, and it is sadness to him now."[66] Throughout the reading, Dwight reported to her brother, Parsons perceived "the visible presence of Fourier in the room . . . [she] says it was real, and her communion with him, by question and answer, as real as any communion she has with any living person."[67] According to Dwight, those who witnessed the reading or saw the notes were generally "satisfied and gratified" by what Parsons had to say.[68] Death's sudden involvement in the character readings fazed no one. So close were psychometry and spiritualism that the *Vanguard*, an occult-friendly paper published in Ohio, repeatedly had to set its readers straight about the differences between them. *Vanguard* coeditor Annie Denton Cridge practiced both psychometry and spiritualism. The two were distinct in her mind, but she strove in vain to get her readers to see why.[69] Cridge's readers, like Parsons, effortlessly made the transition between channeling letters and channeling spirits.

Thus Grimes's personal contribution to Andrew Jackson Davis's practice was just one of many threads connecting mesmerism with spiritualism. Even so, the Poughkeepsie seer's meeting with the skeptical mesmerist condenses something of the overall relationship between these practices, where both rivalry and influence ran deep. Grimes mesmerized by telling his subjects *"you cannot open your eyes,"* and those who obeyed, he believed, had been caught by their credenciveness. Davis insisted he could still open his. He meant literally that Grimes had not succeeded in mesmerizing him.

---

65. "Appendix: A Reading of Fourier's Character by Anna Parsons," in *Letters from Brook Farm, 1844–1847*, by Marianne Dwight, ed. Amy L. Reed (Poughkeepsie, NY: Vassar College, 1928), 185.

66. Ibid.

67. Dwight, *Letters from Brook Farm*, 108.

68. Ibid.

69. Annie Denton Cridge, "Psychometry and Spiritualism," *Vanguard*, Dayton, OH, May 30, 1857, 98; Annie Denton Cridge, "Psychometry-Spiritualism," *Vanguard*, Richmond, IN, February 13, 1858, 373. The distinction, according to Cridge, was that psychometry was accomplished by the medium's unaided intuition and could only determine the letter writer's state at the moment of writing. With spirit help, by contrast, a medium could know the present state of the dead. Cridge and her fellow editors were students of Buchanan: see Dana Luciano, "Sacred Theories of Earth: Matters of Spirit in *The Soul of Things*," *American Literature* 86, no. 4 (December 2014): 719.

Figuratively, though, Davis's open eyes, as opposed to the closed eyes of
Grimes's subjects, also capture the modification he made to Grimes's etherology. Davis believed Grimes had rejected him as a subject because "he recognized a clairvoyant propensity in my mental organism, which would not
serve his public purposes."[70] And unquestionably it would not have done;
Grimes wanted to show how mesmerizing deceived, whereas Davis wanted
to show that it enlightened. With his spirit communications from Galen and
Emanuel Swedenborg, Davis was to take mesmerism in the opposite direction from what Grimes would have wished. Davis's clairvision signified that
he had not passed under Grimes's spell: he was not "credencively inducted."
At the same time, it prefigured that he would fall under a greater spell, the
spell of his own prophetic gifts; that he would pass through the darkness
of credulity and, like other mesmeric clairvoyants before him, see light on
the other side. Spiritualism partially originated in mesmerism in the same
way that mesmerism of the earlier nineteenth century partially originated
in the Franklin commission report. Just as Poyen and other Francophone
mesmerists of the early nineteenth century had argued that credulity was
a useful quality—it conferred both insight and tractability—so spiritualists
would argue, against the more austere view of Grimes and the electrobiologists, that credulity gave access to the spirit world. As Ann Braude has
shown, the prominent spiritualist periodical the *Banner of Light* reasoned
that insight was tied to impressibility: "Hence sickness, rest, passivity, susceptibility, impressionability, mediumship, communication, revelation!"[71]
Davis, and others, *could* open their eyes, much as Loraina Brackett, against
the Franklinian notions of a blind credulity, had opened hers.

"I SEE A RAINBOW"

Grimes regularly lectured against spiritualism from 1850 onward, most often
in Boston, where he debated the spiritualist Leo Miller at the Melodeon in
1860.[72] He reproduced the substance of these lectures in *Mysteries of Human*

70. Davis, *Magic Staff*, 202.
71. Quoted in Braude, *Radical Spirits*, 83.
72. J. Stanley Grimes and Leo Miller, *Great Discussion of Modern Spiritualism, between Prof. J. Stanley Grimes and Leo Miller, Esq.: at the Melodeon, Boston* (Boston: Berry, Colby, 1860); [Advertisements], *Boston Daily Atlas*, January 19, 1850; "Knocking Humbug," *Daily*

Nature (1857) and then revisited the same material in still more detail with *Mysteries of the Head and the Heart Explained* (1875). Sometime between 1845, when *Etherology* was first published, and 1857, when *Mysteries of Human Nature* was published, Grimes had all but recanted on the fluidic component of his theory (*MHN*, 409–10). He still believed that mesmerism amounted to the overstimulation of the conforming social organs, especially creden-civeness, but he had come to doubt that etherium had any role in mediat-ing this stimulation. Instead, he thought that "the language of the operator" alone—what he came to call "magic eloquence," and what others would have called suggestion—stimulated the organs (*MHN*, 348).[73] He was probably in-fluenced by his knowledge of Sunderland's *Pathetism* (1843) and James Braid's *Neurypnology* (1843) in making this change, even though he had been dis-missive of both in *Etherology* (*E*, 263).[74] Grimes's view was that all rapping mediums were imposters, whereas speaking, writing, and table-tipping medi-ums might be self-deceived (*MHN*, 336).[75] These honestly deluded mediums were the victims of their own too-sensitive conforming social organs, includ-ing credenciveness. Speaking and writing mediums responded to suggestions from operators, not to spirit controls, and table-tipping mediums, in whose presence spirits were supposed to move furniture, were actually upsetting the tables themselves by unconscious and involuntary muscle action. Grimes called these mediums "credo-maniacs" (*MHN*, 336).

In his lectures, Grimes laid out his alternate theory of how the illusion of spirit communication was produced by spirit mediums' credo-mania. Much as he had said in 1845 that overstimulated credenciveness produced the

---

Ohio Statesman, July 18, 1850; "Human Nature"; [Advertisement], *Bangor Daily Whig & Courier*, August 26, 1852; "Table Moving," *Boston Investigator*, April 5, 1854.

73. An 1846 lecture ad still calls Grimes's practice "etheropathy" ([Advertisement], *Boston Daily Atlas*, March 25, 1846), while an 1850 ad uses the term "magic eloquence" ([Adver-tisements], *Boston Daily Atlas*, January 19, 1850), so it seems likely that Grimes made the change from a fluidic to a suggestive theory during this window.

74. La Roy Sunderland, *Pathetism* (New York: P. P. Good, 1843); James Braid, *Neuryp-nology; or, The Rationale of Nervous Sleep Considered in Relation with Animal Magnetism* (London: John Churchill, 1843).

75. Grimes had certainly articulated that view by 1854 (see the editor's note to "Table Moving"), and he had most likely articulated it by 1850. In that year he both advertised that he would explain mediumship through "magic eloquence" ([Advertisements], *Boston Daily Atlas*, January 19, 1850) and performed an exposé of the Fox sisters for the New York *Tribune* ("Knocking Humbug"). On Grimes and the *Tribune*, see also Hardinge Britten, *Modern American Spiritualism*, 69.

mesmeric trance, in the 1850s he said that it produced spirit mediumship—
which was only a different name for the same state. "The materials from which
the modern spiritualists have manufactured their miracles and wonderful
manifestations, are all, excepting the jugglery, stolen from mesmerism," he
insisted (*MHN*, 376–77). Onstage, Grimes demonstrated how common spirit
phenomena could be produced through "magic eloquence" alone. This part
of his campaign placed him in the odd position of pretending to speak to
spirits or to see into the spirit land in order to make the appropriate suggestions to his subjects. He was using the old debunking technique of stepping
into the place of the false priest and reproducing all the latter's miracles without any of the mystical explanations.

"To make a vision-seeing medium," he explained in one of several reci-
pes of this sort, "you only have to say to the subject, while his eyes are closed,
'See, yonder in the sky is a beautiful rainbow; there it is! Do you not see it?'
He will point to it and say yes" (*MHH*, 283) (Fig. 10). Like the electrobiologists, he would often progressively embellish the deceptive vision—adding
a "spirit land" under the rainbow, then "one of his own departed friends"
among the spirits (*MHH*, 283). But it was just as easy to make the subject see
"something that is absurd, ridiculous, and impossible, that the spirit land
is full of buffoons and monkeys, or that on the rainbow sits his sweetheart
eating peanuts and throwing the shells at him, and hitting him in the eyes;
he will instantly dream this, and act and suffer accordingly" (*MHH*, 284).
Grimes was not above calling out to spirits in order to improve the effect.
To demonstrate how table turning was the result of involuntary muscle motion, a theory he probably took from Michael Faraday, he would perform
the following scene: "I usually call on the spirit of Sampson to push the
table over, and at the same time urge the young man, the subject, to hold it
up. . . . To give greater effect to the performance, I use encouraging language
to both parties. I say: 'Push, young man! push, spirit! push, both of you!' "[76]
Inexperienced audiences were perfectly capable of mistaking Grimes for
"a wonderful medium," thinking "that a spirit is really moving the table"
(*MHH*, 286). And really, they were almost right: Grimes *was* a wonderful
medium in everything but inward conviction.

Grimes's sham séances resembled the 1784 commission's sham magnetic sessions at Benjamin Franklin's house in Passy, France, except for the
fact that Grimes thought that credenciveness, rather than imagination, was the
effective agent. Grimes's declaration that "the upper front region of the brain

76. *MHH*, 286; "Table Moving."

A VISION SEEING MEDIUM.
"I see a beautiful rainbow, and beyond, beneath the arch, I see the spirit land, and I hear the spirits sing."

Fig. 10. "A Vision Seeing Medium," in J. Stanley Grimes, *The Mysteries of the Head and Heart Explained* (Chicago: W. B. Keen, Cooke, 1875), plate following p. 282. Courtesy, American Antiquarian Society.

is the spirit land, in which all the fairies, witches, superstitions, and wonders of the world are born," might have been the commissioners' own, if "upper front region of the brain" were replaced with "imagination" (*MHH*, 272). What is more, Grimes recognized the resemblance. "I do not wish to be understood as claiming any credit for being the first to perform credencive experiments," he wrote in 1857, "for *Mesmer* himself performed, in effect, the very same experiments" and "the committee appointed, in Paris, to investigate the subject, among whom was *Dr. Franklin*, reported, that the results appeared to be principally owing to the impressions made upon the minds of the subjects, by the people about them, exciting their imaginations"

(*MHN*, 404–5). Grimes even commented later that "it is perhaps not far from the truth to assert that Mesmer's theory, and the report of the commission contain, essentially, all that has been advanced by scientists since that time" (*MHH*, 269). I would agree. But this observation pointed to the futility of Grimes's project. He was trying to end a tradition by repeating the very gesture of debunking that had touched it off—a strategy with little hope of success.

Spiritualists were as much the joint inheritors of Mesmer and Franklin as Grimes himself was, though they remixed their heritage in a rather different way. US mesmerism had annexed the Franklin commission's prestigious object of knowledge, credulity, and had claimed to be able to manipulate it to greater effect than the commissioners had done. Spiritualism would make essentially the same move against Grimes's credenciveness and the mesmeric tradition as a whole. Spiritualists shaped a narrative in which mesmerism was the primitive practice that they had rationalized. When the *Banner of Light* declared that "every profound science has had its primitive martyr," the profound science they meant was spiritualism, and the primitive martyr was "Frederic Anthony Mesmer."[77] To Britten, mesmerism was one of the "rudimental stages of growth" that led to spiritualism's "fully-perfected work"; it was the "germ-thought" to spiritualism's "great discovery."[78] Davis's early series of prophecies, *The Principles of Nature*, represented Spirit as the latest step in a progressively unfolding secularism.[79] "Disenchantment" for Davis, as John Modern notes, "was not the vanquishing of ghosts. Rather, it was a matter of calculating them."[80] Davis opposed "fanaticism," "sectarianism," and "ignorance, superstition, and bigotry."[81] A good heir of the French Revolution, he never uttered the word *institutions* without pausing to express his indignation at the way they confine the mind and body.[82] He condemned "false imagination."[83] Spirit was for him the

77. "The Martyrs of Light: Frederic Anthony Mesmer," *Banner of Light* 1, no. 2 (April 18, 1857): 7.

78. Hardinge Britten, *Modern American Spiritualism*, 21–22.

79. John Lardas Modern, *Secularism in Antebellum America* (Chicago: University of Chicago Press, 2011), 178–79.

80. Ibid., 179.

81. Andrew Jackson Davis, *The Principles of Nature, Her Divine Revelations, and a Voice to Mankind* (Boston: Colby & Rich, 1847), 5, 12.

82. See, e.g., ibid., 12, 13 ("inquisitorial institutions"), 14, 18 ("barbarous and sectarian institutions").

83. Ibid., 6.

future, not the past: "And is this the nineteenth century? And has ignorance so prevailed that the spiritual and internal principle of man has become hidden and obscured? . . . Seven times have I been requested to explain the nature and composition of *Spirit*. What an age to ask such a question!"[84] Spirit was an advanced object of knowledge, something the nineteenth century ought to have progressed far enough to understand.[85] The "universal method of progressive unfoldment" that Hardinge Britten saw manifesting itself across history quite closely resembled the one that mesmerists had seen in what they took to be the primitive prehistory of their own practice.[86] Bumbling false priests of the past gave way to technicians of the present. Only now the false priests were not Egyptians, but mesmerists; and the technicians were not mesmerists, but spirit mediums.

Mesmerists had claimed to rationalize false-priestly practices. Where priests had used magnetism to deceive and had lied about the nature of the power they wielded, mesmerists used it to enlighten—or at least to discipline and modernize. Spiritualism similarly rehabilitated the deceptions that remained in mesmerism. Spiritualism started before electrobiology, but for most of the 1850s, the two practices coexisted. After the electrobiologist G. W. Stone lectured in Ohio, Cridge conjectured in the *Vanguard* that spirits affected mediums through electrobiology.[87] A practice that in G. W. Stone's hands would have caused subjects to see false visions and play fictional characters had a completely different effect in spirit hands. When the dead electrobiologized, they caused subjects to see *true* visions and perform the spirits' own characters—making those characters visible to the living in the only possible way. On one occasion during a séance circle, Cridge saw the spirit of an American Indian mesmerize her brother William Denton by standing with his attention "entirely fixed" on him; "his appearance was exactly similar to that of a biologist operating on a subject." Two other Indian spirits stood at Denton's sides, "making passes under his arms." These manipulations caused him to act out the character of an Indian just as an electrobiological subject might have done: he "sprang to the floor and gave an Indian yell."[88] "It is usually by means of Biology that spirits daguerreotype

84. Ibid., 21.

85. See also, e.g., Annie Denton Cridge, "Necessity of Inner Culture," *Vanguard*, Richmond, IN, November 21, 1857, 284–85.

86. Hardinge Britten, *Modern American Spiritualism*, 21.

87. [Cridge], "Mr. Stone's Biological Lectures," 93.

88. Annie Denton Cridge, "Passages in the Experience of a Skeptical Medium," part 2 of a 3-part series, *Vanguard*, Dayton, OH, October 10, 1857, 254.

on the inner vision of the seeing medium such ideas and information as they desire to convey," the *Vanguard* explained in another article.[89] Thus the Indian biologist had both made Cridge see him and made Denton act out his character. These effects depended on Denton's and Cridge's impressibility. But neither the vision nor the character was false; both accurately reflected the spirit world. What the skeptics of 1784 had called delusion, mesmerists of the early nineteenth century had called a means of managing, controlling, and communicating. Spiritualists had turned the tables on mesmerists: mesmerism, on their view, was merely deceptive, while their refurbishment of its techniques led forward to the truth. Spiritualists were the modern ones now.[90]

89. [Cridge], "Mr. Stone's Biological Lectures," 93.

90. The modernity of Spiritualism has been argued on various grounds. For the argument that spiritualism is modern in its social progressiveness, see Braude, *Radical Spirits*; Alex Owen, *The Darkened Room: Women, Power, and Spiritualism in Late Victorian England* (Philadelphia: University of Pennsylvania Press, 1990); Molly McGarry, *Ghosts of Futures Past: Spiritualism and the Cultural Politics of Nineteenth-Century America* (Berkeley: University of California Press, 2008). In its use of media, see Stefan Andriopoulos, *Ghostly Apparitions: German Idealism, the Gothic Novel, and Optical Media* (New York: Zone Books, 2013); John Durham Peters, *Speaking Into the Air: A History of the Idea of Communication* (Chicago: University of Chicago Press, 1999). For the argument that spiritualism is modern in its secularism or its use of empirical method, see Modern, *Secularism in Antebellum America*, 224–25, 277, and elsewhere; see also David Walker, "The Humbug in American Religion: Ritual Theories of Nineteenth-Century Spiritualism," *Religion and American Culture* 23, no. 1 (2013): 30–74.

CODA: BAGGING THE IDOL

At last extinguishing the fire, he took the idol up very unceremoniously, and bagged it again in his grego pocket as carelessly as if he were a sportsman bagging a dead woodcock.

Herman Melville, *Moby-Dick* (1851)[1]

THERE WAS MORE THAN ONE WAY to be visited by the spirit of Benjamin Franklin during the contentious 1850s. J. Stanley Grimes honored Poor Richard with his debunking zeal. Electrobiologists, like Franz Anton Mesmer before them, did their best to capitalize on the prestige of electricity, Franklin's signature subtle fluid. Spiritualists boldly claimed his endorsement. The *Banner of Light* was not above directly contradicting the truth in its summary of the 1784 French royal commission's results: "D'Eslon succeeded and confounded the persecutors of science to a most palpable extent."[2] Not at all; but by this time, who cared? Spiritualists even went so far as to conjure Franklin. Their version of the ancestral totem spoke audaciously against himself. The presence of "our own practical and unimaginative Franklin" at séances, as Robert Dale Owen put it, was a tacit, but powerful, argument in their favor.[3]

1. Herman Melville, *Moby-Dick; or, The Whale*, vol. 6 of *The Writings of Herman Melville: The Northwestern-Newberry Edition*, ed. Harrison Hayford, G. Thomas Tanselle, and Hershel Parker (Evanston, IL: Northwestern University Press, 1988), 23 (hereafter cited in text as *MD*).

2. "The Martyrs of Light: Frederic Anthony Mesmer," *Banner of Light* 1, no. 2 (April 18, 1857): 7.

3. Owen quoted in Werner Sollors, "Dr. Benjamin Franklin's Celestial Telegraph, or Indian Blessings to Gas-Lit American Drawing Rooms," *American Quarterly* 35, no. 5 (Winter 1983): 461.

Franklin would not have liked the spiritualist appropriation, obviously; but he would not have liked Grimes inventing organs and electrobiologists dreaming up psychological effects for electricity any better. Each of these appropriations did mischief to the founding father, but there was fealty here, too. The practitioners of the 1850s were Franklin's devout followers in that they were all interested in the technical use of credulity. In each case, the manipulation of a credulous person made knowledge possible. Electrobiology and etherology both retained traces of their mesmeric predecessors' claims to benevolent manipulation and cure; more important, they offered their audiences a bird's-eye view of duping, as though watching others being fooled (and watching the puppet shows of primitive religion) could inoculate one against being puppeteered oneself. Spiritualists were dedicated to bringing about a new age through the kind of knowledge that credulous mesmeric sensitives alone could deliver. The impressible medium opened a portal to what Andrew Jackson Davis called "a revolution in the condition of mankind."[4]

Spiritualism's dependence on impressible mediums might seem out of keeping with the practice's modernity. Aren't moderns, on the contrary, free and disillusioned? Viewed in light of mesmerism's history, however, the credulity of the modern medium is not so paradoxical. Extracting knowledge or utility from the raw material of credulity *was* an enlightened activity. Credulity was perfectly at home in enlightenment; enlightenment, in fact, did not leave home without it. But when we insist that the protagonists of our secular histories be empowered and clear-sighted, not disempowered and credulous, we have a hard time opening our own eyes to the fact that mediums belonged to these latter two categories. As long as one is asking whether or not mediums are empowered, it seems that one is fulfilling the obligation to ask whether the practice did the practitioner good or ill. Was she a puppet or a puppeteer? Was he cynically pulling the strings, or was he being had? Devotion to such questions does not guarantee that answers to them are possible, however. Mediums were neither inactive when they channeled others nor irradiated with a perfect self-control when they dropped the aid of spirits and spoke on their own account. The truth lies somewhere in the middle. It has not been my primary aim in this book to answer the question of what the practice does—ethically, politically—for the mesmeric subject. In part that question has not been my focus because I think answers to it, if

4. Andrew Jackson Davis, *The Principles of Nature, Her Divine Revelations, and a Voice to Mankind* (Boston: Colby & Rich, 1847), 13.

available at all, are usually equivocal and always local. Neither mesmerism nor spiritualism had a uniform effect on all its mediums. I have been more interested in describing how the mesmeric tradition used credulity to bring about its own enlightenment, a task that has required spadework enough.

I do want to suggest in closing, however, that there are ways of asking what the practice does for the practitioner without resorting to empowerment as the measure of the good. To open up these other avenues, it is necessary first to engage directly with the book that established the canonical view that empowerment is the ultimate tendency of mediumship, even though the practice centrally involves self-disempowerment in favor of spirits. Not coincidentally, the same book also did much to establish spiritualism as the legitimate subject matter of secular historiography. The text I have in mind is Ann Braude's *Radical Spirits* (1989).[5] Braude's book advances two closely related, but ultimately separable, claims about spiritualism and women's rights: first, that the two movements were closely intertwined, sharing personnel, distribution networks, and position platforms. This claim is impressively supported with evidence drawn mostly from upstate New York, where spiritualism mixed extensively with progressive movements (see *RS*, 56–81).[6] The second claim, that spirit mediumship served as a pathway to empowerment for individual women, relies primarily on an analysis of the career of one medium, Achsa Sprague: what Braude calls "a case study in empowerment" (*RS*, 99). The case study plays a key role in the book as a whole: Braude judges that mediumship was probably "Spiritualism's greatest contribution to the crusade for woman's rights" (*RS*, 82).

Braude's empowerment argument revolves around her judgment that the moment when the medium is a credulous instrument employed by the spirit is merely "a transitional phase" (*RS*, 98). Mediumship, she argues, gave women a chance to try out public speaking without fully identifying with the role (*RS*, 82). As mediums, "women did things they themselves believed women could not do" (*RS*, 83). As soon as they proved their own capacities to themselves, women could "break through limitations on their role" (*RS*, 98). Thus mediumship was an instrument to be discarded as soon as it had played its part "in empowering a woman to assume a public career" (*RS*, 99).

5. Ann Braude, *Radical Spirits: Spiritualism and Women's Rights in Nineteenth-Century America* (Boston: Beacon Press, 1989), hereafter cited in text as *RS*.

6. Robert Cox has raised questions about how well Braude's characterization fits spiritualism as a whole, beyond this milieu. See Robert Cox, *Body and Soul: A Sympathetic History of American Spiritualism* (Charlottesville: University of Virginia Press, 2003), 4.

Trance speakers sometimes became regular speakers, but never, according to Braude, the other way around. "Women who possessed the self-assurance to speak without spirit assistance" would go straight to speaking in their own voices rather than bothering with the intermediate step of having spirits speak through them (*RS*, 98).

On this model, it is progressive to speak by yourself and regressive to speak for a spirit. Mediumship is being recuperated here as a step on the way to secular agency. That ethical or political recuperation is also at one and the same time a historiographical recuperation. If mediums are on the path to choosing pleasure and achieving freedom, then spiritualism is an appropriate topic for a secular historiography that looks for social progress and individual agency. If we can say, as Braude does, that "Achsa Sprague's spirit empowered other women just as her own 'guardians' empowered her during her life," then there is reason to see mediumship as furthering the advance toward political modernity—and thus to bother writing its history at all (*RS*, 116). Early in the book, Braude seems to apply this empowerment claim broadly, but she later expresses doubts about its proper scope. In the postbellum period, mediumship no longer empowers: "Spiritualism distinguished itself less and less among religious groups by fostering female leadership," and mediumship became "a source of humiliation and embarrassment to those who attempted the sensational manifestations expected in the 1870s" (*RS*, 191). Braude's allies and successors have nonetheless found the empowerment argument both compelling and broadly transferable; studies of diverse trance practices, from Protestant Awakening to vodou, have taken it up.[7]

Shying away from mediums' disempowerment disguises the fact that credulity, with its attendant features of impressibility and conformation to others' views, is a constitutive feature of enlightenment. Braude's argument

7. Alex Owen, *The Darkened Room: Women, Power, and Spiritualism in Late Victorian England* (Philadelphia: University of Pennsylvania Press, 1990); Molly McGarry, *Ghosts of Futures Past: Spiritualism and the Cultural Politics of Nineteenth-Century America* (Berkeley: University of California Press, 2008); Deborah Manson, "'The Trance of the Ecstatica': Margaret Fuller, Animal Magnetism, and the Transcendent Female Body," *Literature and Medicine* 25, no. 2 (2006): 298–324; Toni Wall Jaudon, "Obeah's Sensations: Rethinking Religion at the Transnational Turn," *American Literature* 84, no. 4 (2012): 715–41; Nancy Ruttenburg, *Democratic Personality: Popular Voice and the Trial of American Authorship* (Stanford, CA: Stanford University Press, 1998).

seems to betray, if not her own discomfort with the kind of agency that disempowers itself in favor of a spirit, then at least an intuition that her (secularist) audience will not value that kind of agency. There is not much space in this framework for the possibility that the disempowerment of the medium is essential to the spiritualist process of producing knowledge, even though that is clearly the case—mediumship is the only way to know the spirit world. Spirits figure ignobly here, as unconscious ruses employed on the path to women's enfranchisement. The possibility that a medium acts *by and through* her self-disempowerment in favor of a spirit, as an actor or psychometer does, is not one that Braude considers. The give-and-take between mediums and spirits, or the power that clairvoyants exert in interpreting that which they obey, cannot really come under examination as long as our arguments demand that we make the "transition" out of the disempowerment "phase" as quickly as we can—not even passing through it at all, if we have the courage to mount the women's rights platform on our own from the beginning. Moreover, the idea of progress toward empowerment may not even be a coherent one, when one thinks carefully about what secular agency is. We have already seen that the notion of the self-controlled and self-conscious agent is fraught with problems, notably in that it always seems to require a disempowered counterpart. Either there must be a malleable part of the self over which the controlling self has power, or else there must be impressible and credulous people on whom the controlling self exerts his or her will, who serve as fetishistic confirmations that the self's power is real. For a spirit medium to become "empowered," on this view, would only mean that she transferred her fealty from one phantom controller to another: from spirits, to herself-as-secular-agent. She would become, like Hollingsworth in Nathaniel Hawthorne's *The Blithedale Romance*, her own bond slave.

It is possible to measure the good, not by measuring degrees of empowerment but by imagining better and worse ways of being controlled, better and worse ways of relating to those other agencies in favor of which human beings disempower themselves: idols, mesmerists, spirit controls, ego ideals. Herman Melville's *Moby-Dick* (1851) asks the question of what it might mean to have a better or a worse, a benevolent or a malevolent, relationship to one's control, given that being controlled by something or another is inevitable: "who aint a slave?" (*MD*, 6). John Modern has interpreted *Moby-Dick* as a bellwether of secular haunting. Massive efforts to calculate social life, combined with pressure to achieve perfect self-knowledge and self-control, left antebellum secularists oppressed by the near presence of leviathans lurking just underneath the surface.[8] "In its language of steam and electricity," Modern writes, "*Moby-Dick* seems to suggest that a state of enchantment is not the exception that proves the rule of an Enlightened, civilized evolution of human being but rather that enchantment itself is the rule."[9] Modern's secularists have this much in common with idolaters: they feel obliged to propitiate a terrifying power that they cannot quite perceive, one that may or may not be real. *Moby-Dick* has few characters who are not idolaters on this definition. Aboard the whaling ship the *Pequod* there is Queequeg, whose devotions to his effigy Yojo form the backbone of the early chapters. There are the other two "pagan harpooneers," Daggoo and Tashtego, whose religious hygiene, though briefly sketched, is obviously abysmal (*MD*, 523); there is Fedallah, a fire worshipper; and there is the "old Mogul," the crew's name for their captain, Ahab (*MD*, 432; see also 177, 197, 469). If idolatry locates godlike agency where none is, there is no worse offender than Ahab, since attributing malign purpose to the whale who maimed him is the essence of his quest. "To be enraged with a dumb thing . . . seems blasphemous," first mate Starbuck pleads (*MD*, 164), in his attempt to prevent idolatry from becoming the sole object of their "cannibal of a craft" (*MD*, 70).

The strategic adoption of idolatry is one potential solution to the problem of not knowing which agents to blame for one's injuries, as Ahab tells Starbuck in response to his accusation of blasphemy, since at least it gives a person a target:

> Hark ye yet again,—the little lower layer. All visible objects, man, are but as pasteboard masks. But in each event—in the living act, the undoubted deed—there, some unknown but still reasoning thing puts forth the mouldings of its features from behind the unreasoning mask. If man will strike, strike through the mask! How can the prisoner reach outside except by thrusting through the wall? To me, the white whale is that wall, shoved near to me. Sometimes I think there's naught beyond. But 'tis enough. He tasks me; he heaps me; I see in him outrageous strength, with an inscrutable malice sinewing it. (*MD*, 164)

Ahab is agnostic as to whether the whale is the enemy that dismasted him or only an agent (in that older sense of an employee) who carried out the deed

8. John Lardas Modern, *Secularism in Antebellum America* (Chicago: University of Chicago Press, 2011), xv–xvii.

9. Ibid., xvi.

on someone else's behalf. With no satisfactory answer to his question of who is responsible—"sometimes I think there's naught beyond"—Ahab nominates an enemy within his grasp. Ahab is doing just what primitives are supposed to do according to secular descriptions: reaching for the solace of an explanation, even a false one, in an implacable world. From a position that looks like disillusionment, Ahab steps into superstition—not into belief, but actually into *superstition* as understood by the enlightened: the consoling invention of agents that do not exist. This gesture hardly makes the world comfortable for Ahab. But his willful superstition does at least furnish him with a purpose, and with meaning of a sort: it gives him an idol he can destroy.

It is not only Ahab who suffers from the invisibility of whatever tasks and heaps him. The crew also suffers: they adopt the "fiery hunt" for the whale because his whiteness represents the world's deceitfulness about its true colors: "Nature absolutely paints like the harlot" (*MD*, 195). Narrator Ishmael suffers, too. The Fates, in Ishmael's hands, are negligent but inexorable; they do not care enough to assign him anything more momentous than "this shabby part of a whaling voyage," but the assignment is no more flexible for all that. As to their reasons, "this the invisible police officer of the Fates, who has the constant surveillance of me, and secretly dogs me, and influences me in some unaccountable way—he can better answer than any one else" (*MD*, 7). For Modern, these fates express Ishmael's sense that he is "following a script not of his own choosing. He is literally surrounded by words that have nothing, essentially, to do with him. . . . Nevertheless, these words are affective, intimate, prescriptive. These words are auratic, hinting at unseen forces that were shaping and directing them."[10] Those forces are the words, and the words are the forces. The white whale's obtrusive elusiveness captures the obtrusive elusiveness of secular discourse. No one, whether sailing before or behind the mast, escapes the inevitable controls—those agents and shadows who sometimes speak through us, or in whom, maybe, we have hived off some part of the agency belonging to ourselves. Yet also, no one can quite pinpoint where those controls are. The controls insult because they are at once overweening and unreal. The *Pequod*'s quest depends on choosing finite stand-ins for these ineffable powers—choosing idols, that is—and then attacking them.

There are two ways to mount such an attack: credulously, as the crew and its pagan harpooneers apparently do, or knowingly, as Ahab does. Ahab is the novel's clear-eyed and cynical manipulator of enchantment. His "pasteboard

10. Ibid., xxi–xxii.

masks" speech is accompanied by an invented ritual that lies somewhere between animal magnetism and a confidence trick (two categories that substantially overlapped in the mesmeric tradition). He improvises a whaleship *baquet* (magnetizing tool), trying to enthrall his three mates by magnetizing their crossed lances: "It seemed as though, by some nameless, interior volition, he would fain have shocked into them the same fiery emotion accumulated within the Leyden jar of his own magnetic life" (*MD*, 165). His power over Starbuck is his "magnet at Starbuck's brain" (*MD*, 212). When the stars—and a storm—seem against the *Pequod*'s quest, and allegiance flags, Ahab performs false magnetic magic to restore the crew's faith. Lightning has exactly reversed the ship's compasses, and knowing "that to steer by transpointed needles, though clumsily practicable, was not a thing to be passed over by superstitious sailors," Ahab promises to make a new compass out of a sail needle (*MD*, 518). It is one thing to magnetize the needle but quite another to make the process into a "magic" ceremony, designed to appeal to the "servile wonder" of the crew (*MD*, 518). Melville strongly implies that Ahab overdoes anything that might look like an enchanted movement or a magnetic pass. He describes Ahab as "going through some small strange motions . . . whether indispensable to the magnetizing of the steel, or merely intended to augment the awe of the crew, is uncertain" (*MD*, 518). These last gestures were more animal-magnetic than mineral-magnetic— directed toward the men, not toward the needle.

Ahab exercises his control, too, through his all-unifying magnetic totem, the doubloon, which hypnotizes everyone into flights of autosuggestion. While Melville was composing *Moby-Dick* in the first months of 1850, the electrobiologists were explaining to crowds in the thousands how to magnetize by making people stare at a coin. John Bovee Dods instructed his subjects to hold coins in the palms of their hands, a foot from their eyes, and then "the eyes should be placed upon the coin as though they were riveted there."[11] At the beginning of "The Doubloon," it's Ahab who is mesmerized: Ahab's "riveted glance fasten[s] upon the riveted gold coin" (*MD*, 430). Soon everyone else follows, except the mad Pip. Ahab draws his crew's attention to a coin that also draws him. *Moby-Dick*, as a fiction, poses a question that mesmeric manuals would never willingly approach: what is

---

11. John Bovee Dods, *Philosophy of Electrical Psychology, in a Course of Twelve Lectures* (New York: Fowlers & Wells, 1850; repr. (stereotype edition), New York: Fowlers & Wells, 1851), 216. Citation refers to the 1851 edition.

the psychic payoff for the mesmerist himself? Control cannot be the reason that Ahab, false-priest-like, manipulates his crew, because control only gets us as far as the quest to which he welds their wills. And that quest is itself just another false-priest manipulation: Ahab's manipulation of himself, his choice to wreak his hate on a whale-idol that may, or may not, have flukes of clay (Ahab is indifferent). He is doing a travesty of a revenge ritual for himself, just as he does travesties of magic for his crew. His dead earnestness in his hunt for the whale is the dead earnestness not of the naive magician but of the manipulator of wooden "tractors" and other sham devices. He is more a Franklin—in his control of lightning, and in his control of the credulous crew—than a Mesmer.

"Control" proves just as elusive for Ahab as it did for Hollingsworth—a character Hawthorne could have written with Ahab in mind. He composed *The Blithedale Romance* after *Moby-Dick* came out.[12] Melville dedicated it to him (*MD*, vii). Melville expresses Ahab's self-tyranny as monomania: that "special lunacy" that "stormed his general sanity, and carried it, and turned all its concentrated cannon upon its own mad mark" (*MD*, 185). Monomania was, according to Grimes, a self-induced mesmeric state. "Just as one man may induct another," Grimes wrote, "so may one organ induct another organ in the same man."[13] Fedallah, who hardly materializes as a full person, seems the external manifestation of Ahab's madness, connected to him by a rapport or "unaccountable tie" (*MD*, 231). He lets Melville show in pantomime that self-control, which seems like freedom, is actually inseparable from self-ruling. Thus no one can quite tell whether Ahab is the slave and Fedallah the master, or the other way around: "Ahab seemed an independent lord; the Parsee but his slave. Still again both seemed yoked together, and an unseen tyrant driving them" (*MD*, 538). Fedallah is the manifestation of Ahab's iron purpose, his total self-control, as that control enslaves him. There is no special reason why you would be freer from your idol when your idol is your freedom of choice than when it is your little wooden god. The problem with the empowerment argument is that it assumes that freedom is a better master. On the *Pequod*, freedom is the worst master. Ahab never gets out from under its (his own) thumb.

12. Edwin Haviland Miller, *Salem Is My Dwelling Place: A Life of Nathaniel Hawthorne* (Iowa City: University of Iowa Press, 1991), 353–57.

13. J. Stanley Grimes, *Etherology; or, The Philosophy of Mesmerism and Phrenology* (New York: Saxton and Miles, 1845), 34.

There is one character in *Moby-Dick* who has successfully adjusted to life under the difficult conditions Melville thinks we face—where we will be controlled always, but usually not by something we can see or understand. That character is a pagan "idolator," Ishmael's bosom friend Queequeg (*MD*, 52). "Here was a man some twenty thousand miles from home . . . and yet he seemed entirely at his ease; preserving the utmost serenity; content with his own companionship; always equal to himself," says Ishmael of his shipmate (*MD*, 50). Ishmael's earliest encounters with the outlandish Queequeg happen in the modality of religion. There is nothing surprising in the fact that Ishmael describes Queequeg's idol, Yojo, with tongue in cheek; what is more interesting is that Queequeg does not take Yojo altogether seriously, either. In the course of one of his pagan rituals, Queequeg sets Yojo up in the fireplace, burns ship biscuit on a sacrificial pyre of wood shavings, snatches the cracker out of the flames, and makes "a polite offer of it to the little negro" (*MD*, 23). These "strange antics were accompanied by still stranger guttural noises from the devotee, who seemed to be praying in a sing-song or else singing some pagan psalmody or other, during which his face twitched about in the most unnatural manner" (*MD*, 23). It would seem we are in the presence of one of Amariah Brigham's or Grant Powers's witless primitives, until Queequeg does this: "At last extinguishing the fire, he took the idol up very unceremoniously, and bagged it again in his grego pocket as carelessly as if he were a sportsman bagging a dead woodcock."[14] Queequeg can put off his reverence as suddenly as he put it on. Superstition is hardly the onerous chain the Enlightenment imagined. Nor is Queequeg's idol anything like the terrible, yet slippery Moby Dick.

In a novel full of idolaters both civilized and savage, Queequeg stands out less for his devotion to Yojo than for his offhandedness toward him. First he deposits his devotion with Yojo; then, lightly, he deposits Yojo in his coat pocket. Melville, I would suggest, is less interested in the doctrinal trappings of our idols or controls than in their degree of portability. Whale, books, self-will, Yojo: the nature of the control may not matter so much as its size. Melville classes idols the same way he classes cetaceans in the "Cetology" chapter: by cumbersomeness. Folio whales, like the sperm whale Moby Dick, kill; duodecimo whales, like the porpoise, play. Similarly with wooden gods: a good idol is a duodecimo idol, one that fits into a grego pocket and can be bagged like a woodcock when its usefulness expires. Comedy—or to

14. *MD*, 23. A *grego* is a greatcoat.

use a Melvillian word, gamesomeness—separates Queequeg's religious ob-
servances from the earnest primitivity that a lesser Romantic might have
foisted on his savage characters. It also separates them from Ahab's cynical, yet deadly purposeful, magnetization of the ship's needle to control his
crew and achieve his quest. Ishmael says of sighting the Huzza Porpoise—a
duodecimo whale, by the way—"if you yourself can withstand three cheers
at beholding these vivacious fish, then heaven help ye; the spirit of godly
gamesomeness is not in ye" (*MD*, 143–44). The spirit of godly gamesomeness is in Queequeg's believing rites but never in Ahab's unbelieving ones.
Believe in your control or don't, Melville seems to say, but make sure it's something you can stow away. Folio whales are not recommended.

The question of portability might substitute for the question of empowerment as something to ask oneself when faced with a control—spirit-,
self-, or otherwise. Rather than looking for the moment when the controlled
medium becomes the self-controlled women's rights speaker, one could ask
about the quality of the relationship to a control. Perhaps what is interesting
about mediums is not that they moved on from their spirits but that for a
good amount of time, they lived with them. The choice to cohabitate may
indicate that the "spirit-control" is tolerable for the medium: that one feels
one can put it away, as Queequeg does with Yojo. Mediums might possess
the capacity to be unconcerned by the momentary control of the not-me,
because of a trust that the not-me can be stowed away later. Skeptics, perhaps, do not have that confidence. Their refusal to live with idols might
indicate not a laudable wish for emancipation from these chimerical beings
but rather a certain clumsiness with them, a lack of the diplomacy that such
powerful objects require of us. It may be that one calls for freedom mainly
when one finds, like Ahab, that one does not know how to put the wooden
effigy away without destroying it. Skeptics might feel saddled with a folio
idol—an idol one cannot pocket, and cannot escape. At any rate, unbelief
is no better at stowing away its gods than belief is. In *Moby-Dick*, where the
unbeliever is Ahab, it is clearly worse.

J. Stanley Grimes, with his decades of sham spiritualist experiments,
bears comparison to the Ahab whose mastery of both science and false priest-
hood hardly liberated him. The rise of spiritualism embroiled Grimes in a
monomania of debunking; a "skepto-mania" to match the "credo-mania" he
saw in his targets. Putting quietuses on mediums became his more-than-
pastime. "Investigation is my business, my daily labor, and my recreation,
and has been, ever since the day when this modern spiritualism reared its

deformed head. . . . I have never yet met one who has investigated spiritual-ism as much, or as long as I have," he declared in 1857.[15] Given that proponents of spiritualism also called themselves "investigators," Grimes was effectively saying that he practiced more than the practitioners did. He may have been right. As late as 1875, Grimes still played his lonely game of whack-a-mole, hammering away at one false interpretation of his work after another. I hope he took some pleasure in demonstrating his own lucidity by contrast to the credulity of others, but there is little to indicate that he did: injured merit is his usual tone. None of Grimes's quietuses really took; as the Franklin com-mission's own fertile failure exemplified, quietuses seldom do. His quietuses did not do much to free him, either; he was constantly employed with con-juring up controlling spirits in whom he did not believe. Spiritualism was a folio whale for Grimes: unconvinced by it, he still could not stop his sham devotions at its shrine. His devotions were, by his own account, more copi-ous than those of believers. Having burned his fake biscuits, he could not fit the idol—wooden though he believed it to be—into his grego pocket.

Rachael Draper, the Rochester mesmeric clairvoyant who channeled Franklin, seems to have been much more skilled at pocketing idols. Even her act of channeling Franklin was a form of stowing him away, so thorough was her travesty of the living man. The spirit of godly gamesomeness was surely in Draper when she wired to Franklin for telegraphic communica-tions and had him preside over a passing of the baton from mesmerism to spiritualism in 1850. No method of pocketing Franklin—that is, disregard-ing his commands, showing oneself uncontrollable by him—could possibly have been more imperious, more indifferent to his historical wishes, than this one of calling him up and "submitting" to him. On this occasion—and at Franklin's instance on a former visit—Kate and Margaret Fox were also present to help with the communication. Under Franklin's direction through Draper, the company split into two groups: Margaret Fox remained with Draper, her husband, and a few others in one room, while Kate Fox went with a few other observers into another room, "with two doors closed between them."[16] The setup was reminiscent of the Franklin commission experiments

---

15. J. Stanley Grimes, *The Mysteries of Human Nature, Explained by a New System of Ner-vous Physiology: To Which Is Added, a Review of the Errors of Spiritualism, and Instructions for Developing or Resisting the Influence by Which Subjects and Mediums Are Made* (Buffalo: R. M. Wanzer, 1857), 337.

16. Quoted in Emma Hardinge Britten, *Modern American Spiritualism: A Twenty Years' Record of the Communion between Earth and the World of Spirits* (New York, 1870), 53.

in which patients who were magnetized in secret from an adjoining room failed to convulse. They had not known they were being magnetized; hence, their imaginations were not activated; hence, no "magnetic" effects. In this way the commissioners had proven to their own satisfaction that imagination, not magnetism, was the cause concerned.

In this case, though, each room independently decoded the same message, proving that the words really did come from Franklin and not from the medium's heated brain. Here is Franklin's prophecy: "There will be great changes in the nineteenth century. Things that now look dark and mysterious to you will be laid plain before your sight. Mysteries are going to be revealed. The world will be enlightened. I sign my name, Benjamin Franklin."[17] Soon, in the perpetual sunrise of modernity, everyone's eyes would clear. With nearly all specifics boiled away from Spirit-Franklin's message, the eighty-proof rhetoric of modernity remains: change, the present century as the vanguard, the clearing up of mysteries, the sharpening of eyes. Something else remains, too, after content has vaporized: the structure of the communication; the means by which these investigators receive their prize. For this electrifying prophecy to reach the nineteenth century's ears, both credulity and the means of controlling it had to be in the room. The impressible Rachel Draper, the inspired Fox sisters, and a vestige of the double-blind setup the Franklin commission had once used to coax the mesmeric patients' imaginations into appearing: these elements, rightly arranged, made Franklin's message possible. The real Franklin would hardly have wanted to think that the nineteenth century's revelations would come from spirits. And yet the collaboration of the impressible and the disenchanted in the transmitting of this message was loyal to the tradition he had inaugurated. By hooking up his machine to credulity, the spirit of Benjamin Franklin enlightened the world.

17. Quoted in ibid., 53–54.

SELECTED BIBLIOGRAPHY

ARCHIVAL MATERIALS

Archives Nationales d'Outre-Mer, Aix-en-Provence, France (abbreviated ANOM in notes).
———. *Notariat* (notary record) of Guadeloupe.
———. *Série géographique* of Guadeloupe.
———. *Série géographique* of Martinique.
———. *État civil* (register of births, marriages and deaths) of Sainte Rose, Guadeloupe.
Charles Ferson Durant Biographical File. Institute of Aerospace Sciences Archives, Library of Congress, Washington, DC.
Franklin Papers at Yale, Yale University, New Haven, CT, http://franklinpapers.org /franklin//.
———. [J. S. Bailly], "Rapport secret sur le Mesmérisme," August 11, 1784. Unpublished series, July 1, 1784–March 31, 1785.
———. Joseph-Ignace Guillotin to Benjamin Franklin, Paris, June 18, 1787. Unpublished series, May 1, 1787–June 30, 1788.
Perkins School for the Blind Archives, Watertown, MA (abbreviated PS in notes).
———. Incoming and Outgoing Correspondence, 1828–1932.
———. Laura Bridgman journal, 1841–1856.
———. Perkins Institutional Records, Enrollment and Biographies, 1832–1839.
———. Perkins Institutional Records, School Journal, General Abstracts, 1839–1840.
———. Pupil Register no. 2, 1832–1894.
———. Register of Correspondence Sent.
———. Teacher Journals for the Deafblind Department.
Perry-Clarke Collection. Massachusetts Historical Society, Boston.

THESES AND PUBLISHED WORKS

"Account of the Report of the Committee, Appointed by Order of the French King, to Enquire into Animal Magnetism." *Boston Magazine*, May 1785, 163–66.

[Adams, John]. "Animal Magnetism Alias Medical Witchcraft." *Boston Courier*, December 1, 1836.

————. "Boston, Nov. 29: Extract of a Letter Dated September 8, 1784, Auteuil, near Paris." *American Herald*, Boston, November 29, 1784.

Adams, John. "John Adams as He Lived." *Atlantic Monthly*, May 1927.

Adelon, N. P., and F. V. Mérat, ed. *Dictionnaire de médecine.* 21 vols. Paris: Béchet jeune, 1821–1828.

[Advertisements]. *Boston Daily Atlas*, January 19, 1850.

Albanese, Catherine L. *A Republic of Mind and Spirit: A Cultural History of American Metaphysical Religion.* New Haven, CT: Yale University Press, 2007.

Almanach de la Guadeloupe et dépendances. Basse-Terre, Guadeloupe: Imprimerie du Roi, 1832–1836.

Andriopoulos, Stefan. *Ghostly Apparitions: German Idealism, the Gothic Novel, and Optical Media.* New York: Zone Books, 2013.

Archives du magnétisme animal. Paris: 1820–1823. Specific citations of this periodical appear in notes.

Arthur, T. S. *Agnes; or, The Possessed: A Revelation of Mesmerism.* Philadelphia: T. B. Peterson, 1848.

Asad, Talal. *Formations of the Secular: Christianity, Islam, Modernity.* Stanford, CA: Stanford University Press, 2003.

Bacon, Francis. *The New Organon.* Vol. 8 of *The Works of Francis Bacon.* Edited by James Spedding, Robert Leslie Ellis, and Douglas Denon Heath. 15 vols. Boston: Taggard & Thompson, 1860–64. American reprint of Bacon, Francis. *Works.* London: Longman, 1857–1874.

————. *The New Organon.* Edited by Lisa Jardine and Michael Silverthorne. Cambridge: Cambridge University Press, 2000.

Bagnall, William. *The Textile Industries of the United States.* Cambridge, MA: Riverside Press, 1893.

[Bailly, J.-S.]. *Rapport des commissaires chargés par le roi de l'examen du magnétisme animal.* Paris: Imprimerie du Roi, 1784.

[Bailly, J.-S.]. *Report of Dr. Benjamin Franklin, and Other Commissioners, Charged by the King of France with the Examination of the Animal Magnetism, as Now Practised at Paris.* [Translated by William Godwin.] London: J. Johnson, 1785. Issued in December 1784.

Banner of Light. Boston, 1857–1907. Specific citations of this periodical appear in notes.

Barnes, Elizabeth. *States of Sympathy: Seduction and Democracy in the American Novel.* New York: Columbia University Press, 1997.

Bennett, Jane. *The Enchantment of Modern Life: Attachments, Crossings, and Ethics*. Princeton, NJ: Princeton University Press, 2001.

Berlant, Lauren. "Fantasies of Utopia in *The Blithedale Romance*." *American Literary History* 1, no. 1 (Spring 1989): 30–62.

Bibliothèque du magnétisme animal. Paris: Société du magnétisme, 1817–1819. Specific citations of this periodical appear in notes.

Billot, G. P., and J. P. F. Deleuze. *Recherches psychologiques sur la cause des phénomènes extraordinaires, observés chez les modernes voyans . . . ; ou, Correspondance sur le magnétisme vital, entre un solitaire et M. Deleuze*. 2 vols. Paris: Albanel et Martin, 1839.

Borch-Jacobsen, Mikkel. *The Emotional Tie: Psychoanalysis, Mimesis, and Affect*. Stanford, CA: Stanford University Press, 1992.

Borgstrom, Michael. "Hating Miles Coverdale." *ESQ: A Journal of the American Renaissance* 56, no. 4 (2011): 363–90.

Boston Courier. Boston, 1824–1851. Specific citations of this periodical appear in notes.

Boston Daily Atlas. Boston, 1844–1857. Specific citations of this periodical appear in notes.

Boston Investigator. Boston, 1831–1904. Specific citations of this periodical appear in notes.

Boston Medical and Surgical Journal (BMSJ). Boston, 1828–1928. Specific citations of this periodical appear in notes.

Bougerol, Christiane. *Une ethnographie des conflits aux Antilles: Jalousie, commérages, sorcellerie*. Paris: Presses Universitaires de France, 1997.

[Bradbury, Osgood]. *Mysteries of Lowell*. Boston: Edward F. Williams, 1844.

Braid, James. *Neurypnology; or, The Rationale of Nervous Sleep Considered in Relation with Animal Magnetism*. London: John Churchill, 1843.

Branche, H. de. "Plantations d'Amérique et papiers de famille, II." In *Notes d'histoire coloniale*, no. 60. Macon, France: Imprimerie Protat frères, 1960.

Braude, Ann. *Radical Spirits: Spiritualism and Women's Rights in Nineteenth-Century America*. Boston: Beacon Press, 1989.

Brigham, Amariah. *Observations on the Influence of Religion upon the Health and Physical Welfare of Mankind*. Boston: Marsh, Capen, & Lyon, 1835.

Brigham, Josiah. *Twelve Messages from the Spirit John Quincy Adams through Joseph D. Stiles, Medium, to Josiah Brigham*. Boston: Bela Marsh, 1859.

Brodhead, Richard. "Hawthorne and the Fate of Politics." *Essays in Literature* 11, no. 1 (Spring 1984): 95–103.

Brown, William Hill. *The Power of Sympathy*. In *"The Power of Sympathy" and "The Coquette,"* edited by Carla Mulford. New York: Penguin, 1996.

Bryant, William Cullen. *The Letters of William Cullen Bryant*. Edited by William Cullen Bryant II and Thomas G. Voss. 6 vols. New York: Fordham University Press, 1975–1992.

Buchanan, Joseph Rodes. "Animal Magnetism—(Continued)." *Buchanan's Journal of Man* 1, no. 4 (April 1849): 172–74.

———, ed. *Manual of Psychometry: The Dawn of a New Civilization*. Boston: Press of the Roxbury Advocate, 1885.

———. "Psychometry." *Buchanan's Journal of Man* 1, no. 2 (February 1849): 49–62.

———. "Psychometry—(Continued)." *Buchanan's Journal of Man* 1, no. 3 (March 1849): 99–113.

———. "Psychometry—(Continued)." *Buchanan's Journal of Man* 1, no. 4 (April 1849): 145–56.

———. "Psychometry—(Continued)." *Buchanan's Journal of Man* 1, no. 5 (May 1849): 208–27.

———. *Sketches of Buchanan's Discoveries in Neurology.* Louisville: J. Eliot & Co.'s Power Press, 1842.

———. "Sympathetic Impressibility." *Buchanan's Journal of Man* 1, no. 8 (October 1849): 353–68.

Buchanan's Journal of Man. Edited by Joseph Rodes Buchanan. Cincinnati, 1849–1856. Specific citations of this periodical appear in notes.

Burrows, Edwin G., and Mike Wallace. *Gotham: A History of New York City to 1898.* New York: Oxford University Press, 1999.

Carlson, Eric T. "Charles Poyen Brings Mesmerism to America." *Journal of the History of Medicine and Allied Sciences* 15 (April 1960): 121–32.

Cary, Louise D. "Margaret Fuller as Hawthorne's Zenobia: The Problem of Moral Accountability in Fictional Biography." *ATQ* 4, no. 1 (1990): 31–48.

Castronovo, Russ. "The Antislavery Unconscious: Mesmerism, Vodun, and 'Equality.'" *Mississippi Quarterly* 53 (Winter 1999/2000): 41–56.

Chakrabarty, Dipesh. *Provincializing Europe: Postcolonial Thought and Historical Difference.* Princeton, NJ: Princeton University Press, 2000.

Chapin, David. *Exploring Other Worlds: Margaret Fox, Elisha Kent Kane, and the Antebellum Culture of Curiosity.* Amherst: University of Massachusetts Press, 2004.

Chase, Richard. *The American Novel and Its Tradition.* Garden City, NY: Doubleday, 1957.

Chertok, Léon, and Isabelle Stengers. *Le Cœur et la raison: L'hypnose en question de Lavoisier à Lacan.* Paris: Éditions Payot, 1989.

———. *A Critique of Psychoanalytic Reason: Hypnosis as a Scientific Problem from Lavoisier to Lacan.* Translated by Martha Noel Evans. Stanford, CA: Stanford University Press, 1992.

Cheyfitz, Eric. "The Irresistibleness of Great Literature: Reconstructing Hawthorne's Politics." *American Literary History* 6, no. 3 (Fall 1994): 539–58.

Clarke, Mary. *Sarah Maria Cornell, or, The Fall River Murder: A Domestic Drama in Three Acts.* New York, 1833.

Coburn, Frederick William. *History of Lowell and Its People.* 3 vols. New York: Lewis Historical Publishing, 1920.

Cohen, Lara. *The Fabrication of American Literature: Fraudulence and Antebellum Print Culture.* Philadelphia: University of Pennsylvania Press, 2012.

Coleridge, Samuel Taylor. *Biographia Literaria.* Edited by James Engell and W. Jackson Bate. Vol. 7 (2 vols. in 1) of *The Collected Works of Samuel Taylor Coleridge*, edited by Kathleen Coburn. Princeton, NJ: Princeton University Press, 1983.

———. *Lectures 1808–1819 on Literature.* Edited by R. A. Foakes. Vol. 5 (2 vols. in 1) of *The Collected Works of Samuel Taylor Coleridge*, edited by Kathleen Coburn. Princeton, NJ: Princeton University Press, 1987.

Collyer, Robert. *Psychography; or, The Embodiment of Thought.* Philadelphia, 1843.

Conrad, James Lawson Jr. "The Evolution of Industrial Capitalism in Rhode Island, 1790–1830: Almy, the Browns, and the Slaters." PhD diss., University of Connecticut, 1973.

Cook, James. *The Arts of Deception: Playing with Fraud in the Age of Barnum*. Cambridge, MA: Harvard University Press, 2001.

Coviello, Peter, and Jared Hickman, eds. "After the Postsecular." Special issue, *American Literature* 86, no. 4 (2014).

———. "Introduction: After the Postsecular." In Coviello and Hickman, "After the Postsecular," 645–54.

Cox, Robert. *Body and Soul: A Sympathetic History of American Spiritualism*. Charlottesville, VA: University of Virginia Press, 2003.

Crabtree, Adam. *From Mesmer to Freud: Magnetic Sleep and the Roots of Psychological Healing*. New Haven, CT: Yale University Press, 1993.

Cridge, Annie Denton. "Necessity of Inner Culture," *Vanguard*, Richmond, IN, November 21, 1857, 284–85.

———. "Psychometry and Spiritualism." *Vanguard*, Dayton, OH, May 30, 1857, 98.

———. "Psychometry-Spiritualism." *Vanguard*, Richmond, IN, February 13, 1858, 373.

[Cridge, Annie Denton]. "Mr. Stone's Biological Lectures," *Vanguard*, Dayton, OH, March 27, 1857, 93.

Darling, H. G., ed. *Electrical-Psychology; or, The Electrical Philosophy of Mental Impressions, Including a New Philosophy of Sleep and Consciousness from the Works of Rev. J. B. Dods and Prof. J. S. Grimes*. London: John J. Griffin, 1851.

Darnton, Robert. *Mesmerism and the End of the Enlightenment in France*. Cambridge, MA: Harvard University Press, 1968.

Daston, Lorraine. "Fear and Loathing of the Imagination in Science." *Daedalus* 134, no. 4 (2005): 16–30.

Davidson, Cathy. *Revolution and the Word: The Rise of the Novel in America*. 2nd ed. New York: Oxford University Press, 2004.

Davis, Andrew Jackson. *The Magic Staff: An Autobiography of Andrew Jackson Davis*. New York: J. S. Brown, 1857.

———. *The Principles of Nature, Her Divine Revelations, and a Voice to Mankind*. Boston: Colby & Rich, 1847.

"Death of Dr. Poyen." *Boston Medical and Surgical Journal*, September 25, 1844, 166–67.

Debien, Gabriel. *Les Esclaves aux Antilles Françaises, XVIIe–XVIIIe siècles*. Basse-Terre, Guadeloupe: Société d'Histoire de la Guadeloupe, 1974.

Delbourgo, James. *A Most Amazing Scene of Wonders: Electricity and Enlightenment in Early America*. Cambridge, MA: Harvard University Press, 2006.

Deleuze, J. P. F. *Histoire critique du magnétisme animal*. 2 vols. Paris: Mome, 1813.

———. *Instruction pratique sur le magnétisme animal*. Paris: Dentu, 1825.

———. *Practical Instruction in Animal Magnetism*. Translated by Thomas C. Hartshorn. Providence, RI: B. Cranston, 1837.

———. *Practical Instruction in Animal Magnetism*. Translated by Thomas C. Hartshorn. Rev. ed. New York: Appleton, 1843.

Dods, John Bovee. *Philosophy of Electrical Psychology, in a Course of Twelve Lectures*. New York: Fowlers & Wells, 1851. Reprint (stereotype ed.) of New York: Fowlers & Wells, 1850.

———. *Six Lectures on the Philosophy of Mesmerism, Delivered in the Marlboro' Chapel, January 23–28, 1843.* Boston: W. A. Hall, 1843.

Dublin, Thomas. *Women at Work: The Transformation of Work and Community in Lowell, Massachusetts, 1826–1860.* 2nd ed. New York: Columbia University Press, 1993.

Dupuy, [P. S.?]. "Copie du rapport à M. le Ministre de la Marine et des Colonies, sur des expériences faites à la Guadeloupe, concernant la fabrication du sucre." In *Annales de la Société d'Agriculture et d'Economie Rurale de la Martinique,* 439–500. Saint-Pierre, Martinique, 1839.

Durant, Charles Ferson. *Exposition; or, a New Theory of Animal Magnetism.* New York: Wiley & Putnam, 1837.

———. *Grand Aerostatic Ascension, of Charles F. Durant, the First Native Citizen of the United States that Ever Attempted an Ascension in a Balloon, on Thursday, September 9, 1830.* Broadside. New York: J. C. Spear, 1830.

During, Simon. *Modern Enchantments: The Cultural Power of Secular Magic.* Cambridge, MA: Harvard University Press, 2002.

Dwight, Marianne. *Letters from Brook Farm, 1844–1847.* Edited by Amy L. Reed. Poughkeepsie, NY: Vassar College, 1928.

Ebel, Jonathan, and Justine Murison, eds. "American Literatures/American Religions." Special issue, *American Literary History* 26, no. 1 (2014).

Edelman, Nicole. *Voyantes, guérisseuses et visionnaires en France, 1785–1914.* Paris: Albin Michel, 1995.

1850 United States Federal Census. Accessed June 24, 2017. http://search.ancestry.com/search /db.aspx?dbid=8054.

Ellenberger, Henri. *The Discovery of the Unconscious: The History and Evolution of Dynamic Psychiatry.* New York: Basic Books, 1970.

Ellen Merton, the Belle of Lowell; or, The Confessions of the 'G.F.K.' Club. Boston: Brainard, 1844.

Elmer, Jonathan. *Reading at the Social Limit: Affect, Mass Culture, and Edgar Allan Poe.* Stanford, CA: Stanford University Press, 1995.

Emerson, Ralph Waldo. *The Complete Works of Ralph Waldo Emerson.* 12 vols. Boston: Houghton, Mifflin, 1903–1904.

———. *Essays: Second Series,* edited by Joseph Slater, Alfred R. Ferguson, and Jean Ferguson Carr. Vol. 3 of *The Collected Works of Ralph Waldo Emerson,* 10 vols., edited by Joseph Slater and Douglas Emory Wilson. Cambridge, MA: Harvard University Press, 1983.

———. *Journals and Miscellaneous Notebooks of Ralph Waldo Emerson,* edited by William H. Gilman, Alfred R. Ferguson, Harrison Hayford, Ralph H. Orth, J. E. Parsons, and A. W. Plumstead. 16 vols. Cambridge, MA: Harvard University Press, 1960–1982.

Emery, Sarah Anna, ed. *Reminiscences of a Nonagenarian.* Newburyport, MA: William H. Huse, 1879.

Encyclopaedia Britannica: or, A Dictionary of Arts, Sciences, and Miscellaneous Literature; Enlarged and Improved. 6th ed. 20 vols. Edinburgh: Constable, 1823.

English, Thomas Dunn. *1844; or, The Power of the 'S. F.'* New York: Burgess, Stringer, 1847.

"Experiments in Phreno-Magnetism." *Madisonian*, May 26, 1842. Reprinted from the Philadelphia *Inquirer*.

Felski, Rita. *Uses of Literature*. Malden, MA: Blackwell, 2008.

Fessenden, Tracy. *Culture and Redemption: Religion, the Secular, and American Literature*.
Princeton, NJ: Princeton University Press, 2007.

———. "The Problem of the Postsecular." In Ebel and Murison, "American Literatures/
American Religions," 154–67.

Fillassier, Alfred. "Quelques faits et considérations pour servir à l'histoire du magnétisme
animal." Thesis, Faculté de Médecine de Paris, 1832.

Fiske, Theophilus. *Labor the Only True Source of Wealth*. Charleston, SC: Office of the
Examiner, 1837.

Fontenelle, Bernard de. *Histoire des oracles*. Paris: G. de Luyne, 1686.

———. *The History of Oracles, and the Cheats of the Pagan Priests*. Translated by Aphra
Behn. London, 1688.

Foster, Hannah Webster. *The Coquette; or, The History of Eliza Wharton*. Edited by Cathy N.
Davidson. New York: Oxford University Press, 1986.

Fraginals, Manuel Moreno, and Heather Cateau. "The Crisis of the Plantation." In Laurence and Cuesta, *General History of the Caribbean*, 62–103.

Franchot, Jenny. *Roads to Rome: The Antebellum Protestant Encounter with Catholicism*.
Berkeley: University of California Press, 1994.

Frank, Adam. "Valdemar's Tongue, Poe's Telegraphy." *ELH* 72, no. 3 (2005): 635–62.

Franklin, Benjamin. *Experiments and Observations on Electricity*. London: E. Cave, 1751.

Freeberg, Ernest. *The Education of Laura Bridgman: First Deaf and Blind Person to Learn
Language*. Cambridge, MA: Harvard University Press, 2001.

Freud, Sigmund. "Fetishism" (1927). In *The Complete Psychological Works of Sigmund
Freud*, vol. 21, translated by James Strachey, 147–57. London: Hogarth and the Institute
of Psychoanalysis, 1957.

Fulford, Tim. "Conducting the Vital Fluid: The Politics and Poetics of Mesmerism in the
1790s." *Studies in Romanticism* 43, no. 1 (2004): 57–78.

[Fuller, Hiram]. "Remarkable Phenomena of Animal Magnetism." *New Hampshire Sentinel*, December 8, 1836, [1]. Reprint of *Providence Daily Journal*, November 24, 1836.

Fuller, Margaret. *The Letters of Margaret Fuller*. Edited by Robert N. Hudspeth. 6 vols.
Ithaca, NY: Cornell University Press, 1983–1984.

———. "The New Science, or the Philosophy of Mesmerism or Animal Magnetism"
(review of *Etherology; or, The Philosophy of Mesmerism and Phrenology*, by J. Stanley
Grimes). In *Life Without and Life Within; or, Reviews, Narratives, Essays, and Poems*,
edited by Arthur B. Fuller, 169–73. Boston: Brown, Taggard, & Chase, 1859. Originally
published in *New York Tribune*, February 17, 1845.

Fuller, Robert C. *Mesmerism and the American Cure of Souls*. Philadelphia: University of
Pennsylvania Press, 1982.

Gallagher, Catherine. "The Rise of Fictionality." In *The Novel*, vol. 1, *History, Geography,
and Culture*, edited by Franco Moretti, 336–63. Princeton, NJ: Princeton University
Press, 2006.

Garraway, Doris. *The Libertine Colony: Creolization in the Early French Caribbean*. Durham, NC: Duke University Press, 2005.

Gauld, Alan. *A History of Hypnotism*. Cambridge: Cambridge University Press, 1992.

"A Gentleman of Philadelphia" [pseud.]. *The Philosophy of Animal Magnetism, Together with the System of Manipulating Adopted to Produce Ecstacy and Somnambulism—the Effects and the Rationale*. Philadelphia: Merrihew & Gunn, 1837.

Georget, E. J. *De la physiologie du système nerveux et spécialement du cerveau*. 2 vols. Paris: J. B. Baillière, 1821.

Gerber, David A. "The 'Careers' of People Exhibited in Freak Shows: The Problem of Volition and Valorization." In Thomson, *Freakery*, 38–54.

Gersuny, Carl. "'A Devil in Petticoats' and Just Cause: Patterns of Punishment in Two New England Factories." *Business History Review* 50, no. 2 (Summer 1976): 131–52.

Gitter, Elisabeth. *The Imprisoned Guest: Samuel Howe and Laura Bridgman, the Original Deaf-Blind Girl*. New York: Farrar, Straus, & Giroux, 2001.

Goldstein, Jan. "Enthusiasm or Imagination? Eighteenth-Century Smear Words in a Comparative National Context." *Huntington Library Quarterly* 60, no. 1–2 (1997): 29–49.

Gregory, William. *Letters to a Candid Inquirer on Animal Magnetism*. Philadelphia: Blanchard & Lea, 1851.

Grieve, Robert. *An Illustrated History of Pawtucket, Central Falls, and Vicinity*. Pawtucket, RI, 1897.

Grimes, J. Stanley. *Etherology and the Phreno-Philosophy of Mesmerism and Magic Eloquence; Including a New Philosophy of Sleep and of Consciousness, with a Review of the Pretensions of Phreno-Magnetism, Electro-Biology, &c*. Boston: James Munroe, 1850.

———. *Etherology; or, The Philosophy of Mesmerism and Phrenology*. New York: Saxton & Miles, 1845.

———. *The Mysteries of Human Nature, Explained by a New System of Nervous Physiology: To Which Is Added, a Review of the Errors of Spiritualism, and Instructions for Developing or Resisting the Influence by Which Subjects and Mediums Are Made*. Buffalo: R. M. Wanzer, 1857.

———. *The Mysteries of the Head and the Heart Explained: Including an Improved System of Phrenology; A New Theory of the Emotions; and an Explanation of the Mysteries of Mesmerism, Trance, Mind-reading, and the Spirit Delusion*. Chicago: W. B. Keen, Cooke, 1875.

———. *A New System of Phrenology*. New York: Wiley & Putnam, 1839.

Grimes, J. Stanley, and Leo Miller. *Great Discussion of Modern Spiritualism, between Prof. J. Stanley Grimes and Leo Miller, Esq.: at the Melodeon, Boston*. Boston: Berry, Colby, 1860.

Grosz, Elizabeth. "Intolerable Ambiguity: Freaks as/at the Limit." In Thomson, *Freakery*, 55–66.

Gustafson, Sandra. "The Emerging Media of Early America." *Proceedings of the American Antiquarian Society* 115, no. 2 (2005): 205–50.

Hadcock, Editha. "Labor Problems in Rhode Island Cotton Mills, 1790–1940." PhD diss., Brown University, 1945. Typescript; two bound volumes, separately paginated.

Hardinge Britten, Emma. *Modern American Spiritualism: A Twenty Years' Record of the Communion between Earth and the World of Spirits*. New York, 1870.

Harris, Jennifer. "'Almost Idolatrous Love': Caroline Dall, Sarah Knowles Bolton, Mary C. Crawford and the Case of Elizabeth Whitman." In *Women Writers and the Artifacts of Celebrity in the Long Nineteenth Century*, edited by Ann R. Hawkins and Maura Ives, 119–32. London: Ashgate Press, 2012.

Harris, Neil. *Humbug: The Art of P. T. Barnum*. Boston: Little, Brown, 1973.

Hartshorn, Thomas C. "Appendix" to *Practical Instruction in Animal Magnetism*, by J. P. F. Deleuze, translated by Thomas C. Hartshorn, 1–204 (appendix is separately paginated). Providence: B. Cranston, 1837.

———. "Appendix" to *Practical Instruction in Animal Magnetism*, rev. ed., by J. P. F. Deleuze, translated by Thomas C. Hartshorn, 217–357. New York: Appleton, 1843.

———. "New Appendix" to *Practical Instruction in Animal Magnetism*, rev. ed., by J. P. F. Deleuze, translated by Thomas C. Hartshorn, 359–401. New York: Appleton, 1843.

[Hartshorn, Thomas C.]. "The Magnetizer," nos. 1–20, *Providence Daily Journal*, April 19, 1837–August 10, 1837.

Hawthorne, Nathaniel. *The Blithedale Romance and Fanshawe*, edited by Fredson Bowers. Vol. 3 of *The Centenary Edition of the Works of Nathaniel Hawthorne*, 23 vols., edited by William Charvat, Roy Harvey Pearce, and Claude M. Simpson. Columbus: Ohio State University Press, 1964.

———. *The House of the Seven Gables*, edited by Fredson Bowers. Vol. 2 of *The Centenary Edition of the Works of Nathaniel Hawthorne*, 23 vols., edited by William Charvat, Roy Harvey Pearce, and Claude M. Simpson. Columbus: Ohio State University Press, 1965.

———. *The Letters, 1813–1843*, edited by Thomas Woodson, L. Neal Smith, and Norman Holmes Pearson. Vol. 15 of *The Centenary Edition of the Works of Nathaniel Hawthorne*, 23 vols., edited by Thomas Woodson. Columbus: Ohio State University Press, 1984.

———. *Life of Franklin Pierce*. Boston: Ticknor, Reed, & Fields, 1852.

Haygarth, John. *Of the Imagination, as a Cause and as a Cure of Disorders of the Body; Exemplified by Fictitious Tractors, and Epidemical Convulsions*. Bath, UK: Cruttwell, 1800.

Hegel, G. W. F. *Phenomenology of Spirit*. Translated by A. V. Miller. New York: Oxford University Press, 1977.

Hénin de Cuvillers, E. F. de. "Conclusion de l'Introduction aux *Archives du magnétisme animal*." *Archives du magnétisme animal* 1, no. 1 (1820): 215–52.

Herrnstein-Smith, Barbara. "Anthropotheology: Latour, Knowledge, and Belief." Paper presented at the conference "Recomposing the Humanities with Bruno Latour," sponsored by *New Literary History*, University of Virginia, Charlottesville, September 18, 2015.

Hickman, Jared. "*The Book of Mormon* as Amerindian Apocalypse." *American Literature* 86, no. 3 (2014): 429–61.

Howe, Samuel G. *Annual Report of the Trustees of the New-England Institution for the Education of the Blind* (1834–1839, Vols. 1–7). Subsequently titled *Annual Report of the Trustees of the Perkins Institution and Massachusetts Asylum for the Blind* (1840–1852, Vols. 8–20). Boston and Cambridge, 1834–1852.

"Human Nature." *Boston Investigator*, November 20, 1850.

Hurd, D. Hamilton. *History of Essex County, Massachusetts, with Biographical Sketches of Many of Its Pioneers and Prominent Men.* 2 vols. Philadelphia: J. W. Lewis, 1888.

Husson, Henri Marie. *Rapport sur les expériences magnétiques faites par la commission de l'Académie royale de médecine.* Paris, 1831. Reprinted in J. D. Dupotet de Sennevoy, *Cours de magnétisme en sept leçons.* 2nd ed. Paris, 1840.

———. *Report on the Magnetical Experiments Made by the Commission of the Royal Academy of Medicine of Paris.* Translated by Charles Poyen. Boston, 1836.

Inchbald, Elizabeth. *Animal Magnetism, a Farce, in Three Acts, as Performed at the New-York Theatre.* New York: Longworth, 1809.

———. *Animal Magnetism: A Farce, in Three Acts, as Performed at the Theatre Royal.* Dublin: P. Byron, 1789.

"Investigation on Mesmerism at Baltimore." *Daily National Intelligencer*, Washington, DC, May 29, 1843.

Isani, Mukhtar. "Some Sources for Poe's 'Tale of the Ragged Mountains.'" *Poe Studies* 5, no. 2 (1972): 38–40.

Jackson, Andrew. *The Papers of Andrew Jackson.* Vol. 6, *1825–1828.* Edited by Harold D. Moser and J. Clint Clifft. Knoxville: University of Tennessee Press, 2002.

Jackson, Gregory S. *The Word and Its Witness: The Spiritualization of American Realism.* Chicago: University of Chicago Press, 2009.

Jackson, Joseph, ed. "*The Philosophy of Animal Magnetism* Identified." In *The Philosophy of Animal Magnetism*, by "A Gentleman of Philadelphia [pseud.]," 14–31. Philadelphia, 1928.

Jakobsen, Janet R., and Ann Pellegrini. "World Secularisms at the Millennium: Introduction." *Social Text* 18, no. 3 (2000): 1–27.

———, eds. *Secularisms.* Durham, NC: Duke University Press, 2008.

Jaudon, Toni Wall. "Obeah's Sensations: Rethinking Religion at the Transnational Turn." *American Literature* 84, no. 4 (2012): 715–41.

Jefferson, Thomas. *Papers of Thomas Jefferson.* Edited by Julian P. Boyd. 41 vols. Princeton, NJ: Princeton University Press, 1950–.

Jennings, Lawrence C. *French Anti-Slavery: The Movement for the Abolition of Slavery in France, 1802–1848.* New York: Cambridge University Press, 2000.

Josephson, Hannah. *The Golden Threads: New England's Mill Girls and Magnates.* New York: Duell, Sloan, & Pearce, 1949.

Jussieu, Antoine-Laurent de. *Rapport de l'un des commissaires chargés par le Roi, de l'examen du magnétisme animal.* Paris: Veuve Hérissant, 1784.

Kasserman, David. *Fall River Outrage: Life, Murder, and Justice in Early Industrial New England.* Philadelphia: University of Pennsylvania Press, 1986.

Kirby, Georgiana Bruce. *Years of Experience: An Autobiographical Narrative.* New York: G. P. Putnam's Sons, 1887; reprint, New York: AMS Press, 1971.

Kittay, Eva Feder. "Dependency." In *Keywords for Disability Studies*, edited by Rachel Adams, Benjamin Reiss, and David Serlin, 54–58. New York: New York University Press, 2015.

———. *Love's Labor: Essays on Women, Equality, and Dependency.* New York: Routledge, 1999.

"The Knocking Humbug," *Daily Ohio Statesman*, July 18, 1850.

Koestler, Frances A. *The Unseen Minority: A Social History of Blindness in the United States.* New York: David McKay Co. and American Foundation for the Blind, 1976.

Kulik, Gary. "Pawtucket Village and the Strike of 1824: The Origins of Class Conflict in Rhode Island." *Radical History Review* 17 (Spring 1978): 5–37.

Latour, Bruno. *Enquête sur les modes d'existence: Une Anthropologie des Modernes.* Paris: La Découverte, 2012.

———. *An Inquiry into Modes of Existence: An Anthropology of the Moderns.* Translated by Catherine Porter. Cambridge, MA: Harvard University Press, 2013.

———. *Nous n'avons jamais été modernes: Essai d'anthropologie symétrique.* Paris: La Découverte, 1991.

———. *On the Modern Cult of the Factish Gods.* Chapter 1 translated by Catherine Porter and Heather MacLean. Durham, NC: Duke University Press, 2010.

———. *Petite réflexion sur le culte moderne des dieux* faitiches. Paris: Synthélabo, 1996.

———. *Sur le culte moderne des dieux* faitiches, *suivi de* Iconoclash. Paris: La Découverte, 2009.

———. *We Have Never Been Modern.* Translated by Catherine Porter. Cambridge, MA: Harvard University Press, 1993.

Laurence, K. O., and Jorge Ibarra Cuesta, eds. *General History of the Caribbean.* Vol. 4, Paris: UNESCO, 2011.

Lepler, Jessica M. *The Many Panics of 1837: People, Politics, and the Creation of a Transatlantic Financial Crisis.* New York: Cambridge University Press, 2013.

"Letters from Susan: Letter Second." *Lowell Offering*, June 1, 1844, 169–72.

Leverenz, David. *Manhood and the American Renaissance.* Ithaca, NY: Cornell University Press, 1989.

L'Hermès: Journal du magnétisme animal, publié par une société de médecins de la Faculté de Paris. Edited by Pierre-Jean Chapelain. Paris: Lévi, 1826–1829.

Liberator. Edited by William Lloyd Garrison. Boston: 1831–1865. Specific citations of this periodical appear in notes.

Lind, Sidney E. "Poe and Mesmerism." *PMLA* 62, no. 4 (1947): 1077–94.

Lippard, George. *The Quaker City; or, The Monks of Monk Hall: A Romance of Philadelphia Life, Mystery, and Crime.* Edited by David S. Reynolds. Amherst, MA: University of Massachusetts Press, 1995.

Luciano, Dana. "Sacred Theories of Earth: Matters of Spirit in *The Soul of Things*." *American Literature* 86, no. 4 (December 2014): 713–36.

Magnet. Edited by La Roy Sunderland (June 1842–November 1843) and Peter P. Good (January–May 1844). New York, 1842–1843. Specific citations of this periodical appear in notes; see also figure 9.

"The Martyrs of Light: Frederic Anthony Mesmer." *Banner of Light* 1, no. 2 (April 18, 1857): 7.

Manson, Deborah. "'The Trance of the Ecstatica': Margaret Fuller, Animal Magnetism, and the Transcendent Female Body." *Literature and Medicine* 25, no. 2 (2006): 298–324.

Marshall, Megan. *The Peabody Sisters: Three Women Who Ignited American Romanticism.* Boston: Houghton Mifflin, 2005.

Massachusetts, Town and Vital Records, 1620–1988. Accessed June 24, 2017. http://search
.ancestry.com/search/db.aspx?dbid=2495.

Masuzawa, Tomoko. *The Invention of World Religions; or, How European Universalism Was Preserved in the Language of Pluralism.* Chicago: University of Chicago Press, 2005.

McGarry, Molly. *Ghosts of Futures Past: Spiritualism and the Cultural Politics of Nineteenth-Century America.* Berkeley: University of California Press, 2008.

McGill, Meredith. *American Literature and the Culture of Reprinting, 1834–1853.* Philadelphia: University of Pennsylvania Press, 2003.

McGrane, Reginald Charles. *The Panic of 1837: Some Financial Problems of the Jacksonian Era.* Chicago: University of Chicago Press, 1924.

Méheust, Bertrand. *Somnambulisme et médiumnité (1784–1930).* Vol. 1, *Le Défi du magnétisme animal.* 2nd ed. Paris: La Découverte, 2014.

Melville, Herman. *Moby-Dick; or, The Whale.* Vol. 6 of *The Writings of Herman Melville: The Northwestern-Newberry Edition,* ed. Harrison Hayford, G. Thomas Tanselle, and Hershel Parker. Evanston, IL: Northwestern University Press, 1988.

Mesmeric Magazine 1, no. 1 (July 1842). Edited by Robert Collyer. Boston, 1842. Specific citations of this periodical appear in notes.

Midelfort, H. C. Erik. *Exorcism and Enlightenment: Johann Joseph Gassner and the Demons of Eighteenth-Century Germany.* New Haven, CT: Yale University Press, 2005.

Miles, Henry. *Lowell, As It Was, and As It Is.* Lowell, MA, 1845.

Miller, Edwin Haviland. *Salem Is My Dwelling Place: A Life of Nathaniel Hawthorne.* Iowa City: University of Iowa Press, 1991.

Mississippi Free Trader and Natchez Gazette. Natchez, MS. 1843–1850s. Specific citations of this newspaper appear in notes.

Modern, John Lardas. "Commentary: How to Read Literature, Win Friends, Influence People, and Write about American Religion." In Ebel and Murison, "American Literatures/American Religions," 191–203.

———. *Secularism in Antebellum America.* Chicago: University of Chicago Press, 2011.

Mohanty, Gail Fowler. "Putting Up with Putting-Out: Power-Loom Diffusion and Outwork for Rhode Island Mills, 1821–1829." *Journal of the Early Republic* 9, no. 2 (Summer 1989): 191–216.

Moitt, Bernard. "Slave Resistance in Guadeloupe and Martinique, 1791–1848." *Journal of Caribbean History* 25 (January 1991): 136–59.

Monk, Maria. *Awful Disclosures.* New York: M. Monk, 1836.

Monroe, John Warne. *Laboratories of Faith: Mesmerism, Spiritism, and Occultism in Modern France.* Ithaca, NY: Cornell University Press, 2008.

More, Hannah. *The Book of Private Devotion: A Series of Prayers and Meditations, with an Introductory Essay on Prayer.* New York: Leavitt, Lord, 1836.

Munro, Alistair. *Delusional Disorder: Paranoia and Related Illnesses.* Cambridge: Cambridge University Press, 1999.

Murray, Lindley. *Murray's Grammar of the English Language, Altered and Abridged.* [Boston]: Printed at the New England Institution for the Education of the Blind, 1835.

Murison, Justine S. "Obeah and Its Others: Buffered Selves in the Era of Tropical Medicine." *Atlantic Studies* 12, no. 2 (2015): 144–59.

Nathan, Tobie. *L'influence qui guérit*. Paris: Odile Jacob, 1994.

Nathan, Tobie, and Isabelle Stengers. *Médecins et sorciers*. 2nd ed. Paris: La Découverte, 2004.

Negus, Charles, and Jno. [John] W. Tenney. "Letter to Hartshorn." *Providence Daily Journal*, November 10, 1837.

"Neurology." *United States Magazine and Democratic Review* 55 (January 1843): 79–93.

"Neurology; Report of the Sub-Committee." *Wisconsin Democrat*, January 3, 1843.

Newfield, Christopher, and Melissa Solomon. "'Few of Our Seeds Ever Came Up at All': A Dialogue on Hawthorne, Delany, and the Work of Affect in Visionary Utopias." In *No More Separate Spheres! A Next Wave American Studies Reader*, edited by Cathy N. Davidson and Jessamyn Hatcher, 377–408. Durham, NC: Duke University Press, 2002.

New-Bedford Mercury. New Bedford, MA, 1807–1895. Specific citations of this newspaper appear in notes.

New York Commercial Advertiser. New York, 1831–1889. Specific citations of this newspaper appear in notes.

New York Herald. New York, 1840–1920. Specific citations of this newspaper appear in notes.

Ogden, Emily. "Beyond Radical Enchantment: Mesmerizing Laborers in the Americas." *Critical Inquiry* 42, no. 1 (Summer 2016): 815–41.

———. "*Edgar Huntly* and the Regulation of the Senses." *American Literature* 85, no. 3 (September 2013): 419–45.

———. "Mesmer's Demon: Fiction, Falsehood, and the Mechanical Imagination." *Early American Literature* 47, no. 1 (2012): 143–70.

———. "Pointing the Finger." *J19* 1, no. 1 (2013): 166–72.

Osborn, Laughton. *The Critique of the Vision of Rubeta: A Dramatic Sketch in One Act*. Philadelphia, 1838.

———. *The Vision of Rubeta*. Boston: Weeks, Jordan, 1838.

Owen, Alex. *The Darkened Room: Women, Power, and Spiritualism in Late Victorian England*. Philadelphia: University of Pennsylvania Press, 1990.

———. *The Place of Enchantment: British Occultism and the Culture of the Modern*. Chicago: University of Chicago Press, 2004.

Owen, Robert Dale. *Neurology: An Account of Some Experiments in Cerebral Physiology, by Dr. Buchanan, of Louisville, Communicated to an American Newspaper, at Dr. Buchanan's Request*. London: J. Watson, 1842.

"Passenger List for the Brig *Frances Ellen*, May 29, 1834." In *Copies of Lists of Passengers Arriving at Miscellaneous Ports on the Atlantic and Gulf Coasts and Ports on the Great Lakes*. Microfilm ed. Washington, DC: National Archives, 1964.

Perkins, Elisha. *Evidences of the Efficacy of Doctor Perkins's Patent Metallic Instruments*. New London: S. Green, 1797.

———. *To All People to Whom These Presents Shall Come*. [Philadelphia?], [1796?]. Broadside.

Peters, John Durham. *Speaking Into the Air: A History of the Idea of Communication*. Chicago: University of Chicago Press, 1999.

Pietz, William. "Fetish." In *Critical Terms for Art History*, 2d ed., edited by Robert S. Nelson and Richard Shiff, 306–17. Chicago: University of Chicago Press, 2003.

———. "The Problem of the Fetish, I." *RES: Anthropology and Aesthetics*, no. 9 (Spring 1985): 5–17.

————. "The Problem of the Fetish, II: The Origin of the Fetish." *RES: Anthropology and Aesthetics*, no. 13 (Spring 1987): 23–45.

Poe, Edgar Allan. *Collected Works of Edgar Allan Poe*. 3 vols. Edited by Thomas Ollive Mabbott. Cambridge, MA: Harvard University Press, 1969–1978.

————. "The Literati of New York, No. II." *Godey's Lady's Book* 32 (June 1846): 266–72.

Poirier, Richard. *A World Elsewhere: The Place of Style in American Literature*. New York: Oxford University Press, 1966.

Powers, Grant. *Essay upon the Influence of the Imagination on the Nervous System, Contributing to a False Hope in Religion*. Andover: Flagg & Gould, 1828.

Poyen, Charles. "Animal Magnetism (Concluded): Pawtucket, 20th Dec. 1836," *Providence Daily Journal*, January 2, 1837.

————. "Animal Magnetism: Pawtucket, 20th Dec. 1836," *Providence Daily Journal*, December 31, 1836.

————. "Experiments in Animal Magnetism." *New York Commercial Advertiser*, November 23, 1836. Reprint from *Providence Daily Journal*, November 19, 1836.

————. "Experiments in Animal Magnetism." *Providence Daily Journal*, November 23, 1836.

————. Introduction to *Report on the Magnetical Experiments Made by the Commission of the Royal Academy of Medicine of Paris*, by Henri Marie Husson, translated by Charles Poyen, v–lxxi. Boston, 1836.

————. *A Letter to Col. Wm. L. Stone, of New York, on the Facts Related in his "Letter to Dr. Brigham," and a Plain Refutation of Durant's "Exposition of Animal Magnetism."* Boston: Weeks, Jordan, 1837.

————. *The Progress of Animal Magnetism in New England*. Boston: Weeks, Jordan, 1837.

————. "Sketch of the History of Animal Magnetism." *Boston Pearl, a Gazette of Polite Literature*, March 26, 1836, 220–22.

————. "Surprising Phenomena of Animal Magnetism." *New-York Spectator*, November 24, 1836, [2]. Reprint from *Providence Daily Journal*, November 17, 1836.

Poyen de Sainte-Marie, Jean Baptiste. *De l'exploitation des sucreries; ou, Conseils d'un vieux planteur aux jeunes agriculteurs des colonies*. Basse-Terre, Guadeloupe: 1792.

Providence Daily Journal. Providence, RI, 1830–1920. Specific citations of this newspaper appear in notes.

Quinn, Sheila O'Brien. "Credibility, Respectability, Suggestibility, and Spirit Travel: Lurena Brackett and Animal Magnetism." *History of Psychology* 15, no. 3 (2012): 273–82.

————. "How Southern New England Became Magnetic North: The Acceptance of Animal Magnetism." *History of Psychology* 10, no. 3 (2007): 231–48.

"Recherches historiques sur le magnétisme animal, chez les anciens, etc." In three identically titled segments. *Bibliothèque du magnétisme animal* 8 (1819): 60–92, 159–76, 261–74.

Rees, Abraham, ed. *The Cyclopaedia; or, Universal Dictionary of Arts, Sciences, and Literature*. 1st American ed. 41 vols. Philadelphia: Samuel F. Bradford & Murray, Fairman, 1810–1824.

Reese, David. *Humbugs of New-York: Being a Remonstrance against Popular Delusion*. Boston: Weeks, Jordan, 1838.

Regourd, François. "Mesmerism in Saint Domingue: Occult Knowledge and Vodou on the Eve of the Haitian Revolution." In *Science and Empire in the Atlantic World*, edited by James Delbourgo and Nicholas Dew, 311–32. New York: Routledge, 2008.

Reiss, Benjamin. *Theaters of Madness: Insane Asylums and Nineteenth-Century American Culture*. Chicago: University of Chicago Press, 2008.

Report of Dr. Franklin and Other Commissioners, Charged by the King of France with the Examination of the Animal Magnetism as Practised at Paris. Philadelphia: H. Perkins, 1837.

"Report of the Committee." *Daily National Intelligencer*, Washington, DC, May 29, 1843.

Riskin, Jessica. "Eighteenth-Century Wetware." *Representations* 83 (Summer 2003): 97–125.

Robert, Anne-Jean, and Nicolas Louis Robert. *Mémoire sur les expériences aérostatiques faites par MM. Robert frères*. Paris: Imprimerie de P.-D. Pierres, 1784.

Rollason, Christopher. "Poe's 'A Tale of the Ragged Mountains,' Macaulay and Warren Hastings: From Orientalism to Globalisation?" In *India in the World*, edited by Cristina Gámez-Fernández and Antonia Navarro-Tejero, 109–20. Newcastle upon Tyne, UK: Cambridge Scholars, 2011.

Ronda, Bruce A. *Elizabeth Palmer Peabody: A Reformer on Her Own Terms*. Cambridge, MA: Harvard University Press, 1999.

Rossignol, Philippe and Bernadette Rossignol. "De Saint-Affrique à Bordeaux en passant par la Guadeloupe: La Famille Poyen." *Bulletin du Centre d'Histoire des Espaces Atlantiques*, n.s., 5 (1990): 137–56.

———. *La Famille Poyen*, Vol. 1, *Généalogie*. Le Pecq, France, 2013.

Rostan, Léon. "Magnétisme." In Adelon and Mérat, *Dictionnaire de médecine*, 13:421–69.

Rousseau, G. S. "Pineapples, Pregnancy, Pica, and *Peregrine Pickle*." In *Tobias Smollett: Bicentennial Essays Presented to Lewis M. Knapp*, edited by G. S. Rousseau and Paul-Gabriel Boucé, 79–109. New York: Oxford University Press, 1971.

———. "Science and the Discovery of the Imagination in Enlightened England." *Eighteenth-Century Studies* 3, no. 1 (Fall 1969): 108–35.

Rowson, Susanna. *Charlotte Temple*. In *"Charlotte Temple" and "Lucy Temple,"* edited by Ann Douglas. New York: Penguin, 1991.

———. *Science in the Age of Sensibility: The Sentimental Empiricists of the French Enlightenment*. Chicago: University of Chicago Press, 2002.

Rust, Marion. *Prodigal Daughters: Susanna Rowson's Early American Women*. Chapel Hill: University of North Carolina Press, 2008.

Ruttenburg, Nancy. *Democratic Personality: Popular Voice and the Trial of American Authorship*. Stanford, CA: Stanford University Press, 1998.

Saler, Michael. *As If: Modern Enchantment and the Literary Prehistory of Virtual Reality*. New York: Oxford University Press, 2012.

Schaffer, Simon. "Enlightened Automata." In *The Sciences in Enlightened Europe*, edited by William Clark, Jan Golinski, and Simon Schaffer, 126–65. Chicago: University of Chicago Press, 1999.

———. "Self Evidence." *Critical Inquiry* 18, no. 2 (1992): 327–62.

Schlesinger, Arthur Jr. *The Age of Jackson*. Boston: Little, Brown, 1945.

Schmidt, Leigh Eric. *Hearing Things: Religion, Illusion, and the American Enlightenment.* Cambridge, MA: Harvard University Press, 2000.

Schmidt, Nelly. *Abolitionnistes de l'esclavage et réformateurs des colonies, 1820–1851: Analyse et documents.* Paris: Karthala, 2000.

Schuller, Kyla. "Taxonomies of Feeling: The Epistemology of Sentimentalism in Late-Nineteenth-Century Racial and Sexual Science." *American Quarterly* 64, no. 2 (June 2012): 277–99.

Siebers, Tobin. *Disability Theory.* Ann Arbor: University of Michigan Press, 2008.

Smee, Alfred. *Principles of the Human Mind, Deduced from Physical Laws, Together with a Lecture on Electro-Biology, or The Voltaic Mechanism of Man.* New York: Fowlers & Wells, 1850.

Sollors, Werner. "Dr. Benjamin Franklin's Celestial Telegraph, or Indian Blessings to Gas-Lit American Drawing Rooms." *American Quarterly* 35, no. 5 (Winter 1983): 459–80.

Stein, Jordan Alexander. "The *Blithedale Romance*'s Queer Style." *ESQ: A Journal of the American Renaissance* 55, no. 3–4 (2009): 211–36.

Stengers, Isabelle. *L'Hypnose entre magie et science.* Paris: La Découverte, 2002.

Stern, Julia. *The Plight of Feeling: Sympathy and Dissent in the Early American Novel.* Chicago: University of Chicago Press, 1997.

Stewart, Dugald. *Elements of the Philosophy of the Human Mind.* Vol. 1, 5th ed. London: Cadell & Davies, 1814. First published London, 1792.

———. *Elements of the Philosophy of the Human Mind.* Vol. 3. Philadelphia: Carey, Lea, and Carey, 1827. First published London, 1827.

Stoehr, Taylor. *Hawthorne's Mad Scientists: Pseudoscience and Social Science in Nineteenth-Century Life and Letters.* Hamden, CT: Archon Books, 1978.

Stone, G. W. *Electro-Biology; or, The Electrical Science of Life.* Liverpool: Willmer & Smith, 1850.

Stone, William Leete. *Letter to Doctor A. Brigham, on Animal Magnetism: Being an Account of a Remarkable Interview between the Author and Miss Loraina Brackett, While in a State of Somnambulism.* New York: Dearborn, 1837.

———. *Matthias and his Impostures; or, The Progress of Fanaticism.* 3rd ed. New York: Harper & Brothers, 1835.

———. *Maria Monk and the Nunnery of the Hôtel Dieu.* New York: Howe & Bates, 1836.

Stone, William L. II. *The Family of John Stone, One of the First Settlers of Guilford, Conn.* Albany, NY: J. Musell's Sons, 1888.

Sunderland, La Roy. *Pathetism.* New York: P. P. Good, 1843.

"Table Moving." *Boston Investigator*, April 5, 1854.

Taves, Ann. *Fits, Trances, and Visions: Experiencing Religion and Explaining Experience from Wesley to James.* Princeton, NJ: Princeton University Press, 1999.

Taylor, Charles. *A Secular Age.* Cambridge, MA: Harvard University Press, 2007.

Temple, Gale. "'Ineffable Socialities': Melville, Hawthorne, and Masculine Ambivalence in the Antebellum Marketplace." In *Hawthorne and Melville: Writing a Relationship*, edited by Jana L. Argersinger and Leland S. Person, 113–31. Athens: University of Georgia Press, 2008.

Thomas, Dwight, and David K. Jackson, eds. *The Poe Log: A Documentary Life of Edgar Allan Poe, 1809–1849.* Boston: G. K. Hall, 1987.

Thomson, Rosemarie Garland, ed. *Freakery: Cultural Spectacles of the Extraordinary Body.* New York: New York University Press, 1996.

Thornton, Tamara Plakins. *Handwriting in America: A Cultural History.* New Haven, CT: Yale University Press, 1996.

Thouret, Michel Augustin. *Recherches et doutes sur le magnétisme animal.* Paris: Prault, 1784.

Tigner, Steven S. "Magic and Magicians." In *Handbook of American Popular Culture*, 2nd ed., vol. 2, edited by M. Thomas Inge, 671–720. New York: Greenwood Press, 1989.

Townshend, C. *Improved Phreno-Chart . . . According to Grimes's New System of Phrenology.* Boston: White & Potter, 1853.

Townshend, Chauncy Hare. *Facts in Mesmerism, with Reasons for a Dispassionate Inquiry into It.* New York: Harper & Brothers, 1841.

Treitel, Corinna. *A Science for the Soul: Occultism and the Genesis of the German Modern.* Baltimore: Johns Hopkins University Press, 2004.

———. "What the Occult Reveals." *Modern Intellectual History* 6, no. 3 (2009): 611–25.

Trent, James W. *The Manliest Man: Samuel G. Howe and the Contours of Nineteenth-Century American Reform.* Amherst: University of Massachusetts Press, 2012.

Tresch, John. "'The Potent Magic of Verisimilitude:' Edgar Allan Poe within the Mechanical Age." *British Journal of the History of Science* 30, no. 3 (1997): 275–90.

Tucker, Barbara. "The Merchant, the Manufacturer, and the Factory Manager: The Case of Samuel Slater." *Business History Review* 55, no. 3 (1981): 297–313.

———. *Samuel Slater and the Origins of the American Textile Industry, 1790–1860.* Ithaca, NY: Cornell University Press, 1984.

United States Magazine and Democratic Review [alternate title: *Democratic Review*]. Washington, DC, 1837–1851. Specific citations of this periodical appear in notes.

US House of Representatives [Secretary of the Treasury Louis McLane]. *Documents Relative to the Manufactures in the United States.* [alternate title: *McLane Report*]. 2 vols. Washington, DC, 1833.

Vanguard. Dayton, OH, and Richmond, IN, 1857–1858. Specific citations of this periodical appear in notes.

Vital Records of Haverhill, Massachusetts, to the End of the Year 1849. 2 vols. Topsfield, MA, 1911.

Vital Records of Newburyport, Massachusetts, to the End of the Year 1849. 2 vols. Salem, MA, 1911.

Voigt, Irma Elizabeth. "The Life and Works of Mrs. Therese Robinson (Talvj)." PhD thesis, University of Illinois, 1913.

Walker, David. "The Humbug in American Religion: Ritual Theories of Nineteenth-Century Spiritualism." *Religion and American Culture* 23, no. 1 (2013): 30–74.

Warner, Michael. "Was Antebellum America Secular?" *The Immanent Frame* (blog). October 2, 2012. Accessed April 21, 2014. http://blogs.ssrc.org/tif/2012/10/02/was-antebellum-america-secular/.

Weber, Max. "Science as a Vocation." In *From Max Weber: Essays in Sociology*, edited and translated by H. H. Gerth and C. Wright Mills, 129–56. New York: Routledge, 1948.

Wiegman, Robyn. "The Ends of New Americanism." *New Literary History* 42, no. 3 (2011): 385–407.

Williams, Catherine Read. *Fall River: An Authentic Narrative*. Boston: Lilly, Wait, 1834.

Williams, Stephen W. *American Medical Biography*. Greenfield, MA, 1845.

Willich, A. F. M., and James Mease, eds. *The Domestic Encyclopaedia; or, a Dictionary of Facts, and Useful Knowledge*. 5 vols. Philadelphia: William Young Birch & Abraham Small, 1803–1804.

Winsor, Justin. *History of the Town of Duxbury, Massachusetts: With Genealogical Registers*. Boston: Crosby & Nichols, 1849.

Winter, Alison. *Mesmerized: Powers of Mind in Victorian Britain*. Chicago: University of Chicago Press, 1998.

Yelvington, Kevin A. "Caribbean Social Structure in the Nineteenth Century." In Laurence and Cuesta, *General History of the Caribbean*, 283–333.

INDEX